Separate Destinations

Separate Destinations
Migration, Immigration, and the Politics of Places

JAMES G. GIMPEL

Ann Arbor
THE UNIVERSITY OF MICHIGAN PRESS

2002   2001   2000   1999   4   3   2   1

A CIP catalog record for this book is available from the British Library.

Library of Congress Cataloging-in-Publication Data

Gimpel, James G.
    Separate destinations : migration, immigration, and the politics
of places / James G. Gimpel.
        p. cm.
    Includes bibliographical references and index.
    ISBN 0-472-10978-2 (cloth : alk. paper)
    1. Immigrants—United States—Political activity.   2. Minorities—
United States—Political activity.   3. Migration, Internal—United
States.   4. Elections—United States.   5. Political participation—
United States.   I. Title.
JV6477.G55   1999
304.8'0973—dc21   99-28316
                                                                CIP

*To my father,
the late Graydon G. Gimpel, and my
late father-in-law, Abdon Omar Yacobucci,
who were very familiar with the costs
of migration.*

Contents

Figures

Maps

Tables

Preface

I started this project several years ago when I took an interest in reading about population mobility internal to the United States. My interest in the subject stems from my background as well as from interesting books I have read as a social scientist. Having grown up in a family whose history involved considerable internal migration, I have long wondered about the impact of population mobility on people's lives. But a less studied subject in the social sciences is what happens to the places affected by mobility. The strong preference for survey data in the social sciences has made it hard to find works about the effect of mobility on places. An equally strong bias in favor of "topic" oriented studies, and against "area" or "place" oriented studies, has made it more difficult to publish works about political or geographic units below the national level. In spite of disciplinary conventions, here I seek to ask questions such as: What happens to a *place* when half of its population leaves over the course of two decades? Who leaves? Who remains behind? And what happens to the places the people are moving to? Answering these questions requires a heterodox methodology. Individual-level data are important, but aggregate data are also necessary. A large number of cases must be analyzed, along with careful and detailed examinations of important cases, both typical and atypical.

The two books that I count as my starting points on the subject of internal migration come at the topic from very different angles. James N. Gregory's *American Exodus* (1989) is the story of the southwestern migration to California in the 1930s—not the fictionalized version of John Steinbeck but one more true to the facts of migration and resettlement. Thad Brown's *Migration and Politics* (1988) is the best political science work on the subject of internal migration. Brown lays down an indispensable theoretical foundation for considering the effect of mobility on political behavior and takes steps to verify his hypotheses with survey data. I consider these books to be major contributions to the study of internal migration in the United States.

The immigration ideas in this project were stirred up on a Maryland beach in the summer of 1995. There I read a controversial polemic by a well-known journalist against the generous immigration policy the United States had adopted thirty years before. I wanted to test a few of the claims that were made in that book and elsewhere about the settlement patterns of immigrants. The immigration debate is controversial and vitriolic. Those on each side want to know where academic researchers stand. "Open borders or slam the door shut? With whom will you align yourself?" were the demanding questions that so many were asking as I wrote this book and collaborated on another. I have no particular ax to grind. The immigration issue piques my curiosity. Still, I am not a totally disinterested observer. While my own immigrant roots are some distance in the past, I am the spouse of a recent immigrant and the father of another. I am not for slamming shut the golden door. But I don't think we can accommodate everyone who would like to come here either.

I have benefited from the comments and criticism of colleagues who sat in on presentations at professional conferences. Parts of the book were presented at the Midwest Political Science Association meeting in 1996 and the American Political Science Association meeting in 1997. Serious studies of migration must inevitably take one away from political science, however, where very little work is being done on the subject. On the subject of internal migration, I have learned a lot from William Frey of the University of Michigan's Population Studies Center. A demographer and sociologist, Frey introduced me to several of the important ideas I develop throughout the manuscript. Conversations with anthropologists, with their wealth of local or "place specific" knowledge, were very helpful, as were discussions with several labor economists who specialize in population mobility.

Several people provided data, information, and suggestions on particular states and localities. These include Dario Moreno (for Florida), Rodney Hero (for Colorado), Carol Andreas (for Colorado), Don Stull (for Kansas), and Suzanne Parker (for Florida). The University of Kentucky Data Center provided survey data for the 1991 and 1995 gubernatorial elections in that state (free of charge!). At Suzanne Parker's direction, Florida State University provided data from its annual policy surveys, again free of charge.

I interviewed many state and local experts and observers to obtain a ground-level understanding of what was happening in the places where they live and work. Reporters from local newspapers were helpful, but so were city and county planners whose job it is to study population movement and its impact. A partial list of sources includes the following: John Engelenner, *Sacramento Bee;* Don Vest, City of Pueblo Planning Department; Janet Day, *Denver Post;* Randy Olthoff, Elmira County Planning Department; April Hunt, Elmira *Star-Gazette;* Rick Moriarty, *Syracuse Post Standard;* Steve Hughes, Elmira City Council; Joe Salvo, New York City Planning Department; Frank Varty, New York City Planning Department; Tony DiStefano, *Newsday* (New York); Ann Devinney, *Gettysburg Times;* Chris Barber, *Daily Local News* (Chester County, PA); Jim McKay, *Pittsburgh Press;* Dennis Roddy, *Pittsburgh Press;* Fred Rapone, *Daily Press* (McKeesport); Dave Skelly, Erie County Planning Department; Tom Fiedler, *Miami Herald;* Mark Washburn, *Miami Herald;* Mark Silva, *Miami Herald;* Tony Boylan, *Florida Today* (Melbourne, FL); Allen Horton, *Herald-Tribune* (Sarasota); Bill Berlow, Tallahassee *Democrat;* Brett Cott, Kansas State Democratic Party; Rick Aom, *Wichita Eagle;* Steve Nicely, *Kansas City Star;* Bill Bardleman, *Paducah Sun;* Jim Riis, *Kentucky Post;* and Patrick Crowley, *Cincinnati Enquirer.*

Valuable comments, criticism, and encouragement came from departmental colleagues Paul Herrnson, Mark Graber, Irwin Morris, Clarence Stone, and Eric Uslaner and from colleagues at other institutions, including Mark Hansen, Peter Skerry, Rodney Hero, Thad Brown, Jim Edwards, Dario Moreno, and Don Stull. This acknowledgment does not mean that they agree with either my general argument or with anything particular I say in the book. I also thank the students in my seminars at the University of Maryland, who contributed valuable insights and provided generous, if often captive, feedback.

I owe a special debt of gratitude to the John M. Olin Foundation for the generous financial support that permitted me release time and technical resources essential to finishing the book.

My editor, Charles Myers, at the University of Michigan Press was patient and supportive as I finished the manuscript and did not balk at making the extra effort to publish the maps. Based on my experience, I can enthusiastically recommend the Press to anyone.

As always, God was with me from beginning to end and cleared away many real and imagined obstacles to the completion of the book. My loyal and loving spouse, Veronica, has faithfully migrated with me through four states spanning a period of thirteen years. Without her, the journey would have been far less pleasant and the effects of migration far less benign.

CHAPTER 1

Population Mobility and Political Change in the American Electorate

Jumping into a time machine and traveling into the past to 1970, I would get out on the hill overlooking the town where I grew up and instantly recognize the view. Yes, a few buildings have been constructed, a few torn down, a new subdivision has gone up on the east edge of town, businesses have come and gone, people have died and been born, but based on an eyeball inspection things have not changed much. On the downtown streets, I would recognize all of the signs and storefronts and would even recognize some of the faces, although they would be much younger. A look at official statistics would reveal that the population in my hometown is slightly smaller in 2000 now than it was in 1970, but it is nearly identical in terms of its ethnic and economic composition. The population consists almost entirely of local natives—few have moved in from elsewhere. People are better educated than in 1970, but probably not relative to the rest of the nation. The politics, too, has remained pretty much the same, although scrutiny of the figures would reveal a slow drift toward the Republican Party as the generation that came of age during the New Deal has died. Visible differences, though, would be difficult to detect.

While real estate speculators would have found it impossible to make millions in my hometown, they might not have lost much either. There has not been booming prosperity, but the bottom has not completely fallen out of the local economy. In other places in the nation, though, a journey back to 1970 would reveal a far more active, prosperous, and ethnically diverse setting than exists today. The door to the time machine would swing open to busy streets, businesses, factories, and schools that are now either nonexistent, abandoned, or in a pathetic state of disrepair. Whole city blocks of homes and businesses that had vanished by the year 2000 would appear in photographs from that earlier time. These are places where investors could have lost many millions. Several of the depressed old steel towns of the Monongahela Valley in western Pennsylvania come to mind as places that in 1970 would be hard to recognize for any of us whose vision of these towns had been shaped by visits during the 1990s. Compared to 1970, the populations of Homestead, Duquesne, Clairton, and McKeesport are smaller, poorer, older, and more hopeless (Gittell 1992; Serrin 1993). While industrial decline was well under way as early as 1960, the last of the major mills, the Homestead Works, did not close for good until 1986. Even in 1970 these towns had large middle-class populations, ethnically robust neighborhoods, strong main streets, and schools of which the residents were proud. At the turn of the century, these towns will head the list as the most economically and socially distressed places in Pennsylvania, if not the entire Northeast.

Population flight is not the only aspect of mobility that can render a place unrecognizable to the time traveler. I now live in a suburban setting, about halfway between two major East Coast cities in a corridor that has been rapidly developed. Pulling back a curtain to look at my neighborhood as it was in 1970 would reveal not a single familiar vista. Nothing was the same then. Farms and forests have been replaced with strip malls and low density subdivisions that house middle and upper income professionals. An overwhelmingly white population in 1970 is only predominantly white now, as a small black middle class and a sizable population of immigrants have changed the complexion of neighborhoods and schoolrooms. Where a visitor once would have been hard-pressed locate a burger joint or a Dairy Queen, one can now find restaurants named Ak-Bar, Hunan Manor, and Bangkok Delight, to say nothing of the ethnic grocery stores where no English is spoken and smaller restaurants where my ignorance of other languages prevents me from understanding the signs. I do not feel unsettled by these changes since I have contributed to them. My spouse is a Hispanic immigrant, and our children will be bilingual. I have not lived in my neighborhood long enough to experience the changes that have taken place since the 1970s, but I do find myself marveling at how different a place can come to look in less than half a lifetime. And ethnic diversity is not the only conspicuous indicator of change. Even the native-born white newcomers bear little resemblance to the ones who populated the area in 1970. As a white male, I am part of a new population, which earns more money, carries more debt, works longer hours, has younger children, and commutes further than the folks who lived here in the recent past. The political concerns of my neighbors and me bear scant resemblance to those of the residents of thirty years ago—and not just because times have changed. Those who represent my neighborhood in the local, state, and national legislatures at the beginning of the new century face demands that are entirely different from those that were voiced by a very different constituency thirty years ago.

The politics of a place are obviously determined by the people who live there—who they are and how their interests are defined. Because people make demands of the political system in a democracy, significant political change occurs in a place when its population changes. Populations change in myriad ways and at various paces. The pace of change is uneven across space, leading to the social, economic, and political stratification of neighborhoods, towns, and cities. In some places, old populations have been replaced with new ones, as in the rural to urban and urban to suburban transitions that have occurred in so many areas of the country. In other places, the population simply declines as the older residents die. Time brings change even to relatively stable populations as new generations replace the old. Economic booms may bring hordes of interstate migrants to some areas, leaving others untouched. Economic downturns move people out, sometimes leaving no one behind. Overcrowding diminishes the quality of life, and those who can afford to move to greener pastures do so, changing the population composition at both origin and destination. Because politics and population are linked through political participation in a democratic society, population changes produce consequential but rather uneven political changes across places.

In this book, I explore the political consequences of a particular type of population change, that produced by geographic mobility both internal to the nation and across its borders. I ask whether the reshuffling of the native-born population and the influx of immigrants have been politically consequential and whether the two migration flows are related. There are occasional hints from the popular press that internal demographic shifts have some political impact, and there are obvious political reactions to immigrants—as in California's Propositions 187 and 209 (the latter known as the California Civil Rights Initiative or CCRI)—but there have been few studies of what internal and cross-national migration have done to politically stratify and otherwise change the politics of places.

In the existing literature, where the effects or consequences of migration and immigration have been addressed, the emphasis has been on the economics of the sending and receiving areas—what happens to earnings, employment, and the income distribution. In addition, the internal migration of the native born and immigration are usually treated as entirely separate subjects, with some studies specializing in the one and some in the other. There are good reasons for distinguishing the two groups, of course. Natives and the foreign born differ much more today than they did in the early twentieth century (Borjas 1990; Borjas and Freeman 1992). Domestic migrants have much higher skill and educational levels and are more likely to be white. They are led to their destinations by different forces and therefore do not settle in the same locales as the foreign born (Frey 1996, 1995a, 1995b). The native-born migrants are also less concentrated in the areas where they resettle and as a result are far less noticeable than the new class of immigrants. But there is increasing evidence that precisely because native-born migrants and immigrants are so different, these differences may conspire to generate radical changes in the spatial distribution of economic and political interests in the United States. The theoretical basis for this suspicion will be detailed shortly.

In the pages that follow, I will examine explanations of mobility and describe how they may be relevant to understanding the politics of states and localities across the United States. Looking for the political effects of new populations at the state and local levels makes sense because the inflow of foreign-born and native population groups is not occurring evenly across the nation or within states (Frey 1996, 1995a, 1995b; Clark 1995; Bartel 1989). Many states have experienced rather slow growth, or even a decline, in population over the last forty years. Others have been on the receiving end of massive waves of migration. There are differences in the volume and type of migration across the nation as well. In some areas, population change is mostly the result of native in- and out-migration. In others, the influx of the foreign born has altered the demographic composition of cities, regions, and states. There are a few areas to which both foreign-born and native migrants are drawn. Internally, population shifts within states have occurred with the suburbanization of both foreign-born and native residents.

It is entirely possible that by many measures migration within and immigration to the United States have not changed the politics of states and localities at all. In speculating about the consequences of these demographic trends, one must first be clear about the meaning of terms such as *political impact* and *political change*. Politics, after all, takes many forms. Arguably, one could find that almost anything produces political change if the terms are defined broadly enough.

In this study, I will look for specific kinds of political change—all relevant to the electoral foundations of the American political system. First, I am interested in knowing whether population mobility influences levels of voter turnout and political participation in the areas where the migrants settle. Detailed time-series data, complete with annual or semiannual observations, would be best for such an inquiry, but it is generally not available and probably not strictly necessary. If migration does influence turnout, then a cross-sectional study of jurisdictions with varying numbers of migrants should show corresponding political differences. Other things being equal, areas with stable populations could be expected to have high participation rates, while those experiencing an influx of newcomers would exhibit lower turnout. Second, I want to evaluate how migration and immigration influence the relationship between party registration and partisan voting. Places where the electorate has been reconfigured due to migration may show less party loyalty than those where the electorate has remained unchanged. Third, I aim to discover whether population mobility has altered the political party balance of regions and states, either by reconstituting the electorate or by generating political reaction from natives. Partisan change is hypothesized to be uneven across space, varying directly with the influx of newcomers.

The Effects of Population Mobility on Politics

If migration and immigration are a political wash, if they have had no impact, the presence and concentration of migratory populations should do nothing to influence political participation, party voting, or party allegiance in places across the country. In addressing these questions, there is surprisingly little previous research on which to build. Scholars with an interest in politics have been slow in studying the effects of recent migration and immigration in the American context. On the subject of internal migration, the key work has been that of Thad Brown (1988), which elegantly details how migrants' political views change with their new surroundings. Brown's work substantially modified the conclusion of Converse (1966; see also Campbell, Converse, Miller, and Stokes 1960) that partisan attitudes are resistant to geographic mobility. Brown argues that migration's main effect is to slowly unravel the party system by increasing the mover's tendency to defect from his or her party affiliation, perhaps eventually switching parties altogether (Brown 1988, 154–55; McBurnett 1991). At the very least, migration weakens partisanship as voters adopt highly individualized and personal approaches to thinking about politics.

There has been some similarly impressive work on the effects of residential mobility on turnout (Dubin and Kalsow 1997; Squire, Wolfinger, and Glass 1987; Wolfinger and Rosenstone 1980; Rosenstone and Wolfinger 1978). These studies conclusively demonstrate that mobility reduces turnout, especially in the presence of restrictive voter registration laws that obstruct the reregistration of new residents. Another line of original work has demonstrated that the spatial isolation of minority citizens in poor neighborhoods, resulting from the out-migration of wealthier residents, diminishes political efficacy and participation in central city neighborhoods (Cohen and Dawson 1993; Wilson 1996).

Several studies of political partisanship at the macrolevel have credited internal migration with altering the political balance of regions in the United States (Glaser and Gilens 1997; Rice and Pepper 1997; Gimpel 1996; Black and Black 1988, 1992; Frendreis 1989; Brown 1988; Lamis 1988; Stanley 1988; Galderisi, Lyons, Simmons, and Francis 1987; Wolfinger and Hagen 1985; Wolfinger and Arsenau 1978). Along with generational replacement and partisan conversion, population migration has contributed to the nearly complete partisan realignment of the South and the sustained political independence of many voters in the Far West.

As for immigration's influence on American politics, there is a distinguished older body of work on particular ethnic groups (Glazer and Moynihan 1963; Wolfinger 1965, 1974; Handlin 1952). This research has focused on the watering down of ethnic identity over time and the role of immigrants in shaping a new social and political culture (see also Alba, Logan, and Crowder 1997; Ignatiev 1995; Erie 1988; and Alba 1981). While it accurately captures the assimilation patterns of many European immigrant groups, there is only mixed evidence that these works describe the experiences of the newer waves of immigrants from Asia and Latin America.

In response to recent immigration trends and new survey data on particular groups, a growing number of more behaviorally oriented studies has emerged (Tam 1996; de la Garza et al. 1992; Cain, Uhlaner, and Kieweit 1990; Cain and Kieweit 1987). These studies have revealed new facts about the political attitudes of several immigrant groups. For instance, we now know that Mexicans, Puerto Ricans, and Cubans have less in common than previously thought. The three groups have little interaction with each other and Cubans are more politically active than the other two groups. Puerto Ricans, Cubans, and Mexicans do express similar views on many domestic policy issues, and they demonstrate greater trust in government's capacity to solve major problems than Anglos do (de la Garza et al. 1992, 14–15). Cain, Uhlaner, and Kieweit show that over time Latinos in California acquire strong Democratic Party preferences as a result of the discrimination and lack of opportunity they perceive. Because Asians experience less discrimination, they are more divided between the parties (1990, 402).

In a widely read and controversial work on Mexican Americans, Peter Skerry has detailed patterns of assimilation and political attitudes within this large and politically consequential community (1993). Among other things, he documents the gulf between the political attitudes of Mexican elites and the rank and file, finding Latino leaders to be far more liberal than their constituents. But he also details important differences among Mexicans in various parts of the nation—in some areas Mexicans identify themselves and are identified by others as a racial minority, while in other areas their politics is much less racially oriented (318–19). His work offers one explanation for why the backlash against immigrants has been stronger in some states than in others. In California, immigrant minority groups are more likely than elsewhere to make aggressive political claims cast in the language of civil rights and racial discrimination—thus assuming the posture of black Americans. As a reaction against such claims, Propositions 187 and 209 garnered broad-based support in California. In places where the Hispanic population was less aggressive in pressing its demands in racial terms, such as Texas, Florida, and Arizona, restrictionist movements failed to get off the ground.

The political orientations of the new immigrants, and whether their presence in a place generates politically consequential reactions from natives, remains a fertile field for further inquiry. Perhaps we know so little about these topics because the linkage between migration, immigration, and political behavior is seldom direct. Although some immigrants are here for political reasons, natives rarely choose to move for political reasons, and even immigrants do not choose the areas where they resettle on the basis of politics (Glaser and Gilens 1997). So, if there are political consequences to migration, they are a by-product of other forces shaping the demographic destiny of cities, regions, and states. The migration and resettlement pattern of a given group ultimately affects its political power and visibility in the receiving community. For my purposes, altered political patterns are an *effect* of migration and immigration, and I am not especially interested in singling out those cases in which politics, war, or revolution may have caused the relocation to the United States. The causes of population mobility are not trivial, however, as they determine what kind of people will move and where they choose to locate.

Population Mobility and Political Balkanization as an Attribute of Places

Most of the work on mobility in political science has focused on the movers themselves, drawing data on mobility and politics from surveys of voters. There has been much less focus on what happens to the politics of places the movers settle in or leave behind. But the conventional reliance upon survey data is not totally adequate for my purposes because political balkanization is something that happens when places change. To be sure, individual change is at the bottom of changes that occur in places. The attributes of cities, regions, and states are produced by the aggregation of locational decisions by individuals (Schelling 1969, 1972, 1978; Kain and Quigley 1975). Ordinary polling data based on individual responses to survey questions are not capable of determining whether regions and substate sections have been influenced by population movement. It is possible to imagine a survey that could identify such influences, but the sample would have to be extraordinarily large—sufficient to represent substate sections as well as states. In conventionally sized polls, respondents might describe their mobility patterns and political views, but these responses will not provide much insight into whether *locations* are becoming more or less politically active, more Democratic or more Republican, or less loyal to parties altogether. While much of the data analysis in this project draws upon observations of mobility and political change at the aggregate, county, and census tract levels, these are exactly the kinds of studies that tell us whether places are changing. Keeping in mind that the decennial censuses are cross-sectional studies, it is possible to record successive census observations of a set of cases and infer change across the ten-year intervals in much the same way that panel studies of voters are used to discern changes in individual behavior and attitudes. Of course, an exclusive focus on aggregate-level data does not permit detailed examination of the individual-level processes that generate differences in the political behavior of places. Ideally, some mix of aggregate and individual data is optimal for understanding electoral politics (King 1997, 256; Huckfeldt and Sprague 1995, 23). Wherever possible, I draw upon appropriate survey data to provide additional evidence about the individual-level processes that lie behind aggregate-level changes.

In speaking of political balkanization, then, I am referring to inequalities across space in the propensity to vote or identify with one party or the other. States in which inequalities across substate jurisdictions (counties, municipalities) are extreme are said to be more balkanized than those in which jurisdictions are roughly the same in their propensity to turn out or identify with a particular party. Given this understanding of the term, political balkanization is neither a recent nor an uncommon feature of the American political scene. Some areas are dominated by one political party, other areas by the other. Some areas have very high political participation rates, others very low ones. Depending on the level of aggregation, that is, the size of places one examines, political inequalities of this type may be the norm rather than the exception. In the case of two political parties, given a single set of boundaries, one party is going to dominate (Schelling 1978, 141). Unsurprisingly then, neighborhoods are almost never perfectly integrated by partisan preference (or by most other traits) and often take on monolithic characters that sharply demarcate them from places nearby (Lieberson 1963). At times, even entire states will take on uniform political habits and attitudes, as V. O. Key's work on the mid-century South clearly demonstrated (1949; 1956).

The *extent* of political balkanization, however, does change with population trends. Neighborhoods age, decline, or gentrify, driving old populations out and replacing them with new ones. Republican areas go Democratic, and politically lopsided areas become more competitive. With time, even entire states and regions change, as we have witnessed in the southern United States. Not all of these changes in political complexion are driven by population replacement and geographic mobility, but at least some of them are. Linking population mobility to political change requires some understanding of the causes of mobility and the selection process at work in determining who moves and who stays behind.

The Economics and Sociology of Migration

From the voluminous work on the subject by demographers and economists, we have learned a lot about the causes of migration (for a survey, see Long 1988; Ritchey 1976; and Greenwood 1975). Much of the work on population migration has focused on understanding why people move from one place to another. Economists have favored explanations rooted in theories of human capital investment. People pay the financial and psychic costs of moving in hopes of reaping greater future returns. Mobility, then, is seen as an instrument of self-development, like investments in education or the purchase of health care (Cadwallader 1992, 115; Sjaastad 1962; Schultz 1963; Becker 1964). Typically, people move in order to find better paying jobs or avoid unemployment in a market with surplus labor. Certainly the desire to escape economic hardship accounts for the massive waves of rural to urban migration that occurred throughout this century as agricultural employment declined. Movement from one region to another, such as the flow of southwestern migrants to California or the movement of blacks from the rural South to northern cities, can also be understood as a function of economic incentives. International migration, in turn, can be explained in part by economics. The demand to enter the United States by citizens from less developed countries suggests that there are economic motives at the bottom of the decision to emigrate (Rolph 1992; Muller and Espenshade 1985). The economic incentives are so strong that entry into the United States by the foreign born is legally restricted. These restrictions and the risk of arrest by immigration authorities are not enough to deter the many who still want to take advantage of employment opportunities unavailable to them in their countries of origin.

Some do not move to find a better job, but are instead interested in improving their quality of life. The internal migration of elderly retirees to the Sunbelt is mostly a factor of considerations such as climate, low crime, recreation, and better health (Cadwallader 1992; Barsby and Cox 1975). Some movers are apparently willing to trade long-run income gains for improvement in quality of life. Amenities such as good schools, desirable housing, open space, and transportation may draw some residents from city to suburbs (Teaford 1997; Lewis 1996; Burns 1994; Harkman 1989; Peterson 1981; Cebula 1980; Tiebout 1956). Income may actually drop as a result of such moves, but the improvement in public services and amenities is considered to be worth the exchange.

Of course, the economics of labor markets and amenity differentials cannot explain all internal migration and immigration flows. Sociologists have highlighted previous migration patterns and the presence of networks of friends and family as powerful influences on population movement. Movers may be economically motivated, but their decisions about where to relocate are mediated through and influenced by social relationships (Portes 1995; Portes and Rumbaut 1990). A Mexican migrant, for example, may have better economic prospects in one state than in another but be constrained in his choice by family members who are already established in the less advantageous locale. Sometimes, existing social networks enhance a migrant's economic prospects. Family and friends may provide supplementary resources such as no-interest loans, discount housing, and information about jobs (Portes 1995, 12). Immigrants with no skills and little English are particularly drawn to areas in the United States where they are likely to find a warm reception among fellow nationals (Espenshade and Fu 1997). For migrants who face prejudice and discrimination from natives, the only real opportunity to get ahead may be provided by relocation near some compatible social network. In this sense, a migrant's context interacts with whatever skills he or she may bring to determine that person's capacity to prosper at their destination (Portes 1995, 24).

There are, to be sure, migrants who are not drawn to any particular destination but are simply fleeing oppressive conditions in their home countries. Refugees and asylees fall into this special category of migrants. While most political refugees settle in immigrant-dominated states such as California, Illinois, New York, and Texas, they sometimes wind up in an area by virtual accident of where their sponsors are located or as a result of government policy. Many Hmong refugees from Laos and Cambodia were relocated in Wisconsin, Michigan, and Minnesota, in communities that were 95 percent white, because the government desired to limit refugee resettlement in California and midwestern church groups were involved in reuniting refugee families (Hein 1994, 286).

Socioeconomic Mobility, Geographic Mobility, and Political Balkanization

The main reason for suspecting that internal migration may have political effects that alter the political complexion of an area is that the economics and politics of migration are linked. Geographic mobility is frequently the result of upward socioeconomic mobility (Massey and Denton 1993). People who are confident that they can improve their economic position by means of relocation, and have the resources to pack up and move, will relocate. Insofar as political allegiances are related to class and economic position, socioeconomic mobility has implications for the partisan and political balance of cities, regions, and states. Internal migrants in recent times have been people of means who have obtained information about opportunities elsewhere and can afford to pay the costs of relocation. As stated earlier, they are usually choosing to relocate in areas that present economic opportunities coupled with the public services that contribute to a higher quality of life (Peterson 1981; Tiebout 1956). In this manner, movers are self-selected, as they calculate positive and negative factors at origin and destination (Borjas, Bronars, and Trejo 1992; Sandefur, Tuma, and Kephart 1991; Clark and Ballard 1980; Yezer and Thurston 1976; Ritchey 1976; Lansing and Morgan 1967; Blanco 1963; Leslie and Richardson 1961). Depending on what kinds of jobs are being created, specific classes of citizens can be drawn from one part of the country (or state) to another. Many migrants have distinct political preferences that they then import into their new neighborhoods. Most native-born migrants will eventually reregister to vote, although it may take some time. Once registered, these new arrivals can express their views directly at the ballot box. With sufficient numbers, migrants may expand the size of the electorate and reconstitute the mix of interests within it.

Suburbanization is the most obvious pattern of geographic mobility that has had clear political implications. Suburbs first draw upper- and middle-class residents out of central cities, leading to the typical patterns of racial and class segregation visible in metropolitan areas (Morrill 1995; Massey and Denton 1993; Massey 1989, 1988; Kain and Quigley 1975). Poor unskilled workers are the least likely to move (Clark and Whiteman 1983; Sandefur, Tuma, and Kephart 1991). The research on movement to suburbs has demonstrated that the economic attitudes as well as the race and motivation of those who are first to move to suburbia are not randomly distributed. In recent times, these movers appear to be *positively* selected, focusing on considerations at the destination, such as higher wages and amenity differentials, for example, levels of public service (police protection, public schools, open space) that are not available in the old neighborhood (Peterson 1981; DeJong 1977). Positively selected migrants are most likely to be better educated, young, white, and upwardly mobile (Gabriel and Schmitz 1995; Borjas, Bronars, and Trejo 1992; Sandefur, Tuma, and Kephart 1991; Long 1988, 237; Ladinsky 1967; Hobbs 1942), and these traits are strongly associated with Republican Party identification (Wolfinger and Arsenau 1978; Perkins 1974). Bolstering this conclusion about the party leanings of movers to suburbia are results from the American National Election Study Cumulative Datafile showing that Republicans are more likely to report a shorter duration of residence in their current locale even after controlling for age, race, and income (see table 1.1). Apparently Democratic identifiers are less mobile than their GOP counterparts, especially when the distance involved imposes higher costs. This is not an especially new finding. Campbell, Converse, Miller, and Stokes (1960) found in their 1950s election studies that 71 percent of the Democrats raised in a central city still lived there, compared to only 46 percent of the Republicans (465).

The selection process at work in spatial mobility is rendering some cities and regions more demographically homogeneous and geographically segmented by race and class (Cohen and Dawson 1993; Wilson 1996, 1987). The spatial segregation of ethnic groups is also reshaping the politics of places. In spite of the movement of blacks and Hispanics to older suburbs, suburban politics remains overwhelmingly white and committed to maintaining political distance from large central cities (Teaford 1997). By the mid-1990s, inner cities were even more the province of minority political elites and electors than they had been in the 1960s. This segregation has simultaneously made it easier to elect black and Hispanic politicians and in some places has made white suburban politicians safer. But the empowerment of minority political elites has come at the expense of the geographic isolation of ethnic minorities from whites and low-income from upper- and middle-income voters (Massey and Denton 1993, 14). For most of the twentieth century, large central cities have been the predictable home turf of voters who reflexively cast Democratic ballots. The suburbs, particularly the growing suburbs, have been tilting almost as strongly in a Republican direction. There are fewer and fewer truly com-

TABLE 1.1.   The Relationship of Party Identification, Race, Income, and Age to Length of Residence in Present Community

Variable	Coefficient (standard error)
Party identification ($D = 1, I = 2, R = 3$)	−.84***
	(.11)
Income (in quintiles)	−1.05***
	(.10)
Race (1 = white, 2 = minority)	2.56***
	(.34)
Age (in years)	.56***
	(.01)
Constant	−1.69

$N = 22,955$
$F = 2,241.3; p \le .0001$
$R^2_a = .28$

Source: ICPSR, *American National Election Studies, Cumulative Datafile,* 1952–94.
Note: Ordinary least squares estimation; dependent variable = years of residence in current location.
***$p \le .001$

petitive electoral contests in metropolitan election districts. This lack of general election competition, in turn, depresses voter interest and denies citizens the benefit of meaningful choice. With only one real candidate for a given office, elections "become ceremonies which ratify rather than institutions through which choices are made" (Eulau and Prewitt 1973, 451). Officeholders are delighted with these segregated constituencies because in safe districts the threat of electoral sanction for bad leadership is more remote than it would be if there were serious competition. Lacking an effective mechanism to ensure accountability, constituents must depend upon the goodwill and conscience of their incumbent politicians.

The figures for the percentage of voters in each party from central city, suburban, and rural areas across four and a half decades reveal some interesting developments (see table 1.2). First, Democrats and Republicans have fewer voters to draw upon in rural and small town areas, as we begin the new century, than they did in earlier times. While both parties have gained in suburban areas, the Republicans have made the most impressive gains—almost half of their electorate is suburban, compared to less than a third in the 1950s. By contrast, Democratic gains in the suburbs have only risen about ten points since the 1950s. Republicans have experienced their losses in central cities. Their central city constituency has dropped from 25 percent of their party registration base to just 18 percent. The Democrats' central city base has remained a stable 30 to 31 percent of their constituency, even as most central cities have lost population. Independent identification has also risen dramatically in the suburbs (from 29 to 44 percent), while dropping about 8 points in the central city. The rise of independents in the suburbs verifies Thad Brown's contention that mobility often results in an individualized politics characterized by weakened party attachments (Brown 1988, chap. 7).

The geographic separation of the population groups comprising rival electoral coalitions has important implications for the future of both major parties. Within the Republican Party, the geographic isolation of minority and low-income voters from white, middle- and upper-income voters has made it more difficult for Republicans to broaden their base. With homogeneous, white, middle- and upper-income constituencies, Republicans find it to their electoral advantage to advocate policies that benefit a narrowly focused set of interests. Democrats, on the other hand, are threatened internally by having to represent both minority groups and conservative, working-class, white populations clustered in older suburbs who often express virulent racism (Massey and Denton 1993, 94; Cummings 1980; 1977). This balancing of interests has been maintained so far, but as the interests of minorities become more distant from the interests of the majority the disparate components of the rainbow coalition are harder to hold together.

Immigration and Differences in the Mobility of Populations

Internal migration has been a source of political stratification, but it is not the only source of spatial inequalities. High levels of both legal and illegal immigration are accelerating the political balkanization of the nation. A recent body of research has developed the link between contemporary internal labor flows and the influx of immigrants (Frey 1995a, 1995b; Alba, Denton, Leung, and Logan 1994). Evidence from the 1990 census

TABLE 1.2.   Political Party Affiliation by Place of Residence, 1952–94 (in percentages)

Years	Democrat	Independent	Republican	All	Summary Statistics
1950s					
Central city	31.1	29.4	25.4	28.7	$N = 6,250$
Suburban	26.3	28.5	31.9	28.4	$\chi^2 = 44.6$
Rural town	42.6	42.1	42.7	42.9	$p < .0001$
1960s					
Central city	30.1	27.5	20.8	26.7	$N = 6,897$
Suburban	28.7	33.2	36.5	31.5	$\chi^2 = 83.7$
Rural/town	41.2	39.3	42.7	41.8	$p < .0001$
1970s					
Central city	30.7	21.7	21.5	26.6	$N = 10,339$
Suburban	32.1	37.7	36.7	34.4	$\chi^2 = 119.5$
Rural/town	37.1	40.6	41.8	39.2	$p < .0001$
1980s					
Central city	30.9	21.6	18.9	25.3	$N = 9,505$
Suburban	37.5	40.9	45.7	40.9	$\chi^2 = 174.1$
Rural/town	30.6	37.5	35.4	38.1	$p < .0001$
1990s					
Central city	31.9	21.7	18.4	24.2	$N = 6,049$
Suburban	37.6	44.4	48.3	42.9	$\chi^2 = 165.5$
Rural/town	30.4	33.8	33.3	33.0	$p < .0001$

Source: ICPSR, *American National Election Studies, Cumulative Datafile,* 1952–94.

strongly suggests that internal migrants and immigrants are not drawn to the same destinations (Nogle 1996; Kritz and Nogle 1994). Most new immigrants are non-Caucasian, with 85 percent coming from Asia and Latin America. It is also well known that these new residents are less educated and have lower skill levels than natives (Borjas 1990; Borjas and Freeman 1992). Consequently, the natives who are less educated are the most threatened by the arrival of new immigrants in a labor market (Filer 1992, 269). Through preferential hiring practices, immigrant groups create niches that exclude outsiders. "Outsiders lack the traits, histories and relational ties conducive to collaboration or trust; on these grounds alone, rational considerations lead insiders toward economic exchanges with their own" (Waldinger 1996, 26). In New York since the 1970s, native-born blacks have seen a sharp decline in their labor market position while the employment of immigrants has expanded (56). Of course, one solution to bad economic conditions is to leave. If native blacks fare so poorly in urban labor markets, why don't they go elsewhere? The answer to this question takes us back to the selection process at work in determining who is mobile and who is not. Not everyone facing bad economic times can afford to leave. Geographic mobility requires resources and information about opportunities elsewhere. Some groups have the resources and information, while others do not. The ones lacking resources and information are likely to remain stuck in the worst labor markets in the country. Add to this the fact that public assistance programs make it possible for people to remain in a bad labor market long after they should have left it and we can understand how some groups end up immobile in an economy in which only movers get ahead.

Apparently, many native-born whites have both the information and resources to leave surplus labor markets behind. Evidence from the 1990 census indicates that native-born whites leave regions and states that are experiencing an influx of immigrants, leading to a sharp rise in the minority composition and low-income populations of some areas (Frey 1995a, 736; 1995b). In New York, the result of immigration influx has been the expansion of all-minority ghetto areas—all-black and black-Hispanic neighborhoods (Alba, Denton, Leung, and Logan 1994). In California, white lower- and middle-income out-migrants are being pushed out of the state by competition for jobs and housing and the increased social costs associated with immigration (Frey 1995b, 363; Walker, Ellis, and Barff 1992; Muller and Espenshade 1985). Whether the movement of native whites from these areas is the result of displacement or white flight from population groups of color, no one questions that this development will reinforce the existing patterns of geographic segregation by race and class.

The political consequences of the spatial separation of natives from immigrants obviously depend upon where the immigrants find their political home, with Democrats or Republicans, and how politically active they become. There is evidence to suggest that spatially isolated immigrant groups fail to get involved in politics at all. Geographic isolation prevents minorities from voicing demands to outsiders (Kwong 1996; Lamare 1977; Garcia 1973). Members of an ethnic enclave make demands only within the enclave, not on institutions outside their insular community. If we find that newly arriving minorities do become involved in state and national politics in spite of their spatial isolation, then fears of increased political balkanization resulting from sustained immigration have been overblown. Moreover, if a new group's involvement in politics is roughly divided between the parties, then perhaps there is no troubling consequence of the settlement and mobility patterns of native and immigrant groups. But if one party, most likely the Democrats, finds itself becoming the exclusive party of the disadvantaged immigrant population, then a new political sectionalism will result—one that will further undermine the utility of competitive elections as instruments of accountability while further polarizing the American polity by race and class.

The idea that newly arriving immigrants may be totally captured by one party or the other is not as far-fetched as it may sound. Press reports from California during the 1996 elections indicated that newly naturalized immigrants were registering as Democrats by a five to one ratio and that in immigrant receiving cities such as San Jose the ratio was closer to ten to one. Of course the Republican-led U.S. Congress was responsible for pushing many new immigrants away from the GOP with its determined effort to cut most forms of public assistance to legal permanent residents (Gimpel and Edwards 1999). There are serious political risks in alienating any growing population of voters, regardless of their ethnicity. But independent of whether any of the new immigrants naturalize and register to vote, political consequences may follow from the reaction of natives to their presence, with the California referenda of 1994 and 1996 serving as clear examples. Measures intended to cut back on the admission of legal immigrants are popular in many quarters, and they reflect the growing uneasiness of natives and older immigrants with the new wave of foreign-born arrivals.

Political Assimilation and Adaptation of Migrants

Assimilation is customarily thought to mean the gradual erasure of distinct cultural identity, hence the cognate term *melting pot.* Cultural assimilation is thought to work through intermarriage and equal status contact with other groups (Jiobu 1988). By the second and third generations, so the traditional theories would have it, ethnic languages, cultures, and behaviors are lost (Massey 1995; Wolfinger 1965; Gordon 1964). The challenge of assimilating is not something that only the foreign born confront. All migrants, both internal and cross-national, face some degree of difficulty in adapting to their new settings. Not every aspect of a group's ethnic identity is given up in the assimilation process, but some learning of new habits and ways of thinking inevitably takes place in the adaptation process. Ethnic insularity develops whenever sizable groups of newcomers, in distinct geographic locations, assimilate at different rates.

Part of what it means to assimilate is to acquire the civic values and practice the civic virtues prevailing in the new locale. Political assimilation refers to the tendency for a group to adapt its political behaviors and attitudes to conform to the standards of the new community. Granted, sometimes those standards are low. Many native-born citizens of the United States have few of the civic virtues and values so highly prized by democratic theorists. Arguably, in some communities nonparticipation is the prevailing norm and to assimilate would mean to stay home on election day with the majority of the native born. In other words, it is worth asking, from time to time, to what the new populations are assimilating. Nevertheless, concern for the political "Americanization" of new immigrants has been expressed recently by no less an authority than the U.S. Commission on Immigration Reform, which was chaired by Barbara Jordan until her death in 1996. To emphasize Americanization, the commissioners recommended support for English classes, streamlining the naturalization process, and emphasizing individual rights as a component of civic education curricula.

Political stratification occurs when political assimilation occurs unevenly across the migrant population. Some groups acquire the civic values and norms of participation of the host society in less than a generation, while others do not. The populations that are slower to politically assimilate are at a serious disadvantage in a polity in which political power is conveyed through elections that are tied to geographically specific districts.

For some, simply asking whether new populations assimilate is threatening because information about the maladaptation of a group might be used as a justification for its exclusion. The ridiculous doubts that were raised throughout the cold war era about the commitment of Asian immigrants to democracy are an example of how degrees of assimilation can be used as a justification for low visa quotas. Interestingly, internal migrants are suspect for the same reasons. Native-born Californians regularly expressed worries about the political and social values of southwestern migrants during the 1930s.

> "Okie" was soon to become a derogatory term. Private citizens and public officials would, over the next few years, blame the Okies for crime and lawlessness, disrupting the public schools, overburdening the hospitals and social services, draining the state budget and creating a communist menace. Okies would be derided as dirty, lazy, immoral, disease-ridden, lawless and fanatically religious. In short, bigoted Californians ascribed to Okies all the inhuman characteristics once assigned to Irish, Polish, Italians and Jews arriving in the urban centers of the north. (Morgan 1992, 77)

It is noteworthy that the Okies were not simply typecast as dirty, lazy and disease-ridden but also lawless and politically suspect as communists. In other words, their capacity to politically assimilate was forcefully questioned. Doubts about a group's capacity to politically assimilate or adopt American civic values have sometimes served as a justification for nativist policies. Nevertheless, studies of political assimilation should not be avoided for fear that they might show some groups to be less adaptable than others. Research is likely to crush many misconceptions, as the Latino National Political Survey did in showing that English was far more prevalent in the households of Latino citizens than commonly supposed (de la Garza et al. 1992). Inquiry into the political values of Asians showed them to be no more sympathetic to communism than natives, and some, such as the Vietnamese and Koreans, were a great deal less so. Studies of political adaptation yield valuable information about the challenges groups face in their new communities. If migrants have lower political participation rates than nonmigrants, that fact is worth knowing. If new arrivals change the politics of a place by importing new interests and values, generating knowledge about how such change occurs strengthens our capacity to anticipate and cope with changes that are on the way.

A study of the political impact of migration is likely to show that when new populations flow into an area at a sufficiently slow pace, the recent arrivals may be absorbed without much notice and even socialized into the political habits of the established majority. Under such conditions, the political impact of migration may be slight. Even adults are subject to the influence of peers—their new friends and neighbors—who over time reward the adoption of conforming attitudes (Huckfeldt and Sprague 1995; Huckfeldt 1986; Burbank 1995; McBurnett 1991). Upwardly mobile citizens have been found to change their political orientation to suit their new status and location. Presumably this is how many Republican areas maintain their Republicanism in spite of in-migration from Democratic areas. Some political science research has found that migration does not change people's political orientations (Brown 1988, 10; Campbell, Converse, Miller, and Stokes 1960). In the early 1960s, a pair of studies of New York City suburbs found that new arrivals from the city showed no sign of adopting the political views of the older Republican residents (Straetz and Munger 1960; Wallace 1962). The early socialization process is so strong that it stays with a person for life, regardless of socioeconomic or geographic movement.

Some conversion must take place, however, because if it did not New York City's suburban counties would not be nearly as Republican as they are today. Without some partisan conversion, the rapid inundation of the suburbs with former residents of the boroughs would have generated suburban Democratic strongholds. Whether people adapt to new neighborhoods by changing their political orientations or remain steadfast adherents to their political upbringings, is an important question that remains unsettled. Unquestionably it must depend upon individual characteristics such as the strength of one's political beliefs and partisanship at the time of the move as well as the political character of the new community—including the pressures for conformity within it. The more general point, however, is that it is not clear whether places change the politics of migrants or migrants change the politics of places. Most of the evidence points toward the latter, especially when the volume of migration is high. When an area is inundated with those of alien disposition, there will be far less pressure to conform to the existing community's values since those values are likely be challenged by a larger group in which migrants can find compatible social support for expressing divergent views (Berelson, Lazarsfeld, and McPhee 1954, 126; Huckfeldt and Sprague 1995; Huckfeldt 1986). In these circumstances, the migrants change the community. By contrast, when migration is only a trivial part of an area's population growth, the pressure on new arrivals to adapt is much higher. In these cases, migrants are more likely to conform. The foregoing considerations permit the formulation of a reasonable expectation: that the potential for political change due to migration is highest in states where the population of new residents is consequential. To be consequential, the population of migrants and immigrants need not be large by national standards—only large relative to the local population of natives.

Natives, Discrimination, and the Prevention of Assimilation

Migrants and immigrants of color face special obstacles to conformity and assimilation in a predominantly white society. As Massey and Denton (1993, chap. 4) indicate, many want to conform, but whites will not permit their assimilation. The propensity of natives to discriminate against new-comers raises the possibility that movers may generate social and political change by their very presence—independent of whether they become polit-ically involved. Across the nation, townspeople in such out of the way places as Wausau and Appleton, Wisconsin, and Storm Lake, Iowa, have erupted in nativist protest to non-Anglo immigrants whose presence has strained these communities' capacity to deliver public services (Grey 1996).

Native protests are not only directed at those of a different race or those who speak a different language. Even native interaction with inter-nal migrants may provoke hostile reactions, giving the host community a measure of cohesion it had never had in the premigrant period. James N. Gregory's heartrending accounts of discrimination against southwestern migrants by native Californians in the 1920s and 1930s comes readily to mind (1989, chap. 4; see also Morgan 1992). Apparently the maltreatment was so severe that Gregory found elderly Oklahomans who remain ashamed of their origins some fifty years after their arrival on the West Coast (Gregory 1989, 121). In the early 1990s, Oregon became well known for its nationally broadcast television ads, which urged people to visit the state but implored them not to stay. California, Colorado, Oregon, Florida, Arizona, and Washington state have been very aggressive in adopting slow growth initiatives that effectively discourage some would-be migrants by raising the costs of relocation.

Discriminatory barriers to prospective migrants exist in many forms. One of the most common involves legislation governing municipal incor-poration and land use. Nancy Burns chronicles the history of the use of municipal incorporation as a means of preventing racial integration, pointing out that "cities are now more frequently racial boundaries than are neighborhood borders" (1994, 81; see also Teaford 1997). Often, though, discrimination has not taken such a subtle form. One of the strongest barriers to assimilation has been the violence and intimidation practiced by natives against newcomers. Migrants and immigrants of color are particularly vulnerable to exclusion from the mainstream.

The study of the opposition to newcomers by natives involves serious consideration of the well-known "contact hypothesis," which has been the subject of extensive investigation across several disciplines (Hood and Morris 1998, 1997; Sigelman, Bledsoe, Welch, and Combs 1996; Giles and Hertz 1995; Ellison and Powers 1994; Rothbart and John 1993; Hewstone and Brown 1986; Allport 1954; Key 1949). The contact hypothesis has actually been posed as two rival hypotheses. Some have postulated that contact between one group and another reduces negative feelings between groups while others have suggested that proximity breeds hostility and rivalry between the groups. Those believing that contact reduces intergroup tension base this conclusion on the idea that knowledge and hostility are inversely related. Familiarity breeds not contempt but friendship. Others have been less sure about contact leading to peaceful intergroup relations. In the South that V. O. Key Jr. studied, contact with large black populations triggered perceptions of threat among whites and resulted in determined efforts by white elites to preserve Jim Crow. The results of testing the contact hypotheses depend crucially on the way in which contact is operationalized. The use of broad brush contextual variables for contact, such as the population composition of cities and neighborhoods, has generally produced results consistent with the notion that contact breeds rivalry and tension between groups. Lacking detailed individual level data on the quality and type of contact between group members, I am inclined to believe that the aggregate measures of contact utilized in this study will produce results similar to Key's findings. More generally, I expect to find that political changes resulting from population mobility will be most visible in areas of ethnic heterogeneity, for example, where diverse racial and ethnic groups come into contact.

Summary: Population Mobility and Political Change

Admittedly, internal migrants and immigrants may have little in common except for their mobility—but that is a sufficiently common denominator to raise the question of what this mobility does to change the politics of places. There are three ways in which internal migrants and immigrants can change the political landscape in the areas where they resettle. First, there is the element of geographic isolation by race and class that can result from the selection process at work in population mobility. Older inner city neighborhoods are abandoned by suburban-bound Republicans to be replaced with minorities and immigrants whose eventual political allegiances convert the area into a one-party Democratic stronghold. The sorting process in migration clusters poor voters of color in high concentrations in inner cities and white middle- and upper-income voters in suburbs. The evidence showing that immigrants and internal migrants do not settle in the same locations is indicative of a new pattern of geographic clustering that may have profound political implications as politicians emerge who represent highly homogeneous, unidimensional constituencies, leading to a breakdown in electoral accountability and the political extremism encouraged by one-sided electoral districts.

Second, by importing new political preferences, which they express directly at the polls, new residents may alter the political and partisan balance of the neighborhoods where they settle. Relatively competitive areas may become monolithically one-sided as the selection process leaves some groups out. One-party neighborhoods become two-party competitive as new populations mix with old. Southwestern migrants came to be the dominant population group in central California in the 1940s and 1950s, eventually making the Democratic Party a competitive force in a state where it had been weak for decades.

The first two ways in which politics may change assumes that mobile groups will eventually become politically active upon resettlement. But the prospect for political change does not depend upon this assumption. Natives often resent the fact that new arrivals compete for jobs and make claims upon public services for which the established residents must help shoulder the cost. This is particularly true for migrants and immigrants with little means who have school-age families and may eventually come to depend on some form of public aid. Needy newcomers are the least likely to receive a warm welcome from long-time residents. Burns argues that the manipulation of city boundaries is designed to define some as residents and some as nonresidents in order to minimize the costs imposed on the former by needy population groups: "if cities play their boundary cards right, they may not even have citizens in need of social services" (1994, 114).

Selecting Cases for Study

Observers of American politics can be confident, of course, that political change does occur at the macrolevel, even though the microlevel processes that produce it have not yet been pinpointed (Gerber and Green 1998). We can also be certain that at least some of this change within the United States is attributable to the mobility of some populations and the immobility of others. Even those who have recently argued that the political realignment of the American South is primarily the result of the conversion of southern whites do not deny that migration from the North has also played a role in altering the partisan balance of the region (Wolfinger and Arsenau 1978; Wolfinger and Hagen 1985; Stanley 1988; Petrocik 1987). Given the variability of migration and immigration flows, the extent to which population changes alter the electoral politics of an area must be highly variable across the nation. One would expect, for example, that the impact of mobility on the political development of California, Florida, and other Sunbelt states might be much more extensive than, say, the impact in interior states that have experienced lower rates of growth. But simply because some states have more new residents than others does not mean that states with small populations escape the changes that result from mobility. In rural states, it takes fewer strangers to remake the electorate or generate hostile political reactions from long-time residents.

Because I am interested in studying contexts that vary in the scope and nature of their population mobility, the selection of cases cannot be done casually. Areas with few immigrants and internal migrants must be included alongside those with many. My goal in this book is to focus on seven states that show varying degrees and types of population mobility and population growth in order to evaluate the extent to which electoral politics has changed along with the demography. States are important units of analysis in studies of American electoral politics because they are the source of rich and interesting political variation. More specifically to this project, states are relevant because the consequences of immigration and migration fall heavily upon services financed by state government, including infrastructure, environmental protection, growth control, taxation, welfare, and law enforcement. The selection of states is also dictated by convenience. I have chosen to study New York, Pennsylvania, Kansas, Kentucky, Florida, Colorado, and California partly because of the availability of party registration data—changes in partisan balance will serve as an important indicator of political change. Certainly other interesting high- and low-mobility states (such as Texas) could be included, but these were ruled out because they do not enroll voters by party.

The Population Composition of Selected States

A basic description of the population composition of the seven chosen states appears in table 1.3. These figures show that in 1990 New York and California had the highest percentages of foreign-born residents, although a surprisingly low percentage of California immigrants have naturalized. Figures for internal migrants show that Florida has the highest percentage of residents born in other states, although a majority of Colorado's population has migrated from elsewhere too. Kansas and Kentucky are noteworthy for having both a low number and a low percentage of immigrants. Pennsylvania has a significant immigrant population, nearly 370,000, but this figure constitutes a low percentage (3 percent) of the state's total population. Sixty percent of Pennsylvania's foreign-born population is naturalized, the highest of any of the seven states examined here.

Where do these seven fit in the overall distribution of all states on variables such as the percentage of migrants from elsewhere and the size of the foreign-born population? Figure 1.1 shows the univariate distribution of all fifty states (and the District of Columbia) for the percentage of migrants from other states (but not U.S. territories) in 1990. Florida, situated in the right-hand tail of the distribution, is among the few states with the largest proportion of residents from elsewhere, over 55 percent. In the left-hand tail, Pennsylvania and New York have the fewest migrants from other states. Clearly this shows that the deindustrializing Northeast has not been an attractive destination for internal migrants. Kansas is the closest to the mean of the distribution with 35.4 percent, and Colorado is more than one standard deviation above the mean at 51.1 percent.

Figure 1.2 illustrates where the seven states fit in the distribution of the percentage of immigrants residing in each state in 1990. In the far right tail, alone, is California, with 22 percent of its population reporting that they were foreign born. New York is a distant second with 15.9 percent. At the other end of the distribution, Kentucky is among the states with the fewest foreign-born residents. Only two other states, Mississippi and West Virginia, have a smaller proportion of immigrants than Kentucky. Cases that are more typical can be found near the mean, including Colorado, Pennsylvania, and Kansas.

New York and Pennsylvania are in the old industrial core. They are

TABLE 1.3. Population, Foreign-Born Population, and Naturalized Population in Seven States, 1990

State and Variable	California	Colorado	Florida	Kansas	Kentucky	New York	Pennsylvania
Population	29,760,021	3,294,394	12,937,926	2,477,574	3,685,296	17,990,455	11,881,643
Foreign born	6,458,825	142,434	1,662,601	62,840	34,119	2,851,861	369,316
% Foreign born	22	4	13	3	1	16	3
Naturalized	2,017,610	67,277	713,505	27,236	15,890	1,297,020	218,209
% Naturalized	31	47	43	43	47	46	59
% Born in other states or U.S. territories	41	55	65	37	22	20	17

Source: U.S. Bureau of the Census, 1990.

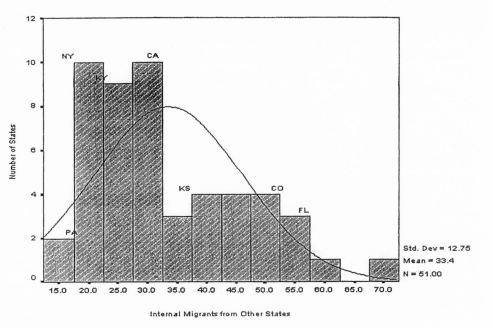

Fig. 1.1.   Distribution of states by proportion of residents born in other states, 1990

important cases because both have experienced economic stagnation and slow growth from internal migration over the past twenty years (*American Demographics,* June 1985, 38–42). Although neither state has seen much net growth in population, there has been considerable internal redistribution with the rapid suburbanization of Philadelphia and New York City. In addition, New York is a major port of entry for immigrants. Between 1985 and 1990, 769,000 foreign-born newcomers settled in New York.

Kansas has also seen very little net growth, mostly due to the gradual decline in agricultural employment. While it ranks low among states as a destination for immigrants (fig. 1.2), it does not take many immigrants to generate political reaction in small rural communities. Parts of rural southwestern Kansas have experienced an influx of Latino and Asian immigrants in the last twenty years. Half of the immigrants in the state have arrived since 1980. Some of this is the result of internal migration of Mexicans eastward across the border from southern Colorado and north from Texas. The attraction is driven by the labor market, especially by

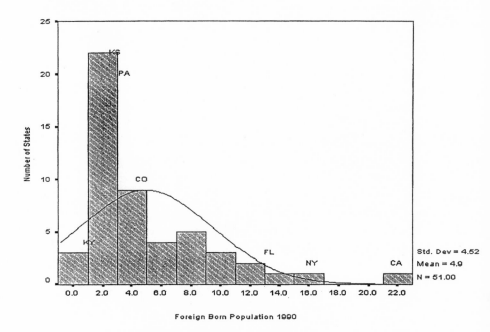

Fig. 1.2.   Distribution of states by proportion of foreign-born residents, 1990

employment in agriculture, food processing (including meatpacking and livestock production), and petroleum production.

Kentucky and Colorado have experienced moderate to high growth due to internal migration over the last twenty-five years. Colorado, in particular, is known for attracting a very highly skilled work force to its high-technology industries around Denver. Neither state is an especially popular destination for immigrants, although southern Colorado has had a large Latino population for most of this century in the working-class town of Pueblo, where the first Mexican immigrants were brought to work in the steel mills after 1910. Sugar growers have long hired cheap Mexican labor to work in the beet fields in the Platte River basin in northeastern Colorado. Accounts of local historians indicate that Anglo-Coloradans have long fought to remain separate from blacks and Hispanics, considering immigrants a "necessary evil" while resisting all forms of integration (Abbott, Leonard, and McComb 1982, 295–98).

Kentucky's growth has occurred in the suburbs of its large cities—Louisville, Lexington, and the Cincinnati area. Migration from northern states, including Ohio next door, is leading to the emergence of the Republicans as a competitive force in state and local politics. The foreign-born population of the state constituted less than 1 percent of the total population in 1990, and only about half of those were naturalized (see table 1.3). Immigration is as close to being a nonissue in Kentucky as it is anywhere in the country.

Finally, California and Florida are extraordinary for their seemingly unstoppable pace of both internal migration and immigration. In Florida, the political impact of population mobility seems clear-cut. Florida's internal migration consists mostly of well-educated northerners in white collar employment and large numbers of elderly retirees. These migrants appear to have slightly more liberal attitudes than the native whites, particularly on racial issues, but most are Republicans (Craig 1991). Florida's most familiar immigrant enclave is Miami's Cuban exile community. During the 1980s, Cubans were joined by 123,000 more of their own from the Mariel boatlift in 1980 as well as 40,000 Haitians. This was followed by substantial waves from El Salvador, Venezuela, Colombia, Nicaragua, and the Dominican Republic (Gannon 1990). The majority of Cubans identify with the Republican Party, but the party loyalties of non-Cuban Hispanics are more evenly divided.

Whereas migration and immigration have aided Republican registration growth in Florida, the political impact of population influx to California is less clear. Most recent internal migrants are like native movers elsewhere: white, well educated, and intending to resettle in wealthy Republican suburbs. But cross-state migration flows to California have not always been Republican. The southwestern and black migrations from southern states between 1920 to the mid-1950s helped resurrect the state Democratic Party from oblivion.

As for immigrants, no state has been more active in searching for ways to deal with massive waves of legal and illegal immigration than California. In spite of their sizable numbers in a state with a long multiethnic history, Latinos and Asians in California remain spatially concentrated in the state's most urban counties. Ethnic conflict is familiar in Los Angeles politics. The riots of May 1992 brought the conflict between Asians and blacks into clear view. Latinos and blacks are also alienated from one another, as blacks consider themselves at a competitive disadvantage vis-à-vis Latinos in the labor force (Wilson 1996; Skerry 1993, 83–84). Latino immigrants are also moving into neighborhoods in once all black areas such as Watts and Compton, putting pressure on housing prices.

Together, these seven states cover varying points on the relevant distributions of internal migration and immigration and should therefore make for meaningful contrasts that are representative of other states and regions. An alternative to comparing the numbers of new residents migrating to these states is to compare growth *rates,* that is, the percentage change in the migrant and immigrant populations from 1970 to 1990. These figures yield the fourfold classification table displayed in figure 1.3. Kansas and Colorado, at the upper right, are representative of states that have registered a surprisingly high immigration rate combined with rather modest growth from domestic sources. While both Kansas and Colorado are home to rather small fractions of the total U.S. immigrant population, the number of foreign-born residents more than doubled between 1970 and 1990. Kentucky, in the bottom left cell of the figure, reflects states where immigration has been limited but internal migration has been high. New York and Pennsylvania are states with low population gains from internal migration and rather low increases from immigration as well. Even though New York's immigrant population increased by 35 percent from 1970 to 1990, this rate of increase is dwarfed by all states except Pennsylvania, where the foreign-born population declined by 17 percent over the same period. Finally, Florida and California (bottom right), are high on both dimensions of population growth. California's immigrant population has increased by 267 percent, and Florida is close behind at 205 percent.

Plan of the Book

In the chapters that follow, I will examine each state's trends in population growth and mobility with an eye toward evaluating whether these trends have had any impact on electoral behavior across places. In each chapter, I will begin by providing an overview of the state's demographic development since 1970. In this opening section, I will determine where various population groups have settled and whether they appear to be responding to economic opportunities at their destination or the existence of prior coethnic communities. The settlement pattern of a group determines the potential visibility and political impact that group may have. Whether immigrants settle in enclaves or disperse into the majority population may also be indicative of their capacity to assimilate.

The next section of each chapter will contain the results of several hypothesis tests of the effect of internal migration and immigration on

Immigration
Growth Rate

		Low	High
Internal Migration Growth Rate	Low	NY, PA	KS, CO
	High	KY	FL, CA

Fig. 1.3. Classification of states by internal migration and immigration growth rates, 1970–90

political participation, partisan voting, and the balance of party registrants at the county level. These aggregate-level results must be interpreted with caution, as ecological data contain many ambiguities. Conclusions about the politics of places can be advanced only tentatively. This data analysis will be supplemented, wherever possible, by available individual-level data from surveys that represent states. Additional data on immigrant and migrant settlement patterns at the subcounty (census tract) level are appropriate for highlighting demographic developments not visible at higher levels of aggregation.

Each chapter will also draw upon appropriate contextual information gathered from secondary sources and interviews. Such material will permit the discussion of particularly important cases and examples of immigrant-native interaction and political behavior. Each chapter concludes with a discussion of what has been learned from the analysis and prospects for the future relationship between immigrants, natives, and internal migrants and their communities.

The final chapter will make comparisons across all seven settings and draw conclusions based on a broader perspective. Here the point will be to mine the large accumulation of factual results in an effort to advance theorizing about the role of population mobility in shaping ethnic relations and political change. The spatial clustering of population groups with homogeneous political interests has important implications for the style and substance of political representation such monolithic communities encourage. I will close with thoughts about how the spatial sorting process resulting from differences in the relative mobility of populations relates to questions of legislative districting and the practice of pluralist politics.

CHAPTER 2

California: Diversity at a Distance

Orange County, California, was once the most predictable Republican stronghold in the nation. Democrats could field only sacrificial lambs in hopeless challenges to GOP incumbents at all levels of elective office. By the mid-1990s, Republicans still held a registration edge that had slipped only slightly since 1970, but many other aspects of the county had changed. About one-quarter of the county's population was of Hispanic origin, and 10 percent were Asian. Twenty-four percent were foreign born.

In 1996, a thirty-six-year-old Hispanic woman, Loretta Sanchez, entered the contest for the 46th Congressional District seat, then occupied by Bob Dornan, a fire-breathing conservative who was finishing his twentieth year in Congress while running a hopeless campaign to become the Republican presidential nominee. Sanchez had no previous political experience and was well aware of Orange County's Republican inclination, but she had taken careful note of the large Hispanic population in the segment of Orange County that is encompassed by the 46th District's boundaries, an area where 50 percent of the population was Latino. She was convinced that Latinos would vote for her because she was one of them, and she won by a narrow 984 vote margin. Dornan immediately made charges of voter fraud, claiming that noncitizens had been improperly registered to vote, but in the end insufficient evidence was found to overturn the result. Dornan had become another political victim of population mobility. His loss was not simply the result of redistricting or the manipulation of district boundaries, although such factors certainly contributed. It was real demographic change in Orange County that led to Dornan's political demise.

In the opening chapter, I offered some good reasons for suspecting that contemporary trends in internal migration and immigration are changing the electoral politics of states and regions. Specifically, internal migration has become the privilege of upwardly mobile, white, well-educated, mostly Republican-leaning natives. This is particularly true of migration across state lines, where the costs imposed by moving are far higher than most moves occurring locally or within a state. A major component of current immigration, on the other hand, involves the movement into the United States of non-Caucasian peoples with few skills, low educational attainment, and little English. These characteristics inhibit the assimilation and integration of immigrants into the social, economic, and political mainstream. Lacking skills, education, and English, the newer immigrants cluster in enclaves, where ethnic distinction is reinforced, rather than dispersing to meld with other elements of the population, including other immigrant groups. Because immigrants are admitted under U.S. law based mainly on family ties, regardless of their skills and education, they naturally form concentrated ethnic pockets in the areas where they settle. Nowhere is this more evident than in California's Santa Clara County (San Jose), where the Asian population increased from 99,000 to 261,000 between 1980 and 1990, or Orange County (Anaheim), where the Asian population increased from 57,000 to 250,000 during the same period. Drawing upon the work of Frey (1996, 1995a, 1995b) and others (Filer 1992; Barff and Walker 1992), I am arguing that the distinct characteristics of foreign- and native-born movers lead to their residential segregation and ultimately to important political changes as substate regions develop monolithic racial and economic interests that eventually translate into political identities. In this manner, population change will catch up to alter the politics of places, as it did in Orange County in 1996.

California's experience of population change is unique in American history and perhaps even in the world. No state has been the destination of such a large volume of both internal migrants and immigrants. In turn, California is an excellent (and relatively easy) case with which to begin an assessment of the political impact of rapid population growth. If population changes have had some impact on turnout, partisanship, and other aspects of electoral politics, that impact should be observable in the Golden State. Map 2.1 shows the areas of highest growth in California from 1950 to 1992. Darker shades indicate counties with the most explosive growth. The map shows that growth has occurred all over the state but especially in the south (Orange, San Diego) and north-central counties (Yolo, Sacramento, Placer, Amador). Several coastal counties south of the Bay Area also rank high, including Santa Cruz, San Mateo, and Monterey. The counties of slower growth are those in the rural north, but even they have grown relative to their 1950 populations.

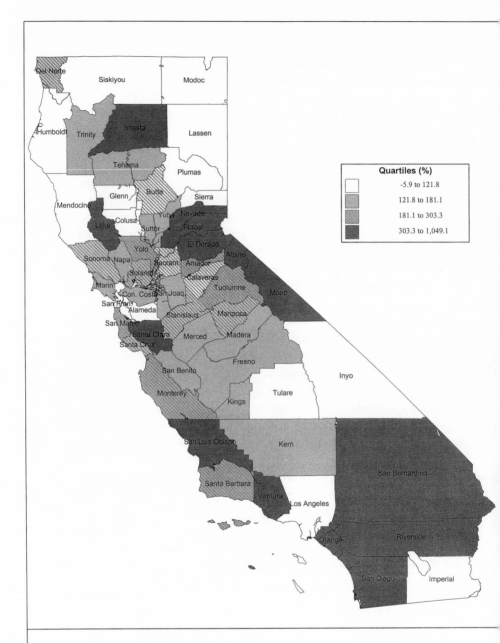

Map 2.1. Population growth in California counties, 1950–92. (Mean = 232.3, Moran's I = 12)

Outside of the northern counties and a few mountain regions along the Nevada border, the growth has been enough to radically realign certain regions of the state. Areas along the coast from Santa Barbara to the Oregon border that voted comfortably for Richard Nixon in the 1960s were voting solidly Democratic by the 1990s (Gimpel 1996). Party registration figures suggest that the electorate is evenly distributed between the two major parties across much of the state, making nearly every area a political battleground. By 1990, only about 15 percent of Republicans (or Democrats) would have had to move for partisan voters to be evenly distributed across the state's fifty-eight counties[1]—a far lower percentage than in the other states discussed in this book. In the Central Valley, once strong Democratic bastions such as Tulare, Fresno, Kings, and Kern Counties became some of the most predictable Republican areas in the state in presidential and gubernatorial races while electing conservative Democrats locally. In Southern California, the increasing racial and economic diversity of Riverside and Los Angeles Counties plunged GOP registration to its post–World War II low point in the mid-1990s. Republicans have remained stronger in Southern California than in the north, and the greater numbers there have helped Republicans control the state's governorship through the 1980s and 1990s, but California's politics is in an evolving, highly unsettled state.

Trends in the growth of the foreign-born population and the change in the percentage of the foreign-born population that is Caucasian provide solid evidence for the rapid changes that have reshaped California's character. The foreign-born population now constitutes about one-quarter of the state's population and a majority of those immigrants are nonwhite. The steep drop in the percentage of foreign-born white residents is particularly worth noting. In 1960, over 90 percent of the foreign-born population in California was white. By 1990, this figure had dropped to about 40 percent. This trend corresponds to both the changes in national immigration

---

1. This figure is based on the calculation of a dissimilarity index for counties that will be used throughout this book to indicate the concentration and spatial segregation of groups across both counties and census tracts. The index of dissimilarity is given by

$$Dxy = .5 * \Sigma\, |(x_i/X) - (y_i/Y)|$$

where
x_i and y_i are the number of X and Y members in census tract or county i.
X and Y are the total number of X and Y members for the entire county (in the case of tracts) or state (in the case of counties) (Massey and Denton 1987, 805–6).

policy that shifted immigration preferences toward less developed nations and the failure to control illegal immigration across the nation's southern border (Gimpel and Edwards 1999). By the early 1990s, 85 percent of California's foreign-born population had entered the country after 1965.

For 1990, the composition of the foreign-born population in California is illustrated by the pie chart in figure 2.1. Of the nearly 6.5 million immigrants in the state in 1990, 31 percent, or just over 2 million, were Asian, with Filipinos, Koreans, Chinese, and Vietnamese the largest groups. Another 2.5 million (38 percent) were Mexican, and this population was seriously undercounted. The remaining immigrants in 1990 included 595,000 Europeans, 706,000 Central and South Americans, and about 66,000 Africans. Continued immigration in the face of a five-year recession during the early 1990s helped fuel much of the nativist resentment that culminated in the Proposition 187 movement to limit public services to legal and illegal residents (Gimpel and Edwards 1999).

The research on migration and internal migration discussed in chapter 1 indicates that there are important demographic distinctions among cross-state migrants, immigrants, and nonmigrants. But many of these research studies have been conducted using national data and surveys rather than data from particular states. In response, one might raise the reasonable objection that what is true for national surveys may not hold for individual states. Could it be the case that migrants, long-term residents, and immigrants are not that distinct in California? To evaluate the differences, I looked at the 1990 Census Public Use Microdata 1 Percent Sample (PUMS) for California. I selected only those Californians over the age of eighteen. Comparisons of the mean age, education level, and income of 213,688 cross-state migrants, immigrants, and native Californians are presented in appendix A (table A2.1). These data show that internal migrants residing in California earn more money, are considerably older, and are more likely to be on Social Security than either native Californians or immigrants. In addition, 80 percent of internal migrants are white, compared to 71 percent of natives and 20 percent of immigrants, indicating that the racial composition of internal migrants and immigrants in California is highly distinct. The age distribution, though, is different from many national studies, as it shows California's newer residents to be older than natives or immigrants. California, like Florida, draws from a migration stream that selects out a disproportionate number of elderly retirees from the national pool of migrants.

What relevance do the 1990 PUMS data have for predicting patterns

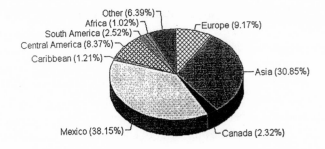

Other (6.39%)
Africa (1.02%)
South America (2.52%)
Central America (8.37%)
Caribbean (1.21%)
Europe (9.17%)
Asia (30.85%)
Mexico (38.15%)
Canada (2.32%)

Fig. 2.1. Composition of the foreign-born population in California, 1990

of spatial balkanization in California? The answer lies primarily in the income, educational, and racial differences between immigrants, internal migrants, and California natives. Nearly $8,000 separated the average income of migrants from that of immigrants in 1990. Immigrants, on average, had 2.2 years less education than did internal migrants and natives. Slightly more than one-fifth of immigrants in California are non-Hispanic white compared to the vast majority of interstate migrants and 71 percent of native Californians. These differences easily predict that immigrants, natives, and internal migrants will not make the same locational decisions about where to live and work. To evaluate whether settlement patterns are different for the migrant and immigrant populations, I will return to the aggregate data.

Settlement Patterns of Migrants and Immigrants

Where are the new population groups settling? The spatial isolation of immigrants from the native born may have an impact on the naturalization rates of the former and the political participation rates of both groups. One version of the contact hypothesis predicts that intergroup interaction will increase political mobilization (Hood and Morris 1997; Stein, Post, and Rinden 1997; Giles and Hertz 1994; Glaser 1994; Key 1949). If groups are clustered in distinct geographical pockets so as to minimize intergroup contact, there will be less of a perception of threat or competition from rival groups and political involvement will be slack (Olzak 1992). The first question to answer, then, is whether migrant and immigrant population groups have become more isolated. One way of evaluating this is to model the locational choices of migrant and immigrant groups. The dominant theories suggest that migrant and immigrant populations are persuaded to settle in certain areas by either the promise of jobs or the presence of family and friends (or at least coethnics). In the absence of comparable state-level survey data on destination choice, I use county-level data throughout this and the next six chapters to evaluate whether those arriving between 1980 and 1990 were drawn by employment prospects, the presence of a community of coethnic prior arrivals, or some combination of both.

The dependent variable is the change in the size of the particular population group as a percentage of the total population from 1980 to 1990. In other words, I am interested in explaining changes in group size relative to the rest of the population of the county. If a county begins the decade with 13 percent of its population of Mexican origin and finishes the decade with 14.5 percent, the change in the size of the Mexican population relative to the rest of the population is equal to +1.5. Constructed in this manner, the dependent variable allows the measurement of whether a group is an increasing or decreasing proportion of the county's population. Time-series data would be best for this purpose, but annual or other appropriate periodic observations for these groups are not available. Realizing that mine is a second-best strategy for modeling population change, I hope to determine whether particular groups became more or less noticeable across the decennial interval between 1980 and 1990.

To reduce the leverage of counties with small populations, I have weighted the model for population. The model also includes a spatially lagged dependent variable to account for spatial dependence among the observations. Spatial dependence is a condition affecting data that are spatially arranged such that the values at one point in space are related to the values at nearby points (Anselin 1988, 11; Haining 1990, chap. 8; see also Appendix B). Since county boundaries are drawn arbitrarily, it is highly likely that one county's values for a variable are related to the values of neighboring counties for that same variable. It would be a mistake to simply assume that the observations are totally independent. By incorporating a spatially lagged dependent variable into a regression model as an explanatory or "right-hand side" variable, one can account for spatial dependence and eliminate autocorrelation in the error term, thereby bringing the model into line with classical regression assumptions. I address the topic of spatial autocorrelation and the strategy I use to correct the problem more completely in appendix B. The variable capturing spatial dependence also serves a useful descriptive function in this particular context because it provides some indication of whether each migrant group is clustering in geographic pockets of California—in counties that are proximate to each other—as opposed to dispersing more evenly or randomly throughout the state.

Among the other explanatory variables, I have included a variable for net change in the population during the decade to account for the possibility that increases (decreases) in a group's share of the county population are controlled by overall population trends. Population density is included to determine whether immigrants are attracted to urban or rural areas of the state, with the expectation that immigrants usually move to cities (Lieberson 1963). Also included in the model is a control for the percentage of college students in a county to account for the possibility that some of the new arrivals are simply university students. A variable for the change in real median family income between 1980 and 1990 is included to capture the changing economic condition of alternative locations within the state during the decade.

The results for this model are presented in table 2.1 for immigrants from several continents as well as for those specifically from Canada and Mexico. A model for the locational concentration of internal U.S. migrants is presented for the sake of comparison. Several interesting patterns emerge from the results. First, compared to 1980 figures, Asians, Mexicans, Central (including Caribbean) Americans, and South Americans are significantly increasing their visibility relative to California natives and other immigrant groups.

The immigrant groups most responsible for reshaping California politics are Asians and Mexicans. Mexicans are becoming a more noticeable presence in the areas where they had established themselves by 1980. For every 1 percent increase in the proportion of Mexicans living in a county in 1980, there is a considerable .21 percent increase in the growth of that population (as a percentage of the total population) by 1990. This finding reflects the fact that newer Mexican arrivals are dependent upon the social networks provided by friends and family members who arrived previously (Portes and Rumbaut 1990). But Mexicans are also likely to avoid areas that began the decade with high unemployment. The Mexican population, then, is growing most noticeably in areas of both previous ethnic settlement *and* economic opportunity.

Map 2.2 illustrates the concentration of the immigrant population in California counties in 1990. The most noticeable pocket of Latino immi-

TABLE 2.1. Influences on Population Concentration in California Counties, 1980–90

Variable	U.S. Migrants	African Immigrants	Asian Immigrants	European Immigrants	Canadian Immigrants	Mexican Immigrants	Central American Immigrants	South American Immigrants
% 1980 group population	-.02 (.19)	.12 (.12)	.37* (.20)	-.30* (.03)	-.49** (.04)	.21** (.06)	1.45** (.04)	.18** (.05)
% unemployment, 1980	2.25** (.85)	-.0003 (.005)	-.14 (.13)	.002 (.013)	.002 (.006)	-.48** (.11)	-.03 (.02)	-.02** (.006)
Change in real median family income, 1980–90	2.00** (.30)	.009** (.003)	.01 (.70)	.04** (.08)	.20** (.10)	-.10* (.07)	-.02* (.01)	.005 (.004)
% net population change	.17 (.05)	-.001** (.0004)	-.002 (.013)	.002 (.001)	.0007* (.0003)	.03** (.009)	.002 (.001)	.001** (.0004)
Population density	-.0006 (.0004)	-.000004 (.000003)	-.0001 (.0002)	-.00001 (.00009)	-.000006 (.000004)	-.00006 (.00006)	-.0002** (.00001)	.000001 (.000003)
% college students	3.33 (2.58)	-.04** (.02)	-.45 (.51)	.03 (.05)	.02 (.02)	.29 (.38)	-.03 (.07)	-.002 (.02)
Spatial lag	.81** (.35)	-.42* (.23)	.38 (.36)	-.29** (.11)	-.006 (.12)	.07 (.17)	.28** (.09)	-.18 (.16)
Constant	-44.10	.11	2.71	-.29	-.007	5.01	.30	.18
N	58	58	58	58	58	58	58	58
R^2_a	.62	.52	.51	.83	.76	.57	.98	.65

Note: Spatial autoregressive model, weighted for population; income coefficients expressed in thousands of 1992 dollars; dependent variable = change in population group as a percentage of total population. See appendix A for a full description of variables.
*$p < .10$.   **$p < .05$.

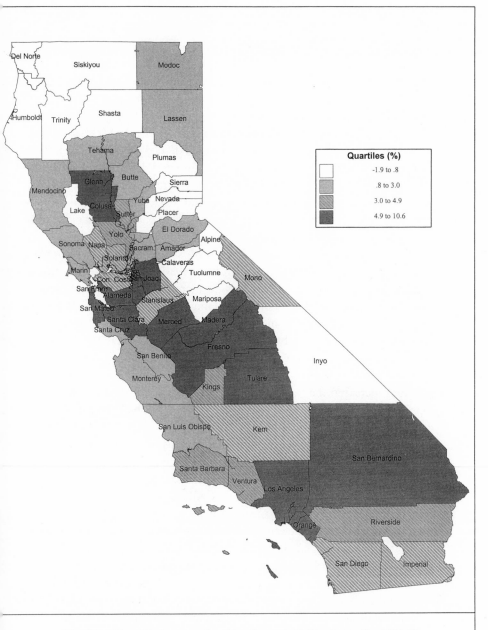

Quartiles (%)
-1.9 to .8
.8 to 3.0
3.0 to 4.9
4.9 to 10.6

Map 2.2.   Change in the proportion of immigrants in California counties, 1980–90.
(Mean = –12.5, Moran's I = .46)

grant presence is in the Central Valley (Fresno, Madera, Merced) where the promise of farm labor continues to attract Mexican migrants (Taylor, Martin, and Fix 1997). There are also significant Mexican immigrant concentrations in the Los Angeles area, including Los Angeles and Orange Counties. Asians are drawn to coethnic enclaves in California much as Mexicans are. But the Asian concentrations are in the darkly shaded Bay Area counties (San Francisco, San Mateo, Alameda, Santa Clara). The regression analysis in table 2.1 shows that for every 1 percent change in a county's 1980 Asian population, there is a .37 percent gain in that group's growth relative to the non-Asian population. The influx of Asian immigrants, coupled with their concentrated settlement patterns, has made this community more visible and politically powerful than ever before.

The proportion of internal migrants constituting the state's population shrunk an average of 12.5 percent from 1980 to 1990 across counties, and the instrument of this decline was the incredible influx of immigrants. The growth in the percentage of internal migrants is occurring not in areas where similar migrants from earlier periods settled but in areas that showed income growth between 1980 and 1990 (table 2.1). They are also an increasing proportion of the population in areas that began the decade with high unemployment. One thing is certain, however: internal migrants have not increased their presence in the areas that are most popular with immigrants. Evidence for this is presented in map 2.3. Note that in the very counties where the foreign-born presence is highest (map 2.2) the presence of out-of-state migrants is lowest. It is certainly possible that areas could attract greater concentrations of the foreign born and a larger proportion of interstate migrants at the same time. This could happen, for instance, in places where the proportion of native Californians shrinks, as seems to have been the case in Modoc County on the state's northern border. But this was a rare occurrence in California during the 1980s. Out-of-state migrants grew *numerically* in many places but not *proportionally* anywhere but in a few rural and mountain counties, which immigrants avoided.

The spatially lagged dependent variable provides some indication of whether there are concentrated growth patterns in California in particular subregions of the state. Positive values indicate patterns of positive spatial dependency—places where the growth of a particular population is occurring not just within a county but across a group of adjacent counties (appendix B). Negative values indicate the rarer condition of negative spatial dependency—places where growth in a particular population is occurring even as that population is diminishing in nearby counties. The

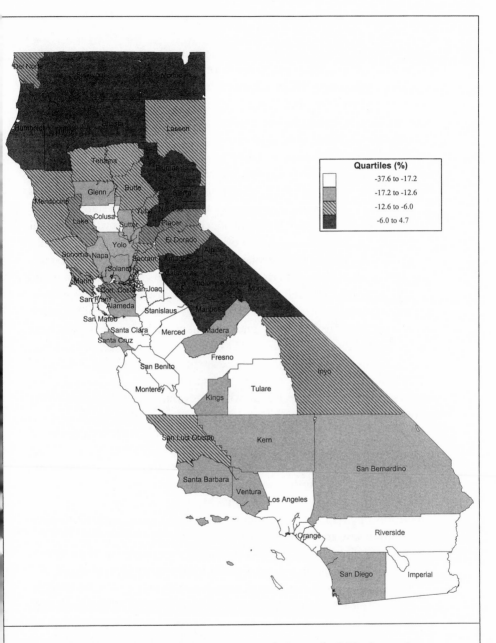

Map 2.3.   Change in the proportion of internal migrants in California counties, 1980–90. (Mean = 3.18, Moran's I = .42)

coefficients in table 2.1 indicate positive spatial dependency for the growth patterns of U.S. internal migrants. In other words, the number of these migrants is growing fastest (or declining more slowly) in counties that are in close proximity—shown as the dark northern counties on map 2.3. Positive spatial dependency is also found in the growth patterns of Central American immigrants, who are clustering in greater concentrations in the state's southern and central counties. Negative spatial dependency can be found in the models for African American and European immigrant growth. These groups are becoming more noticeable in isolated counties but not across entire subregions or "county clusters" in the state.

The models in table 2.1 best predict changes in the growth of Central American, European, Canadian, and U.S. internal migrants. For Canadians and Europeans, there is a strong inverse relationship between their numbers in 1980 and their growth relative to that of other groups. This is not surprising since these movers are highly skilled, well educated, and mobile. They have no need for the social support networks that less skilled immigrants seek. Nor are Europeans and Canadians likely to face the discrimination in the labor market that makes social networks necessary for survival. Canadians and Europeans also show some capacity to move to areas where real income is rising. Central Americans, on the other hand, show a strong propensity to cluster in areas where previous arrivals have established a presence—perhaps suggesting a reliance on social networks.

This overview of migrant and immigrant settlement patterns obviously overlooks important distinctions within these groups. Some Asians are less dependent upon social networks than others. Undoubtedly some interstate U.S. migrants do find themselves in areas of low income growth. But the general picture is clear. Asians, Mexicans, and Central and South Americans, the bulk of the immigrants arriving since changes in the 1965 immigration law took effect in 1968, are drawn to areas in California where their fellow émigrés are concentrating and becoming more noticeable. In 1992, a typical year, four out of ten immigrants settled in Los Angeles County and 75 percent settled in just six counties: Los Angeles, Orange, Santa Clara, San Diego, San Francisco, and Alameda (Bizjak 1993). While Hispanic émigrés show some capacity to avoid concentrating in areas of high unemployment, they are also less likely than U.S. internal migrants to move to areas that are experiencing income growth. These sustained settlement patterns are contributing to the class and ethnic balkanization of the state.

Balkanization within Counties and Naturalization Rates in California

Naturalization is the legal aspect of assimilation (Liang 1994, 407). Obtaining citizenship is important because naturalization entitles an immigrant to vote. Immigrants who naturalize, then, have a measure of political capital that nonnaturalized immigrants lack (Portes and Curtis 1987; Pachon 1987; Garcia 1981). Naturalization is also a "measure of the degree to which immigrants are integrated or assimilated into American life and society" (Liang 1994, 407). Those who naturalize are willing to be identified as citizens and presumably willing to assume the responsibilities that go along with full membership in their new communities.

Several scholars have indicated that the spatial isolation of a group influences the propensity of that group to naturalize (Liang 1994; Portes 1984). Residential segregation increases within-group rather than inter-group interactions (Liang 1994; Blau 1977; Gordon 1964; Allport 1954). Within-group interactions, so the theory goes, reinforce ethnic identity and make immigrants less likely to naturalize than if they had contact with other groups. We can directly assess the impact of ethnic balkanization on naturalization rates with data from California. Of course, counties are geographically large units of analysis, particularly in Southern California. Much of the ethnic balkanization of the state is obscured at this level and can be better captured by data at the neighborhood, census tract, or block group level. Using the index of concentration described in footnote 1 and widely employed by sociologists and demographers for the last forty years (Duncan and Duncan 1955; Lieberson 1963; Taeuber and Taeuber 1969; Jiobu 1988; Massey and Denton 1987, 1993), I computed values indicating the segregation of the Asian and Hispanic populations from the white population across census tracts within each of the state's fifty-eight counties.[2] The result was two indicators of spatial balkanization: one for the

---

2. The dissimilarity index obviously cannot be calculated across census tracts for counties where there is only a single census tract. Ordinarily this means that the most rural counties in many states would have to be excluded from analysis. In some states analyzed in this book there would be so much missing data that I would only be capable of offering a truncated analysis of the most urban areas of the state. To avoid this I decided to code the most rural counties where there was only a single census tract as 0 on the dissimilarity index. Of course, this assumes that ethnic minority populations in the nation's smallest counties are well-integrated, or at least far better integrated than in urban counties. And certainly at the broad level of census tracts, they probably are well-integrated because in the most rural

segregation of the Asian and white populations and a second for the segregation of the Hispanic and white populations. Using these segregation indices as independent variables in two regression models for 1980 and 1990, I evaluated the extent to which ethnic isolation within counties was related to naturalization rates for immigrants residing in those counties. If spatial isolation makes immigrants less likely to naturalize than integration does, a regression analysis should show that the segregation of white from minority groups both within and across counties reduces naturalization rates, thereby retarding the civic engagement of new populations. To control for other influences on naturalization rates, I included variables for population density and the percentage of residents in a county who are college educated.

The results reported in table A2.2 (appendix A) show the expected result that naturalization rates are inversely related to the size of the foreign-born population in a county. In other words, the more populated the immigrant enclave is, the lower naturalization rates will be—although this is less true in 1990 than in 1980. That foreign-born concentrations would be related to a lack of civic engagement conjures up the idea that the visibility of an immigrant population in an area may be positively related to immigrant-native inequality in that area. Blalock (1956) advanced a related idea by suggesting that when a minority population is large the white population will be more likely to discriminate against that population, increasing inequality between the two groups (Beggs, Villemez, and Arnold 1997; Jiobu 1988). Here we have some indication that political inequality across immigrant communities in California—differences in the propensity to civically engage through naturalization—may be related to the size and concentration of the immigrant population. Immigrants who settle in areas populated predominantly by the native born naturalize at higher rates than immigrants who settle primarily among other immigrants.

---

counties outside the Deep South, ethnic minority populations are usually very small. A much less desirable alternative, in my judgment, was to code these counties as 100 on the dissimilarity index—assuming that rural minority populations were much more highly segregated than their urban counterparts. Readers should note that all regression models presented in this book that contain the dissimilarity index as an independent variable are weighted for population so that the influence of the most rural counties, and therefore the influence of these "0-coded" observations on the regression plane, is reduced. There is no doubt that rural minority populations are often very isolated and perhaps the dissimilarity index could be constructed from data at the block-group or even the city block level of aggregation for such places. But in the most rural counties it is often the case that all populations are relatively dispersed and so terms such as *segregation* and *spatial isolation* take on a different meaning than in more urban and suburban settings.

Table A2.2 also indicates that Hispanic segregation from whites within counties has the effect of depressing naturalization in both 1980 and 1990, although less so in the latter year. Interestingly, though, Asian segregation from whites is associated with increased naturalization in 1980 but bears no relationship to naturalization in 1990. The results, then, for the effect of ethnic segregation on turnout are mixed in precisely the way that Liang (1994, 429) discovered. On the one hand, consistent with a variation of the "visibility-discrimination" hypothesis advanced by Blalock (1956) and others, high concentrations of the foreign born within counties are surely not conducive to putting immigrants on a political par with their counterparts who have mixed with the native population. As Liang (1994) found, however, the rate of Hispanic naturalization is more likely to be adversely affected by residential segregation from whites than the rate of Asian naturalization is. This difference in the effect of Asian-white and Hispanic-white segregation can be accounted for by the fact that Asian segregation from whites is not always a sign of poverty, poor education, and lack of English in that community. There are long-standing residential enclaves of established Asian wealth where rates of citizenship and political participation are as high as in any white community. Hispanic segregation, though, is more likely to be the result of characteristics that inhibit Latino mobility such as lack of English, low literacy rates, and poverty.

Migrants, Immigrants, and Turnout in
California Elections

What is the effect of the presence of migrants and immigrants on turnout rates across California's counties? Most of the recent research in political science suggests that internal mobility reduces turnout due to the presence of restrictive registration laws. Movers are hindered in their efforts to reregister by closing dates, inconvenient hours at registration offices, and "procedures shrouded in obscurity" (Squire, Wolfinger, and Glass 1987, 45). With the "motor voter" law, passed by Congress and signed by President Clinton in 1993, many of these barriers were removed (at least in theory) since voter registration is now accessible through state motor vehicle licensing offices. But for most of the period of study here the motor voter legislation had not passed into law, and even after it had passed the California state government delayed implementation while pursuing legal action to enjoin its enforcement.

Many new immigrants also face barriers to conventional political participation. Acquisition of citizenship is a major step, and some immigrant groups show a greater propensity to naturalize than others. Asians generally obtain citizenship rather quickly compared to Mexicans and Central Americans (Portes and Rumbaut 1990, 117). Some researchers have made the very plausible case that noncitizenship is the single greatest obstacle to the political empowerment of Hispanic communities (Pachon 1991; Garcia 1987, 1981). But even when they are naturalized many recent immigrants are not well educated and therefore not inclined to vote (White and Kaufman 1997). In a study of political participation in the 1984 election in California, Uhlaner, Cain, and Kiewiet found that only 60 percent of Latino citizens and 69 percent of Asians voted, compared to 81 percent of blacks and 80 percent of whites (1989). The ability to speak English and longer residence in the United States do increase participation rates among Asians and Hispanic immigrants (210). It is not surprising that established immigrants would be more likely to participate than new arrivals. Older immigrants are more likely to be naturalized and more likely to have acquired a stake in their new country's political future. They may also be inspired to vote by experiences of discrimination that trigger ethnic consciousness. The general expectation, then, is that in areas with recent immigrants, participation will be particularly low. Similarly, places with large migrant populations are expected to have lower rates of political participation after controlling for other variables likely to have an impact on turnout such as education; the residential segregation of whites from Asians, Hispanics, and blacks within counties; the percentage of the population that is African American; and population density.

Average turnout rates for counties across two California gubernatorial elections are depicted on map 2.4. It appears from a simple inspection of this map that turnout rates are inversely related to the concentration of immigrant populations. The lightly shaded counties are those with both low turnout and a strong immigrant presence.

Results of a multivariate analysis of turnout rates in two recent presidential and three gubernatorial contests in California are presented in table 2.2. In the last column of this table, I have also pooled the results from the 1990, 1992, and 1994 elections to facilitate generalization. As one would expect based on well-understood individual-level relationships, education is positively related to turnout across four of the five elections and in the pooled model.

The ecological results correspond to individual-level findings in other ways as well. For instance, turnout is negatively related to the percentage

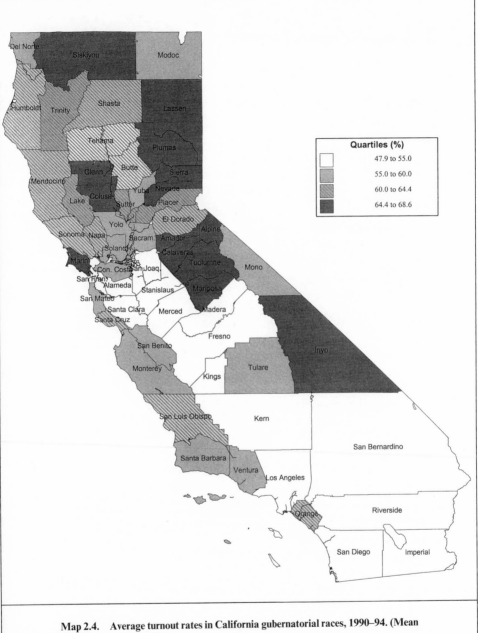

Quartiles (%)

	47.9 to 55.0
	55.0 to 60.0
	60.0 to 64.4
	64.4 to 68.6

Map 2.4. Average turnout rates in California gubernatorial races, 1990–94. (Mean = 59.8, Moran's I = .33)

TABLE 2.2. Impact of Population Mobility on Voter Turnout in California Counties, 1980–90

Variable	1980	1982	1990	1992	1994	Pooled 1990s
% college educated	-.14	.06	.31**	.45**	.25**	.30**
	(.17)	(.11)	(.06)	(.10)	(.08)	(.05)
Isolation of minorities from whites (within counties)	.03	.02	-.05**	-.03	-.01	-.04**
	(.03)	(.02)	(.02)	(.03)	(.03)	(.02)
% post-1970 immigrants	.31	.02	-.03[a]	-.13[a]	-.10	-.05
	(.24)	(.14)	(.09)	(.11)	(.12)	(.08)
% born out of state	.26**	-.10*	.004	-.31**	.11	-.12**
	(.09)	(.06)	(.054)	(.06)	(.07)	(.04)
% black	-.49**	-.16	-.36**	.14	-.48**	-.24**
	(.14)	(.10)	(.10)	(.12)	(.14)	(.09)
Population density	-.001**	-.0005**	-.0001	-.00007	-.0002	-.0001
	(.0003)	(.0002)	(.0002)	(.0002)	(.0002)	(.0001)
Spatial lag	-.80**	.32	.59**	-.23	-.05	.30**
	(.32)	(.23)	(.12)	(.23)	(.19)	(.10)
Presidential race	—	—	—	—	—	7.58**
						(.84)
Constant	128.15	61.58	23.34	81.79	63.71	41.61
N	58	58	58	58	58	174
R^2_a	.48	.35	.70	.53	.36	.68

Note: Spatial autoregressive model, weighted for population; dependent variable = percentage turnout by county. See appendix A for a full description of variable.

[a]Variables with low tolerances and high standard errors due to multicollinearity.

*p < .10.   **p < .05.

of migrants from out of state in three of the five contests, particularly in 1992. In the pooled model, the coefficient for the internal migrant population indicates that a 10 point increase in the percentage of the native born population from outside California drops turnout by about 1.2 points—a substantive difference that could easily determine an election's outcome. Political participation is also lower in areas where there are significant numbers of African American residents. The percentage of the immigrant population arriving after 1970 is associated with lower turnout in the 1990s but not in the 1980s. Of course, by the 1990s the population of immigrants that had entered after 1970 was considerably larger than it was in the early 1980s, indicating that the lack of significance of the immigration variable in 1980 and 1982 was probably due to the smaller proportion of newly arriving immigrants at the time.

The variable for the segregation of minorities from whites within counties in table 2.2 shows a generally negative sign in the 1990s and also for the pooled model. In other words, the more highly segregated whites are from minorities across census tracts within an area, the lower the turnout is likely to be for the entire area. The pooled model indicates that a ten point increase in segregation drops political participation by about .4 percent. This finding is certainly consistent with the contact hypothesis. Interracial contact and proximity generates a concern for the maintenance of political power by whites and a concern for obtaining political power among minorities. This kind of competition produces high participation rates by both minorities and whites. Low turnout, on the other hand, is found in areas where immigrant populations are so distant from native ones that they pose no threat to the values and interests of the majority.

The most consequential finding from the ecological analysis presented in table 2.2 is that places with large populations of both out-of-state and international migrants have lower participation rates than places where natives predominate. Eventually out-of-state migrants may reregister, and they certainly do not face the obstacle of a cumbersome naturalization process. But long after domestic migrants settle down, noncitizens remain politically handicapped. Immigrants are underrepresented in the political system not just because only citizens can vote, but because the foreign born settle in low-income areas where even the *native* population is poor, uneducated, and nonparticipatory. As more of the recent immigrants naturalize, perhaps the differences in participation between areas with many immigrants and those with few will disappear. Even immigrants who have been slower to naturalize have felt the heat of nativist sentiment expressed in movements such as Proposition 187, which threatened to deny public benefits to illegal aliens. There are doubts about whether even legal residency is enough to protect access to government services. Both the Republican Contract with America and President Clinton's own welfare reform legislation (signed into law in August 1996) sought to deny most public benefits to noncitizens even if they were legal residents. In California, the 1994 elections were also followed by Governor Pete Wilson's efforts to roll back affirmative action programs in higher education that were designed to help minority groups. Political mobilization is greatly enhanced by the perception of threat, and these initiatives made it clear that legal residency was not enough. The late-1990s have witnessed a surge in petitions to naturalize.

Migrants, Immigrants, and Partisan Voting

What about the contention that population mobility unravels the party system? Migrants bring political identities and attitudes from elsewhere. Local indigenous political cues have little influence in the short term. The juxtaposition of the imported identities in the new and alien political setting may lead to the weakening of political party identification (Brown 1988). By examining the relationship between party registration and party voting, it is possible to determine whether there is a larger difference between the two in some areas of California than in others. For areas populated with immigrants, many of whom are not naturalized, the expectation is less clear. New immigrants from Mexico and Asia usually identify with the Democratic Party in California once they become citizens. In addition, the lower-class standing of most unskilled immigrants of color strongly suggests that they will locate in urban and suburban neighborhoods where Democrats may be so well entrenched that other parties are not an option. At the county level of aggregation, I suspect there may be significant differences between registration and voting in areas where there has been strong receptivity on the part of white voters to the conservative positions taken by Republican candidates against the use of public services by newer immigrants. In other words, I hypothesize that Republicans will do better than their registration predicts in counties with more immigrants who have arrived since 1970. Control variables have been added for participation rates, percentage African American, education, and population density.

Map 2.5 shows the spatial patterns of party irregularity that must be

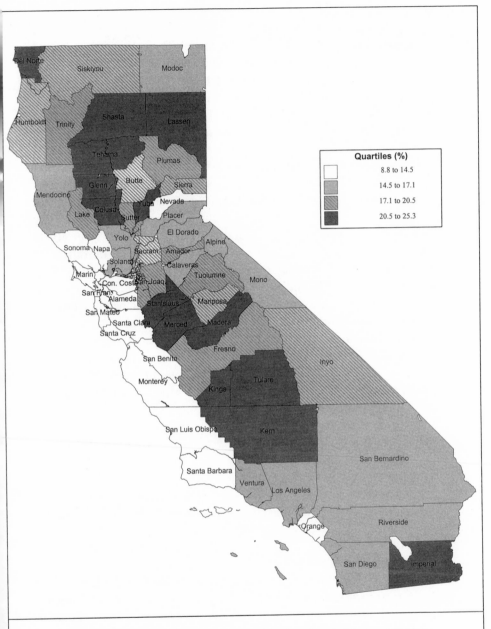

Map 2.5. Average party irregularity in California gubernatorial races, 1990–94.
(Mean = 17.5, Moran's I = .39)

explained by the multivariate regression model. The light streak of coastal counties from Santa Barbara to Sonoma stand out as locations where party registration and party voting match especially well. Areas of party irregularity include Kern, Tulare, and Kings Counties, where many registered Democrats often vote Republican. The northern counties, populated with large proportions of internal migrants, were also highly irregular in their behavior in these elections.

The results of the regression analysis of party irregularity are presented in table 2.3 for five individual election years and a pooled data set that includes 1990, 1992, and 1994. The effect of these demographic attributes on the difference between party voting and registration are evidently dependent upon the election in question. For presidential races (1980, 1992), the percentage of residents born out of state increases the difference between party registration and voting, as Thad Brown's groundbreaking work would predict for individuals. The pooled model also suggests that out-of-state origin is associated with independence of party. Kern and Imperial Counties are good examples of places with high party irregularity coupled with a large nonnative population. In off-year elections, though, there is no statistically significant difference between those places with large migrant populations and those without. In these elections, new arrivals may not have turned out to vote at all. Mobility inhibits the development of political capital. The turnout of migrant groups is likely to be lower in nonpresidential years. When new arrivals, with their weakened party attachments, do not turn out to vote, the difference between party and candidate voting diminishes, thus explaining the change in significance levels between presidential and nonpresidential election years. Low turnout of certain subgroups, such as blacks, also accounts for the difference in signs between the on-year presidential elections and off-year gubernatorial races in table 2.3.

As for new arrivals from abroad, the results show that places with large populations of recent immigrants were productive of highly partisan voting in the early 1980s but not during the 1990s. This change suggests that counties where recent immigrants are concentrated have undergone a political transformation from predictable bastions of party support to volatile and unpredictable places. In the 1992 presidential contest, a 1 percent increase in the percentage of recent (post-1970) immigrants contributed to a .36 increase in the difference between party registration and party voting. Survey data show that many of the recent Asian immigrants are registered as independents. H. Ross Perot's candidacy in the 1992 pres-

TABLE 2.3. Similarity of Party Registration to Party Voting in California Counties, 1980–94

Variable	1980	1982	1990	1992	1994	Pooled 1990s
% college educated	-.60	.66**	-.37**	.18**	-.37**	-.02
	(.11)	(.11)	(.07)	(.07)	(.05)	(.06)
% born out of state	.22**	.02	-.03	.30**	.01	.08**
	(.06)	(.06)	(.04)	(.04)	(.04)	(.04)
% post-1970 immigrants	-.13	-.26**	.09[a]	.36**	.06	.11*
	(.09)	(.11)	(.07)	(.07)	(.06)	(.06)
% black	-.10	.01	.08	-.30**	-.05	-.16**
	(.07)	(.07)	(.08)	(.06)	(.06)	(.07)
Population density	.0003**	.0004**	.00003	-.0006**	-.0002**	-.0003**
	(.0001)	(.0002)	(.0001)	(.0001)	(.0001)	(.0001)
% turnout	.08	.29**	.11	-.11	.01	-.29**
	(.07)	(.13)	(.09)	(.10)	(.07)	(.08)
Spatial lag	.28	.61**	.51**	.39**	.30**	.87**
	(.19)	(.21)	(.18)	(.13)	(.16)	(.05)
Presidential race	—	—	—	—	—	1.40
						(1.16)
Constant	4.64	-6.15	6.08	-3.15	21.42	15.75
N	58	58	58	58	58	174
R^2_a	.72	.65	.68	.71	.77	.79

Note: Spatial autoregressive model, weighted for population; dependent variable = Abs (% Republican vote – % Republican registration); high positive values indicate counties where voting differed from registration. See appendix A for a full description of variables.

[a]Variables with low tolerances and high standard errors due to multicollinearity.

*p < .10.   **p < .05.

idential election probably best accounts for the unusually large discrepancy between registration and voting in that year.

Education behaves predictably across the entire series of elections, and its effect is to decrease the difference between party registration and voting except in 1992 when support for Perot altered the tendency in the opposite direction. The results for education correspond to the individual-level finding that better educated and informed voters are stronger and more consistent partisans (see, e.g., Zaller 1992). In the California context, the areas with the highest percentages of the college educated residents are located on the coast, where better educated residents are committed ideologues, and therefore straight ticket Democratic voting is the norm.

The spatially lagged dependent variable in table 2.3 shows that party irregularity in California follows a pattern of positive spatial dependency. Places that depart from their basic political inclinations are clustered in the north and central regions of the state. Those counties where voting best matches party registration are in the San Francisco Bay area and along the coast, as seen in map 2.5.

To summarize, we have learned that party regularity is a function of internal population mobility, the proportion of recent immigrants in a place, the educational attainment of the population, and idiosyncrasies of individual election years. Patterns of party regularity are important because it is predictably partisan areas that candidates and party organizations can most easily ignore in highly competitive races. California's ideologically liberal and affluent Democrats in Bay Area neighborhoods, for example, need not be the focus of much campaign effort. They are not likely to change. Similarly, those neighborhoods where older waves of immigrants have settled, the large urban counties, are thoroughly socialized and highly predictable. The less predictable places, in presidential election years at least, include those with both a large proportion of out-of-state residents and recent immigrants, many of whom are not politically active. These are the locations where political traditions have been shaken by population growth and where swing voters may determine the outcome of a close contest. Note that the ecological data do not show that migrants and immigrants are directly responsible for independence of party voting. Only surveys of individual behavior could determine this with certainty. It is also possible that waves of migrant and immigrant settlement have stimulated California *natives* to depart from their party affiliations when casting votes. In either scenario, however, both parties in California would be wise to pay close attention to the places where these new arrivals settle, as they are politically erratic if not highly volatile.

Migrants, Immigrants, and Changes in
Partisan Registration

We have so far observed that the impact of migration and immigration on voter turnout at the aggregate level is consistent with commonplace findings from surveys of voters but occasionally depends upon election-specific factors. Areas where minorities are isolated from whites have consistently lower turnout rates, especially in the 1990s, than those areas where there is residential integration. Places with more residents from outside California report lower participation rates than counties populated mostly with native Californians, particularly in off-year elections.

The influence of these indicators of population settlement have a mixed impact on party regularity. Migration across states increases differences between party registration and voting in presidential election years, but party irregularity is not consistently influenced by out-of-state migration in gubernatorial years. By the 1990s, areas with large populations of new immigrants (those arriving after 1970) are less consistent in their political behavior than those with either older waves of immigrants or no immigrants at all. Apparently, the effects of these demographic characteristics of places are mediated through California's candidate-centered elections.

In light of these results, the effect of migration and immigration on changes in the balance of party registration in California counties is worth careful consideration. The independent variables used to predict changes in party registration have been selected based on their theoretical relevance. The dependent variable is the increase in the share of Republican registrants (by county) for the decades 1970–80 and 1980–90. In other words, I seek to explain the variation in Republican registration relative to other parties. This is not the same thing as measuring the change in the *number* of Republican party registrants for each county, since growth in the number of Republican registrants could easily occur alongside growth in party registrants for other parties. Rather, I mean to explain the difference in the percentage of registrants across these ten-year periods. For example, if a county began 1980 with 35 percent registered Republicans and finished the decade (in 1990) with 31 percent, the change (growth/decline) in the share of Republican registrants would be –4.

Put in its simplest and most general form, my main hypothesis is that population growth from sources internal to the United States enhances Republican registration. Areas of population growth are generally associated with expanding economic opportunity and wealth creation. These are middle- and upper-income areas, including suburbs and medium-sized cities where Republicans are already well established and represented. By contrast, older urban areas are associated with brighter prospects for Democrats given their traditional association with population groups that were least mobile during either decade. Areas of population decline, then, are hypothesized to be areas where Republicans took the greatest losses relative to other parties.

The change in Republican registration is thought to be a function of the density of the county population—with urban and densely populated areas less likely to see gains in Republican registration. The percentage of the population born outside the state at the beginning of each decade captures the relative balance of natives and transplants. A variable capturing the *change* in the percentage of the population born out of state will serve in the evaluation of whether the increasing or decreasing balance of non-Californians has influenced Republican registration. Included in the model are variables for the foreign-born population at the beginning of each decade on the supposition that areas with large foreign-born populations are likely to be large cities and Democratic strongholds. The *growth* of the foreign-born population, on the other hand, is likely to be associated with Republican growth, as mobile, better educated immigrants flow to areas of expanding economic opportunity and wealth creation in suburbs and prosperous cities and are less drawn to areas where their ethnic group is spatially concentrated (Nogle 1996; Bartel 1989).

Table 2.4 reports the results of the hypothesis tests on the growth or decline in Republican registration. GOP registration has increased in areas of higher population density across both decades, suggesting that Republicans have done well in certain urban and suburban counties. The population of out-of-state residents in a county at the beginning of the 1980s is associated with strong positive gains in Republican registration in the ensuing ten years. Increases in the proportion of interstate migrants from 1980 to 1990 also contribute to GOP growth rates. In other words, the forces of internal migration are clearly bolstering Republican registration growth. For the foreign-born population, the evidence is different. Areas with large foreign-born populations at the beginning of each decade saw sizable GOP losses, particularly in the 1970s. A one point increase in the proportion of foreign-born residents in a county in 1970 led to a 1.4 percent decline in the percentage of Republicans between 1970 and 1980. These results make sense given that California's most Democratic areas had the largest immigrant populations. In Los Angeles, Alameda, and San Francisco Counties, all with large foreign-born populations, the GOP continues to grow weaker. Places where the foreign-born population *increased as a proportion of the total population,* however, show marked Republican gains in both decades. This is no indication that immigrants are themselves registering as Republicans in the places where they are becoming a larger segment of the population. Without individual-level data, we cannot determine the exact source of the gain in GOP strength— it could also have been produced by the native backlash against the influx of immigrants. But whatever the individual-level process entails, it is note-worthy that places do not necessarily go Democratic in California simply because immigrants become a larger proportion of an area's population.

TABLE 2.4.   Impact of Population Mobility on Changes in Republican Party Registration in California Counties, 1970–80, 1980–90

Variable	1970–80	1980–90
% born out of state, 1970 (1980)	–.29**	.09**
	(.09)	(.05)
Change in % born out of state	–.07	.03[a]
	(.19)	(.13)
% foreign born, 1970 (1980)	–1.41**	–.41**
	(.20)	(.14)
Change in % foreign born	.98**	.25[a]
	(.18)	(.19)
% Republican registrants, 1970 (1980)	–.43**	.23**
	(.05)	(.05)
Population density	.0007**	.0004**
	(.0002)	(.0001)
Spatial lag	–.23**	.69**
	(.07)	(.14)
Constant	28.67	–7.15
N	58	58
R^2_a	.76	.84

Note: Spatial autoregressive model, weighted for population; dependent variable = change in the percentage of Republican Party registrants. See appendix A for a full description of variables.

[a]Variables with low tolerances and high standard errors due to multicollinearity.

p < .10.   **p* < .05.

Finally, the lagged variable for change in Republican registration shows that a different spatial dynamic is at work across California counties in the 1970s than occurred in the 1980s. In the 1970s, GOP growth in a county is negatively related to the growth of Republican registration in neighboring counties. This may indicate that the source of GOP growth during the 1970s was suburbanization, which led to population redistribution within the state. In other words, negative spatial dependency suggests that Republican gains in outlying counties are offset by Republican losses in adjacent core counties. For the 1980s, however, the sign on the spatially lagged variable is positive, suggesting that Republican registration growth is occurring across clusters of adjacent counties. This pattern would reflect GOP gains not from suburbanization but from migration from other states.

Ethnicity and Political Behavior at the Individual Level

The aggregate data examined thus far are informative not for what they suggest about individuals but for what they say about differences among places where individuals reside. Migrant and immigrant groups are drawn to different locations in California. Some groups cluster in the same geographic locations, increasing their visibility relative to other groups, while others disperse. The results describe a state in which turnout is high in areas where there are few blacks and new residents. They show increasing Republican strength in areas where the population from out of state is high in the early 1980s and the foreign born population has increased as a proportion of the total population. Frey (1995) is not only right about California's socioethnic balkanization, but we can go further and conclude that this balkanization has political consequences—it spatially separates people from different parties and with different propensities to participate. Of course, the usual ambiguities of ecological data analysis persist. I have shown that these trends in population mobility and politics are associated but not necessarily traceable to voters. We do not know, for example, whether Asians and Mexicans naturalize, register, and vote Democratic or whether the Republican losses associated with their presence are instead the consequence of white out-migration or nonparticipation. The number of Republicans could be growing more slowly or declining relative to other parties as the result of attrition or generational replacement, not due to real Democratic gains from the addition of new voters.

Studying the political behavior and attitudes of migrants and immigrants at the individual level for specific states is difficult due to the lack of appropriate data. For internal migrants, questions about residential mobility and political attitudes are rarely covered in the same polls. For immigrants, it is similarly difficult to find comprehensive background information together with queries about politics. Immigrants from very different backgrounds are often grouped into broad categories such as Asian and Hispanic. This raises questions about the extent to which most polls and surveys overgeneralize about groups that are internally highly variable. Wendy Tam (1995) has pointed out that the Asian community is highly diverse and the usual polls fail to capture its nuances. In one recent study of the Los Angeles area community of Monterey Park, Chinese Americans were found to be far more Republican than Japanese Americans (Horton 1995). But few polls distinguish the myriad Asian groups. Another drawback of surveys is that they rarely distinguish between resident aliens, naturalized citizens, and undocumented workers. Nor do questions commonly appear about whether a particular ethnic person is native or foreign born. Obviously, most politically oriented surveys are focused on citizens (those eligible to vote). Exit polls only survey those who show up at the polls and therefore capture only ethnic persons who are either naturalized or native born. So in the typical poll there is often no way of knowing whether an ethnic voter is a native-born or naturalized citizen. Of course, birthplace may not matter. Many foreign-born Mexicans are less educated than Mexican American natives. But when they obtain education and find long-term employment many of the differences between the two groups disappear. Differences may also disappear with length of residence in the United States (Cain, Kiewiet, and Uhlaner 1991). If so, then education, income, age, and length of residence may be the critical variables distinguishing the political fortunes of foreign- and native-born residents. Education, age, and income are variables that are readily available in most surveys.

One survey that does record birthplace information is the American National Election Study (ANES). While it is impossible to use this survey to generalize about electorates in individual states, it can be used to evaluate more generally whether it makes much difference if an ethnic voter was born in the United States. Pooling the ANES surveys from recent years (1980–94) provides enough cases to obtain a general impression of the influence of a person's country of birth on his or her political attitudes and voting habits. In appendix A (table A2.3), I present a model of the impact of birthplace on vote choice in presidential elections. I have added control variables for education, income, age, party identification, and length of residence in the country. The results are presented for Hispanic and Asian respondents as well as those with European and Canadian backgrounds. The results show that place of birth makes no difference at all for Hispanics once party identification and the other variables are included in the model. The strength of party identification is extraordinary. Even income is only marginally significant. For Asians, too, party identification is the overriding influence on vote choice.

Given the importance of party identification, one may well want to ask about the acquisition of partisanship, as Cain, Kiewiet, and Uhlaner do (1991). What role does nativity play in the development of party identification? The answer is that nativity does make an important difference to the acquisition of partisanship. First-generation citizens, those who immigrated directly from abroad, are less likely to have experienced discrimination than those of the second or third generation (394–95). Since the 1930s, Democrats have always done well among disadvantaged minority populations. Hence, it is to be expected that the longer an immigrant has been in the United States the more likely he or she is to be a Democrat. This is exactly what we find in examining the ANES data, especially for Hispanics: only 17 percent of the native born identify with the Republican Party, compared to 39 percent of the foreign born ($\chi^2 = 39.2$; $p \leq .0001$). For Asians, the differences are less dramatic: about 38 percent of the native born Asians identify with the Republican party, compared to 51 percent for the foreign born ($\chi^2 = 4.83$; $p \leq .09$). These differences persist even after controlling for income and education.

So what does this do to our ability to use the majority of state-representing polls that fail to differentiate on the basis of nativity and length of residence? Second-best strategies are common in the social sciences, and one such option is to use the available data and describe differences across states, keeping in mind the distinct characteristics of the immigrant populations in those areas. The data presented in the pie chart in figure 2.1 serve as important contextual information. One source of state-level data that is comparable across all of the states studied in this book is the 1990, 1992, and 1994 Voter Research and Surveys Exit Polls (VRS). These polls do not contain the level of detail found in national polls but do contain questions on basic political attitudes and behavior as well as questions on race, education, and other background characteristics relevant to the political

socialization process. Table 2.5 presents the breakdown of party identification by race/ethnic group for the three elections in California. Unsurprisingly, white Californians are divided between the two major parties
about equally, blacks are solidly in the Democratic column, and two-
thirds of Hispanics vote Democratic. Asians, though, are only slightly
more Democratic than Anglo voters. These figures contrast with what
Tam (1995) found for Asians in the San Francisco Bay area, where clear
minorities of each of the three major Asian groups—Japanese, Koreans,
and Chinese—were registered as GOP identifiers. Given the finding that
Asians who are foreign born are more likely to be Republican, perhaps the
high percentage of *recent* Asian immigrants in California is responsible for
their Republican orientation. Higher income and better education appear
to be responsible for the Republican leaning of wealthier Asians, but many
are also foreign born, with a shorter length of residence in the United
States, and therefore less likely to have experienced the kind of discrimination that leads many native-born Asians to identify with Democrats
(Uhlaner 1991). Other explanations for the strong Republican inclination
of Asians in California include the socialization of many new Asian immigrants into a party system dominated by highly visible Republican presi-
dents who took strong stands against communism. Finally, these exit polls

TABLE 2.5.   Party Identification by Race/Ethnicity in Recent California
Elections, 1990–94

Race/Ethnic Group	Year	Democrat	Independent	Republican
White	1990	37.4	18.7	43.8
	1992	36.3	23.4	40.3
	1994	33.5	21.2	45.3
Black	1990	78.4	7.8	13.8
	1992	75.1	16.7	8.2
	1994	81.0	12.0	7.0
Hispanic	1990	61.4	14.8	23.7
	1992	64.3	16.1	19.5
	1994	64.8	17.3	18.0
Asian	1990	41.1	21.4	37.5
	1992	38.7	29.1	32.2
	1994	36.3	24.4	39.3

Source: Voter Research and Surveys, General Election Exit Polls, 1990–94 (weighted
data).

are capturing only Asian *participants* in the elections. As Tam (1995) has pointed out, turnout rates for Asians range from 53 to about 56 percent in off-year elections (237). Hence, the Republican inclination of the Asian electorate may be overestimated by the exclusion of those choosing not to vote. Keeping in mind the surge and decline in participation from presidential to nonpresidential years, it is not surprising that the percentage of Asian Republicans is higher in 1990 and 1994 than it is in 1992 (see table 2.5).

These survey data on the party identification of the Asian and Hispanic electorates in California suggest that the growth of the Asian population may do little to harm Republican prospects. The effects of Asian immigration may well be a wash when considered at a statewide level—with some Asians moving into the Democratic Party and others identifying with Republicans. Attempts to use Gary King's (1997) ecological inference maximum likelihood technique to determine the statewide proportion of Asians who register Republican, based on county level observations, produced estimates that may not be far off. Reflecting the surge and decline of participation across presidential and gubernatorial election years, 27 percent of Asians were estimated to be registered Republicans in 1990, 20 percent in 1992 and 28 percent in 1994. These figures reflect estimates of those Asians who are registered to vote, not of those who actually went to the polls. Asian participants, as the polling data suggest, are more Republican than the total Asian population of registered voters. From this evidence, it seems particularly problematic to suggest that the Asian influx is responsible for any sudden drop in Republican registration across the state. Where the GOP is losing strength in areas of high Asian concentration, it is because Asians are replacing white Republicans who move out of the area. This interpretation is consistent with William Frey's recent studies of the interaction of immigrant and migrant populations (1995). Specifically, Frey has documented the association of immigration and internal out-migration from metropolitan areas across the nation. In California, there is a major out-migration stream induced by immigration, and these out-migrants are less educated, elderly, and white. Asians and high-income white households seem to be staying put (361).

Among Hispanics, though, the VRS polls show a strong Democratic preference that is tempered only slightly by higher income. It is safe to infer that an increased number of Hispanics has led to a direct increase in Democratic registration and a drop in Republican growth, although there may be some population replacement of whites with Hispanics that is also contributing to low Republican growth or even decline.

Political Change and the Internal Composition of
California Counties

Since county boundaries are arbitrarily drawn and often encompass large
and diverse populations, county-level data can obscure internal variations
important to an area's political identity. To bring additional light to bear
on the possible mechanisms of political change, it will be useful to examine
census tract data for several exemplary counties that both have and have
not experienced Republican Party growth between 1980 and 1990. During
this period, GOP registration growth was on an upward curve throughout
the state. In the 1970s, Republicans had taken a beating, losing an average
of five points to Democrats and third parties across California's fifty-eight
counties. The 1980s, on the other hand, reversed this trend, and the average county saw Republicans gain about four points relative to other parties. Los Angeles and Alameda Counties have shown slow to no growth.
As new immigrants have moved in, Los Angeles County's share of Republican registrants has moved up three points—slightly below the state average. Alameda County's proportion of Republican registrants dropped
about a tenth of a percentage point from 1980 to 1990. In Kern County
(Bakersfield), just north of Los Angeles, Republican growth has been
brisk, with the proportion of Republican registrants jumping seven points
from 1980 to 1990 in spite of growth in the Mexican and Asian populations. In Placer County, in northern California just outside of Sacramento,
the proportion of Republican registrants jumped nearly eleven points over
the ten-year period. Might the internal population dynamics of these
counties explain why Los Angeles and Alameda have seen little Republican growth while more rural counties have seen steady to dramatic
improvement in GOP registration?

One possibility is that the counties where Republican growth has been
strongest are those that exhibit the least ethnic diversity. Perhaps Placer
County has seen strong Republican growth precisely because it has not
experienced the kind of demographic change that the more urban areas of
the state have undergone. Placer's population has increased rapidly over
the last fifteen years, but the new residents are the spillover from Sacramento or have migrated from the Bay Area to take advantage of a lower
cost of living and doing business. There are few minorities. The 1980 census reported only 1 percent Mexicans and only .5 percent Asians. These
populations have seen little growth. Local residents report that Hispanics
have had a historical foothold on certain areas of the county, but there are

no Asian enclaves. Thirty years ago, a small Japanese population was involved in the fruit-ranching business, but this group has since dispersed into other walks of life. So it may well be that without the moderating trends of ethnic population change elsewhere, counties like Placer have naturally drifted in a Republican direction in a period that favored Republican growth overall.

What is especially interesting about Placer County is that its small Hispanic population is geographically isolated. The one Hispanic enclave in the county is in the city of Roseville, and there is a small Hispanic population in Lincoln. While the pockets of ethnicity are distinct, these communities have a long history and contain few new arrivals. Ethnic conflict is a relative nonissue in suburban fringe areas like Placer County precisely because of the high degree of spatial separation between groups coupled with the small size of the minority population. When two potentially rival groups do not have much contact, they are less inclined to engage in political combat. This is not a new finding. V. O. Key suggested that black-belt whites in the old South were particularly active in the struggle to maintain Jim Crow, while up-country whites were not (1949). Key's explanation was that black-belt whites had the most contact with blacks and were therefore most likely to be threatened by the empowerment of black voters. Similarly, one early study found that black participation was highest in areas where blacks came into frequent conflict with whites, that is, where the two populations mixed, and lower in areas where blacks constituted the overwhelming majority of the population (Matthews and Prothro 1963a; 1963b). Racial interaction is likely to lead to the experience of discrimination, and therefore ethnicity becomes a salient political cue in more integrated areas (Giles and Hertz 1994; Antunes and Gaitz 1975; Olsen 1970). In a study of turnout in 282 U.S. cities, Robert Alford and Eugene Lee found that political participation was higher in cities with explicit ethnic and class cleavages (1968, 809). If the idea that interethnic proximity leads to political activism applies to race and ethnic relations outside the South, and for intergroup relations other than African American and white, then perhaps the spatial separation between Hispanic and white groups in places like Kern and Placer Counties has resulted in low participation levels among Hispanics and natural, unabated, Republican growth in the rest of the community.

The important methodological question at this point is what constitutes "spatial concentration" and "spatial dispersion"? As with all measures, a certain amount of arbitrariness is involved in the determination of some threshold level or cutpoint. If the cutpoint is set too high, so as to require a neighborhood to contain a majority of an ethnic group for that group to be considered spatially concentrated, then surely few neighborhoods will pass that test outside of the very largest metropolitan areas. Such a stringent measure would understate the degree of spatial concentration of many groups since few neighborhoods contain such high proportions of any minority group. On the other hand, if the standard is set too low, so that a very small percentage of people of color living in an area comprised mostly of whites indicates spatial concentration, then the degree of spatial concentration would be overstated. Every county would contain spatially segregated minority populations. One index that has been derived and widely utilized in discussions of residential segregation is the index of dissimilarity or D (see footnote 1) (Massey and Denton 1987; Jiobu 1988). This measure evaluates the evenness of a group's population across tracts. If a group is unevenly distributed, or segregated, the index values will be high and that group can be described as spatially concentrated. It is spread in even proportions if in each tract it comprises the same percentage of the population that it does in the county as a whole.

The results for the index calculated for the entire state and the four counties discussed are presented in table 2.6. Without question, blacks are the most spatially concentrated group, certainly in California as a whole but even in counties with smaller cities like Kern. This concentration appears to have dropped in all of the counties from 1980 to 1990 but remains highest in Los Angeles (.69). Interestingly, Kern County's Asian and Hispanic populations are at least as spatially concentrated as in Los Angeles and considerably more so than in Alameda.

Placer County
Located to the north and east of the city of Sacramento, Placer County consists of rapidly growing suburban towns and bedroom communities straddling Interstate 80 (see map 2.6). The median home price in the mid-1990s hovered around $150,000, far lower than in the Bay Area or Southern California. The affordable housing and location midway between the mountains and the coast has attracted both younger residents and retirees escaping the high costs, traffic, congestion, and crime of the state's coastal cities. The suburbs of Roseville and Rocklin have been inundated with development spilling over from Sacramento. Light industries, including NEC Electronics and Hewlett-Packard, have been transplanted from Silicon Valley and other parts of the state to Placer's growing number of

TABLE 2.6. Index of Dissimilarity for the Black, Asian, and Hispanic Populations Relative to Whites in Four California Counties, 1980 and 1990, by Census Tract

Variable	California		Alameda		Los Angeles		Kern		Placer	
	1980	1990	1980	1990	1980	1990	1980	1990	1980	1990
Asians	.45	.45	.34	.36	.43	.41	.45	.41	.26	.25
Blacks	.71	.62	.74	.66	.79	.69	.62	.54	.32	.21
Hispanics	.46	.46	.33	.36	.46	.46	.51	.52	.29	.26
N	5857	5857	313	313	1652	1652	109	109	36	36

Source: U.S. Census 1990, and author's calculations.
Note: Figures represent the percentage of each group that would have to move in order for the group to be evenly distributed across census tracts in the county.

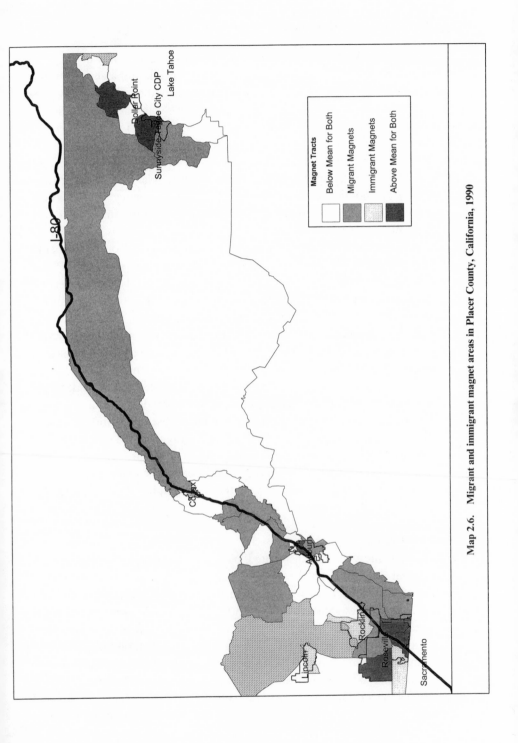

Map 2.6. Migrant and immigrant magnet areas in Placer County, California, 1990

Magnet Tracts

Below Mean for Both

Migrant Magnets

Immigrant Magnets

Above Mean for Both

I-80

Dollar Point

Sunnyside-Tahoe City CDP

Lake Tahoe

Colfax

Lincoln

Rocklin

Roseville

Sacramento

industrial parks. Growth control is a major issue. "No sooner do they settle down than they seek to slam the door on additional newcomers," remarked one local reporter. Local officials are fond of saying to developers proposing multifamily dwellings that "if we wanted to live in Sacramento, we would have moved there." One local initiative in the town of Roseville caps the city's population growth at 96,000 people by the year 2010 partly by cutting down on the density of new housing development.

The cost of living in a place determines, of course, who lives there and what shape politics will take. The strong push for growth control has kept low-cost housing to a minimum, which has isolated the small black and Hispanic populations in older neighborhoods in suburbs lying on the Sacramento County border. Commuting costs to and from Sacramento have also kept low-income minorities close to the city's borders. Placer County's tiny minority population might appear highly dispersed compared to those of the three other counties reported in table 2.6, but the figures are reflective of the small number of minorities in the county rather than the tolerance of the white population. Hispanics settled in Roseville beginning in the late nineteenth century to be near their historical base of employment on the Southern Pacific Railroad. Now many of the former railroad employees are retired, and they remain clustered in the older parts of the town. Outside of a few Roseville neighborhoods, the county is overwhelmingly "white bread." Indeed, one local observer bluntly admitted that people migrate to Placer County to get away from the minorities they feel have taken over other parts of the state. The picture is clear for small monoethnic counties like Placer. This locale has experienced strong Republican growth because few of the demographic forces that temper that growth are operating.

Kern County

"Kern County is a transplanted piece of Oklahoma," said one local reporter. Even though the massive southwestern migration dissipated in the 1950s, many residents still have relatives in Texas, Arkansas, and Oklahoma. They shuttle back and forth on Bakersfield's only wide-bodied jet service to Dallas, Texas. Even the economy is similar. Kern is one of the largest oil-producing areas in the United States. When oil prices dropped in the 1970s, and again in the early 1990s, many of the small towns were devastated. While some residents left the state, many remained behind, driving the local unemployment rate into double digits. Racial tension and segregation are also the results of a transplanted southern culture. The town of Oildale is a haven for white supremacists and hate groups. The black community is clustered in southeastern Bakersfield in the poorest and most blighted neighborhoods. Blacks have taken little interest in local politics, although the Bakersfield City Council did have one black representative as of the mid-1990s.

Aside from oil production, the Kern County economy is based mainly on agriculture and therefore is highly dependent upon immigrant labor. The Hispanic immigrant population is a mix of old and new arrivals. It is concentrated in East Bakersfield and in the rural "ag towns"—small town settlements adjacent to farms at the southern end of the Central Valley (see map 2.7). Second- and third-generation Hispanics are well integrated in the local economy but not in local politics. In spite of its large Hispanic population, Bakersfield has never elected a Hispanic city councilman. Still, Kern County has seen slightly less Republican growth than Placer because the Hispanic population has grown and, while concentrated, it has a history of labor activism. The United Farm Workers organized in this area throughout the 1970s to extract better wages and working conditions from big California growers. Delano, a city of twenty-five thousand on the border of Kern and Tulare Counties (see map 2.7), was the headquarters of labor organizer Cesar Chavez.

Farmers have greeted the political activity of Hispanics with considerable hostility and suspicion. Latino political activity has found its expression overwhelmingly within the Democratic Party. Local polls suggest that as many as 68 percent of the Hispanic voters are Democrats. If ethnics expand their influence over the local Democratic Party apparatus, Republicans are only likely to gain more support among the Central Valley's farmers, generating class cleavages on top of the existing ethnic ones in the local party system.

Los Angeles County
As in many other parts of the nation, California's most urban counties differ from the state's rural counties primarily with respect to their ethnic composition. Unlike Placer and Kern, Los Angeles County has high proportions of all three major ethnic groups: Asians, Hispanics, and blacks, along with an Anglo population that is a steadily declining majority. By tract, the Asian and black populations are highly concentrated in Los Angeles County. The Hispanic population was more concentrated in Los Angeles ($D = .46$) in 1990 than in Alameda ($D = .36$). Whites are more likely to avoid settling in neighborhoods where minorities reside if the

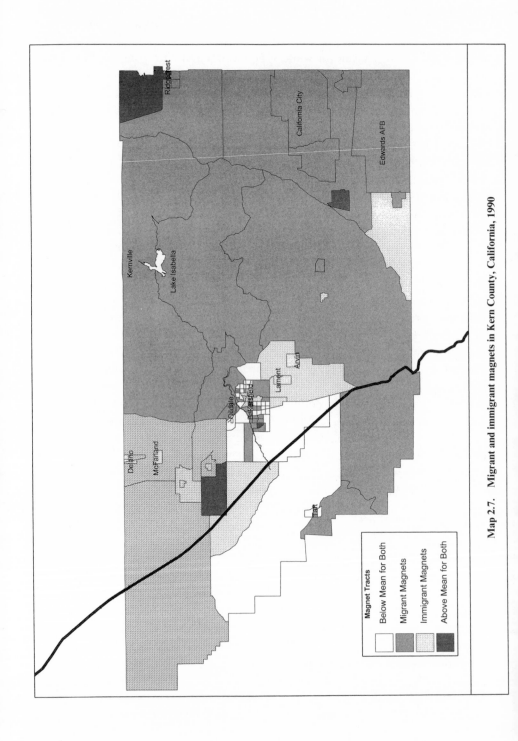

Map 2.7. Migrant and immigrant magnets in Kern County, California, 1990

Magnet Tracts

Below Mean for Both

Migrant Magnets

Immigrant Magnets

Above Mean for Both

population of the minority in question reaches a certain threshold. Similarly, white flight accelerates once neighborhoods undergoing integration reach a certain "tipping point." In many Los Angeles County tracts, these thresholds were reached in the 1950s.

Since the ethnic and white populations in these urban areas are spatially isolated from one another, racial tensions frequently surface in politics. Spatial isolation in the context of densely populated urban settings with district-based elections generates a politics where racial and ethnic advocacy is required for reelection (Clark and Morrison 1995; Skerry 1993). At first this seems to be a contradiction, since I have just argued that the geographic separation of ethnic groups is conducive to low consciousness of ethnicity. Within a neighborhood containing only one's coethnics, a person is less likely to encounter prejudice from outsiders and ethnicity may not become a salient political trait. But California's urban areas contain not only spatially concentrated populations, but also highly dense neighborhoods with extensive transportation links that promote exposure to a variety of nearby places. Citizens rarely stay only within their own neighborhoods. The large populations in these tracts and the casual traffic of people throughout areas of differing social and economic character suggest that the degree of spatial isolation can be easily overstated by looking at residential concentrations in the absence of population density. In highly urban areas, residential segregation and ethnic consciousness can go hand-in-hand because density mitigates the impact of geographic insularity.

The internal composition of California counties, the heterogeneity and density of their populations and their political traditions, help us to understand patterns of partisan change during the 1980s and 1990s. Democratic registration growth in Southern California has been hindered by the low rate of naturalization among Hispanic immigrants. Many Mexicans and Central Americans harbor very little confidence in the political system, perhaps reflecting their experience with government in their home countries. In addition, the Hispanic population is highly mobile and preoccupied with economic necessities (Pachon, Arguelles, and Gonzalez 1994). With no attachment to a particular place, and concerned primarily with the search for work and the payment of rent, political roots never take hold. The result is that predominantly white communities in Los Angeles County have far higher participation rates than recent immigrant communities. Cities where Republicans are registered have much higher turnout than where Democrats are strongest, exaggerating the Republican leaning of Southern California.

Nevertheless, Democrats have remained a competitive force because a small percentage of new immigrants have joined together with white liberals and more established immigrants in Democratic party building efforts. In Los Angeles, the sheer concentration of minorities ensures a strong Democratic political base on the south and east sides of the city even when turnout is low. Although the high level of segregation creates local political districts that are politically safe and encourage an ethnically based politics, liberals in the city's westside neighborhoods supported Mayor Tom Bradley's repeated reelection through the 1980s. Of course, Bradley became mayor of Los Angeles only by shedding a racial orientation and adopting a more pluralist, pro-business approach to city government (Sonenshein 1993). His white support waned as voters in the city's better neighborhoods began to take a dim view of his emphasis on continued commercial development. At that point his support came to rely more narrowly on the minority community. Like many other cities, then, Los Angeles County is far less Democratic than its ethnic and racial composition should dictate. Because so many low income minority voters take no interest in politics, white areas of Los Angeles are disproportionately represented. The ethnic balkanization of neighborhoods helps to create local legislative districts that encompass racially homogeneous areas. The politics following from quite natural and undistorted apportionment schemes ensures that group identities are transferred into politics. The unfortunate result has been that whites remain the controlling force in elections in the face of a growing minority population. Because minorities see a disproportionate number of white faces in state and local office, they assume they have been cheated of representation.

Alameda County
Like Los Angeles, Alameda County contains a heterogeneous population. The western and northern reaches of the county are the most densely populated and racially diverse areas. Large tracts of empty land on the east end of the county in or near the cities of Livermore, Dublin, and Pleasanton are rapidly filling up with single family dwellings that have attracted internal migrants but few immigrants (see map 2.8). In 1990, less than 9 percent of the population in the easternmost tracts was nonwhite. In the most urban settings, including Oakland, the level of interracial contact is high and the black, Asian, and Hispanic communities are large. Immigrants are not confined to inner city areas in northern Alameda. More than one million Bay Area minorities live outside traditional urban enclaves (Viviano 1991).

Some of these are refugees from Southeast Asian countries; others are pro-fessionals drawn by northern California's educational institutions and high-tech employment. Because of the high caliber of the immigrant stock, many of the new Asian immigrant communities in Alameda grew wealthier rather than poorer during the 1980s and 1990s, although the number of families per household has often grown as well. Map 2.8 shows that significant immigrant communities can be found in the southern and cen-tral tracts in or near the cities of Hayward, Fremont, and San Leandro. Notably, these towns have not been as attractive to interstate migrants. The only tracts that have attracted equal internal migrant and immigrant pop-ulations are clustered in the north around Berkeley and the University of California (see dark shaded area in map 2.8).

The black community in Alameda has lost ground economically even as it has gained political power in Oakland and neighboring communities. Isolation in the northern end of Alameda County has conveyed some political representation. Residential segregation, particularly between black and white areas, ensures that race is translated into the politics of state and local legislative bodies—blacks occupied nearly 40 percent of the jobs in Oakland city government by the early-1990s and routinely elected City Council members—but integration and economic progress have been slower. The Latino community is both spatially more dispersed and eco-nomically better off than the black population. Because of its dispersion, however, it has not had the same success in electing Latino representatives. Hispanic politicians elected in Alameda are required to draw upon cross-racial coalitions to an extent that blacks are not. As one Latina assembly-woman from Alameda County remarked, "We have to be careful when people wear their ethnicity on their sleeve all the time. People get uncom-fortable, and they don't want to work with you" (Hull 1994).

The racial consciousness generated by a segregated but densely settled ethnic population has not resulted in much support for Republican candi-dates in Alameda County. Republican registration declined nine points relative to that of Democrats (and other parties) from 1970 to the 1990s, standing at a mere 24 percent by 1994. Republican support for Proposition 187 and the California Civil Rights Initiative, which sought the repeal of affirmative action programs in the state, has done nothing to endear the GOP to lower income blacks and Latinos in Alameda's larger cities. Due in part to the flight of wealthy white residents, the black population of Alameda grew at eight times the rate of the white population from 1980 to 1990.

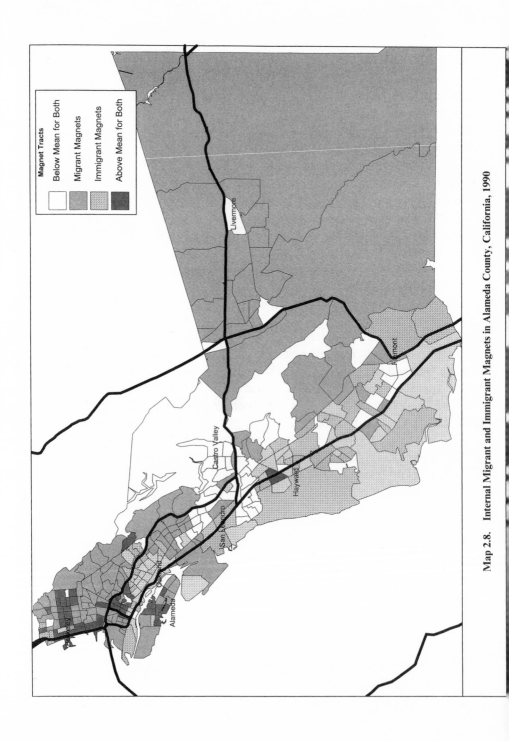

Map 2.8. Internal Migrant and Immigrant Magnets in Alameda County, California, 1990

Magnet Tracts

Below Mean for Both

Migrant Magnets

Immigrant Magnets

Above Mean for Both

Rural versus Urban Isolation

Ethnic heterogeneity and interracial conflict in the East Bay and Los Angeles areas has generated the kind of ethnic consciousness that finds its expression in politics. The segregation of neighborhoods, something that would ordinarily reduce interethnic contact and ethnic consciousness, has been mitigated by the density of settlement. In turn, legislators from the larger minority enclaves practice a racially oriented politics. The rural counties, while generally not as heterogeneous, show how spatial isolation can have a detrimental impact on political participation of any kind, whether politics is racially centered or not (Lamare 1977; Miller 1975; Garcia 1973). In Kern County, Hispanics and new immigrants are located in neighborhoods in the eastern section of Bakersfield and in remote towns in the rural northwestern part of the county (see map 2.7). With a lower degree of interaction with whites than that found in more urban counties, Hispanics are not as likely to be mobilized to naturalize, register, and vote. In this sense, rural isolation is more problematic for democratic politics than urban isolation is (Lamare 1977). Chicano children in rural areas have a stronger Mexican identity than those in urban areas and feel less attachment to the United States and its political institutions (Garcia 1973, 48). Early in life, most Mexican American children have feelings of affection for state and national government, but these feelings erode most rapidly among those living in rural areas. Garcia suggests that this erosion is due to the negative socialization experiences of the rural youth as compared to their urban counterparts (187–88). Rural Hispanics are usually of lower class standing and experience more discrimination from whites than those in urban and suburban settings. An alternative explanation is also consistent with Garcia's evidence, however. Rural Hispanics experience less contact with white political institutions and do not learn that these institutions can possibly work to benefit them. Given their lack of contact with non-Latinos relative to youth in more populated areas, it is difficult to comprehend how rural Mexicans could experience *more* discrimination. Geographic isolation provides some modicum of protection from discrimination by other groups. In fact, it may be that the lack of interaction with other groups as well as isolation from "Anglicizing" institutions in rural areas that depresses political unrest and involvement among rural Latino populations.

The balkanization of urban neighborhoods in Los Angeles and Alameda Counties occurs within a densely populated setting where other parts of town are accessible, albeit with some effort. Some interracial contact will take place, and much of it will not be negative. The black youth's employment in a supermarket in a predominantly white neighborhood two miles from home is the kind of interracial interaction that provides concrete economic benefits. Rural isolation, on the other hand, is far more difficult to surmount. Rural monoethnic communities may experience little racial tension, but they will also find it more difficult to come by the social and economic opportunities that might be available in a different kind of neighborhood. The middle-class white community where there is job growth may be twenty miles away rather than two.

In places like Kern County, with its history of conservative politics and lack of participation by many Hispanics, and at a time when much of the state was leaning toward the Republicans anyway, the GOP has done well. In Placer County, there are too few minorities for them to have been an effective counterweight to the rising Republican tide during the 1980s. The county remains 94 percent white. The few minorities there are dispersed, and, while the number of Asians and Hispanics has increased slightly, there are not enough of them to be consequential to the area's political development.

Peaceful race relations coupled with minority nonparticipation are found in areas where racial and ethnic groups are spatially isolated, where they are scattered over a large, sparsely populated territory, and particularly where the population of nonwhite residents remains small and nonthreatening. The latter description fits Placer County especially well. Placer's population grew by nearly 60 percent from 1980 to 1992, but most of this growth was the result of whites moving in from outside or within the state. Their settlement patterns are shown in map 2.6. The tracts that drew internal migrants are in the northern parts of the county and in the more expensive neighborhoods. Those that were magnets for immigrants are in the older towns near Sacramento. Even in a place like Placer County, the sorting process resulting from population mobility is evident, as it stratifies these small towns. Placer County has become yet another example of a white suburban county filling with residents fleeing large multiethnic central cities. But the ethnics who do make it to Placer still find their mobility restricted.

To say that racial conflict is not likely to break out where there are no minority groups is, of course, as trivial as saying that where there is ethnic heterogeneity conflict is more probable. Diversity is divisive; there is nothing new about that. What is less obvious, though, is the effect of ethnic settlement patterns on the electoral politics of places. Spatially interactive, integrated ethnic minority populations are more likely to get involved in the community. Whether their involvement takes on a racial or nonracial tone depends upon the isolation of the diverse communities. Spatially segregated populations in densely populated areas are particularly productive of a race-based politics since racially homogeneous neighborhoods become the basis of legislative representation. Racial polarization is common in places like Alameda and Los Angeles Counties, where ethnic populations are highly concentrated at the neighborhood level but highly interactive within and across municipalities. Spatially integrated populations, on the other hand, whether in rural or urban areas, may generate political cleavages of some type, but they are not likely to be race based. In racially heterogeneous communities, politicians cannot easily get elected serving an ethnically pure constituency.

While the residential segregation of California's large urban counties has exacerbated the political stratification of the state, the utter hopelessness of ethnopolitical conflict in California has also been overblown. Metropolitan areas may be the places where the most intense racial battles are fought, but they are also the areas where those battles are ultimately to be won. The demobilizing influence of residential segregation in urban communities is easier to overcome than it is in rural areas where distances between homogeneous enclaves can be far greater. The mechanism for integration of ethnic communities in urban areas is the spatial mobility that comes from education and economic advancement. For immigrants, that means overcoming the obstacle of learning to speak English. For native blacks and Hispanics, it means overcoming the considerable disadvantages of low-income neighborhoods through self-effort and government enforcement of antidiscrimination laws. Political winds currently blowing in California threaten to slow progress toward integration. The tone of California politics is one of ethnopolitical separation coupled with trends in party support that increasingly distinguish areas of the state by their ethnic composition.

CHAPTER 3

Colorado: National Crossroads

Immigrant workers from Mexico and Central America are valued in Colorado's mountain resort towns, as they are elsewhere, for their willingness to work hard for low pay. The demand for cheap, exploitable labor, though, has not been matched with an equal concern for affordable housing. Immigrant workers find it nearly impossible to reside anywhere near Aspen, Vail, Keystone, or the other winter playgrounds where they work. In the mid-1990s, the *Rocky Mountain News* reported that families of four were living in tents without water and electricity because they could not afford the pricey rents in the exclusive resort towns (Kelly 1994). The high cost of housing in the ski areas forced many low income workers to commute twenty or thirty miles, snarling traffic and burdening existing infrastructure. The poor housing conditions and low pay prompted the Catholic Archdiocese in Denver to finance the construction of multifamily housing in several mixed income mountain communities while pressuring the recreation industry to increase wages and benefits. Where low-paying service jobs were once held by young white ski bums who came and went seasonally, the immigrant workers have families and are looking to settle down permanently (Kelly 1994; Weller 1994; Frazier 1994). The resort owners and wealthy part-time residents have sent clear signals that cheap temporary labor was welcome but affordable permanent housing for the laborers was not.

Colorado's population growth has been typical of the states in the Mountain West. The state grew by 156 percent from 1950 to 1992, and much of this growth occurred after 1970. In the late 1980s, the state saw a drop in its growth rate as its energy-resource sector experienced the same recession that hit Texas, Oklahoma, and nearby "oil-patch" states. Natural resource extraction has declined steadily since the 1930s, and high-paying jobs in the mining and timber industries are increasingly hard to

80

find. Trade, tourism, and services are the expanding economic sectors (Abbott, Leonard, and McComb 1982; Hamel and Schreiner 1989).

Up until the mid-1990s, Colorado's immigrant population remained small and politically inconsequential. Most of the demographic change in the state's recent history has been the result of interstate migration, drawn to Colorado for employment and the attractiveness of its environment. The foreign born constituted a mere 4 percent of the population in 1990, VS 55% US while the population born in the United States but out of state stood at 55 percent. The Hispanic population is a significant ethnic presence that has had a strong historic foothold especially in southern Colorado. Hispanics amounted to 13 percent of the state's population in 1990, blacks constituted 4 percent, and Asians about 1.8 percent.

Population growth in the state's sixty-three counties is depicted on map 3.1. The demographic sectionalism in Colorado's development is clear. The plains of eastern and southeastern Colorado have become depopulated. The largest city in the state, Denver, stands out as an island of slow growth among exploding suburban counties (Lewis 1996). Like central cities elsewhere, Denver's white population has declined since 1970, while its immigrant and minority populations have increased. Local historians describe the contrast between Denver and its suburbs in terms familiar to scholars of urban development:

> The [income] gap widened in the 1960s, as Denver itself increasingly became an island of old people, poor people and minority group members surrounded by a sea of middle-class white families who found that suburban living allowed the greatest enjoyment of Colorado's space and climate. (Abbott, Leonard, and McComb 1982, 283)

The four counties bordering Denver—Douglas, Jefferson, Adams, and Arapahoe—have led the state's growth. Douglas County's population is now twenty times greater than it was in 1950. Further from Denver, Boulder and Larimer Counties saw their populations more than triple from 1950 to 1992. Growth has also been strong in several of the mountain counties (Eagle, Pitkin, Summit) where resort towns have sprung up to take advantage of the demand for outdoor recreation in the Rockies. The wealthy residents of these counties have been described as "urban corporate dropouts" who leave Wall Street style jobs to work in ski lodges and open small retail businesses (Hamel and Schreiner 1990). Others are wealthy celebrities whose mansions sit empty much of the year (Kelly

1994). The western slope counties are a patchwork of slow- and fast-growing areas. The faster ones (Garfield and Mesa, the latter containing the city of Grand Junction) appear to be growing due to increases in small industry, tourism, service jobs, and retail trade. The slower counties are more dependent on government employment and the winter resort business. Eastern Colorado, sparsely populated to begin with, has experienced depopulation since midcentury due to the decline in plains agriculture and decreasing competition within the meatpacking industry.

The foreign-born population was just under 5 percent of the total population in 1990, but, as in California, a decreasing proportion of the immigrant population is white. In 1970, more than 90 percent of the foreign-born population was white. By the early 1990s, this had dropped to less than 60 percent. The composition of that foreign-born population for 1990 is depicted in figure 3.1. Of the 142,000 immigrants at that time, about one-fourth were from Mexico, with another 5 percent from Central and South America. Twenty-six percent of the foreign-born population is Asian, and about 30 percent is European. This latter figure stands in marked contrast to California, where only 9 percent of the foreign-born population in 1990 hailed from European nations (see fig. 2.1).

Colorado's small Asian population is dispersed. When the dissimilarity index (see chap. 2, n. 1) is calculated to measure the concentration of ethnic groups across the state's counties, it shows that about 24 percent of Asians would be required to move in order for their number to be evenly distributed across the state. Blacks and Hispanics are more concentrated—in 1990, about 49 percent of blacks would have to move, and about 34 percent of Hispanics, for these groups to be evenly spread.

The distribution of political party support in Colorado is also clustered, or "lumpy," making the parties less politically competitive at the local level than they are in California. About 25 percent of Republicans (or Democrats) would have to relocate in order to ensure perfectly even partisan registration across all of the state's counties. This figure reflects the heavily Democratic registration of Denver and certain Hispanic areas in southern Colorado and the one-sided Republicanism of Colorado Springs (El Paso County) and several rural counties.

A comparison of the basic demographic characteristics of migrants, natives, and immigrants shows that the generalizations made in chapter 1 about the wealth, race, and education levels of these three groups also hold for Colorado (see appendix A, table A3.1). The 1990 PUMS data for Coloradans over the age of eighteen shows that those born outside the state

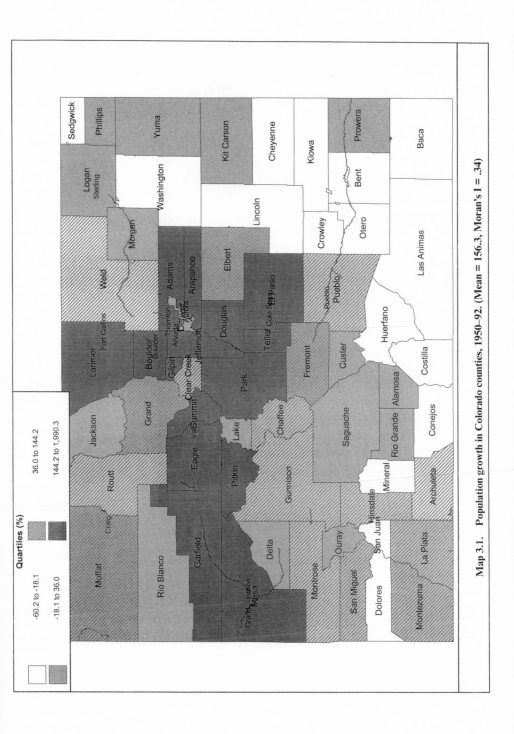

Map 3.1. Population growth in Colorado counties, 1950–92. (Mean = 156.3, Moran's I = .34)

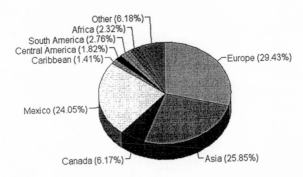

Fig. 3.1.   Composition of the foreign-born population in Colorado, 1990

earned, on average, $3,700 more per year than Colorado natives and $4,500 more than immigrants. Immigrants and native Coloradans were closer together in income, with immigrants reporting slightly higher *median* incomes than native Coloradans. The income figures of native Coloradans are admittedly influenced by the frequent and heavy losses reported by those employed as farmers. Even so, it is clear that internal migration has made the state both wealthier and more white, while immigration has made it poorer and more ethnically diverse. Interstate migrants in 1990 were 89 percent non-Hispanic white, but only 77 percent of natives and 52 percent of immigrants were non-Hispanic white. Table A3.1 also shows that migrants to Colorado from other states are older and have higher Social Security incomes than either natives or immigrants, suggesting that many of the new residents in the state are retirees.

Settlement Patterns of Migrants and Immigrants

Determining where the migrant and immigrant populations are settling is a sure way of evaluating whether they are drawn to expanding enclaves or dispersing throughout the majority white population. The PUMS data for Colorado (table A3.1) indicate that the internal migrant and immigrant populations do not share the same level of wealth and education and are ethnically distinct. Based on these characteristics alone, we would hardly expect them to settle in the same locations. Maps 3.2 and 3.3 serve as useful gauges of the growth in visibility of internal migrants and immigrants from 1980 to 1990. Map 3.2 shows that internal migrants are becoming more noticeable in Denver's outlying suburbs (Douglas and Elbert Counties) and in the mountain counties containing the state's winter resorts. Note that internal migrants have not been drawn to the northeastern section of the state. Immigrants, on the other hand, are a rising proportion of the population in two counties in the northeast, Morgan and Washington (see map 3.3). They are also a more noticeable presence in some of the same mountain counties where the internal migrant population has increased (Eagle, Pitkin, Lake, and Summit).

Following the procedure employed in chapter 2, I model the locational distribution of immigrants and migrants using data to determine whether the changing proportion of immigrants and migrants across the state's sixty-three counties can be explained by local unemployment and income growth, the presence of coethnics, or some combination of both. As in the California case (chap. 2), the dependent variable is the change in the size of the particular group as a percentage of the total population from 1980 to 1990. The goal, then, is not to explain a group's numerical increase but to explain changes in the group's size relative to the rest of the population of the county. Following the strategy of chapter 2, I also take account of spatial dependency in the observations by including a spatially lagged dependent variable among the explanatory variables.

The results for this model are presented in table 3.1 for U.S. internal migrants, Canadians, Mexicans, and immigrants from several of the world's major regions. As in California, Asians and Mexicans are becoming more noticeable components of the population in the areas where they settle. These two groups show the greatest propensity to locate in areas of prior coethnic settlement. For nearly all of the other groups, however, there is an inverse relationship between the size of the group's population in 1980 and the growth in that population from 1980 to 1990. Africans, Canadians, Europeans, and South and Central Americans are especially likely to wind up in areas where their group's presence is *declining* as a proportion of the total population for a couple of reasons. First, their numbers are small; and second, their growth has been outpaced by that of the native-born population. For Canadians and Europeans, in particular, there is no tendency to cluster in areas of prior coethnic settlement.

Most of the economic growth in the state is occurring along the eastern slope of the Rockies (known as the Front Range); the counties running from Larimer (north of Denver) to Pueblo in the south (see map 3.1). Several of the immigrant groups, especially Asians and Europeans, are apparently informed enough about local conditions to avoid concentrating in areas of high unemployment. Growth in the Mexican and Central Ameri-

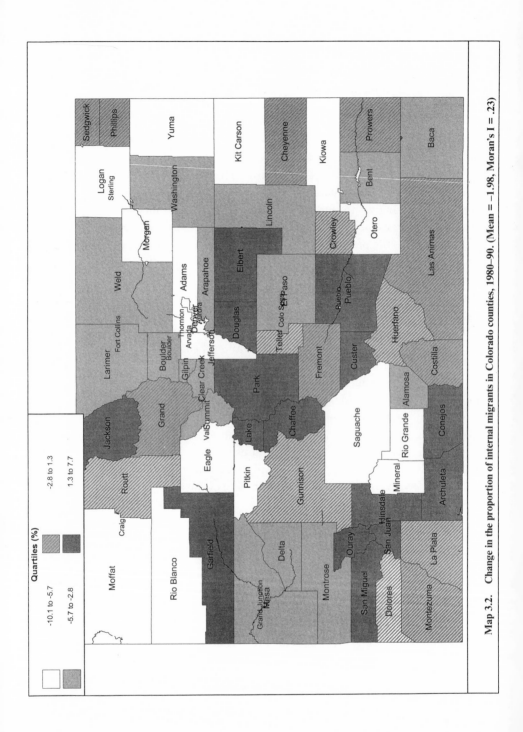

Map 3.2. Change in the proportion of internal migrants in Colorado counties, 1980–90. (Mean = −1.98, Moran's I = .23)

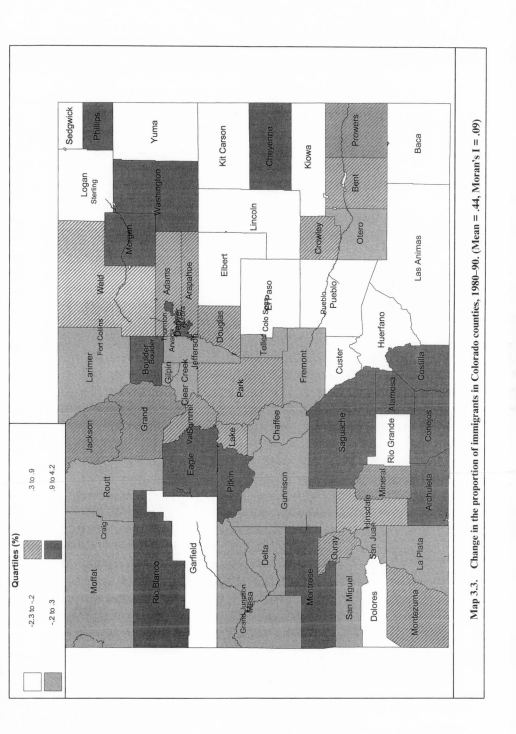

Quartiles (%)

☐ -2.3 to -.2	▨ .3 to .9
▨ -.2 to .3	■ .9 to 4.2

Map 3.3. Change in the proportion of immigrants in Colorado counties, 1980–90. (Mean = .44, Moran's I = .09)

TABLE 3.1. Influences on Population Concentration in Colorado Counties, 1980–90

Variable	U.S. Migrants	African Immigrants	Asian Immigrants	European Immigrants	Canadian Immigrants	Mexican Immigrants	Central American Immigrants	South American Immigrants
% 1980 group population	-.08	-.94*	.29**	-.33**	-.62**	.57**	-.78**	-.55**
	(.05)	(.22)	(.10)	(.04)	(.07)	(.19)	(.45)	(.13)
% unemployment, 1980	.55**	-.006	-.09**	-.02**	-.006	.04	.005	-.003
	(.18)	(.004)	(.01)	(.01)	(.004)	(.04)	(.01)	(.003)
Change in real median family income, 1980–90	-.19	.001	.03**	.04**	.008**	.02	.02	.005**
	(.11)	(.02)	(.01)	(.01)	(.003)	(.03)	(.009)	(.002)
% net population change	.05**	-.0001	.0001	-.001	.001**	.001	-.0002	.0002
	(.01)	(.0003)	(.001)	(.001)	(.0002)	(.003)	(.001)	(.0002)
Population density	-.0008**	-.00003**	-.00007	.00001	.00001**	.0003**	.00005**	.00003**
	(.0003)	(.000007)	(.00006)	(.00002)	(.000008)	(.00009)	(.00003)	(.000006)
% college students	.13	-.005*	-.002	.003	.006**	.03	.04	-.003*
	(.13)	(.003)	(.01)	(.008)	(.003)	(.03)	(.01)	(.002)
Spatial lag	.34**	.47**	-.10	-.005	.38**	.27**	.25	.12
	(.12)	(.17)	(.15)	(.17)	(.10)	(.11)	(.22)	(.11)
Constant	-1.89	.07	.52	.29	.10	-.46	-.18	.06
N	63	63	63	63	63	63	63	63
R^2_a	.53	.57	.51	.70	.68	.57	.01	.40

Note: Spatial autoregressive model, weighted for population; income coefficients expressed in thousands of 1992 dollars; dependent variable = change in population group as a percent of total population. See appendix A for a full description of variables.

*$p < .10$.   **$p < .05$.

can populations, though, was unrelated to employment conditions at the beginning of the decade. This disregard for local labor market conditions is a potentially problematic finding since immigrant use of public services, including welfare, has stimulated much of the recent anti-immigrant sentiment across the country. Map 3.2 illustrates the areas of highest Mexican immigrant concentration in 1990. It ranges from a low of zero to a high of 33 percent in several south-central Colorado counties (Conejos, Costilla, Alamosa). But there are differences between recent Mexican immigrants and the state's long-established Hispanic population. Hispanic settlements in southern Colorado date from the 1600s. Recent Mexican immigrants are a sizable minority within the Hispanic population but still only a minority. Concentrated Hispanic populations of mostly Mexican ancestry are found throughout eastern Colorado, where they have been associated with the sugar beet and meatpacking industries. Starting in the mid-1940s, Colorado farmers directly recruited Mexican immigrant workers as part of the Bracero program. Many stayed on after the growing season to take more permanent jobs in northeastern Colorado's slaughterhouses and feedlots (especially in Weld, Morgan, and Washington Counties; see Andreas 1994, chap. 1).

The newer waves of Mexican immigrants are drawn to cities, especially Greeley, Pueblo, and Denver, where there are established Mexican American communities. Hispanics in Denver, who constituted about one-fourth of the city's population in 1990, are concentrated in the north and west. Early in the century, in both Denver and Pueblo, Hispanics were segregated in poor neighborhoods comparable to the "black ghettos" of the East (Elazar 1970, 343). Their ever increasing numbers translated into political clout in the 1980s and 1990s when a Hispanic candidate, Federico Peña, won the Denver mayoralty twice and a black candidate, Wellington Webb, won mayoral runoffs on the basis of a Hispanic-black coalition (Hero 1987, 1989). Evidence emerged in the early 1990s of a growing immigrant, mostly Mexican, population in the mountain counties, where record numbers of immigrants were being hired in the restaurant and lodging businesses in resort towns (Charland 1995). The movement of low-skill immigrants into the wealthy ski resort areas has generated the serious housing shortage described at the beginning of this chapter. In the mid-1990s, rents in the resort towns were $1,000 per month, while median salaries were only $1,400 per month (Kelly 1994; Weller 1994).

The Asian population is scattered north and south along the most populated areas of the Front Range where there has been impressive growth in real median income. Asian settlements are least likely to develop in areas afflicted with high unemployment (see table 3.1). There are no Asian enclaves of the scale one finds in California, although by standards internal to Colorado the rapid growth of the Asian population in Denver's suburbs could make this subgroup a political force in the twenty-first century.

Interestingly, the settlement patterns of U.S. internal migrants are distinct from those of Asians and Mexicans. Rather than becoming a more noticeable presence in areas where internal migrants have previously settled, they are shrinking as a proportion of the population in such areas. Still, the settlement patterns of internal migrants are not associated with economic conditions in the way I originally hypothesized. Indeed, the concentration of internal migrants increased in areas that began the decade with the highest unemployment rates. Perhaps this is a sign that internal migration to Colorado is driven more by lifestyle considerations than the economic climate. An alternative explanation is that Colorado's unemployment in the early 1980s was confined to specific industry sectors and did not discourage migrants who came to work in other industries.

The spatial concentration of the internal migrant population is illustrated in map 3.3. Internal migrants are a minor presence in the southeastern plains counties where Hispanic concentrations are greatest. Instead, they prefer to locate in the Denver suburbs (Arapahoe, Douglas, and Jefferson Counties) and in mountain resort areas where net population growth has been brisk but population densities remain low.

Finally, the spatially lagged dependent variable (table 3.2) indicates that U.S. migrants, Africans, Canadians, and Mexicans are becoming more noticeable in particular geographic pockets or subregions of the state that cross jurisdictional boundaries. In other words, the growth in the proportion of migrants from these areas is related to similar growth trends in nearby jurisdictions. The other groups show no increase in concentration by subregion when other variables are included in the model.

Ethnic Balkanization and Naturalization Rates in Colorado

The county-level data show that balkanization along ethnic and racial lines has further differentiated areas where immigrants settle from those they avoid. Asians and Mexicans became a more noticeable presence during the 1980s in the areas where they had settled in previous times. This was not true, though, for U.S. internal migrants and other immigrant groups whose settlement patterns were more diffused and whose growth rates were dwarfed by those of other populations. Even at the county level of aggregation, where considerable local variation may be obscured, we see the concentration of some groups and the diffusion of others. Before cities and counties become ethnically distinct, neighborhoods do. Much of the variation in the racial homogeneity of areas is internal to cities and counties. In California, the ethnic isolation of minority from white voters was associated with low naturalization rates among Hispanic immigrants but not for Asians (see appendix A, table A2.1, for California results). The results in table A3.2 help shed light on whether the segregation of minority groups from whites within Colorado counties is related to low naturalization rates for immigrants residing in those counties. As in California, the size of the foreign-born population in a county is inversely related to naturalization in the 1990 data. Specifically, a 1 percent increase in the proportion of the population comprised of immigrants is associated with a two-point drop in the naturalization rate. As in California, places where the foreign born are concentrated are typified by less political capital than those of native concentration. It is not clear from the data in table A3.2 that segregation patterns have a consistent impact on naturalization once the overall size of the foreign-born population is taken into account. Counties with high levels of white-Hispanic segregation definitely show low naturalization rates in 1980 but not in 1990. White-Asian segregation has no relevance to aggregate naturalization rates, probably due to the small Asian population in the state. The spatial lag does indicate that counties with the highest naturalization rates form a distinct geographic pocket that supersedes county jurisdictional boundaries. The counties with the highest naturalization rates are those with the fewest recent immigrants—two sets of counties in the eastern plains and southern regions of the state that have small populations and few employment prospects for Mexican or Asian laborers.

Migrants, Immigrants, and Voter Turnout in Colorado

Political participation rates within states are rarely uniform. Some places in Colorado are characterized by a high level of political empowerment, while others are not, and it has probably always been that way. Average turnout rates for counties across two Colorado gubernatorial elections in the 1990s are shown on map 3.4. It is noteworthy that the depopulated eastern plains counties show the highest turnout rates (darkest shading), while those that have experienced the most rapid population growth, around Denver and in the mountain resort areas, are in the lowest turnout quartile (light shading).

With a small statewide immigrant population, it is not clear that an analysis of county-level data will reveal that current immigration patterns have any significant impact on political outcome variables such as voter turnout. Internal cross-state migrants, on the other hand, constitute a majority of Colorado's population. Perhaps this indicator of population mobility does have the expected impact on turnout, actually decreasing it relative to areas populated mostly with Colorado natives. Results of an analysis of the influence of several variables in predicting turnout rates in five recent Colorado elections appears in table 3.2. As in chapter 2, I have included a model that pools the elections in the 1990s. Control variables have been added for education, the segregation of the minority from the white population, population density, and the percentage of the population that is African American. The results show that the percentage of the population born outside Colorado does not have a consistently negative impact on countywide turnout. The proportion of the population comprised of immigrants who arrived after 1970 is associated with lower turnout levels across all of the elections but especially in the gubernatorial races of 1990 and 1994. The spatial isolation of white from minority voters is associated with higher turnout in the presidential election years of 1980 and 1992, but the signs are negative for the off-year elections. Education does not boost turnout across Colorado as it does in California and other states. This is because education is closely associated with other variables, including internal migration and population growth in Colorado. Douglas County is a good example of a place where the influx of well-educated, wealthy suburbanites has had the effect of depressing participation levels because so many of the newcomers are from outside the state. This rapidly growing county immediately south of the Denver metropolitan area was inundated with migrants from other states and elsewhere in Colorado from 1980 to 1990, and turnout in Douglas is among the lowest in the state—a mere 47 percent in 1990 when the state average stood at 58 percent. Again, in 1994 Douglas County's turnout ran about ten points below the state average.

It is especially noteworthy that the immigrant population is negatively associated with turnout in all five elections. An example of where the

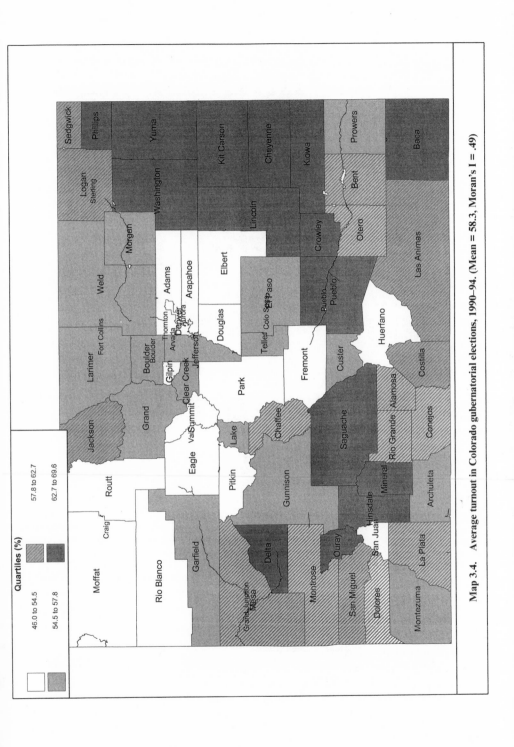

Quartiles (%)

46.0 to 54.5	57.8 to 62.7
54.5 to 57.8	62.7 to 69.6

Map 3.4. Average turnout in Colorado gubernatorial elections, 1990–94. (Mean = 58.3, Moran's I = .49)

TABLE 3.2. Impact of Population Mobility on Voter Turnout in Colorado Counties, 1980–94

Variable	1980	1982	1990	1992	1994	Pooled 1990s
% college educated	-.32*	.15	-.06	-.02†	-.11	-.07
	(.18)	(.14)	(.10)	(.11)	(.10)	(.07)
Isolation of minorities from whites (within counties)	.46**	-.03	-.03	.05*	-.03	-.004
	(.16)	(.02)	(.02)	(.03)	(.03)	(.02)
% post-1970 immigrants	-.15	-.22	-1.00**	-.30	-.88*	-.75**
	(-1.30)	(.93)	(.48)	(.54)	(.51)	(.34)
% born out of state	.06	-.12	-.02	.05	.11	.06
	(.09)	(.08)	(.08)	(.10)	(.09)	(.06)
% black	.59	-.36	.12	.10	-.71**	-.10
	(.46)	(.33)	(.27)	(.32)	(.30)	(.19)
Population density	-.0004**	.001	-.0006^a	-.0004^a	.004**	.001
	(.001)	(.001)	(.001)	(.001)	(.001)	(.001)
Spatial lag	.46**	.44**	.57**	.14	.66**	.60**
	(.16)	(.15)	(.09)	(.21)	(.12)	(.08)
Presidential race	—	—	—	—	—	5.78**
						(.61)
Constant	47.52	42.33	28.74	45.48	18.38	20.44
N	58	58	58	58	58	174
R^2_a	.42	.52	.69	.05	.62	.65

Note: Spatial autoregressive model, weighted for population; dependent variable = percentage turnout by county. See appendix A for a full description of variables.

[a]Variables with low tolerances and high standard errors due to multicollinearity.

*$p < .10$. **$p < .05$.

recent influx of *immigrants* has decreased turnout is Weld County (in which Greeley is located), where participation has run eight to ten points below the state average in nonpresidential election years. Places typified by high mobility wind up with poorer representation than those with greater stability, as the lower turnout ensures that these areas have less influence in statewide elections than their numbers would otherwise dictate.

Finally, the observations for turnout in Colorado are positively auto-correlated, as evidenced by the coefficient for the spatial lag in table 3.2. Lower turnout counties include the fastest growing areas around Denver (Arapahoe, Douglas, Adams, and Weld) as well as the resort counties in the mountains. High turnout areas are those with small and stable populations on the plains and the Western Slope. The statistical significance of the spatial lag indicates that there is a regional basis to patterns of participation in the state, which cannot be captured by conventional demographic variables for education and population migration alone.

Migrants, Immigrants, and Party Regularity in Colorado

Patterns of party regularity in voting at the individual level are an important sign of the utility of partisanship as a cue in general election voting behavior. At an aggregate level, such as a city, county, or state, they are an indication of the predictability of an electorate. The predictability of an electorate has a bearing on the efforts that must be expended by candidates and party organizations in locating and mobilizing voters (Gimpel 1996). As in chapter 2, I hypothesize that migrants from elsewhere serve to unravel the party system (Brown 1988), increasing differences between party registration and actual voting in Colorado jurisdictions. An analysis of the impact of several demographic variables on differences between registration and voting appears in table 3.3. Several variables have a consistent influence on reducing the difference between party registration and party voting: education, population density, and the percentage of the population comprised of recent immigrants. The presence of black voters, though, has the effect of increasing the difference between registration and voting. This is certainly contrary to the California case, in which black populations were often associated with voting in line with registration. The finding is also at odds with individual-level results that show blacks voting consistently and overwhelmingly Democratic. The danger of committing the ecological fallacy looms large when aggregate data produce results so discrepant from survey data (King 1997). The results can be understood as an artifact of aggregation bias. Several of Colorado's

TABLE 3.3. Similarity of Party Registration to Party Voting in Colorado Counties, 1980–94

Variable	1980	1982	1990	1992	1994	Pooled 1990s
% college educated	-.003	.27	-.38**	-.25**	-.66**	-.44**
	(.15)	(.18)	(.11)	(.07)	(.11)	(.07)
% born out of state	.04	-.16	.35**	.12	.22**	.25**
	(.07)	(.10)	(.10)	(.07)	(.11)	(.07)
% post-1970 immigrants	-1.18	-2.69**	-.59	-.54	-.16	-.25
	(1.10)	(1.17)	(.57)	(.35)	(.57)	(.34)
% black	-.03	1.26**	1.16**	.29ª	-.18ª	.42**
	(.36)	(.39)	(.33)	(.22)	(.35)	(.21)
Population density	-.001†	-.002**	-.004**	-.0007	.0004	-.001*
	(.001)	(.001)	(.001)	(.001)	(.001)	(.001)
% turnout	.54**	.05	.06	.22**	-.16	.08
	(.10)	(.16)	(.14)	(.10)	(.12)	(.07)
Spatial lag	.33**	.63**	.43**	.27*	.48**	.52**
	(.11)	(.15)	(.18)	(.16)	(.10)	(.08)
Presidential race	—	—	—	—	—	-1.98**
						(.90)
Constant	-21.55	5.50	17.37	-9.04	18.29	-2.46
N	63	63	63	63	63	63
R^2_a	.77	.52	.80	.59	.75	.65

Note: Spatial autoregressive model, weighted for population; dependent variable = Abs (% Republican vote – % Republican registration); high positive values indicate counties where voting differed from registration. See appendix A for a full description of variables.

ªVariables with low tolerances and high standard errors due to multicollinearity.

*$p < .10$. **$p < .05$.

medium-sized cities with small but significant black populations (*significant* by Colorado standards can be understood to mean any countywide propor- tion greater than the statewide percentage of 4 percent black) have lopsided Republican leanings. One of these is El Paso County (Colorado Springs), where 7 percent of the population is black and Republican voting always runs well ahead of Republican Party registration. The black population in cities like these is just not sufficiently large to redirect these powerful GOP currents even when the minority population is fully mobilized.

Whereas the black population in Colorado's urban areas is not a strong political force anywhere outside of Denver, the influence of the His- panic population is largely captured by the variable for post-1970 immi- gration in table 3.3. This population seems to keep differences between registration and voting to a minimum, thus enforcing party regularity. The places that follow their registration quite closely are the politically com- petitive Denver suburbs and other cities along the Front Range where the Hispanic, African American, and Asian populations are growing rapidly (Patty 1996). In these more densely populated areas, then, the Hispanic population apparently exercises the same influence on the consistency of Democratic margins in Colorado that blacks exercise in many other states. They are active enough to be a predictable Democratic bloc in state and local elections.

The Hispanic counties in southern and southeastern Colorado are dif- ferent from other areas with large Hispanic populations because Republi- cans often do well enough to be competitive in spite of imbalanced party registration figures. In rural Costilla County, for example, Republican registration stood at a mere 9 percent in 1994, but Republicans won 28 percent of the gubernatorial vote that year. Similar figures obtain for the neighboring counties of Saguache, Mineral, and Rio Grande. Apparently the processes that have socialized the Hispanic population into the politics of the Democratic Party in Colorado's more urban areas have not been at work in the southern counties.

Changes in Party Registration in Colorado

As in California and many other states, the 1970s were not kind to the GOP in Colorado. Some of the heaviest losses occurred in rural counties, where just a few departing voters or new arrivals could radically alter the political balance. In Denver and Boulder, Republicans also lost ground to Democrats and independent registrants. The 1980s reversed this trend, with Republicans surging back to retake lost ground. But often their gains did not occur in areas where they had previously lost ground. Republicans continued to lose ground in Denver and Boulder, although they rebounded in many rural counties (see map 3.5).

What explains the gains and losses in these two decades? The impact of population mobility and other demographic characteristics of Colorado counties on changes in Republican Party registration are summarized in table 3.4. As in chapter 2, my central hypothesis going into this analysis is that population growth generally increases Republican registration, especially population growth from outside of the state. The results in table 3.4 suggest, however, that exactly the opposite occurred in the 1970s. In that decade, the increase in the population from out of state diminished Republican registration growth. In the following decade, though, the hypothesis is confirmed, as Republican growth was about 3.5 points higher for every ten-point increase in the percentage of the population moving in from one of the other forty-nine states.

In reference to the result for the 1970s in which population growth appears to hurt Republican registration, one should not necessarily conclude that the Democrats benefited from the arrival of migrants from outside Colorado. Independent and third-party registration increased 61 percent statewide from 1970 to 1980, rising most sharply in the counties with the most out-of-state migrants. Apparently, the growth of the Asian and Hispanic immigrant populations has neither hurt nor helped GOP prospects (table 3.4). The foreign-born population is simply too small to register much impact at such a gross level of aggregation, and the 1980s indicated no widespread political reaction among natives against the influx of immigrants.

The demographic shift toward more non-Coloradans helped the Republican Party in the 1980s but was modestly associated with Republican losses during the 1970s. The losses in the 1970s can be explained by reference to the fact that Colorado began the decade of the 1970s so strongly Republican. Those who track patterns of party change over time have noted the existence of equilibrium cycles in the balance of party strength (Stokes and Iverson 1962; Sellers 1965). In two-party competitive settings, one party's ascendancy is only temporary, as the other party gradually returns to a competitive position and then moves into its own position of superiority for a time. This ebb and flow of equilibrium cycles would predict that if Colorado Republicans reached their peak in the late 1960s subsequent years would witness a GOP decline. Through the 1970s, explo-

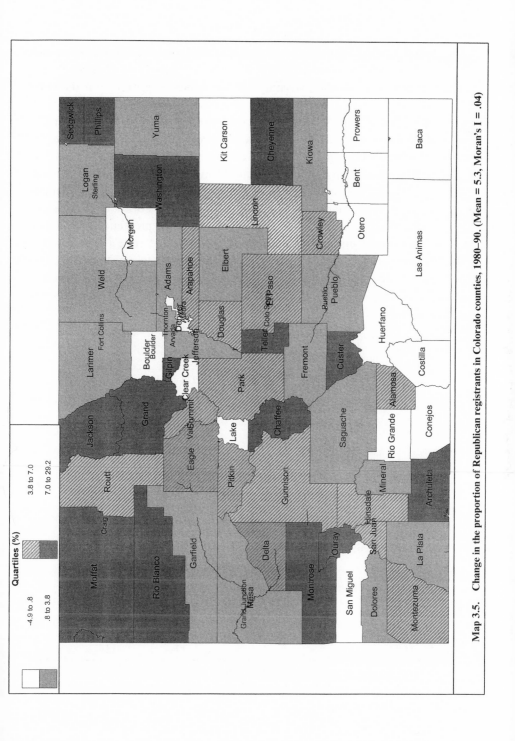

Map 3.5. Change in the proportion of Republican registrants in Colorado counties, 1980–90. (Mean = 5.3, Moran's I = .04)

Quartiles (%)

-4.9 to .8

.8 to 3.8

3.8 to 7.0

7.0 to 29.2

ration of the data indicates that modest population changes were enough to diminish the historically Republican inclination in many areas. A one-point increase in the percentage of Republican registrants on the voter rolls across counties in 1970 was associated with a .14 point drop in GOP registration by 1980. The Denver suburbs were affected by this trend toward weakening Republican strength. Population growth in the Denver suburbs, for example, often came at the expense of Denver itself, the one Democratic stronghold in the state. Denverites of middle-class standing and with ethnic backgrounds wound up exporting their party affiliations to the suburbs. As for the outsiders, Colorado has always been attractive to citizens who are concerned about environmental protection and conservation, including many Californians escaping that state's overcrowding (Ferraro 1994). These migrants are far more likely to register as independents or Democrats than as Republicans because the GOP has historically

TABLE 3.4.   Impact of Population Mobility on Changes in Republican Party Registration in Colorado Counties, 1970–80, 1980–90

Variable	1970–80	1980–90
% born out of state, 1970 (1980)	.05	.06
	(.05)	(.05)
Change in % born out of state	−.09	.35**
	(.09)	(.13)
% foreign born, 1970 (1980)	−.64	.47
	(.56)	(.48)
Change in % foreign born	.08	.05
	(.69)	(.51)
% Republican registrants, 1970 (1980)	−.14**	.21**
	(.06)	(.07)
Population density	−.0003	−.001
	(.0004)	(.001)
Spatial lag	.21	.04
	(.16)	(.11)
Constant	3.96	−6.85
N	63	63
R^2_a	.17	.47

Note: Spatial autoregressive model, weighted for population; dependent variable = change in the percentage of Republican Party registration. See appendix A for a full description of variables.

$*p < .10.$ $**p < .05.$

favored development over preservation and growth control. Outside of Denver and Boulder, the long-time Anglo natives, on the other hand, are the most entrenched Republican identifiers. In fact, the counties with the most rapid Republican growth during the 1980s are those that were untouched by the major internal migration and immigration flows during that decade.

The Colorado case reminds us that one cannot understand the impact of migration on the politics of a place by looking only at the migrants. It is equally important to understand their destination—the places to which they are moving. Suppose that a given migration stream is 70 percent Republican and 30 percent Democratic. In some destinations, say, those that are split evenly between the parties, in-migration of this nature will benefit the GOP because seven out of ten new migrants will import Republican Party identifications. But suppose that a destination is 80 percent Republican at the beginning of the migration influx. In that case, a migration stream that is divided 70–30 in favor of Republicans will either leave the place unchanged or gradually water down GOP strength. In this manner, the characteristics of the migrants interact with the characteristics of the population at their destination to determine the extent and direction of political change. In Colorado, where so many areas began the 1970s with strong Republican leanings, the in-migration of outsiders could only weaken the GOP in the ensuing years.

Ethnicity and Political Behavior at the Individual Level

The aggregate data from the regression analyses in tables 3.2, 3.3, and 3.4 provide an approximate picture of how political outcomes may change as the demographic attributes of jurisdictions vary from place to place and across time. Political stratification across Colorado has been exacerbated by the sorting process that accompanies population mobility. We can see, for example, that the influx of well-educated residents from outside Colorado helps to explain low voter turnout in many elections. We know that in areas heavily populated by recent immigrants political participation is lower than in counties not so populated. It is also the case that the populations in many rural counties do not cling to their Democratic Party registration. In these areas, party registration is a very poor predictor of voting. Finally, we have seen that areas where the non-Colorado-born population grew more noticeable became more Republican in the 1980s but not in the previous decade. Like California, the state can be described as having developed a politics that distinguishes substate regions on the basis of ethnicity and population mobility. But the patterns in these tables and maps are different from those in chapter 2 in some key respects that can only be understood by examining survey data.

Evaluating the political orientation of Coloradans at the individual level is in order if the ambiguities present in the ecological data are to be clarified. Only then can one determine whether the Hispanic population truly is as Democratic as the aggregate data suggest in areas of Hispanic concentration. Figures for party identification by race from the 1990–94 VRS exit polls are presented in table 3.5. The comparison with California (table 2.5) is striking. First, white voters in Colorado are not as Republican as they are in California. Indeed, the gulf between the two states is surprisingly wide. In 1994, 45.3 percent of white voters in California identified themselves as Republicans, while only 27 percent in Colorado did so. For blacks, the figures are similar. Black voters are as hostile to the Republican Party in Colorado as they are anywhere else. Hispanics in Colorado, however, are far more likely to be Democrats than they are in California. In 1994, 77 percent of Hispanic voters identified with the Democratic Party in Colorado, compared to only 65 percent in California. Finally, Asians in Colorado, while constituting only a small percentage of the electorate, are also slightly more likely to be Democratic than they are in California, where they are more evenly divided.

TABLE 3.5.   Party Identification by Race/Ethnicity in Recent Colorado Elections, 1990–94

Race/Ethnic Group	Year	Democrat	Independent	Republican
White	1990	27.1	34.0	38.9
	1992	41.3	31.2	29.0
	1994	44.2	29.0	26.8
Black	1990	77.0	15.1	7.9
	1992	67.8	29.6	2.6
	1994	83.5	9.2	7.3
Hispanic	1990	62.7	15.1	22.2
	1992	75.4	13.2	11.3
	1994	76.7	12.2	11.2
Asian	1990	56.3	26.4	17.3
	1992	60.6	24.2	15.1
	1994	34.2	54.3	11.5

Source: Voter Research and Surveys, General Election Exit Polls, 1990–94 (weighted data).

The differences between the two states are surprising and too large to be ignored as random biases of survey research. In using the ecological inference method developed by King (1997) to come up with estimates of the statewide proportion of Hispanics that register Republican, the results indicated that Colorado's Hispanic population is slightly less likely to support the GOP than the Hispanic population in California through the early 1990s. Similar estimates for the Asian population were unreliable given severe aggregation bias and the limited amount of information available about the Asian population in the state. What accounts for the strongly one-sided Democratic inclination of Hispanics in Colorado and the apparently lopsided inclination of the few Asians in the state? One plausible explanation is that the Hispanics in Colorado are more Democratic than in California because they are more homogeneously of Mexican ancestry (even though a majority may not be *recent* Mexican immigrants, the population is still predominantly Mexican American), spatially concentrated in a few areas of the state, and positioned in blue collar, working-class jobs. Peter Skerry has pointed out that Mexicans in some parts of the country are likely to view themselves as racial minorities and claim special rights (1993). This automatically aligns them with the Democratic Party, long identified with civil rights, labor unions, and the plight of the oppressed. The areas where Mexican American politics takes on an especially racial character tend to be urban and suburban communities where consciousness of minority status can be quite acute—areas where discrimination by whites against minorities is a common occurrence. Colorado, with its mostly white population, much of which was originally rooted in migration from southern states, is one of these areas.

A simpler explanation for the Hispanic inclination to identify with the Democratic Party in Colorado is that the level of affluence enjoyed by Hispanics elsewhere in the country does not exist there. There are far fewer high-income Hispanics (income greater than $75,000 in 1994) in Colorado than in California and therefore far fewer Hispanics who for class reasons can imagine themselves identifying with Republicans. One study conducted during the 1970s suggested that Denver's Hispanics were "poorer, more heavily working class and less well educated than even the disadvantaged blacks" (Lovrich and Marenin 1976, 289–90).

The few Asians in Colorado are a heterogeneous mixture, 70 percent of whom come from six different countries: China, Japan, Korea, Laos, the Philippines, and Vietnam. Slightly over half (55 percent) are very recent immigrants, having entered the country since 1980. Colorado's

Asians are neither as well established nor as wealthy as their counterparts in California. They are scattered across the Front Range but in much smaller pockets than one is likely to find in California or other port of entry states.

Finally, the extent to which ethnic minorities could find themselves fitting into the GOP has a lot to do with the traditions and ethnic makeup of that party in local politics. Republicans in Colorado are far more homogeneously white, suburban, and rural than is the case in California. The Democrats have always been the more ethnic of the two parties, of course, but there is even less of an ethnic tradition within the Colorado Republican Party than elsewhere. Hence, it is not surprising that in such a political setting, where clear signals identify the Republicans as a Caucasian, middle-class group, ethnic, blue collar, and service industry workers would be drawn to the Democrats.

Sustained high levels of immigration from Asia and Mexico will probably hurt Republican prospects rather than help them. Mexicans are well entrenched in the Democratic Party, making it difficult for recently arrived Latinos to develop an affinity for the Republicans. Asians, of course, do not have as strong a tradition in the state, and their small numbers ensure that they will be overlooked as a political force in all but the most local elections. Incoming Asians will have more freedom to develop a political identity independent of their communities. At the same time, the population growth from out of state has had mixed effects on the Republican registration edge in Anglo Colorado. Democrats are more competitive in this state than they have ever been. Colorado appears to be a Republican stronghold that has weakened with demographic change.

Political Change and the Internal Composition of Colorado Counties

Understanding patterns of electoral balkanization and change in places around the country is the primary object of this book. To this end, in chapter 2 I examined several places in California with the aim of shedding light on their political variability by examining the internal composition of their population. In that chapter, I argued that Republican registration growth was greatly enhanced by the absence of forces that would abate that growth, in particular, immigrant and ethnic populations that were more likely to strengthen the Democratic Party than the Republican. The force for Republican growth in Placer County, California, for instance, was in-

migration of white voters from both within and outside the state. Hispanic, black, and Asian voters, on the other hand, have not become much
of a presence in these northern Sacramento suburbs. The instrument of the
exclusion of these groups has been restrictive zoning. In Kern County,
Republican growth was facilitated by the spatial separation of Hispanics
from white voters in a vast and sparsely settled territory. I argued that
such spatial separation diminished the degree of ethnic conflict that would
be translated directly into political mobilization. In Los Angeles and
Alameda Counties, on the other hand, the presence of Asians, whites,
African Americans, and Latinos in close proximity ensured that trends in
Republican Party growth would be offset by corresponding trends in the
growth of the competing party. Proximity breeds political mobilization,
even polarization, of the contending groups in a society.

Does this theory stand up in Colorado? Do we find Republicans
excelling there when their jurisdictions are safe from the encroachment
and mobilization of Democratically inclined ethnics? The models of partisan change presented in table 3.4 suggest that the Colorado picture may be
more complicated. The growth in the proportion of internal migrants is
positively related to GOP growth in the 1980s, but there is no statistically
significant relationship in the 1970s. If any effect is to be found in the
1970s, the data indicate that Colorado Republicans gained ground in
those jurisdictions where native Coloradans maintained a solid majority.
Which party benefits from the influx of migrants is contingent not only on
the characteristics of the migrants, such as their party leanings, but on the
characteristics of the natives.

To obtain a more complete understanding of the state's political
dynamics, I examined five counties in the state with varying degrees of
political party registration change from 1980 to 1990: Denver, Douglas,
Larimer, Pueblo, and Weld (see map 3.1). The average Colorado county
saw the GOP's share of registrants rise a substantial 5.3 percent during the
decade. Denver's Republicans lost ground, dropping by 1.2 percent. Suburban and rapidly growing Douglas county saw growth at the state's average rate. Larimer Republicans gained about 2.7 points over their rivals.
Heavily Democratic Pueblo saw a gain of about one point for Republicans. Finally, Weld County, home of the Colorado meatpacking industry
and a large Hispanic population, saw the Republicans move up two points
from 1980 to 1990.

It is possible that the settlement patterns of rival populations in these
locales may influence patterns of political mobilization and partisan

change. Using a dissimilarity index for the five counties, one can evaluate the extent to which the ethnic population is segregated from the white nonethnic population. As I explained in chapter 2, the dissimilarity index captures the percentage of each minority group that would have to move in order for that group to be evenly distributed across all census tracts. Where there is a high degree of spatial segregation or clustering, one can expect low levels of party activism and turnout among lower income minority groups. Republicans are likely to do well in settings like these, growing at least at the state average. On the other hand, where there is very little clustering, or where ethnic clustering occurs in densely populated areas, the level of partisan activism by minority groups will be much higher. Given this activism, Republicans are likely to do poorly, their numbers growing at a rate well below what statewide trends would predict.

Ordinarily, values of dissimilarity above .60 are considered high, while those under .30 are low. Values between .30 and .60 suggest a moderate level of segregation (Denton and Massey 1988, 806). However, the dissimilarity measure has been customarily applied to metropolitan areas, not to countywide settlement patterns. High values on the dissimilarity index are far more likely when they are calculated for an entire metropolitan area. Dissimilarity values for tracts within the much more limited geography of counties are likely to be lower. For the analysis presented here, then, values of dissimilarity above .50 will be considered high, those below .20 low, and those between .20 and .50 moderate.

The dissimilarity indices show that blacks are most highly segregated from whites in Denver and Weld Counties and only slightly less clustered in 1990 than in 1980 (see table 3.6). Efforts to integrate the schools through busing have done little to integrate Denver. In 1995, school busing to achieve integration was officially ended. Hispanics are highly clustered in Denver and Weld but less segregated from whites in Douglas and Larimer. The small Asian population is most segregated from white voters in Pueblo, Denver, and Larimer Counties and least clustered in burgeoning, predominantly white Douglas. As in other areas of the country, neither Asians nor Hispanics are as segregated as blacks.

Denver
Black-white relations in Denver have been strained in recent mayoral races, as black Mayor Wellington Webb accused his white opponent in the 1995 contest of being racially biased (Weber 1995a). Webb's opponent, Councilwoman Mary DeGroot, had proposed the elimination of racial

TABLE 3.6. Index of Dissimilarity for the Black, Asian, and Hispanic Populations Relative to Whites in the State and in Five Colorado Counties, 1980 and 1990, by Census Tract

	Colorado		Denver		Pueblo		Larimer		Weld		Douglas	
Variable	1980	1990	1980	1990	1980	1990	1980	1990	1980	1990	1980	1990
Asians	.33	.35	.26	.30	.30	.28	.27	.33	.26	.22	.24	.18
Blacks	.68	.65	.71	.66	.40	.34	.35	.35	.83	.66	.45	.22
Hispanics	.44	.41	.51	.47	.28	.25	.26	.21	.27	.28	.16	.11
N	979	979	181	181	48	48	44	44	33	33	17	17

Source: U.S. Census 1990, and author's calculations.

Note: Figures represent the percentage of each group that would have to move in order for the group to be evenly distributed across census tracts in the county.

preferences for an income-based affirmative action scheme (Weber 1995b). It appears from press coverage that both candidates used the race issue to mobilize their respective constituencies. But the black population in Colorado, while segregated, is comparatively small. Even in Denver, it constituted only 12.8 percent of the population in 1990. Webb's support has come from a black-Hispanic coalition (Hero 1989). The same Hispanic neighborhoods that supported Federico Peña's mayoral candidacy in the 1980s supported Webb in his first election and subsequent reelection. Because the black population is small, the residential segregation of the large Hispanic population from whites is more politically consequential than the segregation of blacks from whites. In Denver, roughly half of the Hispanic population would have to move in order to achieve an equal presence across Denver's 181 census tracts. The pattern of Hispanic concentration is illustrated in map 3.6, where the light shading illustrates those tracts that have attracted immigrants. The Hispanic neighborhoods are located on the west and north sides of Denver. These are the areas where black politicians like Webb have had to mobilize voters by playing up minority versus white divisions in local politics.

Hispanics in Denver come into regular contact with members of other groups due to the density of the city's population, and this contact makes the group highly conscious of its ethnicity. There is also a higher degree of social stratification in cities like Denver than in more rural areas. The interaction of distinct ethnic groups and social classes in large cities is likely to contribute to feelings of deprivation or injustice among the underprivileged (McVeigh 1995, 465). This generates a demand for redistributive policies and makes the Democratic Party an attractive instrument for channeling grievances into political action via public policy. Republicans have a hard time benefiting from the kind of segregation that occurs in urban areas when the minority community is aware that class disparities vary directly with the racial constitution of neighborhoods. In short, Democratic dominance and growth in Denver and the appeal of minority candidates like Peña and Webb can be explained by the city's large and active ethnic population.

Pueblo

Pueblo, while not nearly as ethnically segregated as Denver, is similar in many respects. It has an ethnically heterogeneous and politically active population that has shaped the city's politics since the early 1900s. Most of the early Anglo settlers came from southern, Democratic states (Elazar 1970, 165, 176). They were followed first by southern European and then

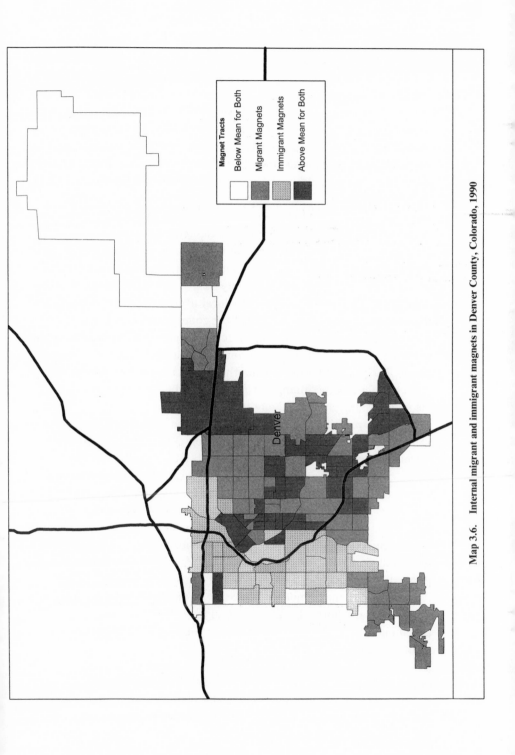

Magnet Tracts

Below Mean for Both
Migrant Magnets
Immigrant Magnets
Above Mean for Both

Denver

Map 3.6. Internal migrant and immigrant magnets in Denver County, Colorado, 1990

by Mexican immigrants who worked in blue collar industries and developed a Democratic identification as a consequence of their class status. As one of the few truly industrial cities in the West, Republicans have been a minority party since the New Deal. Steel was the city's cornerstone industry until the 1980s, when the Colorado Fuel and Iron Corporation (CFI) closed, later to reopen under the ownership of Oregon Steel. Jobs at the reopened plant paid far less than at the old CFI. Labor unions still have a presence in the area, although the service sector is now the fastest growing part of the economy.

Like Denver, Pueblo County's white population has declined in recent years while its Latino population has increased (Vest 1994, 6). Most of the Hispanics are natives, but immigrants have also found their way there. Pueblo's patterns of immigrant and internal migrant settlement are illustrated in map 3.7. Note that in the city itself, on the southeast side, a large number of the tracts are above the local average in their proportion of immigrants. Twenty-two percent of the county's tracts are majority Hispanic, and even the least Hispanic tract is comprised of 5 percent Hispanic residents. There is substantial income variation among these neighborhoods. The poorest Latino neighborhood is in the southern end of the city and contains a large immigrant population, but there are many middle income Hispanic areas. Judging from table 3.6, we can see that the large Hispanic population is moderately segregated, though far less so than Denver (see the dissimilarity index in table 3.6). Pueblo is often represented by liberal Hispanics in the state legislature, and within the county ethnic conflict is not much of an issue. The local election board has drawn upon majority Hispanic election districts for the municipal council with little attendant controversy. There is occasionally some conflict over how many local officeholding politicians are Hispanic, but even Latino leaders are willing to admit that sometimes their underrepresentation in office is the result of having too few candidates. Pueblo's established Hispanic population and its high level of political engagement made it difficult for Republicans to make much headway even during the 1980s when GOP growth was the norm. Local sources suggest that Pueblo's population is becoming less Democratic, but this is because some voters are becoming independents not Republicans.

Greeley and Weld County
Pueblo is a socially stratified, ethnically heterogeneous, and politically active area where Republican growth has been slow. There are, of course,

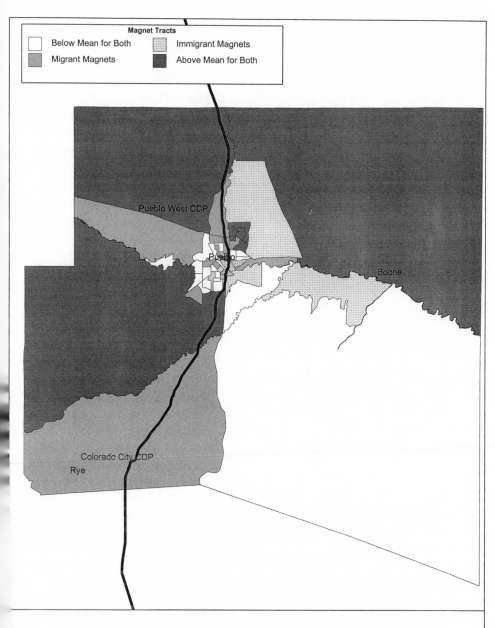

Map 3.7. Internal migrant and immigrant magnets in Pueblo County, Colorado, 1990

socially stratified, ethnically heterogeneous areas in Colorado where Republicans have done well. Certainly Weld County is one of those. The Hispanic population there is only slightly more spatially isolated today than Pueblo's, but the educational attainment of Hispanics ran fully ten points lower in Weld than in Pueblo according to 1990 census figures. The lower education levels undoubtedly dampen levels of political participation (DeSipio and Rocha 1992; Garcia 1987). The Hispanic population in Weld County is not well established. Weld's Mexican immigrant population consists of more recent foreign-born arrivals than Pueblo's, and their ability to speak English and their knowledge of electoral politics are more limited. Fully one-fourth of Weld County's Mexican population reported not speaking English "very well" in 1990, compared to only 13 percent in Pueblo County. This is an important difference because English fluency is a powerful indicator of assimilation, naturalization, and political involvement. Immigrants in Weld County have been pushed to the outskirts of Greeley, to neighborhoods on the north side and towns such as LaSalle, Ault, and Fort Lupton (map 3.8).

Labor organizations have often helped raise the awareness of immigrants and ethnic minorities, seeking to mobilize them for political action. Interestingly, unions have been less of a political force in the Greeley area than in Pueblo. One major meatpacking union that organized some Hispanic workers in Greeley was broken when the Monfort plant closed in 1980 (Andreas 1994, 5). Although it reopened two years later and was purchased by the international conglomerate ConAgra in the late 1980s, the union has never regained its strength. The alternative to meatpacking for Mexican migrants is work in the sugar beet or onion fields. Pay is low in the agricultural sector. The average family of six earned only $7,000 per year in 1988 (Andreas 1994, 24). By contrast, in Pueblo, Hispanics are more likely to find themselves in professional and managerial jobs and far fewer are employed as agricultural laborers. No wonder, then, that the Republicans have done far better in Weld County than in Pueblo. Much of the Hispanic population in the Greeley area remains disenfranchised and without much influence in the political life of the area.

Larimer County

Larimer County, home to the cities of Fort Collins and Longmont, borders Weld County on the west, but the two are light years apart in social and economic terms. Unlike Pueblo and Weld, Larimer has a small Hispanic population, most of which is clustered along the Weld County bor-

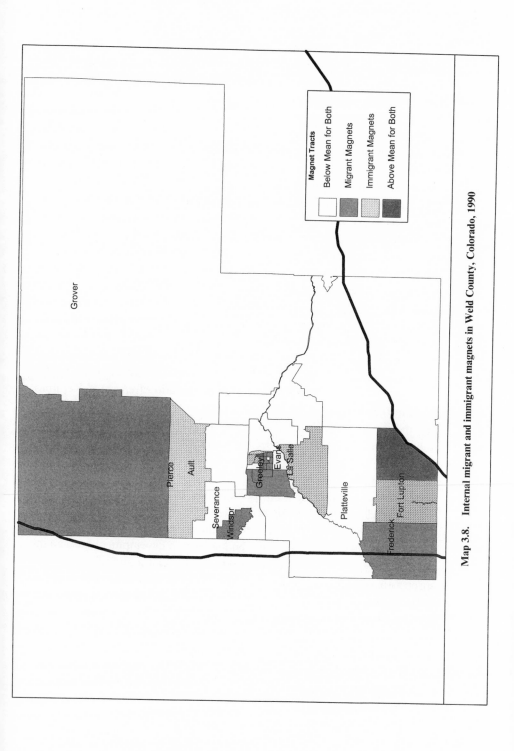

Map 3.8. Internal migrant and immigrant magnets in Weld County, Colorado, 1990

der on the east. In spite of its homogeneous white population, though, Republican gains have been modest. There was a slight 2.7 percent increase from 1980 to 1990, not much larger than the increase in neighboring Weld and only 1.5 points greater than in heavily Democratic and heterogeneous Pueblo. In its ethnic composition, high income, and pattern of development, it looks rather like Placer County, California. Larimer even resembles Placer in its physical geography. The western end of the county abuts the mountains and is the home of Estes Park and wealthy housing tracts. The question for Larimer is why this white-only locale did not experience stronger Republican growth during the 1980s. The answer lies in the nature of white population change in the area. In-migrants to Larimer County as early as the 1970s were far less likely to import Republican Party affiliations than were in-migrants to Placer County. A strong contingent of environmental activists in Fort Collins have mobilized against the county's seemingly unstoppable growth. Many of the new residents of Fort Collins and Longmont are from middle-class Denver neighborhoods and have brought their Democratic inclinations with them. While Larimer is a wealthier county than neighboring Weld, it lags well behind very wealthy areas like suburban Douglas County further south. Entering the 1980s, this part of northern Colorado often voted Republican, but the Democrats were always a competitive force. Those socialized into the prevailing political ways around Fort Collins were nearly as likely to find a home in the Democratic Party as in the Republican.

Douglas County

Just south of the Denver metropolitan area is Douglas County, historically comprised of cattle ranches and several small towns. Bridging the Colorado Springs and Denver metropolitan areas, this county tripled in size between 1980 and 1992. High-end suburban development has caught up with it. Very few large ranches remain. Upscale housing tracts have sprung up, with custom homes on expansive lots dotting the northern part of the county. It is now home to the largest unincorporated homeowners association in Colorado, Highlands Ranch, and in the late 1990s became home to the Denver metro area's largest shopping center, the taxes from which will be used to finance further development. These suburbs remain mostly residential, however, which means that the burden of infrastructure development falls squarely on homeowners, driving up the local cost of living (Kerven 1992).

Republican registration edged up about five points in Douglas County between 1980 and 1990 and this trend can be attributed to the class of residents drawn there: wealthy and white. Unlike Larimer, where white newcomers bring a mix of Republican and Democratic affiliations with them, Douglas County's costs are affordable mainly to those who fit a GOP economic profile. There are almost no ethnic minorities. The population is only 3 percent Hispanic and less than 1 percent Asian, all of whom, judging by the figures in table 3.6, are highly dispersed throughout the seventeen census tracts. In-migrants during the 1980s came mostly from Denver's older suburbs to commute to work in Arapahoe County (Lewis 1996). Local observers claim that Douglas is a haven for those trying to escape crime and gang problems. Only 772 black residents are recorded as having moved in between 1985 and 1990. The mechanism for keeping the minority population to a minimum is development governed by complex restrictive covenants coupled with development impact fees that add to the cost of new housing. There is multifamily housing planned for construction at the northern end of the county, but the rents in these developments, coupled with the costly commute to jobs, place these neighborhoods out of the financial reach of most minority citizens.

Ethnic Settlement Patterns and Political Balkanization

From the comparisons of internal population dynamics across these five counties, some generalizations may be possible. As in California, Republican growth was on an upswing during the 1980s and early 1990s. This growth did not take place evenly across the state. Instead there was significant political variance, which corresponds to the ethnic character of places. At one extreme, Denver, with its dense, ethnically mixed population, saw Republican registration decline during this period. Other areas of ethnic heterogeneity saw only modest Republican growth (Pueblo). If the ethnic population was politically inactive, however, as it appears to have been in the Greeley area, Republicans often made solid gains. Areas with mostly white populations were mixed in their propensity to move into the Republican column. The growing middle income white counties, such as Larimer, saw some Republican growth, but this was tempered by the arrival of many white Democrats. At the other extreme, suburban Douglas County saw impressive Republican gains, as did many parts of rural Colorado. The counties that saw the most rapid Republican growth were not only Anglo dominated and experiencing in-migration from outside the state but also the ones that became even less ethnic over the course of the decade.

Hispanics are spatially concentrated within the four larger counties but most of all in Denver. Like Los Angeles, and other urban areas, Denver's dense population mitigates the impact of the ethnic homogeneity of its neighborhoods on political participation. Interracial contact is high enough to ensure that local politics contains a racial element. The same is true in Pueblo, with its mostly urban but established ethnic population. Hispanic natives with deep roots interact with Anglos regularly and have developed a distinct racial component to their politics. Weld County, on the other hand, has a large rural immigrant population, economically similar to that of Kern County, California. The population is less isolated than in Kern, but it is mostly inactive in politics due to the characteristics of its ethnic population: poor, uneducated, and often migratory. With its population of more recent immigrants, Weld County is not a hotbed of Latino mobilization. For immigrants who are often initially fearful of getting involved in politics, economic empowerment precedes political action. But in the Greeley area immigrants are not even aware of their basic economic rights under state and national law let alone their political rights. According to Carol Andreas, recent immigrants are unaware of the basic protections against discrimination, job safety provisions, and workers' compensation, all of which are guaranteed by law, and that is why the union movement in the Greeley meatpacking industry has been so weak. What will happen in Weld County in the future is a more open question. The education of immigrants is the key to their political acculturation (Garcia 1987). Maintenance of Weld County's traditional Republicanism depends upon the sustained subjugation and inactivity of the growing Mexican American community.

Colorado has become a national crossroads, and the sheer number of out-of-state license plates one sees in the Denver suburbs attests to this inundation. People migrate there from both coasts and from neighboring states, contributing to the electoral volatility of the Front Range (Beatty 1981). Long-term residency in Colorado is worn like a badge of honor. In town meetings, the claim that one is a thirty-year resident gives one's opinion more weight in discussions of growth control and development. The long-term residents are also the most Republican, and controlling growth has become a GOP cry in some counties as natives try to protect an older way of life.

Colorado does show some degree of ethnic balkanization. It comes as no great surprise to learn that of all the state's ethnic groups, blacks remain the most spatially segregated from the white population. But many new Mexican and Asian arrivals move to areas where there are coethnic communities (Carnahan 1992). As a consequence, the Asian and Hispanic populations are becoming larger proportions of the population in the counties where they have settled. Internal to Colorado's counties, though, the degree of ethnic segregation of white from Hispanic and Asian neighborhoods is understated because the immigrant population is either very large and dispersed (Pueblo, Weld) or so small that it remains unnoticed (Douglas, Larimer). Race and immigration issues have not been as controversial in Colorado as in California. Small minority populations are less threatening to whites than large ones. The Hispanics in southern Colorado are well established, with settlements predating Anglo exploration. No one questions their claim to public services, and most speak fluent English. The relatively high level of integration of the white and Hispanic communities in Pueblo County has bred a strong sense of economic and political empowerment among minorities. The Hispanics in northeastern Colorado are subject to more discrimination because they do not have this history. They face barriers Hispanics in southern Colorado do not confront, not the least of which is their limited facility with English. Racism in Greeley is said to be serious, but Weld County residents also realize that this population is an important labor resource for the local vegetable farmers. The Mexican migrants in Weld County will be tolerated as long as they can be exploited. As of the mid-1990s, Coloradans were not on the verge of passing their own version of Proposition 187, but pressure to do so could become a reality in the new century in Denver suburbs and the growing areas along the Front Range.

Since 1970, Colorado's patterns of electoral change have been more influenced by internal U.S. migration than by immigration, and the Anglo outsiders slowly bolstering Republican registration. In the homogeneously white areas where Republican margins have increased, the flood of new residents has accelerated the trend toward GOP domination of the state.

Finally, the long-standing partisan traditions of localities account for some of the growth in Republican and Democratic registration. Republican areas such as Weld, Larimer, and Douglas Counties generated an upswing in GOP registration in the 1980s. The only thing that keeps Denver's suburbs from being even more Republican is the large number of migrants who import independent and Democratic political orientations. Similarly, Democratic areas in southern Colorado have held fast to their traditions, as Republican registration dropped during the 1980s even though GOP candidates performed better than their registration figures would predict.

The data I present contain ambiguities that are not easily cleared up. We do not know from what has been presented how many of the new migrants to Colorado are actually Republicans and how soon they become politically active. Nor do we know how the political affiliations of Colorado natives may change in response to growth pressures. In response, I have tried to talk about the changing politics of places, not of people. In addition, comparisons of the developments in Colorado with those in other states to be dealt with in the remaining chapters are clearly in order. The Colorado case indicates that any generalizations about the ways in which population mobility is thought to influence the political system must be carefully qualified. *Whether internal migrants strengthen or weaken the party leaning of an area depends to a great extent on the political orientation of the natives when the new residents arrive.* In many of Denver's outlying suburbs, including those in Larimer County, long-time Colorado natives are more Republican than their newly arriving neighbors. In these cases, new migrants may leave the balance of party registrants untouched or gradually steer a place away from its traditional moorings.

CHAPTER 4

Kansas: High Growth Islands
in a Sea of Decline

Garden City, Kansas, is not typical of towns on the Great Plains. Signs there come in three languages: English, Spanish, and Vietnamese. Arguably, some of the best Southeast Asian food between California and New York can be found in restaurants along Garden City's main street. Schools are populated with non-English-speaking immigrant children, and on the edge of town, sprawling trailer parks populated with highly mobile immigrant workers have sprung up. In 1970, Garden City was home to just 15,000 people and was growing at a slow pace of less than 1 percent annually. By the mid-1990s, the Garden City population was estimated at 27,000, with most of that growth having occurred since 1980 (Stull and Broadway 1990; Benson 1994). A resident who had left in 1978 would strain to recognize the place at the turn of the twenty-first century. There are places, to be sure, that have grown faster than Garden City, but few have undergone such sweeping ethnic changes in the process. And in the context of Western Kansas, home to stable or declining rural populations, the story of Garden City's growth is even more remarkable.

Kansas does not immediately come to mind when one thinks of population growth and demographic change. Exactly for this reason, it stands as a useful contrast to high-growth states such as California, Colorado, and Florida. The state's population grew by 32 percent from 1950 to 1992, where it stood at 2.5 million. Kansas's population is becoming more urbanized, as almost all of its growth has occurred in its larger cities: the Kansas City suburbs, Wichita, and Topeka. The rural farm population has declined, hitting counties along the Nebraska (northern) border especially hard. Long-term trends in population growth and decline are observable in map 4.1, which illustrates the percentage of population change from 1950 to 1992. Although the largest population gains have

119

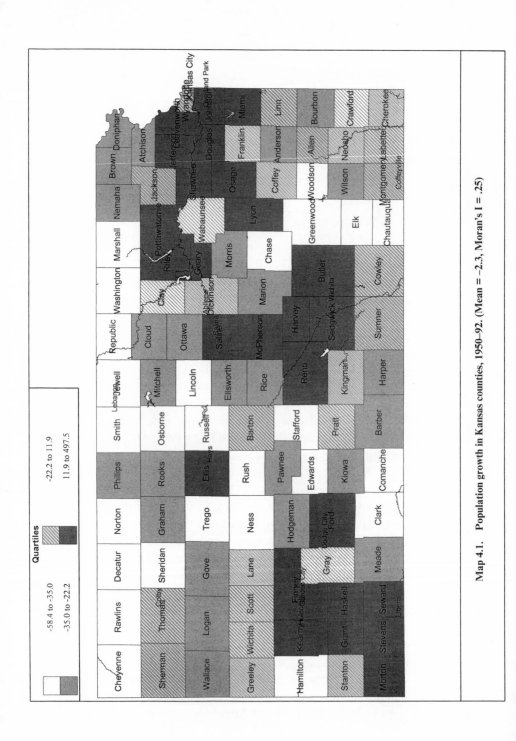

Map 4.1. Population growth in Kansas counties, 1950–92. (Mean = –2.3, Moran's I = .25)

occurred in Sedgwick (home to Wichita) and Johnson (Kansas City suburbs) Counties, another area on the map is particularly noteworthy for its growth—southwestern Kansas, particularly Finney (Garden City) and Ford (Dodge City) Counties. These are rural communities, where the addition of a few people can make a big difference, but that fact should not turn attention away from the extent to which these areas have been transformed by the emergence of a rural industrial economy. During the 1980s, southwestern Kansas added 15,500 people, while in the northwest the population dropped by a slightly greater 18,600 (Berry 1992). The difference between the two areas lies almost entirely in the development of rural industry in several southwestern towns. More than 70 percent of job growth during the 1980s was the result of the aggressive labor recruitment efforts of meatpacking plants. Four of these have been built just since 1969 (Stull, Broadway, and Griffith 1995, 25).

Kansas's immigrant population is not large by national standards, nor by the standards of most states, standing at just over 62,000 in 1990, a mere 2.5 percent of the state's total. There are single communities in California with more immigrants than all of Kansas. But the small number of immigrants makes the foreign-born population quite noticeable when it grows as rapidly as it has. In addition, both the Asian and Hispanic immigrant populations cluster in neighborhoods around the industries where they are employed. Garden City and Dodge City, for instance, are ringed with trailer parks, which serve as temporary low-income housing for immigrants working in the local meatpacking industry. In 1990, 10 percent of the Garden City population lived in a single trailer park (Benson 1990).

The composition of the immigrant population in Kansas in 1990 is shown in figure 4.1. Interestingly, Asians are the largest immigrant group, constituting 38 percent of the state's foreign-born population. This is followed by Mexicans (23.7 percent) and Europeans (19.4 percent). Like other states, the proportion of foreign-born residents who are white has dropped drastically since 1965, from over 90 percent to less than half in 1990.

The state's native Hispanic population does not have the long history it can claim in southern Colorado. After World War I, the drop in European immigration meant more opportunities for Mexicans. Hispanics began arriving in Kansas in the 1920s, settling primarily in cities where they were segregated into barrios (Oppenheimer 1985, 431). Discrimination persisted well into the 1950s, and new arrivals almost always found

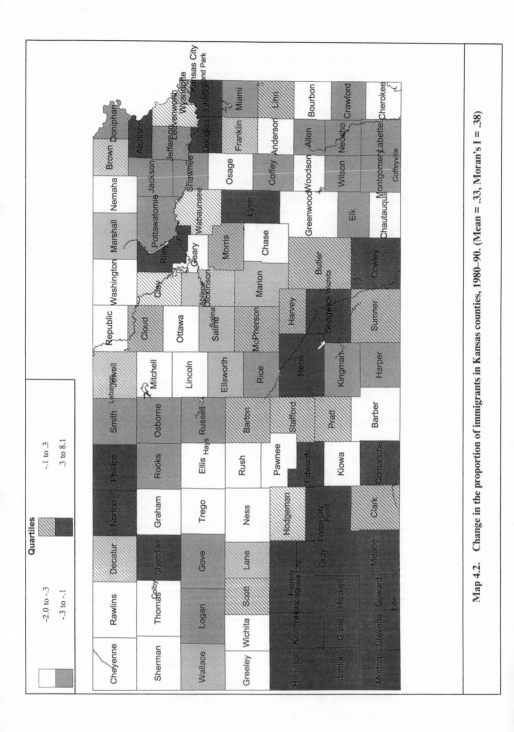

Map 4.2. Change in the proportion of immigrants in Kansas counties, 1980–90. (Mean = .33, Moran's I = .38)

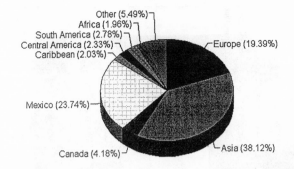

Fig. 4.1. **Composition of the foreign-born population in Kansas, 1990**

themselves in the lowest occupational and income strata. Jobs in meat-packing, agriculture, and the railways were most common, and all were low paying. The spatial distribution of the Hispanic population in 1990 is illustrated in map 4.3. This map clearly shows that Hispanics comprise the largest proportion of the local population in the southwestern counties, although there are also significant pockets in the Wichita area and eastern Kansas.

As in Colorado, once the early Mexican immigrants learned English, naturalized, and raised children of their own, their status improved. The story of their assimilation follows the traditional model (Hirschman 1996). They worked their way out of "immigrant jobs" into small businesses and the service economy. New arrivals, however, still find themselves working in two main industries: agriculture and meatpacking. Surprisingly little has changed about the status of immigrant workers in Kansas towns since the 1920s. The work at the meatpacking plants, where most immigrants are employed, remains dangerous and debilitating. Injury rates are higher than in any other industry (Stull and Broadway 1995). Still, workers are drawn into meatpacking not as a career but as a temporary way to make money above and beyond the main alternative, which is agricultural labor. Entry-level jobs at a packing plant paid in the seven to eight dollar range in the early 1990s, and with bilingual capacity obtaining a better paying management position was not out of the question.

Mexicans in this region were joined in the 1970s and 1980s by immigrants from Vietnam, Cambodia, and Laos, some of whom relocated from California with the help of government-funded relocation programs designed to reduce regional unemployment. The first wave of Vietnamese

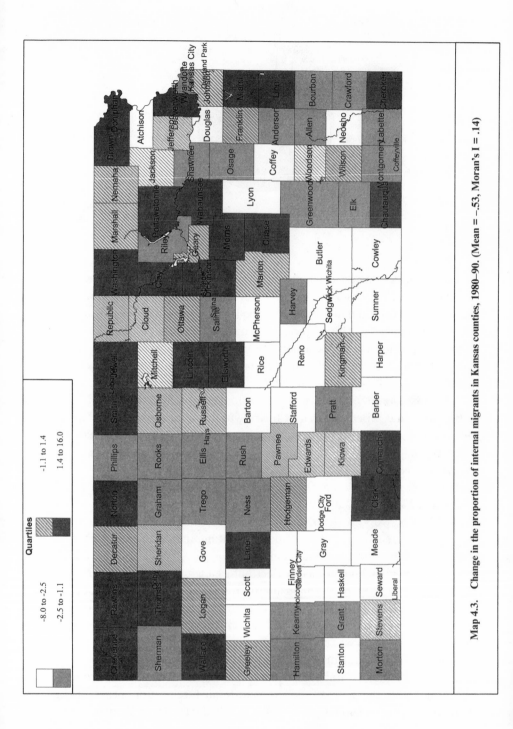

Quartiles

-8.0 to -2.5

-2.5 to -1.1

-1.1 to 1.4

1.4 to 16.0

Map 4.3. Change in the proportion of internal migrants in Kansas counties, 1980–90. (Mean = −.53, Moran's I = .14)

and Laotian immigrants arrived after the Vietnam War. The second wave, generally less educated and poorer than the first, arrived in the early and mid-1980s. These immigrants are described as perfect employees for the arduous work on the "disassembly line" of the meatpacking plants, where no command of English was required (Broadway 1995; Benson 1995; Stull and Broadway 1995). The Asian population in southwest Kansas is highly mobile, and the more recent arrivals are far less likely to settle permanently than were those in the first wave, who have established roots in the area. While the Asian population remains small by West Coast standards, its concentration in just a few towns allows for some evaluation of its social and political impact.

The 1990 Census Public Use Microdata 1 Percent Sample contains information about the income, education level, age, and race of 17,700 cross-state migrants, immigrants, and native Kansas residents over the age of eighteen. The differences between these three groups are not as stark as in other states (see appendix A, table A4.1). Internal migrants are wealthier than the other two groups, but immigrants earn slightly more than Kansas natives. Internal migrants are the youngest and best educated of the three groups, and 88 percent are non-Hispanic white compared to just 42 percent of the immigrants. The fact that many immigrants may have gone uncounted in the 1990 census may explain why immigrants and native Kansas residents are so close to one another in income. In addition, the income of Kansas natives is dragged down by the large number of farmers, who regularly report income losses. A better measure of wealth in farm states might be receipt of public assistance income or even the amount of property taxes paid. These figures reveal that immigrants earned more from public assistance than native Kansans and paid much less in property taxes. Property taxes are an especially useful indicator of wealth for purposes of this research since differences in property tax rates across a geographic area directly reflect the extent of social stratification. The disparities in wealth are still modest, however, compared with other states, so we have reason to expect less racial and class stratification across Kansas neighborhoods and communities than we find elsewhere.

Settlement Patterns of Migrants and Immigrants in Kansas

By determining where immigrants are becoming a larger proportion of a local population, it is easy to tell whether a group is becoming more or less noticeable in an area. Map 4.3 shows the geographic pattern of growth in the proportion of interstate migrants from 1980 to 1990. This growth is concentrated in the northern part of the state, particularly in the northeast. Places where the population of internal migrants has declined relative to other groups include the lightly shaded areas in the southwest and south-central regions. Map 4.2 gives some indication of where immigrants have become more noticeable. The foreign born are a larger percentage of the population in the southwest and in the Kansas City suburbs (Douglas and Johnson Counties) as well as in Wichita (Sedgwick County).

Following the procedure in previous chapters, I use spatial regression analysis to evaluate the influence of several relevant variables on the change in the proportion of the population of counties that consists of émigrés (see table 4.1). For purposes of comparison, the change in the percentage of U.S. internal migrants, depicted on map 4.3, is included with the other results. For most of the foreign born, the 1980 population of the group is inversely related to the prominence of its growth in Kansas. Africans, Europeans, Canadians, and South and Central Americans have all declined as proportions of the population in the counties where they are to be found. In other words, they had become a less noticeable presence by 1990 than they were in the early 1980s. Only Mexican and U.S. internal migrants are becoming a larger proportion of the population in the places where they were most concentrated in 1980. For Mexicans, the effect of previous settlement is striking. For every 1 percent increase in the size of the Mexican population in 1980, there is a .65 percent increase in that population over the decade 1980–90. Growth in the Mexican population is apparently not sensitive to employment prospects or income gains. But growth in the internal migrant population is associated with increases in income across the ten-year period.

Most groups' migration patterns are unrelated to unemployment rates in the early part of the decade, although Asians were particularly adept at avoiding areas that experienced high unemployment. For Asians, these results reflect the secondary migration of Vietnamese, Laotian, and Cambodian refugees to obtain industrial employment in southwestern Kansas (Broadway 1987; see also map 4.2). The coefficient for population density shows that not all immigrant concentrations are developing in the more densely populated urban centers (table 4.1). U.S. internal migrants, in particular, are becoming a larger proportion of the population in many suburban and rural areas in eastern Kansas (map 4.3).

The spatially lagged dependent variable in the model shows that the

TABLE 4.1. Influences on Population Concentration in Kansas Counties, 1980–90

Variable	U.S. Migrants	African Immigrants	Asian Immigrants	European Immigrants	Canadian Immigrants	Mexican Immigrants	Central American Immigrants	South American Immigrants
% 1980 group population	.09**	-1.04**	-.06	-.29**	-.89**	.65**	-.28**	-.26**
	(.03)	(.08)	(.08)	(.04)	(.04)	(.23)	(.07)	(.09)
% unemployment, 1980	.28	-.001	-.07**	-.004	-.01	-.04	.005	.009**
	(.22)	(.003)	(.03)	(.01)	(.006)	(.05)	(.007)	(.004)
Change in real median family income, 1980–90	.54**	-.0003	-.09**	.004	.008	-.21**	-.008	-.002
	(.22)	(.0003)	(.02)	(.0008)	(.006)	(.05)	(.005)	(.003)
% net population change	-.04	.0005	.02**	.002	.0003	.03**	.002**	.0009**
	(.03)	(.0004)	(.002)	(.001)	(.001)	(.007)	(.001)	(.0004)
Population density	-.003**	-.00002	-.00006	-.00003	.00003	-.0002	.00002	.000005
	(.001)	(.00002)	(.0001)	(.00004)	(.00003)	(.0003)	(.00003)	(.00002)
% college students	-.22**	.007**	.04**	.001	.004**	.009	-.000002	-.003**
	(.05)	(.001)	(.007)	(.002)	(.002)	(.01)	(.002)	(.001)
Spatial lag	.53**	.11	-.35*	-.03	-.03	.82**	-.03	.66**
	(.17)	(.09)	(.20)	(.16)	(.06)	(.12)	(.08)	(.21)
Constant	-3.81	-.01	.31	.04	.08	.35	.03	.0013
N	105	105	105	105	105	105	105	105
R^2_a	.30	.70	.56	.54	.86	.65	.20	.38

Note: Spatial autoregressive model, weighted for population; income coefficients expressed in thousands of 1992 dollars; dependent variable = change in population group as a percentage of total population. See appendix A for a full description of variables.

*$p < .10$.   **$p < .05$.

growth of several groups is occurring across regions and that this growth is not confined within county boundaries. Such regional clustering in growth patterns is occurring for U.S. migrants, Mexicans, and South Americans. For Mexicans, the results indicate that a .82 increase in their growth in a particular county follows each one-point increase in their growth in neighboring counties (table 4.1). Interestingly, though, the growth pattern for Asians is negatively associated with growth in immediately adjacent areas ($b = -.35$), indicating that the Asian population is not as geographically diffuse as the Mexican.

These analyses, and maps 4.2 and 4.3, demonstrate that internal migrants and immigrants are not concentrated in the same places in Kansas—not a surprising finding given that domestic movers can afford to be more discriminating in where they live than most immigrants. And among immigrant groups settlement patterns vary widely, with Mexicans expanding their presence in the areas where they had settled previously and most other immigrant groups becoming less noticeable. The destinations of migrants and immigrants are neither randomly nor evenly distributed. The most significant growth in the proportion of immigrants has been in southwestern Kansas. Cross-state (internal) migration has been influential in the counties of eastern Kansas. These distinct migration streams have accentuated differences between the eastern and western regions of the state. Sections within Kansas have always been clearly identifiable based on their economic dependence on one or two principal business sectors: agriculture and oil in the west; aviation in Wichita; industry in Kansas City; finance, insurance, and real estate in Johnson County and Topeka; and mining in the southeast. These separate economies have naturally carved out unique political identities, which only occasionally distinguish regions of the state by social class. Now ethnic balkanization is occurring on top of economic balkanization, and the tendency for immigrants to work at low-wage jobs with no benefits threatens to convert ethnic balkanization into a stronger sense of regional and class disparity than Kansas has ever seen.

Ethnic Balkanization and Naturalization Rates in Kansas

Since neighborhoods become ethnically homogeneous long before municipalities, counties, and regions do, it is useful to study the spatial segregation of the population at a lower level of aggregation such as census tracts within counties. As it turns out, some counties in Kansas are highly segregated, others are not, and the variation in the isolation of ethnic minorities across neighborhoods depends largely on the size of the minority population. The larger the minority population, the more isolated from whites it is likely to be (Tienda and Lii 1987; Frisbie and Niedert 1976). Concentration and isolation may also influence the propensity of foreign-born immigrants to naturalize. Isolation undermines the political and social capital of immigrants, exacerbates economic inequalities, and prevents the learning of language skills necessary for assimilation (Espenshade and Fu 1997, 299; Kwong 1996; Liang 1994; Miller 1975). When put to the test, it is clearly the case that those places with the highest concentration of foreign-born residents have lower naturalization rates than those with few immigrants (see table A4.2). The 1980 census data indicate that a one-point increase in immigrants as a percentage of the total population in a county is associated with a 5.9 percent drop in naturalization. In 1990, the effect is smaller but still statistically significant ($b = -3.45$). The coefficients for Asian and Hispanic segregation are negative, but these variables are too closely related to the size of the foreign-born population to be statistically significant in the regression model. The upshot of these results is that even in states with relatively few immigrants the foreign-born population is not uniformly empowered to express itself in state, local, or national politics. Unequal naturalization rates can, in turn, be explained by the uneven concentration of the immigrant population across the state.

Migrants, Immigrants, and Voter Turnout in Kansas

I have argued that political differentiation across space is the result of social and economic differentiation. In the previous chapters, we have learned that political participation rates are not uniform within or across states. Consequently, some communities have more of a voice in setting the course for local, state, and national politics than others do. Map 4.4 illustrates average turnout patterns across Kansas for two gubernatorial races in the 1990s. As in Colorado, turnout is highest in the most depopulated part of the state, the far western counties abutting the Colorado border. Counties in the lowest turnout quartile are exactly those that have experienced population growth and have large migrant populations. These patterns are prima facie evidence that out-of-state migration and recent immigration are associated with lower voter turnout, especially for off-year (nonpresidential) elections. The reasoning for this is straightforward.

New arrivals may not reregister to vote immediately following a move. Immigrants may not naturalize, and even if they do they may not take much of an interest in politics. These generalizations also appear to hold for Kansas, although the ecological data I present do not yield proof that there is an individual-level relationship. Still, the results do make sense. In four out of the five elections analyzed in table 4.2, increases in the non-Kansas population across Kansas counties help to explain low turnout rates. The three elections in which the relationship is statistically significant occurred in nonpresidential election years, races in which newcomers would be least familiar with the statewide issues, challengers, and incumbents. In all but one election, the percentage of the population comprised of foreign-born residents who arrived after 1970 is associated with lower turnout, especially in 1980 and 1982. Places in Kansas are politically stratified according to whether their populations consist of long-term natives or new arrivals.

The bulk of the new residents in Kansas are internal migrants from other states. Outside of Topeka, a large number of those have settled in the Kansas City suburbs in two counties: Leavenworth and Johnson. The Kansas City metropolitan area is distributed primarily across the border, in Missouri, which means many commuters cross state boundaries every day on their way to work and others move freely back and forth between the Kansas and Missouri suburbs. Inevitably, this movement breeds some apathy on the part of commuters and migrants toward state and local politics. The desire to participate in Kansas politics will generally not be as great for those who spend much of their workday in a different state as it will be for those who both work and live in Kansas. In addition, Leavenworth and Riley counties have large migrant populations made up of army personnel and civilian employees of the military, most of whom are serving temporary stints. Turnout levels in state elections are likely to be lower among this group than among long-term migrants and natives. Certainly these explanations are consistent with the ecological data that report turnout levels. Johnson, Leavenworth, and Wyandotte Counties (see map 4.1) report turnout levels fully one standard deviation below the mean for all counties in 1990. By contrast, just a bit further from the centrality of Kansas City, in counties that are otherwise similar to those closer in (Douglas County, for example), turnout rates jump a full ten points.

Educational levels do not always explain disparities in turnout across Kansas. The relatively low turnout in suburban areas explains why education is not always positively associated with participation in table 4.2. The

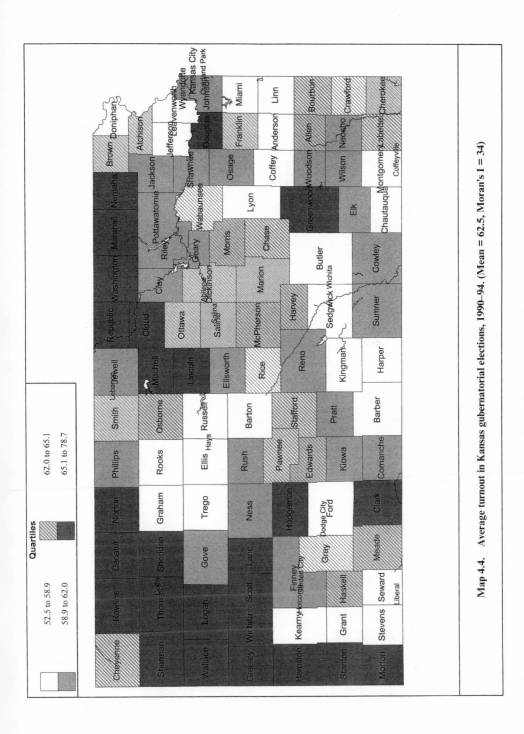

Map 4.4. Average turnout in Kansas gubernatorial elections, 1990–94. (Mean = 62.5, Moran's I = 34)

TABLE 4.2. Impact of Population Mobility on Voter Turnout in Kansas Counties, 1980–94

Variable	1980	1982	1990	1992	1994	Pooled 1990s
% college educated	.004	.53**	.22**	-.16**	-.001	.04
	(.14)	(.15)	(.09)	(.07)	(.07)	(.06)
Isolation of minorities from whites (within counties)	-.03**	-.002	-.02	-.05***	.03*	-.01
	(.01)	(.01)	(.02)	(.01)	(.02)	(.01)
% born out of state	-.02	-.13**	-.14**	.07	-.09*	-.05
	(.04)	(.04)	(.06)	(.04)	(.06)	(.04)
% post-1970 immigrants	-2.30**	-1.88**	-.55**	.53**	-.86**	-.36**
	(.54)	(.53)	(.30)	(.21)	(.24)	(.19)
% black	.14	.68**	.43**	-.22**	-.04	.06
	(.14)	(.15)	(.12)	(.09)	(.10)	(.07)
Population density	.003[a]	-.01**	-.01	.009**	-.008**	-.003
	(.002)	(.003)	(.003)	(.002)	(.002)	(.002)
Spatial lag	.82**	.76**	.65**	.07	.48**	.76**
	(.14)	(.11)	(.13)	(.11)	(.14)	(.08)
Presidential race	—	—	—	—	—	.27
						(.65)
Constant	15.47	14.28	24.51	58.91	36.58	16.63
N	105	105	105	105	105	315
R^2_a	.55	.68	.46	.44	70	.36

Note: Spatial autoregressive model, weighted for population; dependent variable = percentage turnout by county. See appendix A for a full description of variable.

[a]Variables with low tolerances and high standard errors due to multicollinearity.

*$p < .10$.   **$p < .05$.

Johnson County suburbs and Wichita (Sedgwick County) are affluent areas with highly educated populations compared to the rest of the state. But these are also the areas with the largest populations of non-Kansans.

Finally, there is positive spatial dependency in the turnout rates of Kansas counties. Participation patterns in counties are clearly related to the participation rates in neighboring counties. County boundaries appear to be especially meaningless in a state so homogeneous that turnout rates seem to vary more across clusters or groups of counties than across individual jurisdictions.

Migrants, Immigrants, and Party Regularity in Kansas

Party regularity, like turnout, varies within and across states. Differences in the extent to which a place's behavior can be predicted by the underlying partisan predispositions of its population may be explained by the extent to which that place has undergone social change. Rapid social change undermines traditions, including political customs. As in chapters 2 and 3, I hypothesize that party regularity, that is, the extent of congruence between party registration and voting, will be stronger in areas unaffected by the destabilizing forces of population growth. Differences between registration and voting will be much greater in areas where new populations have imported cultures and ways of life from somewhere else and where lower turnout is the norm. The results, reported in table 4.3, indicate strong support for the idea that high turnout areas produce voting in line with registration whereas low turnout areas do not. In all five elections, increases in turnout reduce the extent of party irregularity. Once turnout is controlled, however, it is not clear that places with large proportions of internal migrants will be more irregular. Indeed, locales with non-Kansas residents are more regular in 1982, 1990, and 1992 and in the pooled model for the 1990s. Again this suggests that the reason why some places are irregular in their behavior is because of low turnout by certain segments of the population. The out-of-state migrant population is not necessarily directly responsible for party irregularity through split-ticket voting. In this case, it is because migrants fail to turn out that partisan irregularity is the end result.

The proportion of recently arrived immigrants in an area is associated with departures from basic partisanship in three of the five elections, and the black population also contributes something to discrepancies between voting and registration. This is probably not because the immigrant and

TABLE 4.3. Similarity of Party Registration to Party Voting in Kansas Counties, 1980–94

Variable	1980	1982	1990	1992	1994	Pooled 1990s
% college educated	-.44**	-.20	.11	-.17**	-.05	-.01
	(.20)	(.25)	(.14)	(.08)	(.08)	(.08)
% born out of state	.16**	-.14**	-.15*	-.10**	.002	-.11*
	(.06)	(.07)	(.09)	(.05)	(.05)	(.06)
% post-1970 immigrants	-.20	1.62*	-1.23**	1.28**	.64**	.28
	(.86)	(.92)	(.45)	(.26)	(.27)	(.26)
% black	-.44**	.02	1.09**	.33**	.008	.51**
	(.19)	(.25)	(.08)	(.10)	(.10)	(.10)
Population density	.002	.0007	-.02	.01**	-.002	-.003
	(.003)	(.004)	(.004)	(.002)	(.003)	(.002)
% turnout	-.25**	-.26**	-.44**	-.56**	-.20**	-.10
	(.12)	(.13)	(.13)	(.10)	(.10)	(.07)
Spatial lag	.59**	.90**	.42**	.29**	.62**	.52**
	(.15)	(.09)	(.17)	(.14)	(.13)	(.10)
Presidential race	—	—	—	—	—	1.29
						(1.03)
Constant	29.05	21.85	39.22	43.74	21.14	15.38
N	105	105	105	105	105	105
R^2_a	.20	.60	.41	.73	.37	.24

Note: Spatial autoregressive model, weighted for population; dependent variable = Abs (% Republican vote − % Republican registration); high positive values indicate counties where voting differed from registration. See appendix A for a full description of variables.

$*p < .10.$ $**p < .05.$

black populations split their tickets or vote contrary to their registration. It is more likely the result of low turnout among these Democratically inclined populations.

As with the turnout models in the previous table, the models for party irregularity indicate that positive spatial dependency figures prominently as an explanation of differences across the state in how easily partisanship predicts voting. Counties can be clustered into larger regions for purposes of explaining spatial variation in party regularity. For example, Leavenworth, Sedgwick, Douglas, and Shawnee Counties in northeast Kansas (see map 4.1), all of which have grown rapidly, voted far more Republican in 1990 than their registration figures would have predicted. Not coincidentally, these are also counties where turnout levels are low in off-year elections. High turnout goes a long way toward minimizing departures from party regularity at the aggregate level. In ethnically heterogeneous counties, Republicans generally benefit from lower turnout since ethnic minorities identify with and vote for Democrats and are less likely to participate than whites.

The pattern of spatial balkanization in the degree of party regularity, then, is related to a combination of migratory and ethnic characteristics of places. Those places in Kansas that are ethnically homogeneous and have stable populations are more predictable than areas that are both heterogeneous and growing. In rural Kansas, changes in party registration have occurred very slowly with attrition—the out-migration of residents once tied to the agricultural economy. The remaining voters can be counted on to turn out year after year, and not much work is required to mobilize them. But in the fast-growing counties of eastern Kansas, campaigns have far more work to do. Newly transplanted and ethnic voters must be registered and mobilized. Upscale neighborhoods full of new residents must be sifted for sympathetic partisans and so, too, must the older neighborhoods with black and Hispanic concentrations. The failure to turn out population subgroups in the state's largest cities can mean the difference between a win and a loss in a statewide race.

Changes in Party Registration in Kansas

Population growth is hypothesized to increase Republican registration growth in Kansas. The theory laid down in the first chapter predicted that those who move in from elsewhere in the nation are more likely to have a Republican than a Democratic social profile. Moving costs money and requires information about opportunities at the destination. These costs make migrants a highly select group based on the ability to pay. Hence, internal migrants are likely to be white, upwardly mobile, and have higher incomes than those who do not move. The PUMS data presented in table A4.1 support the notion that recent migrants are wealthier than either natives or immigrants. The coefficients in table 4.4 suggest some support for the idea that the concentration of migrants from outside the state helps Republicans. Areas with higher percentages of out-of-state migrants at the beginning of each decade did see Republican growth at the expense of Democrats and third parties.

The increasing concentration of the Hispanic and Asian populations reduces Republican registration in the 1970s, but the influence is not statistically significant between 1980 and 1990 (table 4.4). Areas of the state where Republicans were strong in 1970 finished with a lower proportion of

TABLE 4.4.   Impact of Population Mobility on Changes in Republican Party Registration in Kansas Counties, 1974–80, 1980–90

Variable	1974–80	1980–90
% born out of state, 1970 (1980)	.11**	.11*
	(.05)	(.06)
Change in % born out of state	.15	−.26*
	(.17)	(.16)
% foreign born, 1970 (1980)	1.08[a]	−.69[a]
	(.73)	(.46)
Change in % foreign born	−1.40**	−.23
	(.53)	(.33)
% Republican registrants, 1974 (1980)	−.24**	.009
	(.05)	(.06)
Population density	−.009**	−.004*
	(.001)	(.002)
Spatial lag	.32**	.04
	(.16)	(.17)
Constant	8.34	3.91
N	105	105
R^2_a	.30	.02

Note: Spatial autoregressive model, weighted for population; dependent variable = change in Republican Party registrants. See appendix A for a full description of variables.
[a]Indicates low tolerances and high standard errors due to multicollinearity.
*$p < .10$.   **$p < .05$.

registrants than those that had only weak to middling Republican registration. This finding can be accounted for by the existence of equilibrium
cycles in two-party electoral politics. Counties at their peak of Republican
registration in one period are likely to move downward in the next simply
as the result of natural trends in party support. Similarly, strong Democratic areas often lose ground as Republicans work their way back into a
competitive position. Finally, Republican numbers appear to have grown
more slowly in the urbanized, densely populated areas of the state, especially in the first of the two decades (table 4.4). The urban counties contain
the cities with the most entrenched and loyal Democratic constituencies,
such as Kansas City (Wyandotte County), and a few Republican areas,
such as Wichita and Johnson County, where the GOP already possesses a
high percentage of eligible voters and equilibrating trends may be operating to limit further Republican gains.

The standard model I have used to predict GOP registration growth
for the 1980s fails to explain much of the variation across the state's 105
counties ($R^2_a = .02$; see table 4.4). The pattern of variation to be explained
is pictured in map 4.5, with registration change blocked by quartile. The
darkly shaded counties are scattered almost randomly, which explains
why conventional accounts fail to address the variation. The spatially
lagged dependent variable in table 4.4 indicates that there is no pronounced regional pattern to the data based on the distance criteria I used
to define the spatial weights. Exploratory methods revealed no striking
nonlinear patterns in the relationship of the existing variables to changes
in party registration, and there are no obvious theories that would suggest
such nonlinear relationships exist anyway.

Another alternative is that the model is poorly specified because
important variables have been omitted altogether. A closer examination of
the cases indicates that changes in Republican registration growth vary
according to urban versus rural characteristics of places that go beyond
mere population density. For example, counties with the highest concentrations of blacks and Latinos were among those least likely to gain
Republican registrants between 1980 and 1990. But high-income suburban
counties in eastern Kansas, including Johnson and Leavenworth, were
characterized by only modest growth in GOP registration. Why would the
rural areas see far faster growth in Republicanism than the wealthier suburban areas? One answer is that Democrats in Kansas are far more willing
to compete for voters in the population centers where their efforts as a
minority party are likely to pay the biggest dividends than they are to

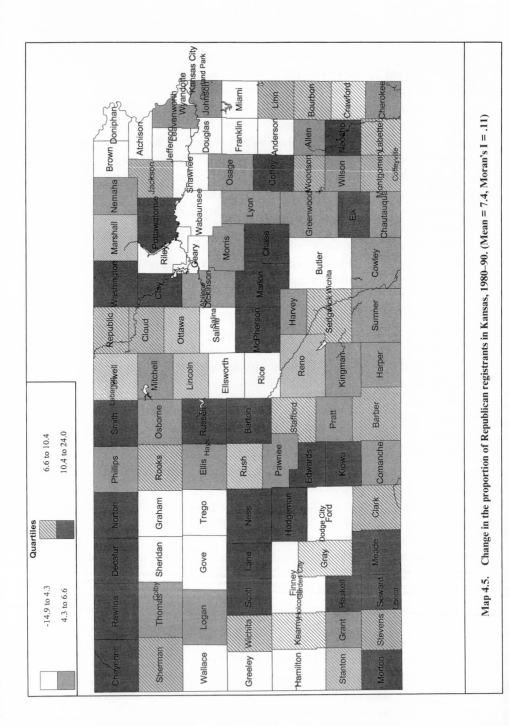

Quartiles

-14.9 to 4.3   6.6 to 10.4

4.3 to 6.6   10.4 to 24.0

Map 4.5. Change in the proportion of Republican registrants in Kansas, 1980–90. (Mean = 7.4, Moran's I = .11)

search small towns for a handful of sympathizers. Registering or convert-ing a few thousand Democrats in Kansas City, Lawrence, Overland Park, or Wichita is also less costly than recruiting the same number of Democ-rats in a dozen small towns scattered throughout western and central Kansas. Consequently, the GOP is left alone to make gains on its already solid base in the state's rural areas, while it runs into more determined opposition where Democrats can concentrate their limited resources.

A second explanation for the GOP growth in the state's most rural counties is generational replacement. The most rural counties in the state are experiencing population losses due to the long-term trend away from agricultural employment. The population that has remained behind is growing older as the children of farmers leave to find employment else-where. As the population has aged, mortality rates have increased relative to fertility rates. The older generation of Democratically inclined voters is being replaced with younger Republican voters. I tested this hypothesis by adding a variable for percentage of the population over age sixty-five in 1970 and 1980 to the models in table 4.4. My guess was that this variable would say nothing about the registration tendencies of the elderly popula-tion but would serve as a mortality indicator. In other words, those coun-ties with large percentages of older residents in 1980 would see strong Republican growth between 1980 and 1990. This did prove to be the case, as a 10 percent rise in the elderly population across counties in 1980 was productive of a 3.1 point surge in GOP registration by 1990. There was no statistically significant relationship, however, for the 1970s. The elderly population is concentrated in Kansas's most rural counties. While the population in these places has declined, Republicans have become a larger proportion of party registrants. Hence, the older the rural population the better the prospects are for the Republicans at the county level. Statewide, however, these gains do not mean much for the GOP since these rural counties contain a smaller share of the state's population than in the past.

Ethnicity and Political Behavior at the Individual Level

Political balkanization occurs when there are vast differences in the polit-ical behavior of areas, including differences in the propensity to partici-pate in politics and variance in aspects of political behavior such as party regularity. These differences translate into who is elected to represent and govern a community and ultimately what policies are enacted. All other things being equal, representatives elected on the basis of turnout by a small and select group of citizens will be inclined to pursue a less pluralistic form of politics than those elected on the basis of high turnout. This is why the spatial balkanization of electorates is an important subject for study and why homogeneous electorates may be undesirable as a foundation for electoral representation. Similarly, the separation of areas that are regular in their voting from those that are not undermines the capacity of politicians to run coherent, responsible, party-centered campaigns. Partisanship has one meaning in one community and a quite different meaning in another. Candidates of the same party cannot band together to cooperate in a legislative body such as a county council or a state legislature when their electorates have separate and rival conceptions of the content of the party label.

The data presented in tables 4.1 through 4.4 present a picture of a state that is politically stratified in ways related to population mobility and demographic change, albeit far less so than in California or Colorado due to the much smaller volume of population influx. In 1990, two-thirds of the Mexican immigrants in the state were clustered in just five counties, where their presence is growing more noticeable. Asians are equally concentrated, but their numbers did not grow larger relative to the rest of the population. Many remain noncitizens and therefore politically uninvolved, but even if they were involved it is not clear that their small numbers would change much about Kansas politics except, perhaps, at the local level.

Internal U.S. migration, on the other hand, is balkanizing Kansas, and here the numbers are sizable and harder to ignore. Northeastern Kansas and the counties around Wichita (Sedgwick, Reno, Butler) have benefited from employment and income growth. This growth has drawn internal migrants from many states, dividing a new, growing, mostly urban Kansas from an older, declining, agricultural one. Evidence from table 4.4 shows that areas where the out-of-state population was especially large in 1970 and 1980 did see GOP growth in the following decade. But these areas of migrant settlement, such as Johnson County, are less regular in their political behavior than the older, more stable counties around the state. Table 4.3 paints a picture of a Kansas as a state with distinct political tendencies. One, that of rural Kansas, is characterized by the stable, high turnout of regular partisans (usually Republicans) who have a long history in the state. The other is characterized by the much weaker party attachments of more urban and suburban voters as well as the nonparticipation of many would-be Democrats. Suburban and urban Kansas usually votes far more

Republican than its registration figures would predict due mostly to the low turnout among ethnic minorities.

Verifying that these patterns of political stratification and differentiation have roots at the individual level is no easy task. Network exit polls, sampled by state, are a good source of data for comparing states by ethnicity, partisan identification, and party regularity. While exit polls only survey those who show up to vote, their accessibility and standard format makes them superior to surveys in which question wording and varying sampling frames do not facilitate comparison. Figures from the 1990s show that Kansas is a mostly Republican state, with roughly half of the population identifying with the Republican Party (see table 4.5). Even blacks are surprisingly likely to report Republican Party identification. For Hispanics, whose numbers remain small, independent party identification is especially strong. The figures for Asians in table 4.5 are not reliable given the small number of Asian respondents surveyed. Estimates of the proportion of Hispanics registered as Republicans across the state's counties, based on the ecological inference model developed and advanced by King (1997), show that like elsewhere, Hispanics in Kansas are more Democratic than non-Hispanics (29.6 percent to 42.9 percent in 1992), but in some contests, these differences fade. For instance, in the context of the lower turnout of the 1994 gubernatorial contest, an estimated 43.1 percent of Hispanics were registered as Republicans, compared to 43.7 percent for non-Hispanics.

On the matter of Kansans' party regularity, survey data from the 1990 gubernatorial race show that voters in the Kansas City and Wichita areas are slightly more likely than rural voters to abandon their party identifications (table not reported). This suggests that the absence of party regularity in counties in urban Kansas is not only a function of turnout but of the independent sensibilities of the voters in these areas, many of whom come from other states.

Comparing the polling data in table 4.5 with similar data from other chapters reveals some striking contrasts. First, Kansas's white and black populations are far more Republican than in either California, Colorado, or New York. But, unlike these other states, minorities are not much of a force in statewide elections. The influx of Asians and Hispanics into the state has not made a decisive difference given that most of them are nonparticipants and show little interest in politics. Indeed, the state's traditional Republican bias may encourage more minorities to declare Republican Party affiliation than they would if the Democrats were more viable.

Since the number of migrant minorities is small relative to the number of natives, the native political culture exercises influence on the attitudes and behavior of the new arrivals.

Political Change and the Internal Composition of Kansas Counties

Political differences across places within states can be understood with reference to variability in the population composition of cities, counties, and substate sections. Given the Democratic leanings of blacks and Hispanics, Republicans do best in areas where such Democratically inclined ethnic groups fail to gain a political foothold. The political influence of ethnic minorities is obviously minimized when their numbers are small (minority status is acute). But it is also minimized when they are highly segregated from the majority white population. Table 4.2 showed that the degree of white from minority segregation was negatively associated with turnout, particularly in presidential years. Similarly, foreign-born concentration depresses the naturalization rate in immigrant communities (see table A4.1).

Residential segregation is associated with many traits that conspire to depress political participation and community involvement: poverty and

TABLE 4.5.   Party Identification by Race/Ethnicity in Kansas Elections, 1990–94

Race/Ethnic Group	Year	Democrat	Independent	Republican
White	1990	29.8	21.5	48.7
	1992	28.3	23.1	48.6
	1994	28.0	20.3	51.8
Black	1990	59.0	19.4	21.7
	1992	58.2	18.6	23.2
	1994	74.1	16.1	9.8
Hispanic	1990	27.8	38.2	34.0
	1992	60.2	39.8	0.0
	1994	42.7	26.4	30.8
Asian	1990	29.0	16.8	54.3
	1992	46.4	36.5	17.2
	1994	0.0	100.0	0.0

Source: Voter Research and Surveys, General Election Exit Polls, 1990–94 (weighted data).

welfare dependency, lack of access to burgeoning labor markets, and inferior schools (Miller 1975). By reducing interracial contact, highly segregated communities may keep interethnic conflict to a minimum, but opportunities to resolve the tensions that do arise are lost. In this respect, highly segregated communities are adverse to the practice of pluralist politics and instead foster a politics dominated by the interests of monolithic groups. As V. O. Key repeatedly noted in the 1940s and 1950s, political party competition is also minimized in homogeneous communities. Such electoral one-sidedness marginalizes the value of an individual's vote in deciding electoral outcomes, depresses turnout, and undermines the accountability of officeholders to the electorate. In settings of fierce electoral competition, the value of one's vote is maximized, turnout is high, and so is accountability to the voters.

When considered in isolation from other states, Kansas provides a difficult challenge for this thesis because ethnic minorities and immigrant groups are such a small proportion of the state's population. While table 4.4 did show that the proportion of domestic migrants at the beginning of each decade is associated with modest Republican gains, the size of the foreign-born population had no definite influence on changes in party registration. Notably, though, *growth in the proportion* of foreign-born residents was associated with diminished Republican registration. Political party competition is strong, in spite of heavy Republican biases, and Democrats have repeatedly overcome the statewide Republican edge. Certainly, if the presence of immigrants is important for politics, it is in closely contested races and a few local areas where minorities constitute a sizable voting bloc.

To complete the investigation of this chapter, I have selected three counties and one county area within the state that exhibit a variety of demographic and political characteristics. These are Wyandotte, Johnson, Sedgwick, and four rural counties in southwestern Kansas: Hodgeman, Finney, Ford, and Gray (see map 4.1). Republican registration growth was stronger in Kansas during the 1980s than in Colorado, rising an average of 7.5 points. Sedgwick County's Republican registration exceeded the state average, moving up about 9 points from 1980 to 1990, and Johnson's Republican strength was boosted by 6.4 points. The GOP in Wyandotte made only modest gains, a mere .6 point increase over the course of the decade. The four-county area in southwestern Kansas varied. The most rural of the four counties, Hodgeman, saw impressive Republican growth—a full 14 points. Finney County (Garden City) and Ford County

(Dodge City), on the other hand, home of the largest meatpacking opera-
tions, saw slow Republican growth, 3 and .2 points, respectively. Finally,
Gray County Republicans moved up about 6 points from 30 to 36 percent
of all registered voters.

As in the previous chapters, I hypothesize that aside from the sheer
number of ethnic minorities the activation of the ethnic population goes a
long way toward explaining political trends and behavior. Counties that
are characterized by ethnic homogeneity and spatial isolation are likely to
have lower levels of political activism among minority and low-income
voters. The argument is not only that political activism is low in areas of
residential segregation because minorities are poor, uneducated, and do
not feel politically efficacious. Rather, it is their lack of interaction with
the majority white society that retards their mobilization (Lamare 1977).
Those new to the community may feel more secure interacting only with
members of their own group, but this separation does not facilitate assimilation, political or otherwise (Kwong 1996; Miller 1975). Balkanized in an
enclave of their own making, the making of their employers, and/or the
making of planners and developers, ethnic minorities are less likely to seek
solutions to community problems through politics or the political party
system. Since lower income ethnics are more likely to express their political preferences within the Democratic Party, the spatial segregation of
minorities from whites usually improves Republican electoral prospects.

The mechanism for ethnopolitical balkanization in Kansas is slightly
different than for other states, as it involves migration from out-of-state
sources rather than rapid growth in the ethnic population. By choosing to
live in areas where the costs of housing are higher than minorities can
afford, internal migrants inadvertently contribute to the racial segregation
of the areas where they move. Predictably, Republican growth has been
very strong in these parts of the state. In other areas of Kansas, such as
Wyandotte County (Kansas City), growth in the immigrant and ethnic
minority populations has played a role in keeping Republican registration
to a minimum. The model of party change in table 4.4. does suggest some
tendency for Republican growth to be smaller in areas with significant and
growing immigrant populations. By constructing a dissimilarity index for
each county, one may be able to determine whether the areas where
Republicans did well were areas where ethnic integration was especially
low.

Spatial segregation for each area, as indicated by the dissimilarity
index, is described in table 4.6. Like other urban areas in the United

TABLE 4.6. Index of Dissimilarity for the Black, Asian, and Hispanic Populations Relative to Whites in Kansas Counties, 1980 and 1990, by Census Tract

	Kansas		Wyandotte		Johnson		Wyandotte and Johnson		Sedgwick		Southwest Kansas	
Variable	1980	1990	1980	1990	1980	1990	1980	1990	1980	1990	1980	1990
Asians	.45	.47	.40	.48	.22	.21	.64	.28	.37	.40	.36	.42
Blacks	.68	.63	.65	.58	.34	.28	.73	.72	.73	.63	.36	.37
Hispanics	.41	.44	.34	.40	.15	.17	.39	.40	.32	.33	.40	.39
N	684	684	75	75	75	75	150	150	101	101	15	15

Source: U.S. Census 1990, and author's calculations.
Note: Figures represent the percentage of each group that would have to move in order for the group to be evenly distributed across all census tracts.

States, at the tract level blacks are the most spatially segregated group in Wichita (Sedgwick County), Kansas City (Wyandotte), and the Kansas City suburbs (Johnson). Segregation has diminished some since 1980, but over half the black population in both Wichita and Kansas City would be required to relocate for this population to be evenly distributed across census tracts. In the rural counties of southwestern Kansas, there is less difference in the degree of segregation of the three groups from white residents. Blacks, Asians, and Hispanics are about equally isolated. In Johnson County, the low degree of segregation is mostly an artifact of the county's affluence and its very small minority population.

As in Colorado, the black population is tiny—less than 2 percent of the state's population in 1990—and it is not growing. The Hispanic population, while only 4 percent in 1990, has grown more rapidly, especially in the southwestern counties, where Mexicans have been recruited to work in the meatpacking business. It is noteworthy that the spatial concentration of Asians and Hispanics in the four southwestern counties did not diminish from 1980 to 1990 and that Asians have become even more concentrated. Not coincidentally, Hodgeman and Gray have the fewest minorities and the strongest Republican growth. Hodgeman is typical of the rural Kansas counties that have lost population in the last few decades (see map 4.1). Several of the darkly shaded neighborhoods in map 4.6 consist of low-cost trailer park housing in Dodge City and Garden City, which was built to accommodate workers at the meatpacking plants (Gouveia and Stull 1995, 90; Benson 1990). While at the broad level of tracts and block groups the degree of spatial segregation may seem modest, the concentration of lower status minorities in trailer parks should not be overlooked. When the dissimilarity index is calculated at lower levels of geographic aggregation, the spatial concentration of Asians is more acute. Within the Asian community, spatial segregation is highest for Laotians and Cambodians and lowest for the Vietnamese, who have a longer history in the community and have worked their way into permanent jobs and housing. The established residents in Garden City stigmatize the newcomers in the mobile home parks and fiercely resist efforts at integration (Benson 1990; Campa 1990). Observers of life within the trailer courts report that they are also highly segregated internally, with Asians, Mexicans, and Anglos clustered in separate sections (Benson 1994, 372).

Southwestern Kansas

The Garden City area (Finney County) grew by 43 percent in the decade of the 1980s, and as a rare example of rural multicultural society it has been extensively investigated by sociologists and anthropologists (Lamphere, Stepick, and Grenier 1994; Stull, Broadway, and Griffith 1995; Lamphere 1992). The growth came largely as a result of the recruitment of laborers for the meatpacking plants in the towns of Holcomb and Garden City. In the mid-1990s, the two plants employed about 4,500 workers. Lacking a local labor force willing to take the hazardous jobs in meatpacking, company personnel offices advertised around the country and in areas of high unemployment within Kansas. Nearly two thousand Southeast Asians moved in to take the jobs, many coming from Wichita (Stull, Broadway, and Erickson 1992, 42), where the aircraft industry experienced a recession in the early and mid-1980s. In 1988, Hispanics were estimated to hold about 50 percent of the jobs in Monfort's Garden City plant (50).

Most of the migrants to southwestern Kansas do not expect to stay, so their direct political impact on the communities has been minimal. Migrants come and go "at an amazing rate. And their attachment to and influence on the community is little felt" (62; see also Benson 1994). A 1987 study by the local school district discovered that 44 percent of all newcomer households left the community within one year and only a third remained after two years (Stull 1990). The Garden City School District's student population was 51 percent minority by 1997 (Lessner 1997). Similar to Weld County, Colorado, Finney and Ford Counties have attracted a low-skilled labor force that takes little interest in the community. This inactivity has not kept resident Anglos from resenting their presence. The political reaction to ethnic diversity in Garden City has varied with the class standing of the residents. Upper income professionals are more tolerant than lower income workers, who are often competing for the same jobs and housing. Many Anglo residents suspect that increases in crime and traffic congestion can be tied to the meatpacking plants and their foreign-born workers.

Map 4.6 illustrates the settlement patterns of immigrants and internal migrants in southwestern Kansas for block groups in 1990. Note that immigrants have mixed well with internal migrants in a number of the neighborhoods on the outskirts of Garden City but the central and northern neighborhoods of the town are more attractive to financially better off internal migrants than to immigrants. In Dodge City, internal migrants

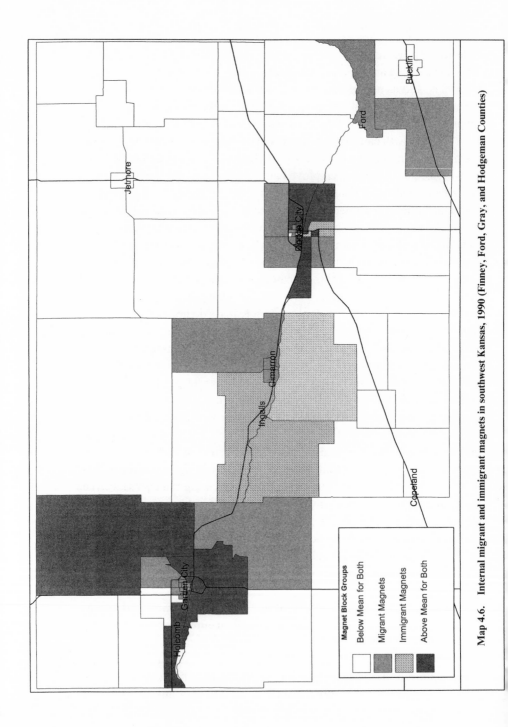

Map 4.6. Internal migrant and immigrant magnets in southwest Kansas, 1990 (Finney, Ford, Gray, and Hodgeman Counties)

Magnet Block Groups

Below Mean for Both

Migrant Magnets

Immigrant Magnets

Above Mean for Both

have thoroughly mixed with the immigrant population except in one area on the south side of town where immigrants have concentrated. There are also rural areas between Garden City and Dodge City, in the towns of Ingalls and Cimarron, that are attractive to immigrants but not to internal migrants.

There is a permanent population of ethnic minorities not tied to the meatpacking plants, and they have set down roots and established a long-term presence. The established Hispanic population in Garden City originally came to work in the sugar beet fields and on the Santa Fe Railroad in the early 1900s (Oppenheimer 1985; Smith 1981). The descendants of these farm and railway workers have become the core of the permanent Hispanic community in southwestern Kansas (Campa 1990, 349). While lacking the roots of the Hispanic population in southern Colorado, these Mexican Americans are established enough to earn high school diplomas, speak fluent English, and compete for better jobs than the newer arrivals. Intermarriage between the Hispanic and Anglo populations has helped integrate the two communities. Their presence in local politics has provided the Democrats with a political base in an area that is predominantly Republican. Hispanics have held City Council seats and are commonly elected to the local school board. As in Colorado, the native Hispanics disassociate themselves from the poorer classes with shorter tenure. "Immigrant Hispanics are much more likely to interact in the workplace with Southeast Asians than with native Hispanics. Relatively few local Hispanics work at the meatpacking houses, and these are likely to be in managerial positions" (Campa 1990, 357).

The state Democratic Party has a Hispanic caucus, which has sought to activate the native-born Latino community in southwestern Kansas. A major registration effort aimed at Hispanics took place during the 1996 presidential election. New issues in Kansas politics have spurred this effort, including the attempt to pass English only legislation and restrictions imposed on enrollment in the state universities. But local sources suggest that many Mexicans and Asians are afraid to get involved in politics, thinking that taking sides in the system may result in some kind of retaliation, targeting, or even repatriation of themselves or their relatives. Although they may be legal residents, or even citizens, many have relatives who are not. As a consequence, the overriding cultural tendency is to try to solve problems within the community of coethnics rather than outside it. The mobilization of Hispanics and Asians into the ranks of the Kansas Democratic Party promises to be a slow process that may not pay statewide dividends until well after the turn of the century. But Republican growth in this area was considerably slower during the 1980s and early 1990s than the state average. The barons of beef, never friendly to the Democratic Party, may be setting the stage for a Democratic resurgence in southwestern Kansas.

Wichita and Sedgwick County
Wichita (Sedgwick County), is Kansas's largest city and one of the most conservative in the nation. It is the only major U.S. city that has resisted the fluoridation of its water. City blocks are still required to pay for the upkeep of their streets, and consequently many residential streets remain unpaved. The Republicans have traditionally been the dominant party, although the city of Wichita's black and Hispanic neighborhoods are solidly Democratic. The city's industrial workers in the aircraft industry have provided some support for the Democratic Party and there is a large machinists' union, but the white working-class voters are conservative populists, hostile to people of color, trade agreements, and immigrants who compete for their jobs. The union rank and file commonly abandon the Democratic Party in statewide and national elections.

Sedgwick County's population influx during the 1980s and 1990s, much of which has come from outside the state, has contributed to a rising Republican tide. The GOP share of registrants moved up a full nine points from 1980 to 1990 and an additional three points from 1990 to 1994. Yet the county's population is 9 percent black, and Hispanics and Asians are a growing presence. What accounts for such rapid Republican growth in the midst of an expanding ethnic minority population? The answer is that the minorities are highly segregated and therefore not as politically active as they might be if they were more dispersed. Following the path taken by older central cities, Wichita is becoming a city of ethnic minorities and poor whites who cannot afford to move out (Broadway and Snyder 1989). The forces of internal migration and immigration have balkanized Wichita. Map 4.7 illustrates the spatial patterns well. The small proportion of new immigrants is concentrated in scattered tracts on the south and west sides of the downtown area, areas of internal migration are on the far eastern side of the county, and in between are about ten tracts where the two populations have mixed. Native-born Kansans, on the other hand, dominate the western tracts of Sedgwick County, displayed in white on the map. While there is no ghetto, locals admit that it is difficult to find an integrated neighborhood in Wichita. This impression seems well founded.

Until 1954, the black population was segregated by law and forced to live on the northeast side of town. The dissimilarity index reveals that the city's black population is as spatially concentrated as any in the nation (see table 4.6). The Hispanic and Asian neighborhoods are less segregated from white neighborhoods than from black, but there are distinct enclaves of these groups also. The few Hispanic and black representatives in the Kansas state legislature have come largely from majority-black districts within the city, but the concentration of the minority population would ensure the election of these politicians regardless of minority turnout, so votes for them do not have much value. When black politicians seek higher office, their racially conscious affiliation with majority-black districts dampens their appeal to the broader community. In this manner, the spatial concentration of a minority population that has been hailed as an instrument for the election of a few minority politicians to local office provides only an illusion of empowerment. Even local African American politicians recognize that race-based, "superliberal" politics has held them back (Flynn 1991). Sedgwick County Commission chair Billy McCray, a black politician from Wichita, admitted in the early 1990s that budgetary restraint was necessary to prove to the broader community that blacks can be trusted in higher government offices (Flynn 1991). The isolation of the white and minority populations has ensured internal political balkanization within Sedgwick County, which limits the political influence of minorities while giving Republicans increasingly lopsided victory margins in the areas in which they are dominant.

Helping to balkanize the Wichita area is the arrival of affluent white migrants from out of state, nearly all of whom choose to live in the suburbs. This new population is employed in white middle management jobs connected to the aircraft industry and its spin-offs. Growth east of Wichita, in Butler County, has consisted of fewer out-of-state migrants and more native Kansans who have exited the city. Since these short-distance migrants are more likely to be lower income, working class whites, the number of Butler County Republicans has declined slightly as a share of total registration.

Kansas City

Kansas City (Wyandotte County) is an aging industrial center. While the meatpacking plants that were the core of the economy forty years ago have long since gone out of business, tire and auto plants remain major local employers. It has many of the characteristics of rust belt cities further east.

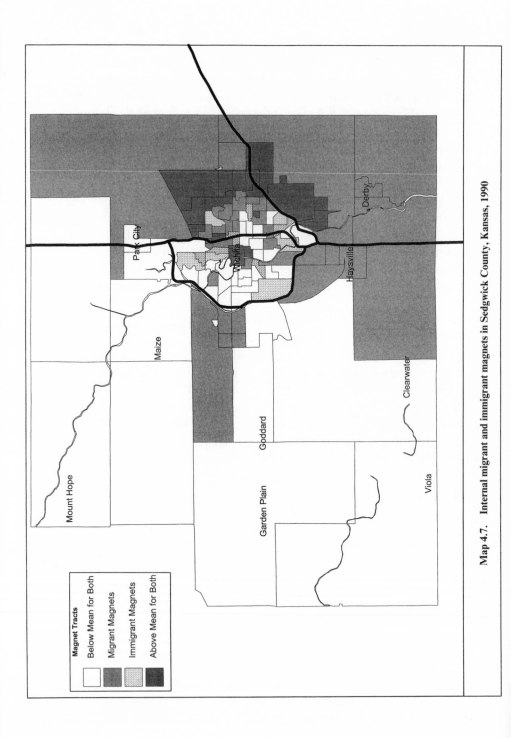

Map 4.7. Internal migrant and immigrant magnets in Sedgwick County, Kansas, 1990

Magnet Tracts

Below Mean for Both

Migrant Magnets

Immigrant Magnets

Above Mean for Both

Mount Hope

Maize

Park City

Garden Plain

Goddard

Wichita

Haysville

Derby

Viola

Clearwater

Besides having a large concentration of blacks (28 percent of the population in 1990), this area contains an ethnic enclave of older immigrants
from Southern and Eastern Europe. Locals describe it as a quiet, hard-
working community where voters are preoccupied with getting the bills
paid. Issues of economic well-being dominate their political thinking. In
response to long-term job loss, the population has declined as residents
have moved southward to Johnson County or out of the area altogether.
Like cities elsewhere, the middle class white population has gradually been
replaced by a poorer black and Hispanic population.

As for residential segregation, table 4.6 shows that Wyandotte's Hispanic and Asian communities became more segregated from the white
population from 1980 to 1990. The major black enclave is in the northeast,
and Hispanics are concentrated in the southeast. The working class white
population lives predominantly in the western tracts and the town of
Edwardsville (see map 4.8). There are occasional ethnic tensions between
black residents and the local police department, but race relations are not
as volatile as in larger cities. Kansas City was one of the first places in the
nation to integrate its public schools.

Wyandotte is the strongest Democratic county in the state. It is the
one place in Kansas where Democrats can mobilize voters on a block by
block or geographic basis. Indeed, a machine-style organization has controlled city government for decades based on an alliance between white
and black elites. Local politicians are described as having a siege mental-
ity. Facing an overwhelmingly Republican state, they have grown defen-
sive and inbred. Serious political party competition does not exist. The
Republican Party has been moribund for years and often cannot slate candidates. Turnout is often below the state average—a reflection of the one-
sidedness of elections as well as the lower education and income levels of
residents. As in other densely populated communities, though, there is
sufficient interaction between minority and white neighborhoods to give
ethnic minorities a sense that they have a stake in community politics.
Population concentration mitigates the adverse impact of residential segregation on political participation. Unlike ethnic populations that are isolated in rural areas, whites and blacks are in contact in Kansas City as a
function of everyday life.

Johnson County
Immediately south of Kansas City lies Johnson County, a collection of
affluent, white suburbs, including Overland Park and Mission Hills (see

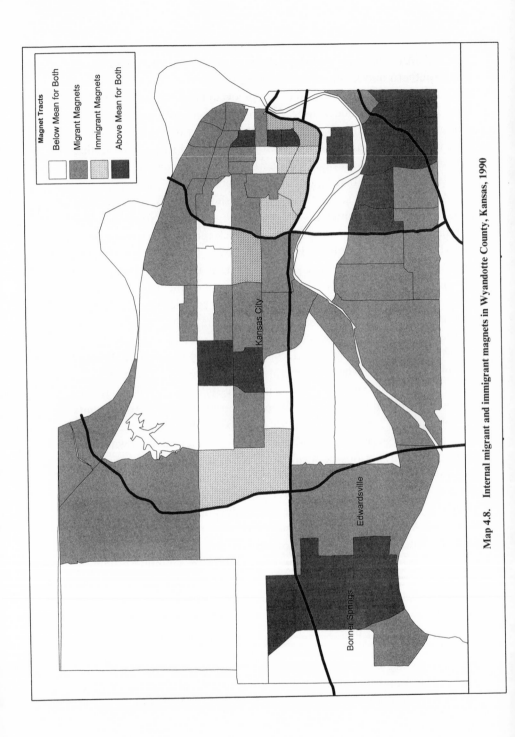

Magnet Tracts

- Below Mean for Both
- Migrant Magnets
- Immigrant Magnets
- Above Mean for Both

Kansas City

Edwardsville

Bonner Springs

Map 4.8.   Internal migrant and immigrant magnets in Wyandotte County, Kansas, 1990

map 4.9). Many of its residents are Wyandotte County exiles and their children. When Johnson County residents look north, they see a population they consider poor, uneducated, unsophisticated, and of the wrong color. "Not many people from Johnson even come to Wyandotte," said one local newspaper man. "They feel that their life is in danger when they come near Kansas City." Politically, Johnson's suburbs are exactly contrary to Kansas City. Democrats moving to Johnson County often register as Republicans because the Democratic Party has traditionally been so weak that it cannot field candidates for many offices. The overriding concern of voters in these affluent suburbs is the avoidance of higher taxes. For years, the state government has relied mainly upon property taxation, which weighs heavily on the rural farms and ranches of western Kansas. Talk of shifting more of the burden of state revenue collection to an income tax is anathema to Johnson County's wealthy residents. This is one of the most rapidly growing areas of the state, and it has attracted many residents and businesses from Missouri. In 1990, 22 percent of the population had come from other states in the previous five years. Consistent with Thad Brown's (1988) theories about the role of migration on the weakening of partisan identification, the number of independent voters is rising. In 1992, 48 percent of the population were registered Republicans and 21 percent were Democrats, but one-third were independents. Ross Perot did better in Johnson County than he did nationally in the 1992 race, winning 26 percent of the vote. Because of its highly informed electorate, turnout is high in these affluent suburbs in presidential years. Off-year races, though, show substantially lower turnout as the result of the large percentage of non-Kansans who are unfamiliar with state issues, candidates, and parties.

Like Douglas County, Colorado (chap. 3), Johnson County shows relatively little geographic isolation of its ethnic minority population from whites (see table 4.6). Hispanics and Asians are themselves very affluent, and their numbers are small. Map 4.9 shows that many tracts in the southern part of the county contain both migrant and immigrant concentrations that exceed the local mean. When considered as a two-county area, however, it is clear that the degree of spatial clustering across Johnson and Wyandotte Counties is at least as high as in Wichita (table 4.6) due largely to the sparse number of minorities in Johnson. The dissimilarity index calculated for the combined counties shows that blacks and Asians were about as segregated in 1990 as they were in 1980. Only Asians became significantly less segregated from whites from 1980 to 1990. Local reports

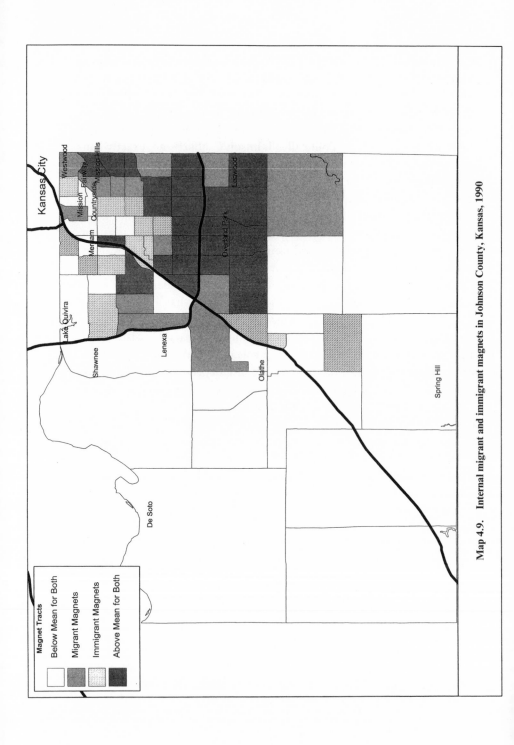

Magnet Tracts

☐ Below Mean for Both

▨ Migrant Magnets

▨ Immigrant Magnets

■ Above Mean for Both

Kansas City

Westwood
Mission
Fairway
Countryside
Mission Hills
Merriam
Leawood
Lake Quivira
Overland Park
Shawnee
Lenexa
Olathe
De Soto
Spring Hill

Map 4.9. Internal migrant and immigrant magnets in Johnson County, Kansas, 1990

suggest that blacks and other minorities are beginning to trickle into the older suburban towns of Merriam and Shawnee in the northern reaches of Johnson County. Even so, the dissimilarity index for the two-county area shows that 72 percent of blacks would have to relocate for them to be evenly distributed across the area's 150 census tracts.

Isolated and Politically Irrelevant Minorities

At a statewide level, race relations and ethnic politics have been an inconsequential part of most Kansas elections. Blacks, Hispanics, and the foreign born have not been a large enough voting population to decide many elections. Nor has the immigrant population in Kansas generated much in the way of a political backlash among natives. Locally, however, patterns of interaction among whites, blacks, Asians, and Hispanics are similar to many other places. Generalizations about ethnic politics that hold elsewhere also apply to Kansas. For example, the longer the ethnic population has been established in the community the more likely it is to be assimilated into the political life of that community. Naturalization, turnout, and political involvement by ethnic minorities are also contingent upon the racial composition of areas, with lower participation in southwestern Kansas where there is geographic isolation and low population density coupled with recent immigration streams. In areas of residential segregation and high population density, as in Kansas City, the level of interethnic interaction that exists ensures that minorities are more actively involved in politics than in the state's most rural counties.

As in Colorado and California, Republican registration growth has been strongest in areas where the migratory trends that facilitate it have worked unaffected by countervailing pressures such as the presence of a growing and active Hispanic or black community. The Kansas City and Wichita areas, characterized by upscale interstate in-migration to white suburbs and an increasing proportion of blacks and Hispanics in older city neighborhoods, are examples of locales where ethnic balkanization has generated political stratification. Wyandotte County is as monolithically one party as Johnson County. Democrats are as disadvantaged in one area as Republicans are in the other. For democratic theorists and those practicing politics in the trenches, the areal balkanization of neighborhoods, suburbs, cities, and counties in a place as white as Kansas is a subject for careful thought and further study. It reminds us of how arbitrary geographical boundaries can be and yet how important such boundaries are in determining a group's level of political engagement. Ethnic minorities may not be much of a force in Kansas politics for many years to come, but they are sure to be marginalized as long as they remain in isolated residential pockets.

CHAPTER 5

Kentucky: Biracial Balkanization

In May of 1998, the Immigration and Naturalization Service raided a tobacco company warehouse in Lexington, Kentucky, and deported 86 illegal immigrants to Mexico (Herron 1998). The following month, the mayor of Lexington announced several new policy initiatives aimed at dealing with a growing immigrant population, including new grants for providing healthcare to legal and illegal immigrants (Honeycutt 1998). The number of immigrants seeking public benefits in central Kentucky remains small by California standards, but it is growing. Why would immigrants be attracted to central Kentucky in the first place? The answer: agricultural labor. In the mid-1990s, about 8,000 Mexican workers were given temporary visas as part of a Department of Labor guest worker program. Only a few years earlier there were no immigrant laborers in Kentucky, when tobacco farmers relied exclusively on local labor markets. But the ease with which immigrants cross the border—and the low wages they will accept to work here—proved to be too great a temptation for Kentucky's tobacco producers to resist. For the near future, Kentucky's immigrant population is likely to remain small by the standards of larger states, but the state's agricultural employers are turning down the same path blazed by farmers in border states in the 1940s and 1950s.

As a Sunbelt state with the attractions of a nonunion, low-wage labor force, proximity to major national markets, and a pleasant climate, Kentucky has benefited from moderate economic growth in the last half of the twentieth century. The state's population stood at 3.7 million in 1990, up from just under 3 million in 1950. Due partly to the state's geographic isolation from the nation's major ports of entry, the population influx has not included many immigrants. By 1990, Kentucky had fewer foreign-born residents than Kansas, totaling only 34,119, less than 1 percent of the state's population. As map 5.1 shows, most of the population growth has occurred in the urban and suburban counties of central Kentucky, includ-

159

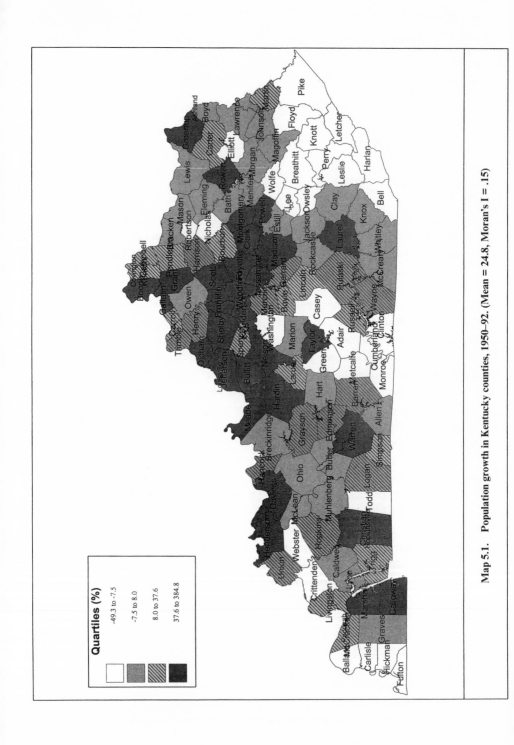

Quartiles (%)

-49.3 to -7.5

-7.5 to 8.0

8.0 to 37.6

37.6 to 384.8

Map 5.1. Population growth in Kentucky counties, 1950–92. (Mean = 24.8, Moran's I = .15)

ing those around Louisville (Jefferson, Oldham, Bullitt), Lexington (Fayette, Jessamine, Woodford), and Cincinnati, Ohio (Boone, Kenton). This area has benefited from an excellent transportation infrastructure, including proximity to the Ohio River, along which major highways and rail lines were built. Central Kentucky is also the region where immigrants have chosen to concentrate. Sixty-eight percent of the foreign-born population lives in Kentucky's metropolitan areas, and half of those live in central city neighborhoods in Louisville and Lexington-Fayette, where housing is cheapest. Mexican immigrants are increasingly recruited to work in central Kentucky's tobacco fields, taking positions once worked by migrants from the poor counties of eastern Kentucky.

Rural eastern Kentucky, part of the well-known and thoroughly studied Appalachian region, has been in a state of economic decline since the 1950s (see map 5.1). Appalachia is culturally, geographically, and economically isolated from the rest of the state (Bowman and Haynes 1963, 25–26). Mountainous terrain cuts the area off from the urban centers that surround it. As a result of its inaccessibility, eastern Kentucky's poverty is a striking contrast to the wealthy horse farms and thriving suburbs to the north and west. In 1990, this region's median income averaged only 68 percent of that in the rest of Kentucky. Thirty percent of the area's families lived below the poverty line, compared to only 15 percent in the rest of the state. These counties continue to have the highest proportion of citizens on public assistance. Not well suited to agriculture, coal mining was the backbone of the economy until midcentury when competition from better located fields and an international coal market shut down many of the mines. Since the 1940s, people have been moving out (Bowman and Haynes 1963; Schwarzweller, Brown, and Mangalam 1971; Deaton and Anschel 1974), primarily to find work in the industrial areas of southern Ohio. Aside from its poverty, the population of southeast Kentucky is noteworthy for two extraordinary traits: it is homogeneously white and certain counties have a strong Republican tradition (Jewell and Cunningham 1968; Miller and Jewell 1990). Due to out-migration, however, the region's importance in state elections has declined.

Kentucky was largely bypassed by the black migration from the Deep South to northern industrial cities in the first half of the twentieth century. The black population of the state, at 7 percent of the total population in 1990, is located in just a few counties but is most highly concentrated in Louisville, where the population is 30 percent African American. Outside of Louisville, the most notable concentration of blacks is in a rural area known at the turn of the century as "the black patch" in the southwestern counties along the Tennessee border (especially Fulton, Trigg, Christian, Todd, Logan, and Simpson Counties). While the black patch is far more white today than it was in the early 1900s, there are still significant African American concentrations there. The counties of eastern Kentucky, by contrast, have minuscule black populations.

Almost nothing has been written about Kentucky's small and still politically inert immigrant population. For most of the twentieth century low-skilled immigrants would find it difficult to compete in a state that has so much native white labor willing to work for low wages in nonunion employment (Wright 1986; Cobb 1982; Serow 1981). The reason why so much industry has decided to move to the South since World War II, namely, the search for cheap labor, has made the southern and border states unattractive destinations for low-skilled immigrants from Asia and Latin America. Only in the 1980s and 1990s have local tobacco and vegetable growers drawn on immigrant labor to work their fields. Kentucky is one of the few states where a majority of the foreign born are still Caucasian, although this has steadily fallen since the immigrant preference system was changed in 1965. Of the immigrants in the state, though, it is noteworthy that a plurality of them are Asians (see fig. 5.1), 60 percent of whom have entered the country since 1980, mostly to settle in Louisville and Lexington. Europeans are the next largest group, and they are a much older population. Mexicans remained a very small proportion of the population, numbering less than a thousand in 1990. While Kentucky is not likely to become a major immigrant destination state anytime soon, farmers and food processing industries are changing the ethnic composition of certain counties through their recruitment efforts. Newly constructed chicken-processing plants in the western part of the state are in constant search for Mexican laborers.

Until recently, the state has not received much by way of internal migrants either. Prior to the 1970s, Kentucky was a net loser of population through migration, and its growth was mostly the result of natural increase (Long 1988; Shryock 1964). In stark contrast to California, Colorado, and Florida, fully 78 percent of the population had been born in the state as late as 1990, and this figure has fallen only since 1970. Where in-migration has occurred, it is in the predictable areas where it is found in Kansas (chap. 4): in prosperous cities and suburbs and bedroom communities that often lie on the borders with other states (see map 5.2). Boone,

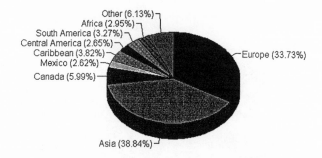

Fig. 5.1. Composition of the foreign-born population in Kentucky, 1990

Kenton, and Campbell Counties, for instance, have predictably large populations of Ohioans who have left Cincinnati for suburbia. Louisville's development has spilled over into nearby counties—Meade, Bullitt, and Oldham—which have attracted a large nonnative work force looking to settle in transitional rural-suburban neighborhoods. Hardin County's large non-Kentucky work force, like that of Leavenworth, Kansas, is entirely the result of military employment at Fort Knox.

The state's counties are racially segregated, with eastern Kentucky having few minorities. Blacks, Asians, and Hispanics are concentrated in just a few areas. Growth in the ethnic population is occurring in the Cincinnati and Louisville suburbs, in Fayette County (Lexington), and in scattered other places. Map 5.3 shows the change in the proportion of immigrants in Kentucky counties between 1980 and 1990. The spatial pattern is nearly random given the small number of immigrants attracted to Kentucky. Growth in the proportion of immigrants across the state's 120 counties has been much slower than in most other states.

While immigrants may not be much of a force behind the social and political stratification of the state, there is a strong element of partisan balkanization. Many counties lack close two-party competition due mostly to Kentucky's Democratic heritage. When a diversity index (see chap. 2, n. 1) is calculated to measure the concentration of Republicans (or Democrats), it reveals that 36 percent of Republican (or Democratic) registrants would have to move for them to be evenly distributed across the state's counties. Nearly one-third of Republican votes come from the poor mountain areas of eastern Kentucky—an area that suffers from chroni-

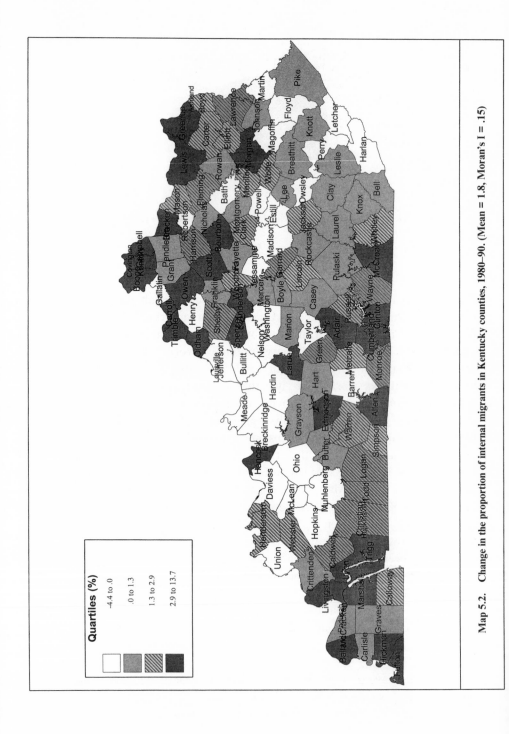

Map 5.2. Change in the proportion of internal migrants in Kentucky counties, 1980–90. (Mean = 1.8, Moran's I = .15)

Quartiles (%)

- -4.4 to .0
- .0 to 1.3
- 1.3 to 2.9
- 2.9 to 13.7

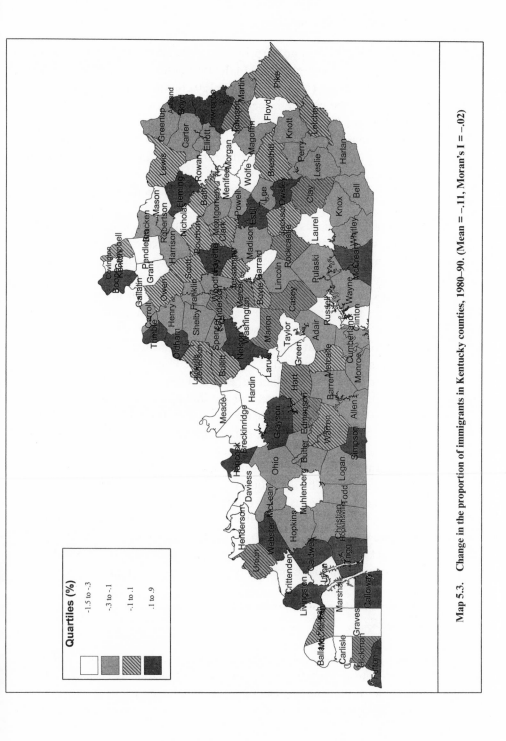

Map 5.3. Change in the proportion of immigrants in Kentucky counties, 1980–90. (Mean = –.11, Moran's I = –.02)

cally low turnout. It is no surprise that Republicans have had difficulty competing in statewide elections. In the 1991 gubernatorial race, for example, only 11 percent (13) of the state's 120 counties were two-party competitive. Eighty percent of the counties were solidly in the Democratic column, with only 8 percent going lopsidedly Republican. This segregation of ethnic groups and political party identifiers has little to do with immigration, although new internal migrants have improved Republican prospects.

The smaller the immigrant population in a state, the better off it seems to be. In Kentucky, immigrants reported higher average earnings than either internal migrants or those who were born in the state (see appendix A, table A4.1). Immigrants over the age of eighteen earned an average of $14,045 in 1989, compared to $13,823 for cross-state migrants and $10,250 for native Kentuckians. The figures for median income show that internal migrants do considerably better than either natives or immigrants. That Kentucky's native population is especially poor is not surprising. Rural Kentucky is known for its low standard of living. What is different about this border state is that immigrants fare well by a variety of different standards. Immigrant respondents in the Public Use Microdata Sample had higher levels of education than either internal migrants or natives. As for racial characteristics, 57 percent of the immigrants in Kentucky in 1990 were non-Hispanic whites (table A5.1). Immigration will change the ethnic complexion of the state because natives and internal migrants are likely to be white, but this change will occur at a far slower pace than in states such as California or Florida with their far higher proportion of Hispanic and Asian newcomers. The selection process that determines where migrants and immigrants settle has made Kentucky an outpost for a relatively small number of well-educated and affluent immigrants, a majority of whom in 1990 were white. Because they have been so small in number, immigrants in Kentucky have not faced the level of discrimination and the same barriers to assimilation that more conspicuous immigrant communities face.

Settlement Patterns of Migrants and Immigrants in Kentucky

Because the population of immigrants to Kentucky is so small, it is worthwhile to consider whether any immigrant population is becoming more noticeable. Following the examples set out in the previous chapters, I model the change in a group's *proportion* of the population, rather than its actual numerical growth, from 1980 to 1990. In Kansas, Colorado, and California, the Mexican population was growing and becoming more concentrated. In Kentucky, however, the evidence in table 5.1 shows that none of the immigrant groups became a more significant presence relative to the rest of the population between 1980 and 1990. Indeed, the opposite occurred: Africans, Europeans, Canadians, Mexicans, and South Americans, became considerably less noticeable than they were in earlier times because the size of their communities was shrinking relative to the rest of the population. In some places, the *number* of immigrants has increased, but population growth from internal sources and natural increase has made these groups a smaller *proportion* of the population than they were in previous decades.

The state of the local employment market early in the decade is not clearly related to an immigrant group's changing concentration except in the instance of Africans—their presence shrank in areas where joblessness was high in the early 1980s. Increasing income in an area is associated with growth in the proportion of Europeans and Mexicans but not with any other group. Population density, reflecting the appeal of urban areas, is significantly associated with growth in the proportion of Asians and Canadians but not with any other group (see table 5.1). Apparently, émigrés from most parts of the world are becoming a smaller proportion of the population in the state's larger cities because growth in the native population has outpaced the growth of these foreign-born groups. Given the rather low appeal of Kentucky as a place to find low-skill immigrant work opportunities, some immigrant groups are growing merely as a function of their attendance or employment at the state's colleges and universities (see table 5.1). Finally, the spatially lagged dependent variable indicates positive spatial dependency in the growth pattern of U.S. internal migrants and South American immigrants and negative spatial dependency for Mexicans. Growth is occurring across county boundaries or in adjacent county clusters for both U.S. migrants and South Americans. For Mexicans, though, the growth is more concentrated within isolated counties than across groups of counties.

Kentucky's immigration flows suggest that if the state is balkanized by ethnicity and race, immigrants are not contributing significantly to that stratification. It is important to underscore the fact that internal migration has been a force for change in the most urban areas of the state but that many immigrants are a declining presence in such places. Of course, in most cities immigrants are becoming less noticeable, and many jurisdic-

TABLE 5.1. Influences on Population Concentration in Kentucky Counties, 1980–90

Variable	U.S. Migrants	African Immigrants	Asian Immigrants	European Immigrants	Canadian Immigrants	Mexican Immigrants	Central American Immigrants	South American Immigrants
% 1980 group population	-.05	-1.00**	.04	-.27**	-.88**	-.46**	-.05	-.24**
	(.03)	(.02)	(.10)	(.03)	(.06)	(.11)	(.08)	(.08)
% unemployment, 1980	-.12	-.002**	-.007	-.001	-.001	.0007	-.002	-.0005
	(.09)	(.001)	(.008)	(.004)	(.002)	(.001)	(.002)	(.001)
Change in real median family income, 1980–90	.15	-.001	.002	.009*	.001	.006**	.003	-.006
	(.09)	(.001)	(.002)	(.005)	(.01)	(.002)	(.003)	(.004)
% net population change	.03	.0005	.003	.0003	.0006	-.0004	-.0003	.0003
	(.03)	(.0003)	(.003)	(.001)	(.001)	(.0004)	(.001)	(.0003)
Population density	-.002**	-.00002**	.00009**	.00001	.0002**	-.00004	-.00001	.00001
	(.0006)	(.00001)	(.00005)	(.00006)	(.00001)	(.00004)	(.00003)	(.000005)
% college students	-.09	.003**	.007	-.003	.004**	.002**	.0005	-.00004
	(.07)	(.001)	(.007)	(.003)	(.001)	(.001)	(.002)	(.001)
Spatial lag	.32*	.03	-.18	.08	-.02	-.71**	-.08	.69**
	(.19)	(.03)	(.21)	(.17)	(.08)	(.15)	(.27)	(.22)
Constant	3.12	.04	.04	.06	.02	-.003	.03	1.00
N	120	120	120	120	120	120	120	120
R^2_a	.18	.96	.11	.42	.61	.33	.06	.13

Note: Spatial autoregressive model, weighted for population; income is expressed in thousands of constant 1992 dollars; dependent variable = change in population group as a percentage of total population. For a full description of variables, see appendix A.
*$p < .10$.   **$p < .05$.

tions report having no immigrants at all. But these differences in the migratory flows of internal migrants and immigrants do suggest a path toward greater ethnic balkanization of the kind found in populous port of entry states. As of the 1990s, however, Kentucky's ethnic composition was still pronouncedly biracial, and segregation by county, city, and neighborhood was a function of white and black attitudes.

Ethnic Balkanization and Naturalization Rates in Kentucky

Immigration may be coming to Kentucky belatedly, but other aspects of population mobility clearly help explain residential settlement patterns within Kentucky jurisdictions. The isolation of minorities from whites is related to the size of the minority groups and to the percentage of residents who have moved in from outside the state. Segregation is not only the consequence of white flight or out-migration. It is the consequence of in-migration as well, as the selection process brings white upper income settlers into the state who then choose to reside in neighborhoods that are inaccessible to lower income groups.

In other chapters we have observed that the concentration and isolation of immigrant groups within states depress naturalization rates. In this manner, the residential separation of newly arriving immigrants from the native born has an adverse impact on the assimilation of the former (Lieberson 1961). This might not be true of a state such as Kentucky given that true immigrant enclaves are hard to find. While the immigrant population is drawn to just a few places in the state, these concentrations are too small to bear much of a relationship to naturalization rates. Surprisingly, though, when put to the test even this state's rather modest concentrations of immigrants are associated with low levels of citizenship (see appendix A, table A5.2). For 1980, in particular, a 1 percentage point increase in the proportion of immigrants across counties drops the naturalization rate about 4.7 points. Even in a state where immigrant concentrations are modest at best, the same relationship holds between the size of the immigrant population in an area and the propensity to naturalize. Asian and Hispanic segregation from whites within counties also contributes to lower naturalization rates, although multicollinearity in the model has undermined the statistical significance of the coefficient estimates. In 1990, naturalization rates are highest in the most densely populated areas of the state and in places where the general population is poorly educated. These results reflect the fact that the older, more established immigrant population is found in Kentucky's urban areas and in places that have been less attractive to more recent immigrants, who are slower to naturalize.

Migrants, Immigrants, and Voter Turnout in Kentucky

Places in Kentucky, as in other border and southern states, are highly stratified in their political behavior (Miller and Jewell 1990). Much of the time, race and poverty are blamed for differences in turnout across the state, but mobility is also relevant. The presence of non-Kentucky natives in an area decreases participation. Map 5.4 shows average turnout rates in Kentucky counties for the 1991 and 1995 gubernatorial elections. There is an obvious difference between the high-turnout counties in north-central Kentucky and the low participation of the rural eastern and southern counties. The object of the analysis in table 5.2 is to provide an account of this variability in turnout. In Kansas (chap. 4), the presence of out-of-state residents in the eastern part of the state was associated with lower turnout, especially in state-level elections. In Kentucky, the same pattern is observable, although it is not always statistically significant once related variables (such as education) are included in the model (table 5.2). Still, it is no accident that in the 1979, 1983, 1991, and 1995 gubernatorial contests, turnout was lower in those areas with the most out-of-state migrants. For the presidential contests of 1980 and 1992, turnout is positively related to the proportion of out-of-state migrants. The reasoning behind the disparate patterns for presidential and state contests is the same as in chapter 4. For newcomers, especially those who commute to jobs across state borders, Kentucky state politics is not likely to be a burning issue. Presidential elections, though, are of much higher salience across the country and will generate high participation as much, if not more, among the highly educated newcomers as among natives (Miller and Jewell 1990, 279–80).

Another noteworthy pattern is that areas with large black populations are apparently far more active than those with predominantly white populations. In the pooled results, a 1 point increase in the percentage of black residents in a county is associated with a .14 increase in the participation of registered voters (see table 5.2). This is contrary, of course, to the usual individual-level findings, which show blacks to have lower participation rates than whites. In the Kentucky context, however, the very low turnout in the poor white counties of eastern Kentucky explains this bizarre pat-

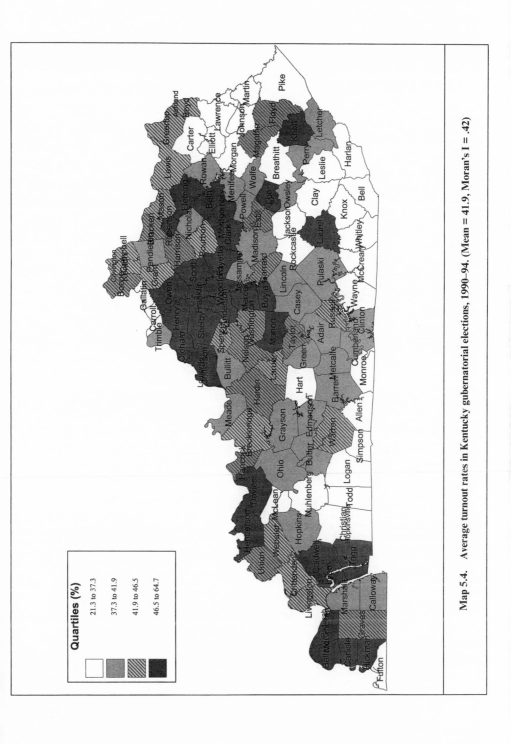

Quartiles (%)

21.3 to 37.3

37.3 to 41.9

41.9 to 46.5

46.5 to 64.7

Map 5.4.   Average turnout rates in Kentucky gubernatorial elections, 1990–94. (Mean = 41.9, Moran's I = .42)

TABLE 5.2. Impact of Population Mobility on Voter Turnout in Kentucky Counties, 1979–95

Variable	1979	1980	1983	1991	1992	1995	Pooled 1990s
% college educated	1.15**	.60*	.68**	.60**	.34**	.71**	.54**
	(.37)	(.36)	(.28)	(.19)	(.09)	(.11)	(.08)
Isolation of minorities from whites (within counties)	-.04	-.01	.008	-.01	-.002	.006	-.004
	(.03)	(.03)	(.02)	(.03)	(.01)	(.02)	(.01)
% born out of state	-.31**	.05	-.08	-.11	.02	-.08	-.05
	(.14)	(.14)	(.11)	(.09)	(.05)	(.06)	(.04)
% post-1970 immigrants	5.34	1.39	2.25	-1.81*	-.75	-2.57**	-1.77**
	(3.50)	(3.48)	(2.61)	(2.00)	(1.00)	(1.21)	(.87)
% black	.008	.17	-.13	.22	.07	.10	.14**
	(.20)	(.20)	(.16)	(.17)	(.08)	(.10)	(.07)
Population density	.0003	.001	.005**	.002	.004**	-.002*	.001
	(.002)	(.002)	(.002)	(.002)	(.001)	(.001)	(.001)
Spatial lag	.22*	.31**	.57**	.40**	.61**	.62**	.54**
	(.13)	(.15)	(.11)	(.13)	(.09)	(.09)	(.06)
Presidential race	—	—	—	—	—	—	8.26**
							(1.16)
Constant	44.44	43.11	19.57	22.30	18.91	11.07	15.35
N	105	105	120	105	105	105	360
R^2_a	.18	.22	.55	.45	.78	.61	.81

$*p < .10.$ $**p < .05.$

tern. It is not uncommon for turnout in rural Kentucky counties to run 10 to 12 points behind those of the Louisville and Lexington metropolitan areas, where much of the black population is concentrated.

The immigrant population is so uniformly small that it is not likely to have much influence on turnout patterns aggregated at the county level. Even so, after 1983 the proportion of recently arriving immigrants is negatively associated with participation. In the pooled model for the 1990s, a one-point increase in the proportion of recent immigrants drops participation a substantial 1.8 percent.

High levels of political participation are an important sign that citizens are engaged with their political system. This state's counties are obviously cleaved according to their level of interest in politics. Kentucky's participation patterns show a separation between high and low turnout areas that corresponds to familiar class patterns in American politics. Counties with some combination of high education and income have higher turnout rates than poor areas with low educational attainment. Because the poor white areas of rural Kentucky are often inactive, there is less of a racial component to the political stratification of places than in other states. In gubernatorial contests in off years, the state's turnout patterns are also separable between locales with many out-of-state migrants and those with few. This corresponds to the individual-level finding that migrants have difficulty getting involved in the political system once they have moved. Aside from barriers to reregistration, local parties and candidates may have a difficult time getting the non-Kentuckians interested in local politics. In presidential contests, turnout is higher in the cities, where minorities are concentrated, and lower in the rural white areas.

The spatially lagged turnout variable is included in the models in table 5.2 to account for the possibility that the participation rates of places are related to the participation rates of areas nearby. In every instance, the observations show a highly significant pattern of positive spatial dependency. Turnout in Kentucky is not stratified by county as much as it is by region, with groups of adjacent counties displaying similar turnout rates.

The implications of these spatial patterns of participation are not trivial. Kentucky's poor rural areas wind up underrepresented relative to the urban areas of the state in presidential contests. In 1992, for instance, turnout in the most rural counties in the state ran twelve points behind the most urban counties. In state-level contests, fast-growing counties are underrepresented relative to areas with higher proportions of natives. Established residents have probably always voted in higher numbers than newcomers, but state government and policy are important to all residents regardless of their tenure. The net effect of weak turnout in southeastern Kentucky's Republican counties, and among residents new to the state who have imported Republican affiliations, is to reduce Republican voting margins in these areas. Of course, many Democratic registrants regularly abandon their party affiliation to support Republican candidates, but this occurs far less often in state-level contests than in presidential ones. By the year 2000, Republicans had not held the state's governorship since 1967 and the state legislature was controlled by overwhelming Democratic majorities.

Migrants, Immigrants, and Party Regularity in Kentucky

As in previous chapters, party regularity refers to the extent to which an area's voting can be predicted from the balance of its Democratic and Republican Party registrants. Its relevance to this discussion is that it is an indicator of the volatility of an electorate and the durability of its underlying partisan attachments. Those areas where party voting neatly matches the balance of registrants are said to be regular. These relatively regular locations are pictured by the lightly shaded areas in map 5.5 for two gubernatorial races in the early 1990s. Party irregularity is pronounced in Kentucky, where as many as 40 points separates party registration from voting in the darkly shaded counties. To explain the variation described by map 5.5, I model party irregularity as a function of the variables in table 5.3. Several consistent and statistically significant results stand out in the table. First, places with highly educated populations are more irregular in their behavior than those with less well educated populations. In 1980, for example, a 10 point increase in the percentage of residents with a college degree was associated with a 5.8 point rise in the difference between party registration and actual gubernatorial voting across counties. In 1995, the effect was even greater and still significant. This is an unusual finding because education is often associated with high-turnout elections. High-turnout elections, in turn, generate electoral margins that are usually closely related to the balance of party registrants.

To understand why Kentucky is different, a closer examination of the observations is in order. A useful comparison is that of impoverished Pike and Letcher Counties in southeastern Kentucky, on the one hand, and Boone County, near Cincinnati, on the other (see map 5.5). Pike and Letcher, with the highest poverty rates in the state, saw George Bush run

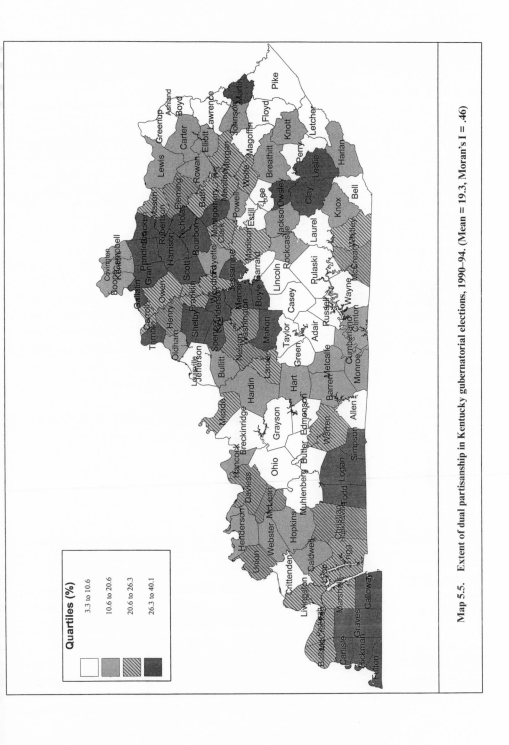

Quartiles (%)

3.3 to 10.6
10.6 to 20.6
20.6 to 26.3
26.3 to 40.1

Map 5.5. Extent of dual partisanship in Kentucky gubernatorial elections, 1990–94. (Mean = 19.3, Moran's I = .46)

TABLE 5.3. Similarity of Party Registration to Party Voting in Kentucky Counties, 1979–95

Variable	1979	1980	1983	1991	1992	1995	Pooled 1990s
% college educated	.58**	.38	.18	.26	.43**	.84**	.48**
	(.35)	(.37)	(.34)	(.18)	(.16)	(.21)	(.11)
% born out of state	-.04	.19	.09	.04	.19**	.09	.10*
	(.13)	(.15)	(.12)	(.09)	(.08)	(.10)	(.06)
% post-1970 immigrants	-1.74	-2.47	1.53	-4.27**	-8.32**	-9.26**	-7.23**
	(3.30)	(3.52)	(3.10)	(1.92)	(1.76)	(2.04)	(1.12)
% black	-.09	.17	.02	.45**	.61**	.58**	.51**
	(.19)	(.21)	(.18)	(.17)	(.16)	(.18)	(.10)
Population density	-.01**	-.01**	-.007**	-.009**	-.01**	-.01**	-.01
	(.002)	(.002)	(.002)	(.002)	(.002)	(.002)	(.001)
Turnout	-.05	-.20**	.25**	-.09	-.02	-.05	-.05
	(.09)	(.10)	(.10)	(.09)	(.14)	(.14)	(.06)
Spatial lag	.71**	.68**	.75**	.47**	.64**	.74**	.72**
	(.11)	(.09)	(.11)	(.11)	(.10)	(.08)	(.05)
Presidential race	—	—	—	—	—	—	1.05
							(1.31)
Constant	7.27	-10.01	-10.53	9.16	1.03	-.91	1.22
N	120	120	120	120	120	120	360
R^2_a	.43	.46	.36	.44	.56	.60	.57

Note: Spatial autoregressive model, weighted for population; dependent variable = Abs (% Republican vote – %Republican registration); high positive values indicate counties where voting differed from registration. See appendix A for a full description of variables.
*$p < .10$.   **$p < .05$.

about ten points ahead of what a strict party line vote would have predicted, although he lost both counties. In Boone County (suburban Cincinnati), an area with a far better educated population, Bush ran eighteen points ahead of Republican registration, winning a majority of the vote (52.2 percent) in a three-way contest. In both poor and wealthy counties, Republicans did better than their registration figures would have predicted, but the counties with the highly educated migrants, including Boone, were far more likely to abandon traditional party cues. This finding is clearly consistent with the individual-level study conducted by Thad Brown (1988), which showed that voters are more likely to abandon party labels when they have relocated than when they have remained in the same place.

The GOP is usually capable of winning the state's presidential vote, but Republicans have had consistent difficulty in statewide races (Miller and Jewell 1990, 291–93). With few exceptions, areas of high population density are more consistent in the aggregate than rural areas are because rural counties are more likely to be one-party strongholds, usually Democratic, where Republicans are an attractive choice because rural Democrats are more conservative (297, 307). In all six elections, increasing population density is associated with a propensity to vote in line with party registration. In the most urban areas, Republicans and Democrats more evenly divide the electorate (Miller and Jewell 1990). There was only a 3 percent difference between Republican registration and voting in Jefferson County (Louisville) in the 1991 gubernatorial contest.

In locales with high proportions of black voters, the balance of party registrants bears little resemblance to voting outcomes (table 5.3). In 1991, for example, a 10 point increase in the proportion of black residents across counties is associated with a corresponding 4.5 point increase in the gap between party registration and the party vote. This result can be best understood by both the low turnout of black voters in statewide elections and the correspondingly high turnout of white voters in areas of black concentration. The Democratic candidate in 1991, Brereton Jones, won an overwhelming victory over a scandal-tainted opponent, Larry Hopkins, who mustered only 35 percent of the total vote. But in the counties where there was a large black population, such as Logan, Todd, Christian, and Fulton in southwestern Kentucky (see map 5.5), Hopkins did far better than Republican registration figures would have predicted. Again, in 1992, George Bush won a plurality in heavily black Christian County (Hop-

kinsville), with 47.5 percent of the vote, even though Republican registrants constituted a mere 15 percent of the electorate there.

In counties where black voters participate in high numbers, they boost
party irregularity by making these places less Republican than party registration would predict. Major turnout efforts in Louisville funded by
Washington-based groups in 1995 ensured a narrow Democratic victory in
the governors' race when the tide was running in the Republican candidate's favor. Jefferson County's Republican percentage of the vote ran
thirteen points below its Republican registration that year. Blacks have
rarely played this decisive a role in Kentucky elections. As Penny Miller
and Malcolm Jewell have indicated, Kentucky is a Democratic state, but it
is also one characterized by low turnout (1990). The dismal participation
rates of Democrats sometimes makes Republicans far more competitive
than they would be otherwise. This is why high turnout is generally associated with party regularity in table 5.3, although the association between
high turnout and regular party voting is still weaker than in Kansas and
other states.

**Migrants, Immigrants, and Changes in Party
Registration in Kentucky**

Republicans improved their share of party registrants in the state by a
slight 2 percent from 1980 to 1990, bouncing back from losses during the
1970s. The improvement is associated with strong population growth
across more areas of the state during the 1980s than in the 1970s. Internal
migration from other states to Kentucky is associated with lower turnout,
but it is also associated with improved Republican registration shares
according to the findings in table 5.4. From 1970 to 1980, and again from
1980 to 1990, Republican registration grew as a proportion of total registration in those counties with a rising tide of out-of-state migrants. Map
5.6 shows where the GOP made its most dramatic gains during the 1980s.
Gains were particularly significant in suburban Louisville and Cincinnati,
in Lexington (Fayette County), and in a cluster of rural counties in southeastern Kentucky directly north of Knoxville, Tennessee. In places where
population growth was especially low, as in the easternmost counties, the
proportion of GOP registrants declined.

Net population growth, a variable I did not include in table 5.4, is also
associated with Republican growth, especially in the latter period. In
Boone County, for example, just across the Ohio River from Cincinnati,

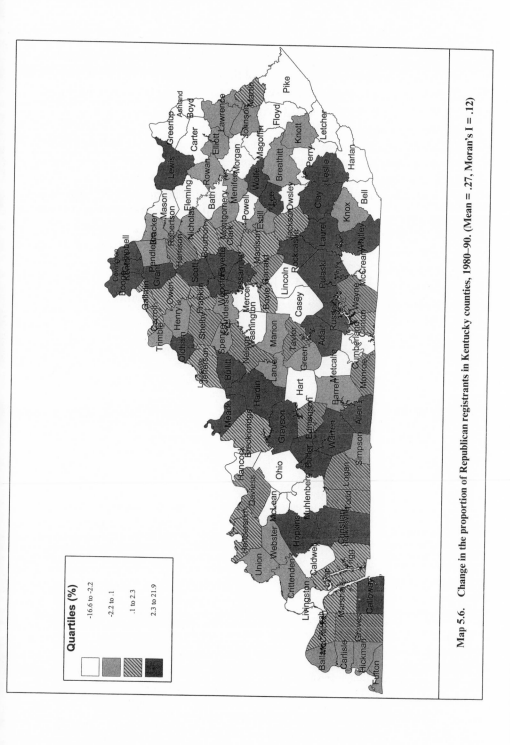

Quartiles (%)

☐ -16.6 to -2.2
▨ -2.2 to .1
▨ .1 to 2.3
▨ 2.3 to 21.9

Map 5.6.   Change in the proportion of Republican registrants in Kentucky counties, 1980–90. (Mean = .27, Moran's I = .12)

the population grew by 30 percent during the 1980s, and Republicans finished the decade with one-third of the registered voters, up from only 23 percent in 1980. Similarly, in suburban Louisville (Oldham County) population growth contributed to a six-point rise in the share of Republican registrants during the 1980s.

The variation in GOP growth across Kentucky does bear some relation to the concentration of the foreign-born population (table 5.4). Places that had a large proportion of immigrants in the early 1980s saw their share of GOP registration rise significantly. The precise relationship in exploratory scatterplots is nonlinear. Republican registration growth rises quickly when immigrants are from zero to 1 percent of a county's population, then it levels off once immigrants reach a threshold of 1 to 2 percent. The data are consistent with the notion that once the foreign-born population reaches a threshold it begins to restrain Republican growth. One should not be convinced that the relationship of immigrant concentrations

TABLE 5.4.   Impact of Population Mobility on Changes in Republican Party Registration in Kentucky Counties, 1970–80, 1980–90

Variable	1970–80	1980–90
% born out of state, 1970 (1980)	.15[a]	–.06
	(.13)	(.07)
Change in % born out of state	.06	.63**
	(.15)	(.14)
% foreign born, 1970 (1980)	–1.98	3.04**
	(3.14)	(.87)
Change in % foreign born	.14	.82
	(2.09)	(1.03)
% Republican registrants, 1970 (1980)	–.10**	.01
	(.03)	(.02)
Population density	–.004**	–.001
	(.001)	(.001)
Spatial lag	.27	.28**
	(.17)	(.14)
Constant	–.84	–1.17
N	120	120
R^2_a	.22	.24

Note: Spatial autoregressive model, weighted for population; dependent variable = change in Republican Party registration. See appendix A for a full description of variables.
[a]Indicates low tolerances and high standard errors due to multicollinearity.
*p < .10.   **p < .05.

to Republican registration growth at the county level signifies anything causal at the individual level. The connection could be entirely spurious given the small number of immigrants in Kentucky. But the relationship does not disappear when related variables, such as population density and percentage African American, are included.

The association between increasing numbers of out-of-state migrants and improved Republican prospects is clearly consistent with the theoretical considerations laid out in chapter 1 as well as the findings in other chapters. Those who can afford to move are upwardly mobile and able to finance the costs associated with relocation. They most often seek to relocate in middle and upper income communities, particularly in suburbs. Although Kentucky seems to be following this pattern, Republican growth from out-of-state sources has not contributed to Republican victories in many local elections. This is probably the consequence of low turnout in these communities (see table 5.2). Even well-educated, upper-income migrants may take time to develop an interest in local affairs and reregister to vote. And, while Kentucky's patterns of population growth are clearly benefiting the Republicans, the GOP is starting from a sizable deficit. By 1994, the average county was composed of 68 percent registered Democrats and only 29 percent Republicans. Sustained growth will be required to bring Republicans into a truly competitive position vis-à-vis the Democrats locally. At the statewide level, the Republicans are fortunate that they have gained considerable ground in the heavily populated suburban and urban counties, where 2 or 3 percent growth is enough to overcome the Democratic bias of many sparsely populated areas of the state.

Ethnicity and Political Behavior at the Individual Level

The aggregate-level findings show a pattern of development common to states in the South. Republicans are taking ahold of the region's burgeoning suburbs. There is still a legacy of the one-party-dominated rural jurisdictions described so clearly in V. O. Key's *Southern Politics* (1949) in reference to other states, but usually these places have resisted political change because they are remote and untouched by demographic change. As a biracial state, where even the black population is a small minority, immigration has not had any sweeping consequences. Whatever political changes have taken place in the state, they have been the result of the conversion of long-time residents and the in-migration of non-Kentuckians.

Survey data that would accurately identify the partisan leanings of Kentuckians are scarce due to the scheduling of gubernatorial races in off years when networks do very little political polling. A 1995 poll conducted by the University of Kentucky's Survey Research Center is of some help. By selecting only those respondents who reported voting in the 1995 gubernatorial race, I have tried to render the responses in this poll comparable to the VRS exit polls reported in table 5.5. The polling figures do show that there are major differences between off-year and on-year elections as to who shows up to vote. In 1990, only 18.8 percent of the white voters surveyed leaving the voting booth claimed to be Democrats. More than half of the white voters that year were Republicans, in spite of the Democrats' lopsided two to one registration edge statewide. In presidential election years like 1992 and highly salient gubernatorial contests like the one in 1995, however, the true colors of the Kentucky electorate emerge. The Republican share of the white electorate drops and the Democratic share jumps to at least half. The number of reported independents also drops off from 1990 to 1992 and 1995.

For black voters, too, judging from the figures reported in table 5.5, low turnout in off-year elections gives Republicans an edge relative to their actual registration figures. In presidential election years, however, the black vote is at least two-thirds Democratic, and 19 percent Republican. The small number of Hispanics sampled makes conclusions drawn from

TABLE 5.5.   Party Identification by Race/Ethnicity in Kentucky Elections, 1990–92

Race/Ethnic Group	Year	Democrat	Independent	Republican
White	1990	18.8	26.8	54.4
	1992	49.3	14.3	36.4
	1995	55.6	11.2	33.2
Black	1990	30.2	22.3	47.5
	1992	67.8	13.6	18.6
	1995	76.5	11.8	11.8
Hispanic	1990	24.3	41.3	34.5
	1992	65.7	0.0	34.1
	1995	—	—	—

Source: Voter Research and Surveys, General Election Exit Polls, 1990–92; University of Kentucky Survey Research Center 1995 Poll.

Note: Figures for Asians are not included since so few were polled. The 1995 poll includes only those respondents who reported voting in the 1995 election.

table 5.5 highly tentative, but the pattern is similar to that of blacks. In highly salient elections, the Hispanic vote is solidly Democratic.

As for party regularity, the aggregate results in table 5.3 indicated a relationship between urbanization and a propensity to vote according to one's party identification. In the 1992 U.S. Senate race, the VRS exit polls reveal that voters were more likely to cast ballots contrary to their party identification in rural eastern and western Kentucky than in either the Lexington or Louisville areas. This confirms the results in the aggregate data showing that densely populated areas are more regular in their political behavior than the rural ones (see table 5.3). This pattern occurs not simply because the cities and suburbs are more evenly divided in their party registration than the one-party-oriented rural counties. The causes of party irregularity in rural areas are mostly a function of the ideological leaning of rural Kentucky Democrats. Conservative Democrats are often attracted to Republican candidates, particularly in national elections (Miller and Jewell 1990). By contrast, urban Democrats, like those elsewhere in the country, are more likely to be liberal and less inclined to vote for Republicans.

Other findings from the 1995 survey suggest that voters with a shorter duration of residence in the state are less likely to vote Democratic or identify with the Democratic Party (controlling, of course, for the age of the respondent). This would correspond to the findings of Petrocik (1987) and Wolfinger and Arsenau (1978), who have pointed out that the Republican realignment in the South can be attributed to the arrival of new voters as well as the conversion of natives. While the questions on the University of Kentucky survey do not permit detailed proof of generalizations made at the aggregate level, these results do support the idea that as Kentucky's out-of-state population increases Republican prospects will improve.

At the aggregate level, there is an ongoing sorting process in Kentucky that will segment the state into pockets of interest and behavior even as it slowly betters GOP prospects for winning office. Areas of population growth in central Kentucky are showing signs of Republican strength, regardless of the precise microlevel interactions that are generating the growth. High-income areas with well-educated populations in central Kentucky show higher turnout rates than poor areas in the rural east and west. This means that the politically competitive and highly populated areas of central Kentucky will continue to dominate in state and national elections.

Political Change and the Internal Composition of
Kentucky Counties

The argument I have been making about populations and politics has tried
to clear a place for discussions of economic and ethnic stratification across
space as a factor to consider in evaluating an area's political development.
Given the prominence of race in the history of southern and border states,
Kentucky presents a particularly good case for understanding the role that
residential segregation may play in influencing patterns of participation
and electoral change. Kentucky has only two racial groups of any political
consequence: whites and African Americans. So Kentucky provides a
good setting for evaluating communities that have not been touched by
noticeable waves of immigrants but have varying proportions of blacks.

Given the high salience of race in American politics, I have hypothesized that areas in which there is considerable spatial isolation of white
from minority voters will see lower levels of political activism. The results
in table 5.2, predicting turnout levels across the state, are only weakly consistent with this idea. Residential isolation of whites from minorities has a
generally negative impact on countywide participation rates, although it is
not statistically significant here. It is education, more than race or residential segregation, that stratifies the state by its propensity to participate. Segregation does not appear to matter because participation in Kentucky is so
uniformly low. Even many white voters with deep roots in the state fail to
turn out. This fact strongly suggests that Kentucky is politically stratified
by socioeconomic status more than race. The Hispanic and Asian populations are sufficiently small that measures of residential segregation for these
populations are not likely to affect overall turnout rates. Even so, the
activism of minority groups in Kentucky benefits the Democratic rather
than the Republican Party in general elections, so the segregation of white
from black voters should benefit the GOP after controlling for the size of
the black population. By contrast, in areas where the black and white populations are more integrated, the contact hypothesis predicts that the level
of political activism among both populations will be much higher.

I investigated several areas in Kentucky and calculated a dissimilarity
index for the racial concentration of population groups for each area's census tracts. For comparison purposes, the dissimilarity coefficient was also
calculated for the entire state (table 5.6). The most urban county in the state
is included, Jefferson (Louisville), along with the Cincinnati suburbs
(Boone, Kenton, and Campbell Counties), a four-county rural area in

TABLE 5.6. Index of Dissimilarity for the Black, Asian, and Hispanic Populations Relative to Whites in Kentucky Counties, 1980 and 1990, by Census Tract

Variable	Kentucky		Cincinnati Suburbs		Jefferson		Christian		Southeast Kentucky	
	1980	1990	1980	1990	1980	1990	1980	1990	1980	1990
Asians	.50	.50	.34	.33	.34	.35	.56	.44	.38	.50
Blacks	.64	.64	.76	.67	.76	.71	.45	.42	.54	.58
Hispanics	.38	.27	.25	.24	.24	.23	.54	.54	.18	.27
N	995	995	77	77	178	178	15	15	31	31

Source: U.S. Census 1990, and author's calculations.
Note: Figures represent the percentage of each group that would have to move in order for the group to be evenly distributed across all census tracts.

Appalachia comprised of Leslie, Harlan, Perry, and Letcher Counties, and finally Christian County on the Tennessee border in the west (See map 5.1).

Together these places cover a variety of demographic settings and conditions. The eastern Kentucky counties have experienced notable population losses over the last thirty years and net out-migration. In three of the four counties, Republican prospects have faded with the population loss. Only in Leslie County, the strongest Republican county in the area, have Republicans enlarged their share of the electorate in the face of economic decline. Further north, directly across the Ohio River from Cincinnati, lie three prosperous counties where Republicans have expanded their share of the electorate substantially, corresponding to a growing suburban population. In central Kentucky, Jefferson County is home to the state's largest city, Louisville. Jefferson has seen very little Republican growth. Finally, in western Kentucky, Christian County (Hopkinsville), with a large black population, enjoyed modest Republican growth throughout the decade.

Can the internal composition of these counties help explain patterns of electoral competition, participation, and political change? The dissimilarity index (table 5.6) shows that, as in other parts of the nation, the black population is the most highly segregated from white voters in three of the four areas. Segregation is especially pronounced in Louisville and the Cincinnati suburbs and slightly less so in the rural counties. Indeed, the small Hispanic and Asian populations are more segregated than blacks in Christian County, one of the few areas in the country where that is the case. Hispanics in Kentucky are also less segregated than Asians. More noticeable populations are easier targets for discrimination, and by 1990 Hispanics had not yet relocated to Kentucky in sufficient numbers to produce a widespread political reaction.

Northern Kentucky

The three Cincinnati suburban counties are not clearly a part of the state. Cincinnati media dominate the airwaves. People read Cincinnati-based papers, the *Kentucky Post* and the *Enquirer*. Because the Kentucky suburbs provide better access to the downtown business district than the Ohio suburbs, many Ohioans have chosen to relocate there. Historically immigrants to the other parts of Kentucky were primarily Protestants from southern states, but northern Kentucky's settlers were like those in Cincinnati, Catholics of Irish and German ancestry. The only Kentucky governor to be elected from this part of the state was assassinated in 1900 on the day of his inauguration, and his German ancestry may have contributed to his becoming a target (Reis 1994).

Since the Civil War, northern Kentucky has always been more Democratic than southwest Ohio. When President Franklin Roosevelt provided funds to build the Cincinnati airport, he sent the project to Boone County rather than Ohio since the Kentucky delegation in Congress was solidly Democratic, while the Ohio side was Republican. What Roosevelt did not know at the time was that the airport would fuel the economic development that would change the political character of Cincinnati's Kentucky suburbs. In the 1980s, the area was transformed by industrial parks and corporate relocations. The airport became a major hub for Delta Airlines. Other corporations, such as the Heinz food company and Fidelity Investments relocated their headquarters to northern Kentucky. By the mid-1990s, these counties had been inundated with upwardly mobile, white collar workers who had moved in from elsewhere: Atlanta, Dallas, the West Coast, and other parts of Kentucky. The population influx caused by the expansion of white collar employment has eroded the hold of the Democratic Party on the electorate and elected office. Republican registration has soared in all three counties. Whereas Republican Party identification was once stigmatized, Republicans are now highly competitive. In 1986, major league baseball player Jim Bunning won the area's congressional seat running as a Republican, and his subsequent election to the U.S. Senate was based on the loyal support of northern Kentuckians.

The prosperity of the Cincinnati suburbs has left the established black population isolated in the older towns of Covington and Newport. These contain the lowest income neighborhoods in the region, and they were originally segregated by law. With desegregation, established black neighborhoods remained black but grew poorer as black professional workers moved elsewhere. In Covington, home to the largest black neighborhoods, there have been frequent ethnic tensions, hostility toward the police, and racist incidents, including vandalism of black-owned property and intimidation of black residents. Blacks are politically active but in an irregular manner, often depending on whether there is a black candidate running. They have occasionally elected city council and school board members in Covington, but the population is still small and easy to ignore in county-wide politics. There are wide income disparities between the older and newer suburbs in northern Kentucky. New internal migrants drawn by white collar employment move to the newer developments further from Covington to live in neighborhoods with low crime, low poverty rates, and predominantly white schools. Immigrants have fared well in northern Kentucky compared to native blacks. While blacks remain clustered in older neighborhoods near Cincinnati, immigrants have shown some propensity to migrate to outlying tracts in wealthier areas (map 5.7). The internal migrants have imported Republican Party identification and attitudes, but reportedly they have been slow to develop a stake in their communities. In Edgewood, the city administration converted the fire department from a volunteer to a paid force mainly because newcomers refused to volunteer. Typically the new residents oppose further development, including the construction of multifamily housing (DeVroomen 1995).

The gravitational pull of Cincinnati has given this area a distinctive culture, which has separated it from the rest of the state and gradually watered down Democratic influence. Although black political weakness and growing GOP strength in this area is more a function of the small size of the black population than its segregation from whites, it is fair to say that segregation has played a role in denying this population the opportunity to influence elections outside the rather small area that has been conceded by whites as black territory. Segregation also denies blacks the opportunity to take advantage of economic opportunities that stimulate upward mobility, leading to greater civic and political involvement.

Louisville and Jefferson County

In contrast to rapidly changing northern Kentucky, Jefferson County's population has been stagnant since the 1970s and Democrats have maintained a solid registration edge and an iron grip on local offices. Unlike northern Kentucky, Louisville has not attracted white collar employment. The city is less industrial now than it was at midcentury, but the transition to a service economy has mostly generated lower paying and/or part-time jobs. United Parcel Service, for example, employed nearly 13,000 people in the mid-1990s at its major air transit hub, but many were part timers, including students and local residents who worked more than one job. The relative population stability has meant that Kentucky's Democratic tradition has not been eroded here, and Republican operatives confess to simply trying to minimize their losses. Louisville's Democrats are far more reluctant than elsewhere in the state to abandon their fundamental party cues. Labor union sympathies are stronger in Louisville than in other parts of the state, and much of Kentucky's black population is concentrated here. Democrats in Louisville act very much like Democrats in liberal northern cities.

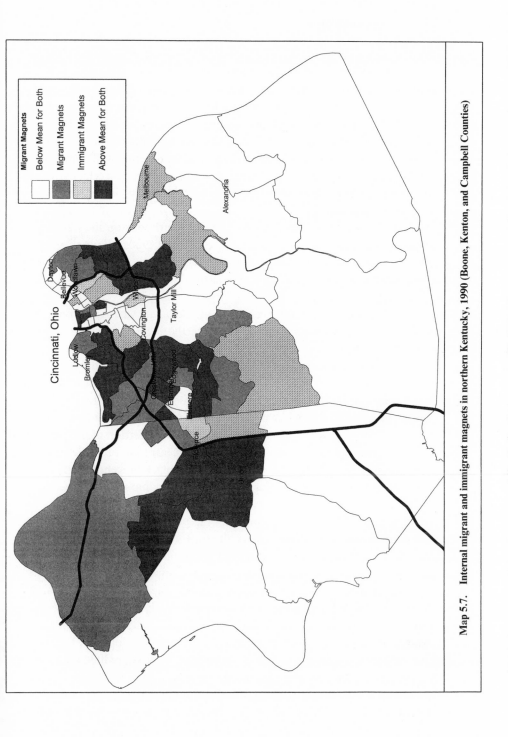

Migrant Magnets

Below Mean for Both

Migrant Magnets

Immigrant Magnets

Above Mean for Both

Cincinnati, Ohio

Dayton
Bellevue
Woodlawn
Melbourne
Ludlow
Bromley
Covington
Wilder
Taylor Mill
Glassy... Hills
Elsmere Edgewood
Elsmere
Florence
Alexandria
Dr. ... rt

Map 5.7. Internal migrant and immigrant magnets in northern Kentucky, 1990 (Boone, Kenton, and Campbell Counties)

Louisville's population dynamics have followed a familiar northern pattern. Blacks are a larger proportion of the population since whites have fled. Immigrants have only a small presence here, but they show a capacity to penetrate the suburbs that blacks do not. The darkly shaded areas in map 5.8 show tracts where the population of both internal migrants and immigrants is above the local mean. The most dramatic pattern of balkanization on the map is not the separation between migrant and immigrant tracts but the separation of both migrant and immigrant tracts from tracts where native Kentuckians predominate (the tracts shaded in white). There is a pronounced east versus west split in the pattern of growth from population mobility. Once middle-class white neighborhoods on the west side of the city became black enclaves in the 1950s and 1960s. While there are many white natives in the southern part of the city and county, white newcomers from outside the state flooded eastward toward the dark gray areas on map 5.8.

White flight could have been far worse than it was. An important development in the history of the city was the local response to court ordered busing in 1975. Upon receiving the order to integrate, the city merged its school system with that of Jefferson County. The entire county was then forced to integrate its schools, and that left many white residents with fewer places (outside of private or parochial schools) to flee. The effect is that Louisville's white population was more likely to stay put than in cities like St. Louis, where integration led to the desertion of the city by white residents (Teaford 1997). The spatial concentration of blacks in certain areas of Louisville has led to the election of black officeholders but no mayor. By the mid-1990s, four of the twelve aldermanic seats were held by blacks, and all twelve of the seats were Democratic.

The rise of black influence in statewide politics has been a relatively recent development. For many years, the state's one-party tradition meant that the Democratic Party did not need to mobilize the black vote to win elections. As Republicans have become more competitive, the predictably Democratic black vote has become more valuable to party leaders and candidates. In the 1995 gubernatorial contest, Washington-based interest groups poured money into mobilizing the black vote in Louisville to ensure a Democratic victory in a hard fought race. The lopsided Democratic inclination of black voters in Louisville was widely credited for electing the governor by a slight 22,000 vote margin.

Compared to white precincts, voter turnout in the black community is still low (Wright 1995), and the high value of the black community in most

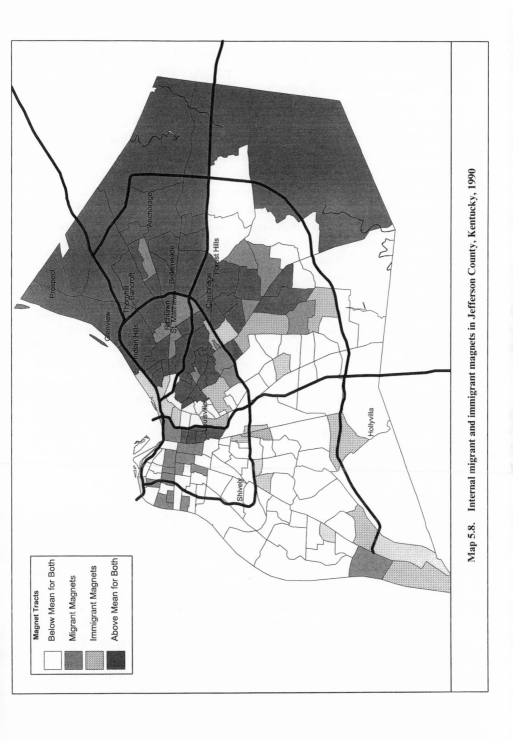

Map 5.8. Internal migrant and immigrant magnets in Jefferson County, Kentucky, 1990

Magnet Tracts

Below Mean for Both

Migrant Magnets

Immigrant Magnets

Above Mean for Both

Prospect

Glenview

Indian Hills

Thornhill

Bancroft

Anchorage

Richlawn

St. Matthews

Bellemeade

Cambridge

Forest Hills

Louisville

Shively

Hollyvilla

elections comes with its predictability more than its actual turnout. In local elections, turnout by black voters isn't important at all since the county is monolithically one party. There is no need to sift a black neighborhood for loyal partisans in the way most white neighborhoods must be sifted. As we have learned, in many areas of Kentucky Democratic registrants are not truly Democratic in their behavior. This irregularity raises the cost of party mobilization efforts and complicates the task of turning out favorable voters. Democratic strategists face no such difficulties when they look at Louisville's black wards.

Table 5.6 shows that blacks are more segregated in Jefferson County than in any of the other Kentucky counties evaluated. As elsewhere, it is the geographic isolation of African American from white areas that has contributed to the economic disadvantage of the black community as well as its political cohesion. The density of the population mitigates spatial segregation to some degree, but the concentration of blacks in just a few areas ensures that the value of their votes is only realized in statewide contests where their predictability may be of some value to the Democrats in a closely contested race. Locally, however, general elections have been far less competitive and there is little need for black input at the polls. In local primaries, black Democrats have run racially oriented campaigns seeking to represent black interests (Wright 1995). This has inhibited construction of the kind of cross-racial coalitions that have successfully elected black and Hispanic mayors in other cities. Residential segregation has thus contributed to both low levels of turnout and a special interest politics that alienates white voters.

Christian County and Western Kentucky
Christian County is home to Fort Campbell, the home of the U.S. Army's elite 101st Airborne Division and some of the best trained and well-educated soldiers in the military. Fort Campbell and the local economy have been joined at the hip since the base opened in 1941. Soldiers live off the base in Hopkinsville and other towns, and many return at the end of their careers to retire there. Politically the military population is as conservative as the native white population, and the area votes strongly Republican in presidential contests. The state legislators from this area, though, are all Democrats, giving rise to the contention that voters in southwest Kentucky are dual partisans—Republicans at the presidential level but Democrats locally (Miller and Jewell 1990, 297, 309–10).

In contrast to this large population of migrants is the native black population, about 25 percent of the total in 1990, which is clustered in the highly segregated city of Hopkinsville. The segregation of the black population dates to the antebellum period when the local populace was divided between southern planters and slaveholders in the south end of the county and nonslaveholding Union sympathizers north of Hopkinsville. Officially the state remained neutral during the Civil War, but Kentuckians from Christian County fought on both sides. In the postbellum period, the county gradually went Democratic, and the New Deal created a one-party county as Republican blacks switched parties and the Roosevelt administration established several major public works projects in the region.

Harry Truman's vice president, Alben Barkley, was a native of western Kentucky, and the older generation can still remember his powerful presence. In 1980, only 11 percent of the population was registered as Republican. Since that time, population growth from outside Kentucky, the generational replacement of older voters with younger ones, and the slow conversion of natives has contributed to improved Republican prospects. By the fall of 1995, Republican registration stood at 17 percent of the electorate. As the model for party change suggests (table 5.4), outsiders have contributed to Republican growth. Mitsubishi Motors has located a plant there, bringing in white professionals with GOP sympathies. But migration is not the only factor changing the county's political complexion. Older Democrats have died. The younger voters do not remember the issues that made this region the Democratic stronghold that it was during the 1940s and 1950s. Considerable Democratic support was won through the New Deal's provision of federal public works projects in counties nearby. Old-fashioned Democratic pork-barreling disappeared with the federal budgetary crises of the 1980s and 1990s.

Here, as elsewhere in the state, the high level of segregation (table 5.6) between the black and white communities is a symptom of the quiet racism that persists. White attitudes have led to an equally high level of political stratification, as the black areas of the county are far less likely to abandon their Democratic partisanship than the white areas are. In 1992, George Bush did some thirty-two points better than strict Republican Party registration would have predicted, but this was mainly because conservative whites turned out in force while many blacks stayed home. As in Louisville, residential segregation has also devalued black votes except in the very closest races where their turnout can make a difference for the Democrats. Mostly, though, black turnout levels are very low. The population is poor, not well informed, and often divided in the Democratic primary. Black churches are the focus of political mobilization, but these churches are often rivals for position and influence rather than unified in coordinated political efforts.

Appalachian Kentucky

Eastern Kentucky is a world away from the rest of the state. The counties in this region are typically one-party strongholds of either Republican or Democratic inclination. There are few black voters, no towns of substantial size, and the rural population is evenly dispersed across thirty-six counties that abut and straddle the Appalachian mountains. Rural, poor, and uneducated, with extended kinship networks, politics has very little substance and old traditions die hard. The Democratic counties were originally tied to coal mining, and the United Mine Workers Union is still a powerful influence in the more mountainous counties. Republican Party affiliation dominates where there is no labor union tradition and the families are predominantly Baptist. Family traditions are important, and parents pass their partisanship down to their children. Stories are told of Democratic fathers-in-law who make their Republican daughters-in-law convert so that their grandchildren will grow up in a Democratic household. There is an economic caste system that keeps upward mobility to a minimum. Stigmas are inherited and sustained through extensive informal relationships (Schwarzweller, Brown, and Mangalam 1971; Duncan 1992). The son of a banker is likely to become a banker. The son of a bricklayer is likely to become a bricklayer. It is difficult to overcome the disadvantages of a bad family name. "Those from poor families are least likely to have either the reputation or political connections necessary to find steady work in this social structure" (Duncan 1992, 111). This rigid stratification promotes societal stability, as class and party traditions do not fade quickly.

Industry has not been attracted to this area. The terrain prevents development, as plants and factories cannot be located easily in the rugged hill country (Bowman and Haynes 1963). People do leave to find work, and the population has declined across the entire region (see map 5.1). The population loss occurs among the younger generations, which would be most likely to develop alternative political views and traditions. The elderly population stays behind, and this promotes stability in the balance of partisanship. Partisan change due to generational replacement occurs far more slowly than change due to conversion or migration (Green and Schickler 1996).

Patronage politics has not died out in rural Kentucky as it has elsewhere (Miller and Jewell 1990, 31; Duncan 1992). The scarcity of jobs gives public officials with a few patronage slots a degree of power almost unheard of in the 1990s. Voter turnout in Appalachia is a function of "vote hauling"—paying a few locals a small premium to drive voters to the polls. Since people are poor, the cost of hiring vote haulers is modest. Cultivating the support of key families can also pay off on election day. Locals indicate that having the active support of a family member is often enough to win a hundred or more votes. Even so, turnout in these counties is considerably lower than elsewhere in the state. Through the early 1990s, the percentage participating in the thirty-six counties of eastern Kentucky averaged nine to eleven points lower than in the remaining counties.

The four counties of Appalachian Kentucky depicted in Map 5.9 are politically heterogeneous in spite of their uniform poverty and population loss. Leslie County is perhaps the most Republican in the entire state. By 1995, fully 77 percent of its population were registered GOP supporters. The other three counties are nearly as Democratic as Leslie is Republican. Comparisons from the 1980s and 1990s suggest that while there is no significant difference in family income, the Republican counties do have slightly stronger economic bases with more jobs in manufacturing and lower unemployment rates. Map 5.9 shows that there are virtually no blacks in Leslie County, suggesting that its homogeneous white population may be one explanation for its Republican record. In this four-county area, the black population, averaging 1.8 percent across census tracts, is too small to be of much political consequence. In only three block groups does the black population exceed 10 percent. In recent years, race relations have been peaceful, something locals attribute to the shared history of hardscrabble poverty and the trust built between blacks and whites working side by side in the coal mines (Associated Press 1995). Race relations have not always been so placid. Hazard (in Perry County) was home to the state's last public lynching. The black population originally migrated there to work in the mines, where they were often recruited to forestall unionization by white workers in the late nineteenth and early twentieth centuries (Bailey 1985). By the mid-1980s, the black population had declined to less than 10 percent throughout eastern Kentucky (Turner and Cabbell 1985; Turner 1985). Those who remain are aged, unschooled, and politically lethargic (Turner 1985; Cabbell 1985; Billings 1974). They are also highly segregated, especially in Harlan County, although not as much so as in more densely populated areas where their proportion of the popula-

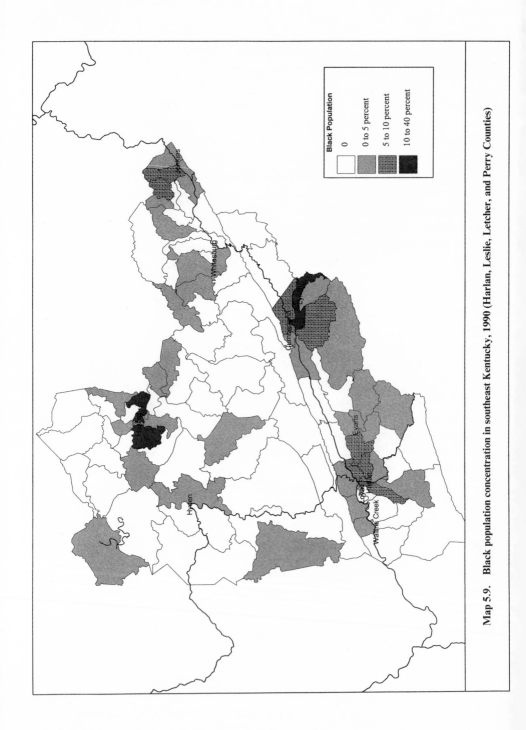

Map 5.9. Black population concentration in southeast Kentucky, 1990 (Harlan, Leslie, Letcher, and Perry Counties)

Black Population

0

0 to 5 percent

5 to 10 percent

10 to 40 percent

tion is much higher (Marshall and Jiobu 1975; see table 5.6). Their isolation and small numbers have served to keep the black population even poorer and more inactive than the white population.

It is difficult to detect any equilibration process occurring in the counties of eastern Kentucky that would eventually restore two-party competitive politics. The population is growing older, which may lead to some eventual change. But generational replacement has not contributed to much partisan change because younger voters who might stand a chance of developing political attitudes and beliefs independent of those of their parents leave the area. Population loss leaves behind the elderly and the poor—groups that are highly averse to risk taking and new patterns of life and thought. This area provides an interesting contrast to the faster growing parts of the country. What happens to the politics of places afflicted with out-migration? Eastern Kentucky shows us that their population ages and the politics becomes even more resistant to change. Places like Harlan County remain isolated from the social and economic changes that have occurred elsewhere in the country. With no infusion of business capital on the horizon, the population is as dependent on government aid as it has been since the mid-1960s. For years, the government has been subsidizing people to remain in areas that, were it not for the government's intervention, many of them would probably leave. Locals insist that people remain in eastern Kentucky because they choose to stay. "They like the familiarity and safety of their small towns. They are afraid of big-city life, the traffic, the noise, the pace, the crime," said one local observer. The population there will continue to age and shrink, and with the help of its ubiquitous extended family ties its politics is likely to remain in the same New Deal mold.

Biracial Balkanization and Isolated One Partyism

Kentucky is a good example of a state that is ethnically and politically balkanized without immigrants. The immigrant population was still so small in the early 1990s that Asians and Hispanics were not a major force even when they were politically active. This is the only state of the seven investigated in this book in which Asians are more spatially segregated than Hispanics. The Hispanic population declined between 1980 and 1990. While Mexican immigrants appear to be an increasingly important source of labor for central Kentucky's tobacco fields and several new poultry plants in western Kentucky, they are still migrants with almost no permanent communities. Kentucky's balkanization is similar to that of many other rural, interior states, which have remained largely unaffected by the many immigrants who have arrived since the late 1960s. The state and its counties are not balkanized between native and immigrant areas, as in California, but in an older, more familiar pattern of segregated black and white communities. While Kentucky had few slaveholders, a majority of Kentuckians had strong southern sympathies. These remain and contribute to the climate of separation.

Of the seven states examined in this study, Kentucky contains the one rural region that has undergone the most out-migration, as the population in the rural eastern counties has declined. The isolation of Appalachia from the rest of the state has reinforced a long-standing class divide between poor, rural, native whites and blacks and their wealthier cousins in the larger cities of central and western Kentucky. This divide has a generational component, as the younger generation leaves the mountain country behind and the older folks remain. These geopolitical aspects of Kentucky's development are not diminishing. In the 1980s and 1990s, population trends highlight rather than obscure the differences between eastern, central, northern, and western Kentucky.

Settlement patterns contribute to the political activity of a group and the nature of the demands it makes. While observers have occasionally pointed out that Kentucky's black population would get further by pursuing a deracialized politics (Wright 1995), the spatial isolation of that population from the majority in the cities has ensured that demands will be voiced in the terms of black interests and concerns. With few other minorities in Kentucky's cities and towns, the opportunity to form interracial coalitions with other minorities is slim to none. But because black communities are so highly homogeneous and spatially clustered, the pressure on a politician to represent only that constituency overwhelms sentiment favoring a broader, nonracial orientation.

Elsewhere, in the rural areas of the state, the segregation of white from black communities closely tracks class differences, with blacks being far poorer and less educated than whites, far less mobile and less interested in political affairs. The plight of blacks in Appalachia is likely to worsen. Their spatial isolation from better labor markets in Kentucky, Ohio, North Carolina, and Tennessee aggravates the problem of their unemployment (Milne 1980). For blacks in Louisville, Covington, and other large towns, the degree of segregation is mitigated somewhat by the density of settlement and the shorter distance between home and job leads.

Not coincidentally, it is in the cities that a higher value is placed on political activity.

The political power of Kentucky's black population has also been hindered by its isolation in traditionally one-party Democratic municipalities and counties, in a traditionally one-party state, where its voice only counts in the occasional close election. The 1995 gubernatorial race signaled the end of the state's long tradition of noncompetitive gubernatorial contests, but close elections at the local level are likely to remain rare, as Kentucky's one-party localities seem to generate interest only in primaries. Local Democratic primaries often split the black community among rival candidates, dampening enthusiasm for the eventual nominee, who everyone knows is likely to win by an overwhelming margin anyway. Of course, the political stratification of Kentucky is optimal for its incumbent politicians, each one of which develops a separate, monopolistic sphere of operation (Key 1949, 79–80). Voters, though, wind up cheated, as one-party factionalism is poorly suited to recruiting quality leaders or sustaining a program of action (Key 1949, 304, 308). Fortunately, the one-party system has eroded in presidential and congressional elections, as white voters have abandoned their sworn Democratic affiliations in exchange for dual partisanship. While population growth in northern and central Kentucky is likely to generate partisan change well into the twenty-first century, it is likely to be many years before dual partisanship leads to competitive elections on a routine and widespread basis.

CHAPTER 6

Florida: Segregated Heterogeneity

In 1949, V. O. Key observed of Florida with characteristic understatement that there is "plausibly a relation between a diverse, recently transplanted population and mutable politics" (86). One could hardly expect politics in a state whose population has quadrupled in forty years to be unaffected by such amazing growth. Because of its highly mobile population, Florida never had the consistent anchorage to old-fashioned Democratic politics that other southern states had (Key 1949; Dauer 1972). The sources of growth include both immigration and internal migration. A major port of entry for immigrants since the 1960s, and a haven for elderly retirees and warm weather seekers, the flood of new residents has radically reshaped the state's electoral foundations. Not one of the state's sixty-seven counties lost population from 1950 to 1992, and several South Florida counties are now twenty times the size they were in the early 1950s. Map 6.1 shows that the state's most rapid growth has occurred in South Florida, including Broward, Collier, Lee, Charlotte, and Sarasota Counties. Central Florida counties have also experienced high growth, including several along the Gulf Coast and Brevard County on the Atlantic. The slowest growing areas are in northern Florida and the panhandle. These counties contain high proportions of native Floridians and most resemble the Old South.

By 1990, 13 percent of the state's population was comprised of immigrants and 71 percent of those had entered the country since 1965. The composition of the state's immigrant population shows a heavy Latin American–Caribbean influence (fig. 6.1). Fully 43 percent of the immigrant population is from the Caribbean, with two-thirds coming from Cuba and another 12 percent from Haiti. Seventeen percent of the immigrant population is from South or Central America, and this proportion is growing. European and Canadian immigrants, many of whom are retirees, are another significant group, amounting to 22 percent of the total. Asians

200

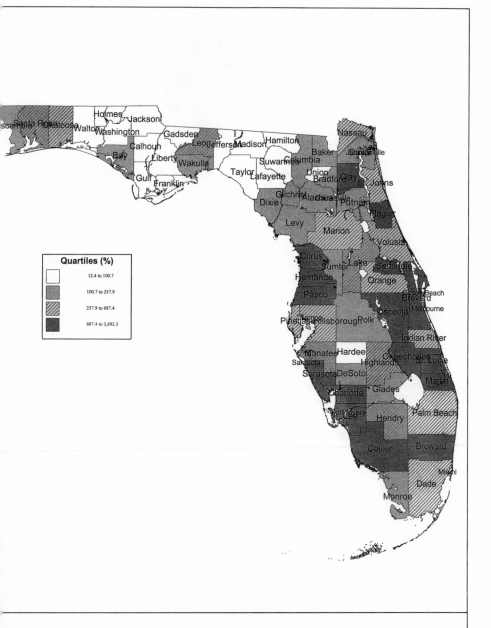

Map 6.1. Population growth in Florida counties, 1950–92. (Mean = 480.2, Moran's I = .35)

Quartiles (%)

- 12.4 to 100.7
- 100.7 to 237.9
- 237.9 to 687.4
- 687.4 to 2,682.3

Escambia Santa Rosa Okaloosa Walton Holmes Jackson Washington Gadsden Leon Jefferson Madison Hamilton Nassau Calhoun Liberty Wakulla Bay Gulf Franklin Taylor Lafayette Suwannee Columbia Baker Duval Jacksonville Union Bradford Clay St. Johns Gilchrist Alachua Gainesville Putnam Dixie Levy Marion Flagler Volusia Citrus Sumter Lake Seminole Hernando Orange Pasco Cocoa Beach Brevard Osceola Melbourne Pinellas Hillsborough Polk Indian River Manatee Hardee Okeechobee St. Lucie Sarasota Highlands Martin Sarasota DeSoto Glades Charlotte Fort Myers Lee Hendry Palm Beach Collier Broward Miami Dade Monroe

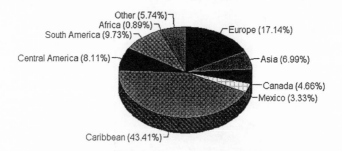

Fig. 6.1.   Composition of the foreign-born population in Florida, 1990

are a growing presence (7 percent in 1990), with especially large populations of Indians, Filipinos, and Vietnamese (Bouvier, Leonard, and Martin 1994). Contrary to settlement patterns in other states, immigrants from Spanish-speaking countries and the Caribbean are far more likely to reside in Florida's central cities than those from Asia or other world regions. As elsewhere, Mexicans are the most rural immigrant population from Latin America. In 1990, just 1 percent of Florida's Cuban population lived in rural areas, compared to 27 percent for Mexicans. The geographical pattern of Mexican settlement reflects the agricultural origins of that population (Aguirre, Schwirian, and LaGreca 1980, 52).

South Florida's population growth on both sides of the peninsula is a function of both internal migration and immigration. Immigrants predominantly settle in the Atlantic Coast counties, particularly in Dade and Broward (Miami and Fort Lauderdale). Internal migrants constitute a larger share of the population on the Gulf Coast than on the eastern side, and a majority of them come from midwestern and southern states (Winsberg 1993).

The bulk of the foreign-born arrivals are Cubans, who fled the Castro regime in two massive waves, the first in 1959, the second with the Mariel boatlift in 1980. Cubans originally settled in South Florida mostly because it was close to Cuba, other Cubans had already settled there, and many hoped to one day return (Portes and Mozo 1985; Garcia 1996; Portes and Rumbaut 1990, 114–15). Naturalization rates among the initial wave of Cubans exiles was very low, but vastly increased over time as the likelihood of an overthrow of the Castro regime diminished. Among second-generation Cubans, most of whom have never seen Cuba, the desire to return is not nearly as strong, and many among the first generation are so well established in the United States that they have lost interest in returning.

By 1990, 45 percent of the Dade County population was foreign born and 87 percent of those had entered the country since 1965—less than half of the Dade County population was born in the state. In recent years, mass migrations from Haiti, Nicaragua, Columbia, Venezuela, and other parts of South and Central America have added to Miami's international flavor and correspondingly reduced the influence of natives in the politics of the community (Mohl 1988; Dunn 1997). The mix of cultures is at once rich and volatile. Miami's explosive ethnic milieu is best described by anthropologists Alex Stepick and Guillermo Grenier—"the only U.S. city to have had four black riots in the 1980s and to receive 125,000 new immigrants at the beginning of that decade, many reputed to be criminals, homosexuals and mental patients" (1992, 1; see also Stepick, Grenier, Morris, and Draznin 1994).

Even though the population of South Florida is growing more ethnically diverse, it is not necessarily growing more *racially* diverse. Most Cubans are white, and many refuse to be identified with Hispanic groups of color. Still, the immigrant population is concentrated in the peninsula, as map 6.3 illustrates. Racially these counties are relatively homogeneous since most Cubans are white. But in ethnic terms, the counties of South Florida are the most diverse in the state.

Elsewhere in South Florida, immigrants are a smaller proportion of the population, and the new arrivals consist largely of internal migrants. Broward County is noteworthy for having a large population of Jewish migrants from New York and New Jersey, so large, in fact, that they succeeded in electing one of their own, Peter Deutsch, a Democrat, to Congress in 1992. Sarasota and Lee Counties on the Gulf Coast are also good examples of areas inundated by interstate migrants. By 1990, nearly three out of four people in these two counties had moved in from elsewhere in the United States. Between 1980 and 1990, internal migrants became a less influential presence in several South Florida counties because their growth was outstripped by that of the immigrant population. In Dade, Broward, and Palm Beach Counties, internal migrants are a smaller percentage of the population in the 1990s than they were in the past (see map 6.2) not because internal migration slowed but because immigrants constituted a much faster inflow (see map 6.3). Internal migrants became a significantly larger proportion of the population only in central and northern Florida and along the Gulf Coast, where immigrants have less of a presence. South

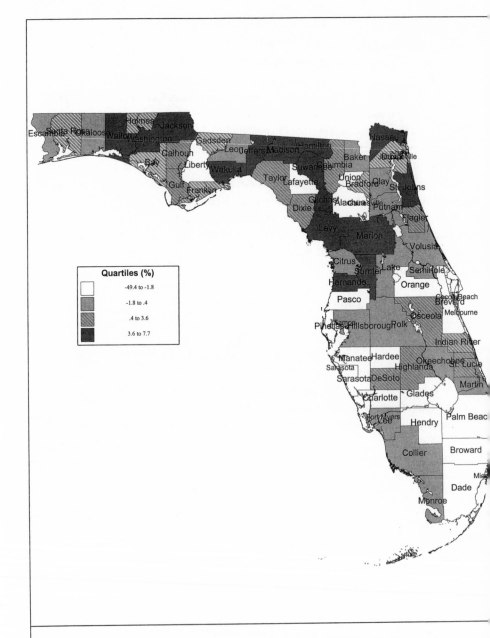

Map 6.2. Change in the proportion of internal migrants in Florida counties, 1980–90. (Mean = –.22, Moran's I = .12)

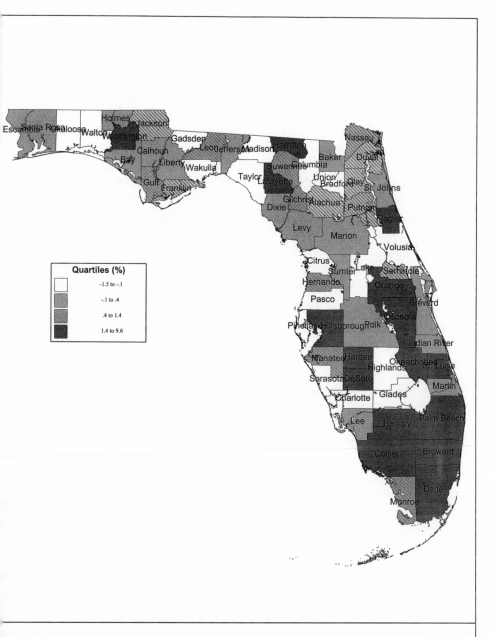

Map 6.3. Change in the proportion of immigrants in Florida counties, 1980–90. (Mean = .97, Moran's I = .12)

Florida's increasing population density has made central Florida a more attractive destination for internal migrants (see map 6.2).

Central Florida was described in the 1970s as a "giant suburbia" and a "big franchise mall," jammed with tourists, with new subdivisions and municipalities sprawling across the countryside (Dauer 1972). By the early 1990s, central Florida was suburbia on an even grander scale. Agriculture maintained an important and profitable presence, however, as large tracts of land were still occupied by citrus and vegetable growers. Most of the state's population of Mexican immigrants (55,000 in 1990) reside in central Florida near the farms. The Cuban and Asian populations are growing, but not nearly as fast as in South Florida. Central Florida has been the wealthiest and most Republican area of the state for thirty years (Dauer 1972; Bass and DeVries 1976). This region has voted presidentially Republican at least since 1948.

The northern and panhandle counties have been least transformed by the state's growth. These counties are most like the Old South; rural, uneducated, poor, and Democratic (Button 1989, 27). Several northern counties are home to large black populations, including Leon (Tallahassee), Madison, and Jefferson Counties on the Georgia border. These counties are highly residentially segregated by race, and school desegregation has been a prolonged and continuing battle (Button 1989). The economic growth in the Florida panhandle has occurred along the Gulf Coast, leaving the interior towns poor and isolated. Race- and class-based voting is particularly pronounced in northern Florida. The white population, like elsewhere in the South, is culturally conservative and prone to dual partisanship. Republicans do well in the Florida panhandle in presidential contests but less well in congressional and state elections.

Politically, the balkanization of the counties by party affiliation is far less extreme in Florida than in Kentucky (chap. 5). In Kentucky, political balkanization was a function of many one-sided Republican and Democratic counties. But in Florida more places are politically competitive, containing nearly equal numbers of GOP and Democratic registrants. By the 1990s, a comparatively low 18 percent of the Republicans (or Democrats) in the state would be required to move if partisans were to be evenly distributed across counties, compared to twice that proportion in Kentucky.

Simply because Florida's localities are more politically balanced than those in other states does not mean that the migrant, immigrant, and native populations are mixing well. The 1990 PUMS data reveal an $1,800 difference in average income between internal migrants and immigrants who are over the age of eighteen (see appendix A, table A6.1). As in California, many of the internal migrants residing in Florida are retirees. The median income figures, however, suggest that internal migrants lag behind both native Floridians and immigrants—indicating that many of the retirees are living on modest fixed incomes and that the mean income figures reflect the influence of a few super wealthy interstate migrants. Moreover, the average age of internal migrants (those over age eighteen) is fifty-one, compared to forty-eight for immigrants and a much younger thirty-nine for those born in the state. Consistent with the findings of studies cited in chapter 1, immigrants are less well educated than either internal migrants or natives, and only 28.4 percent are non-Hispanic white, compared to 89 percent of internal migrants and 68 percent of natives. Based on these racial and economic differences (table A6.1), one is led to ask how likely it is that migrants, natives, and immigrants are settling in the same locations and neighborhoods. Based on mountains of previous research on the mobility and settlement patterns of distinct ethnic and economic groups, the prospect for finding well-integrated communities in Florida are not very bright.

Settlement Patterns of Migrants and Immigrants
in Florida

Evaluating whether immigrants and internal migrants are becoming a larger proportion of the population in the areas where they settle is one way of determining the degree to which these groups are dispersing or clustering and, more importantly, of determining whether each group is becoming a more noticeable presence than in the past. Because the inflow of immigrants to Florida has been of such incredible volume, we should not be surprised to find many of these arrivals finding one another and settling down in the same neighborhoods. As in previous chapters, we should expect some groups to be drawn to preexisting populations of coethnics while others are not. Immigrants who are poorer, of color, and with limited English would be most likely to cluster in expanding ethnic enclaves. Maps 6.2 and 6.3 show the geographic distribution of growth in the internal and immigrant populations between 1980 and 1990. Table 6.1 presents the results of a spatial effects regression analysis predicting where various immigrant groups are becoming a larger or smaller proportion of the population. In Florida, as in other high-immigration states, Asians and Latin Americans cluster in ever more noticeable pockets in the areas where they

TABLE 6.1. Influences on Population Concentration in Florida Counties, 1980–90

Variable	U.S. Migrants	African Immigrants	Asian Immigrants	European Immigrants	Canadian Immigrants	Mexican Immigrants	Central American Immigrants	South American Immigrants
% 1980 group population	-.32**	-.62**	.19*	-.28**	-.21**	.65**	.36**	1.00**
	(.13)	(.11)	(.10)	(.02)	(.03)	(.27)	(.02)	(.07)
% unemployment, 1980	5.46**	-.02**	-.02	.02	.01	-.05	-.17	-.05
	(1.43)	(.004)	(.02)	(.03)	(.01)	(.05)	(.13)	(.04)
Change in real median family income, 1980–90	.008**	-.0008	.02*	.10**	.009	-.02	-.10	.05
	(.001)	(.002)	(.01)	(.02)	(.007)	(.02)	(.08)	(.03)
% net population change	-.01	.0001	.0008	.001	.0001	-.0007	-.002	-.0009
	(.06)	(.0002)	(.001)	(.001)	(.001)	(.002)	(.005)	(.002)
Population density	-.003**	.000001	.0001**	-.00004	.000004	-.00007	-.00008	.00004
	(.002)	(.000007)	(.00004)	(.00005)	(.000002)	(.00008)	(.0002)	(.00006)
% college students	-1.13**	.009**	.01*	-.0008	-.005	-.01	.03	-.03**
	(.39)	(.002)	(.009)	(.009)	(.004)	(.02)	(.03)	(.01)
Spatial lag	.43	.38**	.38**	-.12	-.10	.17*	.56**	.48**
	(.44)	(.12)	(.13)	(.08)	(.11)	(.10)	(.15)	(.16)
Constant	-46.55	.11	-.15	-.47	-.07	.62	.93	.18
N	67	67	67	67	67	67	67	67
R^2_a	.74	.45	.46	.84	.38	.21	.94	.91

Note: Multiple linear regression, WLS estimation; income coefficients expressed in thousands of 1992 dollars; dependent variable = change in population group as a percentage of total population. See appendix A for a full description of variables.

$*p < .10.$ $**p < .05.$

have settled previously. A one-point increase in the percentage of South Americans living in a county in 1980 is associated with a corresponding 1 percent increase in the proportion of that population by 1990 (see Table 6.1).

U.S. migrants, Africans, Europeans, and Canadians, on the other hand, are becoming a smaller proportion of the population in the areas where they had a strong presence in the early 1980s (table 6.1). Even where their numbers may have increased, their share of a place's total population has decreased. Since U.S. migrants, Canadians, and Europeans are not inclined to settle in enclaves, their decreasing proportions in areas of previous settlement are also an indicator of their geographical dispersion.

Economics plays a familiar role for many groups but apparently not for the bulk of U.S. internal migrants, who cluster in areas that began the decade with high unemployment. This finding can only be the result of the specific character of internal migration to Florida. Elderly retirees do not move there to find work, so the selection process behind migration is slightly different in Florida than for other states. In spite of this important difference, though, interstate migrants did become more of a presence in areas that had rising incomes across the decade. The growth in the proportion of Asians and Europeans across counties is also associated with rising income. Africans, Mexicans, and South Americans have avoided increased concentration in areas where economic opportunities were limited in the early 1980s, but their increasing presence is not associated with rising income.

Finally, population density is linked to the growing proportion of Asian immigrants but not for any of the other groups. Asians are drawn to cities—only 6 percent lived in Florida's rural areas in 1990—often to areas where there are other Asians. Internal migrants become a more noticeable population in the less densely populated suburban and rural counties. This settlement pattern reflects the growth of retirement communities throughout central Florida and along the Gulf Coast.

These results lead to one conclusion. The primary mechanism for ethnic balkanization in Florida is Latin American immigration coupled with the internal migration of elderly native-born whites. These two populations have not mixed well. When both populations pour into an area, their settlement patterns become "lumpy" or "clustered" rather than "smooth." In many areas of the state, Hispanics are more highly segregated from the white population than either blacks or Asians, and the results in table 6.1 show the reasons why. Hispanics are drawn to areas of

prior Hispanic settlement to a much greater extent than other groups. Hispanics go where their coethnics are located. Political balkanization by
partisanship would undoubtedly create many one-sided Democratic jurisdictions if so many of Florida's Hispanics were not Republican. Because
of the Republican leanings of the Cuban population, Florida is one state
where ethnic balkanization has created safe Republican seats in areas of
Hispanic concentration.

Ethnic Balkanization and Naturalization in Florida

Internal to counties, ethnic segregation is the product of both the size of
the immigrant population in an area and the lifestyle choices of internal
migrants from outside of Florida. Internal migrants make predictable
locational decisions much as immigrants do. Elderly migrants desire to
live in homogeneous communities such as Sarasota, where minorities are
excluded by the high property values and scarcity of multifamily housing
near upscale seashore developments. Segregation, whether it is deliber-
ately exclusive or simply an artifact of groups' residential choices, is of
concern because it has long been considered an obstacle to the assimilation
of immigrant and minority groups (Liang 1994; Portes and Curtis 1987;
Lieberson 1961, 1963).

Naturalization is one indicator of assimilation, albeit not the only
one. Most naturalized immigrants have no interest in returning permanently to their countries of origin once they have taken the steps necessary
to acquire citizenship. More importantly, naturalization is also the path-
way to political participation. The biggest obstacle to the political empowerment of immigrants is their noncitizen status. Obstacles to naturalization, then, are also barriers to political empowerment.

In previous chapters, we have observed that naturalization rates are
lowest in places of foreign-born concentration. Table A6.2 shows that this
is also true in Florida for both 1980 and 1990, although less so in the latter
year. For 1980, for example, a 10 point increase in the percentage of immigrants across counties is associated with a 6.9 point drop in the naturalization rate compared with a 4.1 point drop in 1990. For 1980, places
where Asians are highly segregated from whites have lower naturalization
rates than areas where Asians and whites are residentially integrated. Hispanic-white segregation has no obvious connection to naturalization rates,
perhaps because many of the Hispanics in Florida are themselves Caucasian. The magnitude of the effect varies from state to state, but a consis-

tent finding throughout this book is that the concentration of the immigrant population is not conducive to high naturalization rates.

Migrants, Immigrants, and Voter Turnout in Florida

With the tidal wave of immigrants and migrants continually washing over Florida, one would expect to see lower turnout rates than in states where the population is more stable. The path to conventional participation in politics is beset with obstacles and costs voters must overcome (Squire, Wolfinger, and Glass 1987; Rosenstone and Hansen 1993). I have pointed out in previous chapters that substate regions can frequently be divided into those with high turnout and those with low turnout. High participation areas, especially in nonpresidential election years, are typically settled by persons native to the state or at least by long-term residents. These places may also be characterized by some combination of high income and education. Low turnout areas, on the other hand, are found where the population is highly mobile or there are high numbers of poor and uneducated citizens. These aggregate-level generalizations are understandable given the individual-level relationships that have been found to hold between education, income, mobility, and participation (Rosenstone and Hansen 1993).

For Florida, patterns of turnout averaged across two gubernatorial elections in the early 1990s are shown on map 6.4. Somewhat surprising is the darkly shaded patch of central and Gulf Coast counties, which apparently have the highest turnout rates in nonpresidential elections in spite of their large and growing migrant populations. Also of note is the low participation rate in Broward County (Fort Lauderdale), home to some of the wealthiest migrants on the Atlantic Coast. To explain the geographic variation in turnout depicted on map 6.4, I estimated the same regression model corrected for spatial dependency that I used in previous chapters to evaluate turnout percentages for Florida counties in five recent elections (see table 6.2). There is very little consistency in turnout rates across the five elections. The signs on the variables change direction from year to year, making it difficult to generalize. Looking at the pooled model for the 1990s reveals that education and recent immigration are related to higher turnout, whereas the proportion of a county's population comprised of African Americans is associated with depressed turnout. Participation is also lower in the state's most densely populated urban areas.

The tendency for the presence of internal migrants to reduce partici-

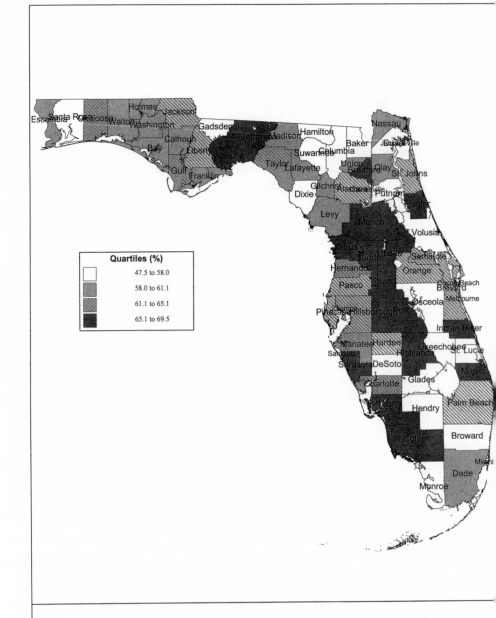

Map 6.4. Average turnout in Florida gubernatorial elections, 1990–94. (Mean = 60.9, Moran's I = –.04)

TABLE 6.2. Impact of Population Mobility on Voter Turnout in Florida Counties, 1980–94

Variable	1980	1982	1990	1992	1994	Pooled 1990s
% college educated	.08	-.23	.19	.35**	.12	.23**
	(.20)	(.21)	(.12)	(.11)	(.09)	(.08)
Isolation of minorities from whites (within counties)	.08**	.02	.005	.02	.03	.008
	(.02)	(.03)	(.04)	(.03)	(.03)	(.03)
% post-1970 immigrants	-.65**	.10	-.42**	.39**	-.03^a	.13**
	(.17)	(.12)	(.17)	(.12)	(.03)	(.06)
% born out of state	-.07	.20**	-.09^a	.11^a	.05^a	-.02
	(.07)	(.07)	(.07)	(.07)	(.06)	(.05)
% black	-.03	.05	-.36**	.24**	-.18	-.17*
	(.09)	(.10)	(.13)	(.12)	(.10)	(.09)
Population density	-.002**	-.0009	-.00009	.000002	-.0002	-.0003
	(.001)	(.001)	(.001)	(.001)	(.001)	(.001)
Spatial lag	-.06	.59**	-.29	-.17	.42**	.19**
	(.15)	(.09)	(.18)	(.11)	(.16)	(.08)
Presidential race	—	—	—	—	—	4.37**
						(.79)
Constant	73.33	8.60	82.24	53.99	84.77	47.99
N	67	67	67	67	67	201
R^2_a	.42	.74	.19	.48	.27	.17

Note: Spatial autoregressive model, weighted for population; dependent variable = percentage turnout by county. See appendix A for a full description of variables.

^{a}Variables with low tolerances and high standard errors due to multicollinearity.

*p < .10.   **p < .05.

pation is not uniform, as it is in other states, and internal migrants are associated with significantly higher turnout in 1982, 1992, and 1994. In these instances, the difference between Florida and other states is to be found in the high volume of migration nearly everywhere on the peninsula contrasted with the extreme inactivity of the electorate in the impoverished rural counties of the Florida panhandle. Unlike northern Kentucky, Florida's in-migration is not an especially recent flow, and migrants have settled in almost all of the counties in the peninsula, with a very high concentration in central Florida. In contrast to areas with more recent migration flows, many of Florida's migrants in the early 1980s were not new arrivals and were therefore well established in their communities. "The more South you go, the more North you get," is a popular saying among long-term Floridians. Many are elderly residents who have settled permanently and have the leisure time to get involved in politics (Rosenbaum and Button 1989). This has led some observers to comment that in Florida "age, not youth, is in charge" (Edmundson 1987).

A second reason for the higher turnout in migrant areas during the 1980s and 1990s is that the places with the highest proportions of native-born Floridians are in the rural, poor, and uneducated parts of the panhandle. Here turnout suffers for some of the same reasons one finds in eastern Kentucky. Voters are simply not aware that participation is important or that politics is of any concern to them. Turnout rates generally run three to five points lower in the twenty-five counties in the panhandle than in the rest of the state. The counties in central Florida have the highest participation rates, and the large, politically informed, elderly population has much to do with this (Rosenbaum and Button 1989; Weaver 1976). The relative size of the elderly population is positively associated with turnout in all but the 1992 presidential election.

Florida's foreign-born population has no consistent impact on countywide turnout across the five elections. In the pooled model, the proportion of recent immigrants in a place is associated with *higher* turnout. But in two of the three *gubernatorial* elections one finds lower turnout in the areas of immigrant concentration. These results may indicate that the newer immigrant population is more active in presidential contests than in state-level races. That the foreign-born population would be more associated with presidential than state-level participation comes as no great surprise. Cuban exiles take exceptional interest in foreign policy concerns and have developed sophisticated political organizations to navigate the waters of official Washington (Garcia 1996). Other politically active exile groups joined Cubans in South Florida in the 1980s, including Nicaraguans, Haitians, and Salvadorans. State politics is dominated by the political participation of nonimmigrant populations in central and northern Florida, whereas presidential politics is much stronger in South Florida. Throughout the 1980s and 1990s in off-year elections, the twelve southernmost counties typically turned out 44 to 45 percent of the Florida electorate, with Dade County itself accounting for about one-fourth of the state's total turnout. This participation drops, however, in off-year races by 3 to 4 percent (perhaps as many as fifty to sixty thousand votes), and central Florida and the panhandle counties therefore gain more influence.

Migrants, Immigrants, and Party Regularity in Florida

If patterns of turnout in Florida are unique, so must be the patterns of party regularity. At the county or precinct level of analysis, party irregularity can be a function of two things: (1) low turnout, which causes patterns of voting to be different from the balance of party registrants; and (2) split-ticket voting or dual partisanship, where voters are unfaithful to their party when they go to the polls. In many states, high turnout reduces the differences between party registration and actual voting. This explains why, in Florida at least, the larger proportion of out-of-state residents, the greater the party regularity. Because migrants vote at higher rates than many natives, party registration figures predict voting for major offices with considerable accuracy—far more so than in Kentucky, where migrants were responsible for departures from the predictions one could make from party registration figures. For instance, in the 1994 Florida gubernatorial race, a ten-point increase in the percentage of migrants from other states dropped the difference between registration and voting by six points (table 6.3). The difference between regular and irregular counties is captured in the contrast between places where partisanship has been transformed through long-term growth and those counties in northern Florida where partisanship is still heavily Democratic. Like rural western Kentucky, the upstate counties are often one-party Democratic but vote Republican in many elections. The counties in the peninsula, on the other hand, are more regular precisely because their electorates are more evenly divided between the parties and they consistently show up at the polls.

There are a couple of other consistent indicators of party regularity in table 6.3. Counties with high proportions of black voters are also associated with voting consistent with party registration. In the Florida case, this

TABLE 6.3. Similarity of Party Registration to Party Voting in Florida Counties, 1980–94

Variable	1980	1982	1990	1992	1994	Pooled 1990s
% college educated	-.79**	-.38**	-.12	-.31**	-.20*	-.30**
	(.29)	(.18)	(.24)	(.14)	(.12)	(.11)
% born out of state	-.35**	-.25**	-.21[a]	-.14*	-.62**	-.29**
	(.08)	(.06)	(.16)	(.08)	(.08)	(.07)
% post-1970 immigrants	.29*	-.09	-.57[a]	-.32**	-1.26**	-.09
	(.18)	(.09)	(.37)	(.17)	(.16)	(.07)
% black	-.21	-.17**	-.48*	.03	-.18	-.14
	(.14)	(.08)	(.27)	(.14)	(.14)	(.12)
Population density	-.004**	.002**	.004	.002*	-.0009	.002**
	(.001)	(.001)	(.003)	(.001)	(.001)	(.001)
% Turnout	-.11	.08	-.80**	-.19[a]	-.41**	-.24**
	(.17)	(.09)	(.25)	(.15)	(.17)	(.10)
Spatial lag	.22**	.34**	.69**	.36**	.03	.37**
	(.09)	(.08)	(.19)	(.12)	(.07)	(.08)
Presidential race	—	—	—	—	—	.46
						(1.13)
Constant	62.70	19.50	70.25	31.05	86.44	45.55
N	67	67	67	67	67	67
R_a^2	.71	.62	.45	.43	.76	.44

Note: Spatial autoregressive model, weighted for population; dependent variable = Abs (% Republican vote − %Republican registration); high positive values indicate counties where voting differed from registration. See appendix A for a full description of variables.
[a]Variables with low tolerances and high standard errors due to multicollinearity.
*p < .10.   **p < .05.

may be due to the very high proportions of blacks in some northern counties and the influence they can therefore exercise on local electoral margins. In eight northern Florida counties, blacks constitute at least one-fourth of the population, including Duval County (Jacksonville). The black vote is such a strong Democratic influence in these counties that they are often surprisingly regular in their behavior—in spite of the white inclination toward dual partisanship described in chapter 5. In Kentucky, the black population is as predictably Democratic as it is in Florida, but it is not a sizable enough population to exercise much influence on overall countywide balloting.

Migration and immigration have had some impact on both turnout and party voting in areas across Florida. Interstate migration is associated with party regularity because the out-of-state population is older and more established in Florida than it is in other states. By the early 1990s, the counties receiving the largest inundation of new residents were being filled with people who were far more inclined to participate than many of the long-term Florida natives. Hence, we also see that turnout is instrumental in reducing party irregularity in the pooled model (see table 6.3). Unlike other states, the areas of highest turnout also had the highest proportions of interstate migrants. This distinguishes Florida from, say, Kansas (chap. 4), where areas settled by internal migrants had lower rates of participation than those with stable and declining populations.

Judging from the ecological data, the effects of demographic change have not been politically neutral in Florida. While the out-of-state population in the state has not always been associated with low turnout and higher party irregularity, as it has in other states, it is safe to infer that when those cross-state migrants are newly arrived and younger, as opposed to long established and older, the usual pattern of political stratification will emerge: high migrant counties will fail to turn out while low migrant counties will participate in high percentages. In this sense, the Florida case demonstrates that there is some variation across states in the type of internal migrants a state receives. Places of high mobility in Florida are exceptional because they appear to be overrepresented in elections relative to areas of population stability. At the same time, areas of high mobility are also more predictable in their patterns of party support than areas where natives are the predominant population—partly because the turnout of new voters is so high but also because elderly migrants are not as likely as younger migrants to change their party affiliation upon relocation.

Changes in Party Registration in Florida

Unlike other states, where Republicans did poorly in the 1970s, in Florida the GOP made amazing gains in the three final decades of the twentieth century. Republican registration averaged 4 percent growth in the 1970s and nearly 10 percent from 1980 to 1990. The spatial patterns of GOP growth in the latter decade are displayed on map 6.5. Republicans made registration gains on Democrats and third parties in every county in the state. Those counties in the highest growth quartile include Dade and Monroe in South Florida and Hillsborough (Tampa) in central Florida. In the lowest growth quartile (shown in white) are the rural panhandle counties and Broward and Palm Beach in South Florida.

In the opening chapter and subsequent ones, I have argued that changes in party registration are traceable to migration and immigration. The results in table 6.4 lend support to the argument. In this table, changes in party registration from 1970 to 1980 and from 1980 and 1990 have been regressed on relevant indicators of demographic change for the same periods. The dependent variable, then, is the rate of Republican registration growth. Interstate migration from 1970 to 1980 is strongly associated with high Republican registration growth. Surprisingly, once other variables are included in the model we see that the foreign-born population has not had a dramatic impact on party registration. One would think that the growth in the Hispanic population would have had a pronounced impact on Republican registration rates given that newly naturalized Cubans in Miami were registering as Republicans by a ratio of nine to one in the mid-1980s (Mohl 1988). But the regression model in table 6.4 shows that GOP registration growth across counties is inversely related to the proportion of immigrants in a location at the beginning of each decade. Counties where natives were the predominant population in the beginning, then, proved to be the fastest growing Republican pockets ten years later.

Places that begin each decade with high proportions of Republican registrants wind up with lower GOP growth rates than counties that are one-party Democratic strongholds. The most Democratic counties, in other words, appear to be changing the most rapidly as a function of both conversion and new arrivals. Some of these counties are also very rural, so the addition of a few new residents can have a more dramatic impact on the balance of registration than would be the case in a more populated county. As areas reach an increasingly competitive balance between Republicans and Democrats, the rate of Republican growth slows. The

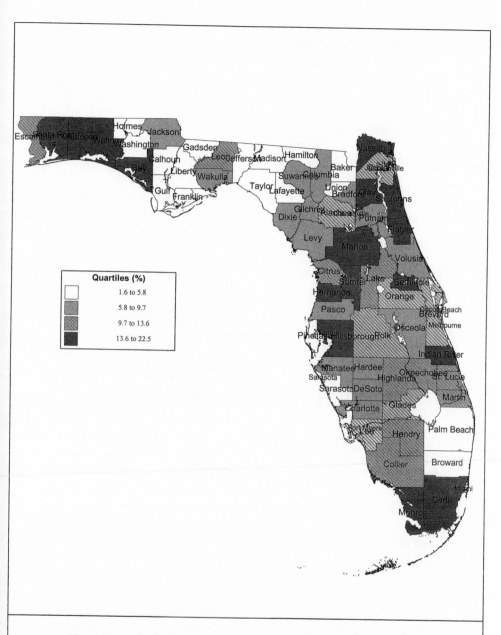

Map 6.5. Change in the proportion of Republican registrants in Florida counties, 1980–90. (Mean = 9.9, Moran's I = .45)

Quartiles (%)

1.6 to 5.8

5.8 to 9.7

9.7 to 13.6

13.6 to 22.5

TABLE 6.4.   Impact of Population Mobility on Changes in Republican Party Registration in Florida Counties, 1970–80, 1980–90

Variable	1970–80	1980–90
% born out of state, 1970 (1980)	.25**	−.07[a]
	(.09)	(.09)
Change in % born out of state	.66**	−.07[a]
	(.19)	(.24)
% foreign born, 1970 (1980)	−.19[a]	−.12[a]
	(.23)	(.38)
Change in % foreign born	.08[a]	.09
	(.69)	(.37)
% Republican registrants, 1970 (1980)	−.44**	−.02
	(.09)	(.09)
Population density	−.0006	−.002**
	(.001)	(.001)
Spatial lag	.53**	.47**
	(.14)	(.11)
Constant	−4.63	12.44
N	67	67
R^2_a	.61	.47

Note: Spatial autoregressive model, weighted for population; dependent variable = change in Republican Party registration. See appendix A for a full description of variables.
[a]Variables with low tolerances and high standard errors due to multicollinearity.
*$p < .10$.   **$p < .05$.

Democrats have not gained any ground relative to other parties, although there has been some growth in the share of independent identifiers. Finally, there is considerable evidence that party registration change has a strong regional dimension that is not explained by the other variables. In both models in table 6.4, the spatially lagged dependent variables have statistically significant coefficients (.53 and .47, respectively). GOP growth is occurring in distinct substate regions across county boundaries, particularly in central and South Florida.

While immigration has undoubtedly been influential in reshaping the politics of South Florida, internal migration has had a more direct impact on the balance of party registrants across the entire state. While many native Floridians have changed their party identification (Beck 1982), not all of the Republican growth can be accounted for by conversion alone (Parker 1988; Wolfinger and Arsenau 1978). Suzanne Parker (1988, 27) has shown that Republicans outnumbered Democrats among new residents (those migrating to the state between 1960 and 1980) by nearly two to one. In Dade County, the realignment in favor of the GOP has been greatly aided by the arrival, naturalization, and Republican inclination of Hispanic, mostly Cuban, immigrants.

Population growth and change have occurred so uniformly across the peninsula that the only area left behind by the political changes wrought by these population trends are the counties in the northern panhandle (see map 6.5). In 1994, Republican registration in twenty-five counties in Florida's panhandle averaged just 16 percent compared to 43 percent in central Florida and 28 percent in the southernmost counties. Outside of the panhandle, Florida appears to be one of the least politically balkanized states judging by the distribution of party registrants, which is nearly even in most counties. The relative absence of one-party, noncompetitive geographic areas is astounding given the state's ethnic diversity. The inability of the Democratic Party to make much headway in Dade County's Cuban neighborhoods has prevented political balkanization from following on the heels of ethnic segregation.

Ethnicity and Political Behavior at the Individual Level

The aggregate data on immigration patterns suggest that Florida's population is mainly segregated between Hispanic and non-Hispanic areas, with Hispanics, mostly Cubans, becoming larger proportions of the population in the counties where they settle. Similarly, the turnout figures show differences between immigrant and nonimmigrant areas depending on the election year. In presidential years like 1992, the counties with large immigrant populations register higher turnout than those with few immigrants. In off-year elections, however, the reverse is true. The nonimmigrant areas have higher turnout (see table 6.2). As for party regularity, the regression models show that areas with high percentages of migrants from out of state are more regular in their behavior than those with few migrants. I have suggested that this is due to the lower turnout of native populations in northern Florida and also the tendency toward dual partisanship in the panhandle. We also observed in table 6.4 that both the populations of internal migrants and Hispanics are associated with robust Republican registration growth.

Determining whether these ecological patterns reflect real differences at the individual level requires survey data. Fortunately, several Florida polls with the questions that permit such study are available. The break-down of party identification by race appears in table 6.5 for 1990, 1992, and 1994 from exit polls. There is no question that the Hispanic popula-tion is far more Republican in Florida than in most states—certainly far more so than in California (table 2.5). In the 1994 off-year elections, for example, 59 percent of the Hispanic population in Florida claimed to be Republican identifiers, compared to only 18 percent in California and 11 percent in Colorado (see table 3.5). The black population, though, is about as Democratic as it is everywhere else. The small number of Asians polled makes the figures reported for this group of questionable value, but Asians voting in the 1994 elections appeared to be far more Republican than Democratic (table 6.5).

Breaking down the survey results by region does verify that central Florida has the largest Republican bloc and the northern counties provide the most lopsided Democratic vote. There is also some evidence suggesting that, while black voters are overwhelmingly Democratic, Florida's rural blacks, most of whom are located in the northern counties, are slightly more Democratic than either suburban or urban blacks. Hispanics, on the other hand, are more Republican in the large cities and suburbs and Democratic in rural areas and small towns. Again, this pattern is the opposite of what one would find in California. It reflects the difference in the ancestry of the Hispanic population, with the Cubans in Dade County

TABLE 6.5.   Party Identification by Race in Recent Florida Elections, 1990–94

Race/Ethnic Group	Year	Democrat	Independent	Republican
White	1990	34.2	23.2	42.6
	1992	37.7	39.1	23.2
	1994	32.7	23.4	43.9
Black	1990	80.9	8.6	10.6
	1992	81.5	8.9	9.6
	1994	86.2	11.1	2.6
Hispanic	1990	30.9	13.9	55.2
	1992	32.3	42.5	25.2
	1994	27.0	14.5	58.5
Asian	1990	81.9	0.0	18.1
	1992	19.2	52.3	28.5
	1994	37.7	10.4	51.8

Source: Voter Research and Surveys, General Election Exit Polls, 1990–94 (weighted data).

being strong GOP supporters, while more rural Hispanic groups, including Mexicans, are drawn to the Democratic Party.

Results from the 1990 poll decisively demonstrate that voters moving into Florida from out of state are far more Republican than the natives. Among Florida natives, 53 percent were Democrats and only 30 percent were Republicans, with the balance claiming to be independents. Among nonnatives of short tenure (less than ten years), 34 percent were Democrats and 42 percent were Republicans. Among nonnatives of longer tenure, the figures were nearly the same: 43 percent Republican and 35 percent Democrat. Such figures confirm the results from an estimation of King's (1997) ecological inference model for the Republican registration of the out-of-state population based on county level observations. These estimates revealed that about 55 percent of the population born outside Florida were registered with the GOP in 1990, 56 percent in 1992, and 62 percent in 1994, compared with between 15 and 20 percent of the combined population of natives and immigrants. Taken together, this evidence explodes the myth that all, or even most of the partisan change in Florida, is the result of the conversion of Florida natives. Migrants were more likely than natives to vote Republican for governor in 1990, too. Retired voters, however, were slightly more Democratic than Republican, even among those who migrated to Florida to spend their final years. This suggests that it may be the migration of younger voters that is so strongly benefiting the Republican Party. Exit polls reveal that the most Republican age cohort in the early 1990s was the eighteen to thirty-five group. Finally, migration theory predicts that those who have moved to Florida would have higher incomes than those who are native to the state. Once one controls for the large number of elderly pensioners on fixed incomes, this finding holds in the polling data.

The individual-level results mostly conform to the patterns of the county-level data. Hispanics and new migrants to the state really are more likely to be Republican than Democratic identifiers. The Republican Party in Florida is far more ethnically heterogeneous than it is in most states. We can infer from the polling data that the inflow of new U.S. internal migrants to Florida has bolstered Republican prospects but that these new Republicans are not necessarily the elderly, who are more Democratic than Republican. The northern counties, which have been least affected by migration and immigration, are far more Democratic in party identification and voting than the rest of the state, especially central Florida. Because of the high volume of migration, Florida is an especially good case for testing whether and to what extent in-migration contributes to political change.

Political Change and the Internal Composition of Florida Counties

The dynamics of party change in Florida are traceable to the internal composition of the state's counties and the extent to which their populations have changed due to immigration and internal migration. Patterns of ethnic segregation within counties are also politically relevant. A large body of theoretical and empirical work suggests that concentrated and spatially isolated ethnic populations are less likely to get involved in politics than those that are more integrated. This finding was borne out for Florida in the naturalization data (appendix A, table A6.2).

The spatial isolation of white and minority groups did not have an adverse impact on county-level turnout in Florida in table 6.2 once related variables were held constant. Even in bivariate plots, there was certainly no straightforward linear relationship between turnout and the internal segregation of counties. Apparently much of the politically relevant segregation in Florida occurs across counties rather than within them. Counties with large proportions of blacks and newly arrived immigrants do show lower turnout rates in gubernatorial elections than those populated mainly with white Anglos (see table 6.2). But residential settlement patterns internal to counties have no clear impact on countywide turnout.

Several aspects of population growth contribute to the spatial isolation of minority groups within and across counties. In some cases, like northern Kentucky and northeastern Kansas, the mechanism for the entrapment of blacks in older cities and suburbs is the in-migration of whites and the subsequent inflation of housing prices in areas outside the older core. In this respect, racial segregation is enhanced by economic factors that permit or inhibit mobility. In previous chapters, we have seen that the isolation of Hispanic and black populations from white populations serves to undermine the participation and political influence of the minority groups, often strengthening Republican prospects.

In Florida, blacks remain the group most residentially segregated from whites judging from the dissimilarity index calculated in table 6.6 for Florida census tracts in 1980 and 1990. Hispanics are highly segregated in the state as a whole, and especially concentrated in South Florida, but within certain counties Hispanic and white neighborhoods are relatively

TABLE 6.6. Index of Dissimilarity for the Black, Asian, and Hispanic Populations Relative to Whites in Four Florida Counties, 1980 and 1990, by Census Tract

Variable	Florida		Dade		Brevard		Sarasota		North-Central Florida	
	1980	1990	1980	1990	1980	1990	1980	1990	1980	1990
Asians	.36	.35	.29	.34	.27	.22	.23	.21	.25	.28
Blacks	.73	.65	.78	.71	.71	.52	.84	.74	.32	.41
Hispanics	.59	.55	.32	.21	.18	.20	.32	.31	.16	.25
N	2,447	2,447	267	267	89	89	42	42	15	15

Source: U.S. Census 1990, and author's calculations.
Note: Figures represent the percentage of each group that would have to move in order for the group to be evenly distributed across census tracts in the county.

well integrated. In Dade County, for example, the dissimilarity index for whites and Hispanics in 1990 is .21, down from .32 in 1980. Of the counties reported in table 6.6, Sarasota has the most highly segregated Hispanic population in 1990 and also the most segregated black population.

The counties evaluated in table 6.6 are racially and politically very different. Dade County, the most populous and ethnically diverse in the state, has the strange distinction of being one of the fastest growing hotbeds of Republican strength in urban America. Republicans gained a full sixteen points on Democrats and third parties during the 1980s. If Dade County were in any other state, it would almost certainly be a Democratic fortress. Sarasota County, on the Gulf Coast just south of Tampa, has experienced rapid population growth but is typified by population homogeneity; an elderly, mostly white population; and high incomes. In most states, the population composition of Sarasota County would predict healthy Republican gains. Yet Republicans gained only five points from 1980 to 1990, considerably less than the state average of ten points for the decade. Brevard County, on the Atlantic Coast in central Florida, is one of the fastest growing areas in the state (see map 6.1). Republicans have done exceptionally well there, increasing their share of party registrants a full twelve points during the 1980s. With an elderly population below the state average and few minorities, Brevard appears to be a more typical "suburban" county than other areas of Florida, and a high percentage of its population, nearly three out of four people, are from out of state. Finally, the four-county region in northern Florida described by the dissimilarity index in table 6.6 is comprised of Hamilton, Lafayette, Madison, and Suwannee Counties (see map 6.1) located directly south of Valdosta, Georgia, and northwest of Gainesville. These counties are typical of northern Florida for having large black populations, few Hispanics, few elderly residents, a high proportion of native Floridians, and low to moderate population growth. Republican gains in these counties have been well below average, especially in Lafayette and Hamilton, suggesting that the Old South is dying a prolonged death in northern Florida.

Miami and Dade County
Miami's domination by Cuban Americans is resented and envied by both blacks and non-Cuban Hispanics in South Florida. The Cubans are resented both for their economic success and their political cohesion. They are described as an industrious people who in the early 1990s managed to displace Anglos as the most potent force in local politics (Dunn 1997,

320–21). The sizable black community, about 20 percent of the population in 1990, is considerably less powerful and much poorer than the Hispanic population. As the dissimilarity index shows (table 6.6), the black population is also spatially segregated, but these figures tell only part of the story. This segregation, coupled with the relative dispersion of these black neighborhoods around the Dade County metropolitan area (Rose 1964), has made it especially difficult to mobilize voters (Stack and Warren 1992). Political demands by racial minority groups do not smoothly translate into the political sphere when there is a high degree of neighborhood isolation. When politicians represent homogeneous, ethnically pure communities, their politics takes on the tone of special interest centeredness that alienates other populations. They have difficulty claiming that they speak for the entire community. Their attempts to pursue a nonracial politics in order to reach that broader community are often halfhearted and usually held in contempt by their core supporters.

The black community in Miami has less political power than it does in other major cities mostly because of its smaller numbers relative to rival groups. But it is also powerless because the spatial segregation of the black community produces black politicians who have difficulty communicating a vision for the entire city instead of the singular constituencies from which they come. Finally, black progress has been slowed because this constituency is drawn to a different party than the one that generally runs Miami. While the mayoralty is officially nonpartisan, recent Cuban mayors have had strong Republican inclinations (Xavier Suarez was a registered independent, but his politics were Republican). In the politics of most major cities, blacks can at least claim a role in the election of the mayor and often are able to gain influence by throwing their support to one Democratic primary contender over another. In Miami, blacks are almost never on the winning side. As the most frustrated group in Miami politics, black protest has often erupted in violence. Four riots were precipitated in the 1980s mostly as the result of incidents involving police and black citizens (Dunn 1997; Dunn and Stepick 1992; Porter and Dunn 1984). The most serious of these, the riot of 1980, left eighteen people dead.

Black leaders argue that Miami's economic growth has bypassed their community and that political leaders in the Cuban American community are exclusive in their governing philosophy. Since much of Miami's business is conducted in Spanish and blacks in the city are least likely to be bilingual, the black population is disadvantaged by both skin color and language. Bilingual requirements for employment are concentrated in entry-level positions in the local labor market (Castro 1992). Thus, many of Miami's African American citizens are trapped in an area where their job prospects are especially poor. Even black Cubans are the victims of discrimination, partly because older Cuban exiles perceive blacks in Cuba as having been supportive of the Castro regime (Aguirre 1976; Aguirre, Schwirian, and LaGreca 1980). Cuban firms employing mostly Cuban workers often compete successfully for construction work because they are not unionized whereas the older firms that employ black and Anglo workers are forced to pay higher union wages. (Grenier et al. 1992).

If Cubans are exclusive in their hiring practices, they are even more so in their governing style. Of course, given the spatial clustering of Cubans in Miami, it is rarely necessary for their politicians to pursue a politics of inclusion. Election districts generally encompass distinct constituencies, and the disadvantage of blacks is exacerbated by the fact that Cubans gravitate toward a different party than the one that is home to most blacks. Traditional Cuban politics consists mostly of anti-Castro demagoguery. Local observers talk about the key litmus test for even trivial local public offices as being the candidate's willingness to denounce Castro. This fierce anti-communism led most Cubans to enroll as Republicans, particularly in the 1980s in response to the cold war rhetoric of Ronald Reagan (Perez 1992, 102). Republican positions on foreign policy can be viewed as an extension of the community's broader concern with its homeland.

It is surprising that a community so interested in Cuba would take any interest in local politics given the expressed desire to eventually return to a post-Castro Cuba. But as the community developed its identity and roots in Miami it became less and less interested in returning (Portes and Mozo 1985). This transition in consciousness occurred during the 1970s, a time when the upper and middle class immigrants put their capital and skills to work in new business ventures (Garcia 1996, 108–9). Second generation Cubans are even less interested in Cuba, and most prefer to speak English (Perez 1992; Portes and Schauffler 1996). Miami has become so Cuban that few will ever return even if the opportunity arises. Miami is the new Havana, and locals will privately admit that it is far better than the old one.

Between Anglos and Cubans, conflict has been mitigated by the flight of the former northward into Palm Beach and Broward Counties. The Cuban and Anglo populations are closely integrated in many neighborhoods. The more exclusive Anglo areas include large settlements of migrants in the "condo canyons" of Miami Beach and North Miami Beach. These are mostly elderly retirees from New York, New Jersey, and

Connecticut, more Democrat than Republican, with time to be politically informed and active. Locals speak of the "condo political guys," South Florida precinct captains, who are responsible for organizing and turning out friendly partisans on election day. Every large retirement home has one of these political operatives, and his or her activity can generate hundreds and sometimes thousands of votes for the Democratic Party. Aside from the city's black voters, the most significant Democratic population in Dade County is the predominantly Jewish northeasterners, who have developed a political identity specifically opposed to the domination of Cubans (Moreno and Rae 1992). Party labels are being appropriated by rival ethnic groups, with Jews aligning themselves with Democrats and Cubans with Republicans (Moreno and Rae 1992, 201).

Brevard County
The results in table 6.4 predicted that areas receiving out-of-state migrants would become more Republican in the 1970s and 1980s. Brevard is one of the counties that fits the model well, as its population growth has coincided with a twelve-point rise in Republican registration relative to other parties during the 1980s. Brevard is the home of the "Space Coast," Cape Canaveral, and major Air Force and NASA installations. Republican strength has been built on military employment, engineering and high-tech employment at NASA, and some very large white evangelical churches. Military assignments at Patrick Air Force Base, outside of Melbourne, are considered "cushy," and many retired military officers have permanently settled there. Grumman Aircraft relocated a plant from Long Island to Brevard County in the mid-1980s, and thousands of New Yorkers were transferred. For a time during the mid-1980s, the Brevard area economy was stagnant as a result of the Challenger disaster, which raised serious questions about the future of the space shuttle program. When the shuttle resumed flying thirty months after the accident, investment in the county began increasing once again. Even so, the local economy has a tentative feel about it. If the space program loses favor in Congress, investment may dry up. The economy cannot survive on the strength of elderly migration alone.

The black population is small (8 percent of the county in 1990) and concentrated in the older town of Cocoa and in the rural northern tip of the county around the small towns of Mims and Scottsmoor. The town of Mims is split down the middle between white neighborhoods on the west side of U.S. Route 1 and black neighborhoods to the east. A well-known civil rights activist was murdered there in the 1950s (Button 1989, 70–71), and the perpetrators escaped punishment. The migration of northerners to the Cape eroded the hold of southern white prejudice on the community, but the economic position of blacks has not improved much. The black population remains politically inactive, mostly powerless, and attached to a minority party in a heavily Republican county.

There is a small Mexican community involved in agricultural labor in the orange groves. This settlement is illustrated on map 6.6 at the southernmost end of the county. While not nearly as residentially segregated as blacks, many Hispanics live in Palm Bay, a hastily constructed and sprawling residential development with poor infrastructure built by a corrupt housing corporation in the 1970s. Cheap housing in Palm Bay has attracted Mexican and Puerto Rican immigrants but almost no blacks. Cuban residents are not considered "Hispanic" in the same sense that Mexican migrant workers are. Cubans who settled this far north are from the first wave of migrants—mostly in the professions and business, affluent pillars of the community. They are well integrated into the Anglo population and are as active and Republican as Cubans further south.

If the Democrats have one solid constituency in Brevard County it is the elderly northeasterners. Melbourne has some of the largest "Century City" retirement communities in the state, and when President Clinton visited early in his first term touting his health care plan it was as if the Pope had arrived. Thousands of elderly people turned out in ninety degree heat to pay homage to their new Roosevelt. Republican plans in Congress to cut Medicare benefits have polarized the Brevard County population by generation. The elderly will remain a minority interest in the area unless the Space Coast's economy collapses and the legions of Republican migrants flee for greener pastures.

Sarasota County
The Florida Gulf Coast population is considerably different from the population on the Atlantic. In Sarasota County, in particular, the elderly are more likely to come from the Midwest than the Northeast, with Michigan and Illinois being the leading origin states. Some of Florida's wealthiest retirees have settled there, preferring it to the east coast for its slower pace, white sand beaches, lower density development, and the perception of lower crime rates. The city of Sarasota is very proud of its reputation as Florida's center for the arts and is known for its annual French film festival. Strict growth control plans were put in place in the late 1970s to limit development and protect existing investments. A local initiative to place a

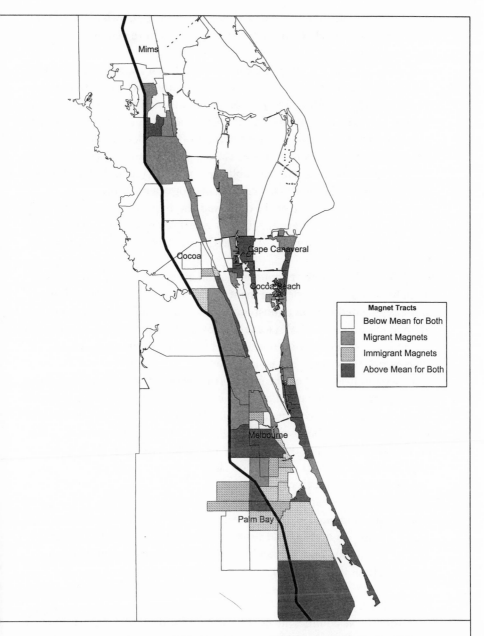

Map 6.6. Internal migrant and immigrant magnets in Brevard County, Florida, 1990

three-year moratorium on new development was narrowly defeated in a 1990 referendum. There are no major industries in the county, and most employment is strictly in the service sector.

Sarasota became a Republican county almost overnight in the 1952 presidential election when all of the area's Democrats were swept out of office on the strength of Eisenhower's coattails and the growing population of northern transplants. In the 1990s, the area's strong conservatism was productive of only one Democratic officeholder, a state legislator from the city of Sarasota who was elected on the basis of her personality and her ability to work with Republicans. In recent years, Republican registration growth has been slower than that of other counties because the area's tight growth controls have slowed the population influx. In addition, the Sarasota area attracts mostly elderly people, and some of those are migrating from Florida's Atlantic Coast, bringing Democratic affiliations with them.

The mechanism for racial segregation along Florida's Gulf Coast has been high-end housing development. Sarasota's small black population is more segregated than in almost any other county in Florida and more so than in the state as a whole (see table 6.6). Ordinarily, when minority populations are small, they go unnoticed and are therefore easily integrated. This is not the case in Sarasota County, where the black population is almost entirely located on the near north side of the city of Sarasota. Some recent immigrants have settled there as well (see map 6.7). The city has a ward-based election system, and all of the black votes are concentrated in a single ward. The black population is overwhelmingly Democratic, but, as in Brevard County, the one-party Republican nature of local politics prevents the minority population from having much of a political influence given its partisan orientation. The Hispanic population is located well inland on the east side of the city of Sarasota. These residents are primarily Mexicans and Caribbean islanders who work on fruit and vegetable farms. As a small and isolated population, they have no political influence. Internal migrants and wealthier immigrants prefer living on the coast south of the city of Sarasota, as shown on map 6.7.

Rural North Florida
The four rural counties in north-central Florida that I have evaluated (Hamilton, Suwannee, Madison, and Lafayette) show a higher degree of residential integration than the more urban counties in table 6.6, but appearances can be deceiving since the census tracts cover much larger

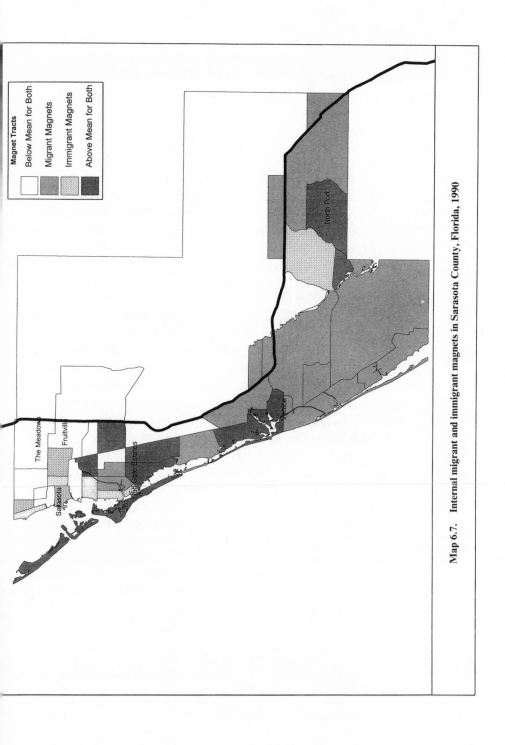

Map 6.7. Internal migrant and immigrant magnets in Sarasota County, Florida, 1990

land areas than in urban Florida. The mechanism for political and social stratification in these areas is not population growth and economic development, as it has been elsewhere, but the Jim Crow system that has been so slow to die in the rural South. The conservative white Democrat is still alive here and sharply distinguishes this region's politics from Democratic strongholds in the state's urban areas. As late as the 1990s, most of the white Democrats from this region were ideologically as conservative as the Republicans. Democratic politicians are not elected on the basis of promises of racial inclusion. School prayer and gun rights legislation were repeatedly introduced in Tallahassee not by Republicans but by North Florida Democrats. In its ideology, North Florida's politics has been more like that of Georgia and Alabama, where political control has remained firmly in the hands of white elites.

Integration of blacks into the economic and political system of North Florida has been hindered by the out-migration of the most able, upwardly mobile blacks. With the collapse of cotton plantations and the mechanization of agriculture (described in Wright 1986), many blacks moved north or migrated to large southern cities nearby. Those who remained behind have been particularly victimized by the low demand of local labor markets. Given that the Democratic Party was supportive of Jim Crow, it is worth asking why rural blacks did not find expression for their views within the Republican Party. The Republicans were not much of an alternative since they could never win a general election. In order to vote in the Democratic primary, nearly everyone, black or white, had to register as a Democrat. The power structure at the local level remained white and Democratic well into the 1990s simply because Democrats could automatically draw upon a larger pool of voters. Even in counties where blacks constitute a majority, or nearly a majority, of the population, most local offices are still in white hands. Today there is increasing evidence of party switching on the part of white Democrats, who have voted Republican in presidential contests since the 1960s. The GOP stigma as the Yankee silk stocking party has steadily eroded. Suwannee County's Republican registration increased by seven points during the 1980s in spite of population growth that lagged well behind the state average.

The few interstate migrants to North Florida are not as wealthy as those who move to the Gulf and Atlantic Coasts. They come to North Florida because land and housing are cheaper and settle mostly near the two interstate highways that run through the area (see map 6.8). Newcomers have been slow to fit into North Florida's small town life and are

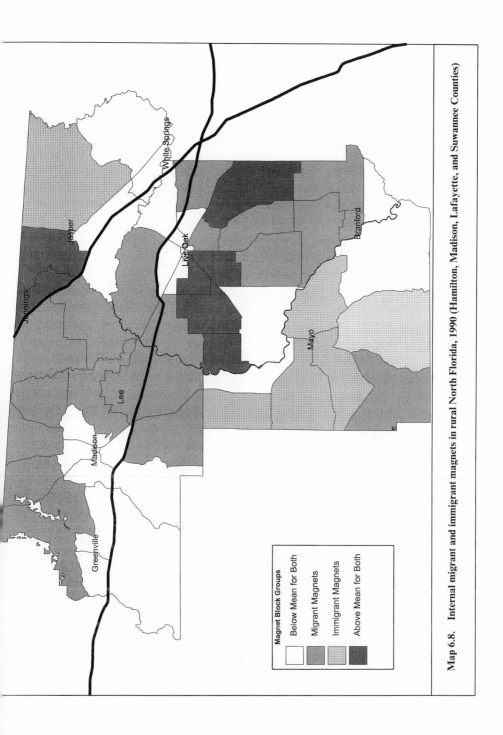

Map 6.8. Internal migrant and immigrant magnets in rural North Florida, 1990 (Hamilton, Madison, Lafayette, and Suwannee Counties)

not always welcome. The social conventions of the rural South are alien to these northerners, who are often retiring from industrial jobs in Michigan and Ohio. Natives are suspicious of the new arrivals and worry about how they may alter the racial and political complexion of the region, including Democratic hegemony. White Democratic politicians from North Florida are often dubbed "he-coons," a southern "cracker" term for male raccoons who protect their turf and eye outsiders with suspicion and hostility. A growing number of Hispanics has settled near the town of Mayo to work in agriculture, but they have not become a political force in state and local politics. Mexicans in north-central Florida have been stigmatized by native whites as involved in marijuana smuggling and drug crime. It is common in this part of Florida for whites to believe that minorities cannot be trusted and are unfit for public office (Button 1989, 229).

Segregated Heterogeneity in Florida

To the extent that Florida is politically balkanized, both migration and ethnicity are responsible. Cuban settlement in South Florida has created a distinct Republican politics in Dade County and the southeast coast. Jewish migration to Broward County and North Miami has given these areas a pronounced Democratic leaning. Sarasota, and the Gulf Coast, has become a one-party Republican stronghold stimulated by the arrival of wealthy, elderly midwesterners. The politics of aged migrants appears to depend mainly upon their states of origin. The elderly are not as politically cohesive as they are often assumed to be (Rosenbaum and Button 1989, 1993). Elderly migration from the Northeast is far more likely to bring Democrats than Republicans to the state's retirement communities. That northeastern migrants have been more attracted to the Atlantic than the Gulf Coast (Winsberg 1993) explains how regional migration streams have contributed to the state's political balkanization. The Space Coast of Brevard County has made this area highly dependent upon defense spending and NASA procurement. This has attracted white, well-educated migrants who vote Republican. The much slower population growth of rural North Florida and the attitudes of the entrenched white power holders there have left it the last bastion of the Old South.

While the political parties in Florida counties are more closely competitive than they were forty years ago, Republican gains due to migration have created many new one-party-dominant areas for the GOP. Most of the South Florida Republicans in the U.S. House occupied very safe seats in the early 1990s, and several consistently ran unopposed in general elections. While Florida's political balkanization is not as great as that of Kentucky, population groups in the Sunshine State are sufficiently segmented and interests of the balkanized groups sufficiently well defined to undermine the practice of pluralist politics and encourage instead the kind of special interest centeredness that is characteristic of so much of contemporary American electioneering. While the redrawing of election boundaries to create more competitive and ethnically heterogeneous districts would counteract the balkanization generated by residential segregation, there is a limit to how extensive the redrawing of boundaries can be. Spatial segregation inevitably affords some politicians the luxury of representing monolithic, single-interest electorates.

The effect of Florida's spatial balkanization has been to exclude blacks and non-Cuban Hispanics from the political process. Blacks remain the minority everywhere except in rural North Florida, where the vestiges of official segregation have excluded them from office. Their monolithic identification with the Democratic Party and the almost equally monolithic identification of the Cuban community with the Republicans have continually frustrated the attempts of blacks to redress grievances in Miami. Spatially segregated populations are consigned to a politics that often awards the spoils to only one or a few dominant groups. Those left out of the process have no other voice but unconventional protest. Rioting and violence have sometimes resulted (Button 1989, 233–37). While violence occasionally wins concessions, these come at a very high cost and are no substitute for meaningful input at the community bargaining table. There is more to representation than electing someone who looks like you, but politics in South Florida has fused the ethnic to the political in such a way that it is increasingly difficult to imagine the separation of the two.

CHAPTER 7

Pennsylvania: Deindustrialization and Division

As a state that is closely identified with deindustrialization and the rust belt decline of the post–World War II period, Pennsylvania has not grown much in the last four decades of the twentieth century. Once the heartland of coal, apparel, and steel production, by 1990 only 20 percent of the labor force was employed in manufacturing. The shipbuilding industry in Philadelphia died soon after World War II. The steel industry in western Pennsylvania completely collapsed by the early 1980s, with only 14 percent of Pittsburgh's employment accounted for by manufacturing by 1988 (Giarratani and Houston 1989; Serrin 1993). In Bethlehem, the home-grown Bethlehem Steel Corporation employed only 3,600 workers by the mid-1990s, down from nearly 32,000 at its peak during World War II (Deitrick and Beauregard 1995). The coal industry in northeastern Pennsylvania also died, stranding long-time industrial workers in a postindustrial economy (Marsh 1987, 339; Kolbe 1975).

In spite of the deindustrialization process, the state has grown, though very slowly. The Pennsylvania population was just 14 percent larger in the mid-1990s than it was in 1950. Between 1980 and 1992, the average county grew by only 3.8 percent, and in thirty-five of the state's sixty-seven counties the population declined. None of Pennsylvania's jurisdictions have grown as fast as those of Florida or California. This is no surprise, of course. Migrants and immigrants base their choice of destinations partly on the availability of employment. Pennsylvania's stagnant economy has not been inviting in this respect.

For years there has been a cultural divide separating the people of eastern and western Pennsylvania. This divide has become demographic and economic, too, as map 7.1 illustrates. Eastern Pennsylvania has weathered the process of deindustrialization far better than the west and has completed the transition to the service economy without the long-term unemployment that still plagues the western counties (Gimpel 1996). The

238

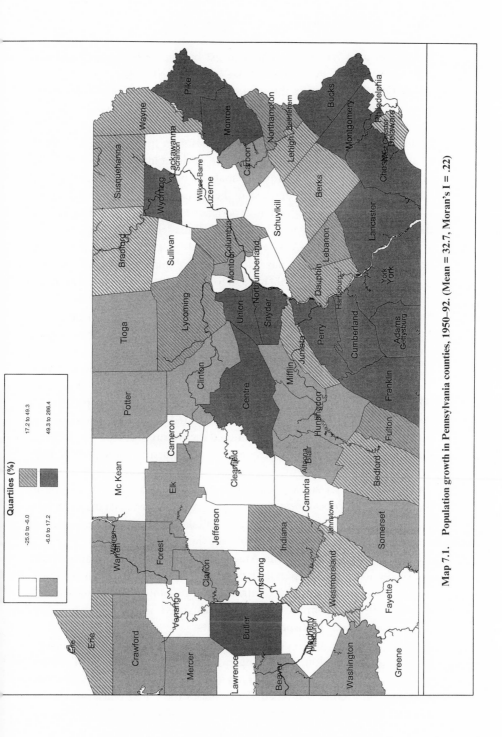

Map 7.1. Population growth in Pennsylvania counties, 1950–92. (Mean = 32.7, Moran's I = .22)

Quartiles (%)

-25.0 to -6.0

-6.0 to 17.2

17.2 to 49.3

49.3 to 286.4

shading in map 7.1 displays the contrast between growing and declining regions. Western Pennsylvania has experienced stunning population losses. Only one county in this area shows rapid growth from 1950 to 1992, Butler County, north of Pittsburgh. Allegheny County (Pittsburgh and its immediate suburbs) was 12 percent smaller in the 1990s than it was in the 1950s. Since white people of means are among the first to abandon a locality when jobs disappear and the poor are the least likely to move, the population loss has contributed to the spatial isolation of blacks and poorer ethnics in the worst labor markets in the state (Bodnar, Simon, and Weber 1982). Eastern Pennsylvania has experienced the most rapid growth, with the expansion of the suburbs around Philadelphia leading the way. Wealthy Montgomery County has doubled in size since the 1950s, and next door Bucks County has led suburban Philadelphia in population growth, moving from 145,000 in 1950 to over half a million by 1992. Some of this growth in the suburbs is due to out-migration from Philadelphia, but the economy of the region has also attracted migrants from out of state, in particular from the neighboring states of Maryland, New Jersey, and New York.

Little of Pennsylvania's growth can be accounted for by the arrival of new immigrants. It is one of the few states where a majority of foreign-born residents were still Caucasian in 1990. The ethnic composition of Pennsylvania's 370,000 immigrants is illustrated in fig. 7.1. Forty-two percent of the immigrant population entered the country before 1965, the year that the nationality preference system was changed by Congress, making Pennsylvania's immigrants much older on average than those in other states. As figure 7.1 shows, nearly half of the foreign-born population in the state is of European origin. An increasing number of Asians have been moving into the state, mostly to settle in Philadelphia, Pittsburgh, and the Philadelphia suburbs (Goode 1990), but their numbers in 1990 remained small. Immigration from Latin America also constituted a small percentage of the foreign-born population, only 11 percent for South America, Mexico, the Caribbean, and Central America combined. Pennsylvania is therefore distinct from the other states discussed in this book with their much larger shares of Hispanic immigrants.

Adding to the state's ethnic diversity, though, is a large and concentrated black population, numbering more than a million in 1990. This bloc is highly concentrated in Philadelphia and to a lesser degree in Pittsburgh. Together, these cities contained 72 percent of the state's black population in 1992. When a racial dissimilarity index is calculated to determine the

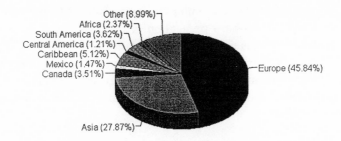

Other (8.99%)
Africa (2.37%)
South America (3.62%)
Central America (1.21%)
Caribbean (5.12%)
Mexico (1.47%)
Canada (3.51%)
Europe (45.84%)
Asia (27.87%)

Fig. 7.1.   Composition of the foreign-born population in Pennsylvania, 1990

concentration of the black population across the state's counties, the index reveals considerably more concentration and segregation of blacks from whites than in Florida (chap. 6). In Pennsylvania, nearly two-thirds of blacks would have to move for them to be evenly distributed across the state's sixty-seven counties. The Asian and Hispanic populations, while much smaller, are not nearly so segregated. The same diversity index indicates that only about one-third of Asians and 46 percent of Hispanics would have to move for them to be evenly distributed. Politically, too, the state is spatially balkanized, as there are many one-party counties of either strong Republican or Democratic inclination. As in Florida, an index of dissimilarity suggests that about one-third of Republicans (or Democrats) would have to move in order for the parties to have equal strength across all counties.

Differences between immigrants, native Pennsylvanians, and internal migrants residing in the state in 1990 closely reflect the findings of many national studies. Migrants earn considerably more than either immigrants or natives (see appendix A, table A7.1). Internal migrants are also the best educated of the three groups. Natives and immigrants, though, are only several hundred dollars apart in average wage and salary incomes. Table A7.1 shows considerable difference between mean and median incomes for immigrants, indicating that immigrant earnings are especially concentrated at the lower end of the income distribution. An important difference between Pennsylvania and other states lies in the age of the foreign-born population. Immigrants were several years older, on average, than either natives or internal migrants in 1990. Pennsylvania has attracted so few recent immigrants from Latin America and Asia that fully 67 percent of foreign-born residents there are non-Hispanic whites. The data strongly suggest that the foreign-born population in Pennsylvania arrived in the United States early. It is well established relative to populations in other states, although it is certainly not wealthy. Given the racial and economic profile of the immigrant population, we can reasonably expect it to be better integrated with the native and internal migrant populations than it is in many other places.

Settlement Patterns of Migrants and Immigrants in Pennsylvania

The darkly shaded areas of map 7.2 show where the growth in the proportion of internal migrants has been strongest in recent years. The south-central and northeastern counties stand out in the highest growth quartile, having benefited from migration from adjacent states, including New York, New Jersey, and Maryland. The counties of western Pennsylvania stand out because the proportion of out-of-state migrants in these places has declined. In western Pennsylvania, internal migrants have been slow to flow into the state, and many who were there in the 1960s and 1970s have left. In Philadelphia and its suburbs, the proportion of internal migrants shrunk during the 1990s because the native population increased faster than the foreign-born or migrant population. Growth in the proportion of immigrants across Pennsylvania during the 1980s can be characterized as sluggish at best (see map 7.3). Once again, western Pennsylvania stands out as an area increasingly dominated by natives whose familial attachments keep them in place. The lightly shaded counties near Wilkes-Barre and Scranton indicate that few recent immigrants have been attracted to the depressed anthracite coal region of northeastern Pennsylvania. In Philadelphia, the immigrant population has become slightly more visible but not in most of its suburbs.

Table 7.1 displays the results of regression models predicting where immigrants and U.S. internal migrants are becoming a larger or smaller proportion of the population in the areas where they have settled. The dependent variable, as in previous chapters, is the increase or decrease in the proportion of the population comprised of the particular group from 1980 to 1990. In other words, for a particular observation (county), if the proportion of Mexican migrants began the decade as 2 percent of the population and finished the decade at 4 percent, the dependent variable for that case would take on the value, +.2. By constructing the variable in this

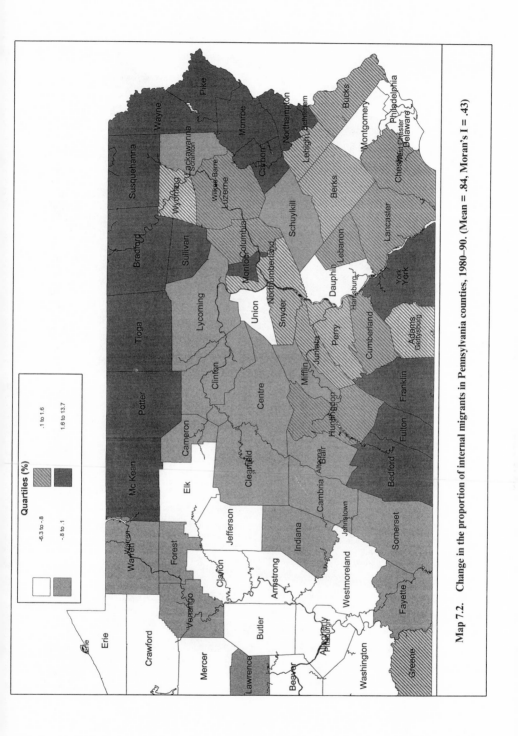

Map 7.2. Change in the proportion of internal migrants in Pennsylvania counties, 1980–90. (Mean = .84, Moran's I = .43)

Quartiles (%)

- -6.3 to -.8
- -.8 to .1
- .1 to 1.6
- 1.6 to 13.7

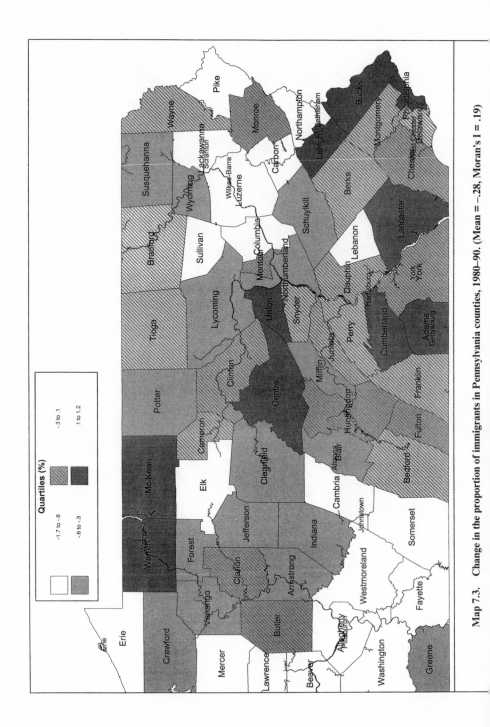

Quartiles (%)

▨ -1.7 to -.6	▨ -.3 to .1
☐ -.6 to -.3	▓ .1 to 1.2

Map 7.3.   Change in the proportion of immigrants in Pennsylvania counties, 1980–90. (Mean = –.28, Moran's I = .19)

TABLE 7.1. Influences on Population Concentration in Pennsylvania Counties, 1980–90

Variable	U.S. Migrants	African Immigrants	Asian Immigrants	European Immigrants	Canadian Immigrants	Mexican Immigrants	Central American Immigrants	South American Immigrants
% 1980 group population	.10**	-1.06**	.61**	-.42**	-.28**	1.36**	-.18	.06
	(.04)	(.13)	(.11)	(.03)	(.08)	(.33)	(.21)	(.19)
% unemployment, 1980	.24**	-.004	.03*	-.03**	-.001	-.005	-.009	.0001
	(.10)	(.003)	(.01)	(.01)	(.002)	(.006)	(.006)	(.004)
Change in real median income, 1980–90	-.13**	.003*	.01*	.02**	-.0005	-.002	-.007*	-.003
	(.05)	(.002)	(.005)	(.006)	(.001)	(.003)	(.004)	(.002)
% net population change	.14**	.0006	-.0007	.004*	.0005	.002*	.003**	.002**
	(.03)	(.001)	(.002)	(.002)	(.0004)	(.001)	(.001)	(.001)
Population density	-.0005**	-.00001**	.00002**	.00003**	.0000001	.000001	.00003**	.00001**
	(.00008)	(.000002)	(.00001)	(.000007)	(.00001)	(.000003)	(.000007)	(.000003)
% college students	-.09**	.006**	-.03*	.001	.003**	-.003	.005**	-.004**
	(.05)	(.002)	(.005)	(.005)	(.001)	(.003)	(.003)	(.002)
Spatial lag	.46**	-.05	.22**	-.18**	-.03	-.31*	.42	.38**
	(.09)	(.19)	(.09)	(.09)	(.15)	(.18)	(.33)	(.18)
Constant	-2.47	.03	-.53	.21	.014	.07	.09	.02
N	67	67	67	67	67	67	67	67
R^2_a	.89	.67	.94	.89	.21	.34	.45	.55

Note: Spatial autoregressive model, weighted for population; income coefficients expressed in thousands of 1992 dollars; dependent variable = change in population group as a percentage of total population. See appendix A for a full description of variables.

$*p < .10.$ $**p < .05.$

manner, areas where the group population has increased do not necessarily register a positive value. It is important that the variable here shows positive gains for the population in question only when it has grown relative to the rest of the population.

The independent variables have been selected mostly on the basis of what economic and sociological theory has taught us about the reasons migrants and immigrants choose to settle where they do. The two principal hypotheses to be tested are (1) that groups concentrate where there are friends and family members—for example, coethnics—who can help them to gain a foothold in the new society; and (2) that groups concentrate where the job prospects are strongest or at least in areas where unemployment is most easily avoided.

The results are consistent with the notion that Asian and Mexican settlement patterns are most dependent upon existing coethnic communities. The areas where Asians and Mexicans are growing relative to the rest of the population are places where there were sizable populations of Asians and Mexicans at the beginning of the decade. Africans, Europeans, and Canadians, on the other hand, have been shrinking as a proportion of the population in areas where they have settled in the past. This is a reflection of both the declining proportion of immigrants from these world areas and their independence of coethnic enclaves.

European émigrés show some propensity to avoid increasing their presence in areas of high unemployment, but this is not the case with the other groups. Asians and U.S. internal migrants are a growing proportion of the population in areas that began the decade with high unemployment rates. This is unusual for internal migrants, who generally have the kind of information about local conditions that directs them to avoid areas with poor employment prospects. Some of the strongest growth in the out-of-state population occurred in northeastern Pennsylvania along the New York and New Jersey borders. Some of this growth is the result of development in the Pocono Mountains in Monroe and Pike Counties east of Scranton. The reason this growth is unrelated to employment in these areas is that northeastern Pennsylvania has not attracted as many job seekers as it has retirees and commuters from northern New Jersey and the New York City suburbs lured there by low-cost housing, open space, lakes, and mountains. Migration models that only consider economic conditions are likely to miss the important component of migration motivated by lifestyle considerations.

Several groups are growing as a function of net population increase.

These include internal migrants, Europeans, South Americans, Central Americans, and Mexicans. In other words, these groups are growing larger even in areas that are experiencing growth from other sources. These are sometimes, but not always, the more densely populated areas of the state, as the coefficients for population density show (table 7.1). Africans, Asians, Europeans, and South and Central Americans are all drawn to Pennsylvania's larger cities and suburbs. Asians increased their presence in both Philadelphia and suburban Montgomery County. Mexicans became a more significant presence in Berks (Reading) and Chester (suburban Philadelphia) Counties. Internal migrants are actually drawn to areas of low-density development, especially Monroe, Pike, and Wayne Counties. These results make it clear that the destinations of migrants and those where immigrants are concentrating are very different. The immigrant population is growing larger in Pennsylvania's urban centers and older suburbs. The population of out-of-state migrants is growing in rural areas of eastern Pennsylvania and in less densely populated suburbs.

Ethnic Balkanization and Naturalization in Pennsylvania

The fact that the internal migrant and immigrant populations are drawn to different areas of the state is of some consequence. Concentrated populations are much more noticeable than dispersed ones. While internal migration is not always of sufficient volume in Pennsylvania to influence the residential segregation of groups within counties, it is distinguishing counties from one another, strongly suggesting that the population of mostly white migrants from out of state, and that of immigrants, are not mixing well. The segregation accompanying increasing ethnic heterogeneity is occurring on top of the more familiar separation of the white and black populations that has helped to identify Philadelphia as a city with special interests and needs on the basis of its racial composition alone.

Concentrated immigrant populations are slower to assimilate politically than dispersed populations are, but naturalization rates also vary directly with duration of residence in the country. Given Pennsylvania's older stock of immigrants, the percentage of immigrants who are citizens is likely to be far higher there than in areas with more recent immigration—and at 59 percent in 1990, the state's naturalization rate is among the highest in the nation. Still, duration of residence is not the only important variable. Naturalization rates are a function of immigrant concentration and isolation, as table A7.2 shows. In 1980, however, it is noteworthy that foreign-born concentration was associated with high naturalization rates because the immigrant population in Pennsylvania remained predominantly of European origin. These European immigrants were concentrated in the state's urban areas but had immigrated prior to 1970. Where more recent Hispanic and Asian immigrant populations were clustered, naturalization rates were much lower. Hence, the segregation of Asian and Hispanic from white neighborhoods depressed naturalization rates according to the 1980 census data (table A7.2). By 1990, with Europeans shrinking as a proportion of the immigrant population, immigrant concentrations in Pennsylvania were associated with lower naturalization rates. Asian and Hispanic isolation are not statistically significant in 1990 because these variables are closely related to foreign-born concentration (table A7.2).

Migrants, Immigrants, and Voter Turnout in Pennsylvania

Has population migration and immigration helped to politically stratify the state? One might evaluate this by looking directly at levels of voter turnout across Pennsylvania jurisdictions. Trends and patterns of political participation have important implications for politics and policy because turnout ultimately determines who is elected to govern. One scholar of urban politics has noted that there are more avenues for citizen involvement and participation in central cities than in suburbs or "edge cities" (Scavo 1995). This dearth of participation in local politics by suburban residents may have broader implications for state and national politics. If a much smaller fraction of the suburban than the rural electorate participates in gubernatorial races, this undoubtedly gives rural areas a stronger voice in choosing statewide officeholders than they would have otherwise.

Participation rates averaged across two gubernatorial elections are shown by quartile on map 7.4. Interestingly, the area of the state that has experienced the most population growth, suburban Philadelphia (except for Delaware County), is in the lowest turnout cohort. Other areas of growth, including Butler County outside Pittsburgh, have lower than average turnout rates. The highest turnout areas, on the other hand, are those characterized by population stability or decline, including the rural northwest.

To explain these turnout patterns, table 7.2 presents a regression analysis of the influence of several demographic variables on the percent-

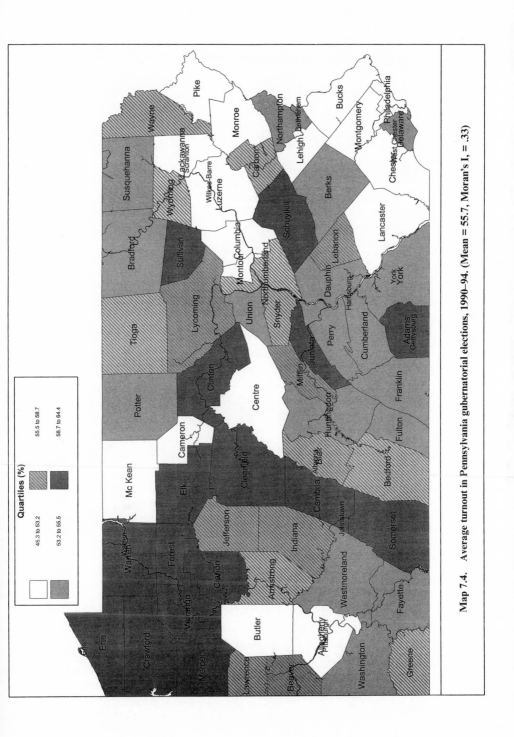

Quartiles (%)

45.3 to 53.2

53.2 to 55.5

55.5 to 58.7

58.7 to 64.4

Map 7.4. Average turnout in Pennsylvania gubernatorial elections, 1990–94. (Mean = 55.7, Moran's I, = .33)

TABLE 7.2. Impact of Population Mobility on Voter Turnout in Pennsylvania Counties, 1980–94

Variable	1980	1982	1990	1992	1994	Pooled 1990s
% college educated	.31*	-.04	-.09	.15*	-.04	.01
	(.17)	(.24)	(.11)	(.08)	(.10)	(.09)
Isolation of minorities from whites (within counties)	-.0001	-.03	-.02	.03*	-.006	-.007
	(.02)	(.02)	(.02)	(.02)	(.02)	(.02)
% post-1970 immigrants	-5.17**	-3.75	.22	-.23	-.25	-.30
	(1.52)	(2.20)	(1.15)	(.84)	(.93)	(.88)
% born out of state	-.09	-.21**	-.18**	-.07	-.07	-.09*
	(.06)	(.09)	(.07)	(.05)	(.05)	(.05)
% black	-.35**	.32	.10	.20[a]	.09	.01
	(.14)	(.22)	(.21)	(.14)	(.15)	(.09)
Population density	-.001**	-.001*	-.001[a]	-.001[a]	-.0007[a]	-.0001
	(.0001)	(.0005)	(.001)	(.001)	(.001)	(.001)
Spatial lag	.28*	.04	.25*	.02	.55**	.61**
	(.17)	(.16)	(.15)	(.16)	(.14)	(.10)
Presidential race	—	—	—	—	—	4.35**
						(1.44)
Constant	56.42	73.65	48.54	60.87	46.53	23.47
N	67	67	67	67	67	201
R^2_a	.72	.76	.65	.26	.54	.69

Note: Spatial autoregressive model, weighted for population; dependent variable = percentage of turnout by county. See appendix A for a full description of variables.

[a]Variables with low tolerances and high standard errors due to multicollinearity.

*$p < .10$.   **$p < .05$.

age of registered voters who have participated in recent elections. My central hypothesis is that population growth from outside Pennsylvania reduces the political participation of eligible voters given various barriers to reregistration. Control variables for education, population density, the segregation of white from minority neighborhoods, and the percentage of the population that is African American are designed to evaluate whether population mobility has an impact on county-level participation once these other variables are added. The results show that the percentage of the population born out of state is negatively associated with turnout in all of the elections. This corresponds to the findings in other states, including Kentucky (chap. 5), which suggest that migrants may be slower to take an interest in politics than long-term residents. Corresponding to this is the finding that the percentage of recent immigrants (those who immigrated since 1970) is associated with lower turnout in four out of the five races considered in table 7.2. In the 1980 presidential contest, for instance, a 1 point increase in the percentage of recent immigrants across counties was associated with a 5.2 point drop in voter turnout. The key insight here is that the exercise of social and political power by a population lags well behind that population's arrival in a new place. There are considerable costs involved in learning about the politics of a new location.

The population of college educated residents promotes turnout in presidential elections but depresses it in gubernatorial contests. Apparently areas with well-educated populations such as Chester, Montgomery, and Bucks Counties in the Philadelphia suburbs are far less interested in local politics than in major national elections. Not coincidentally these are also the counties with the most interstate migrants.

The black population has no consistent impact on an area's turnout, increasing it relative to predominantly white areas in most races but dropping it in 1980. Black turnout in cities such as Philadelphia and Pittsburgh may depend upon the competitiveness of the contest and the mobilization efforts of particular candidates and campaigns. Population density is negatively associated with turnout in all five elections. On average, urban and suburban areas do turn out a smaller percentage of eligible voters than the more rural counties. Finally, the spatially lagged dependent variable indicates that turnout patterns have a regional basis in Pennsylvania that reaches across county boundaries in the most recent elections.

These results clearly show that turnout across Pennsylvania counties is highly variable both across the state and across election years. Still, the state is stratified in some consistent and predictable ways. In most elections, urban areas do not have the representation at the polls that rural areas do. Suburban areas with well-educated populations vary more from election to election, often generating higher turnout than nonsuburban counties in presidential elections but then lagging behind the other counties in off-year contests. Not coincidentally, it is the suburbs that have the highest proportion of out-of-state migrants, who are slow to develop interest in local and statewide elections (Muller, Meyer, and Cybriwsky 1976). Turnout rates are occasionally cleaved along native-immigrant lines, with areas of large immigrant concentrations having lower levels of political participation than those with large native concentrations, especially in the early 1980s.

Much has been made of the rise of suburban power in American politics, and rightly so, for a plurality of voters in most states now live in suburban communities. For purposes of legislative apportionment, it is not at all trivial that the membership of Congress and the state legislatures is more suburban than it has ever been. But in statewide elections suburban power may not be fully realized due to the transient nature of the suburbs and the reluctance of well-educated migrants to involve themselves in state and local affairs. A further factor may also be relevant to the Pennsylvania case in particular. Several recent gubernatorial contests have been won by popular politicians who were well ahead in the polls in the weeks before election day. The perception that a race is not competitive gives voters the impression that their votes will make little difference to the outcome. Many suburban voters may respond by skipping the consensus contests such as the 1990 reelection of popular governor Bob Casey.

Migrants, Immigrants, and Party Regularity in Pennsylvania

Areas of heavy in-migration are more likely to be irregular in their political behavior than those with highly stable populations. By party irregularity in this context, I mean the extent to which party registration figures predict actual balloting. Those counties where there is little correspondence between the two are said to be irregular. Which counties might be irregular can be predicted based on studies done at the individual level of analysis (Brown 1988). Political attitudes and party affiliations often change with migration as people sort out how traditional cues apply in novel, unfamiliar settings. The percentage of migrants from out of state is highly associated with independent party registration in Pennsylvania (table not reported). Counties with more nonnatives, whether immigrants or internal migrants, should be more irregular in their behavior, often departing from party registration figures when actual ballots are cast.

Alternatively, counties may be irregular because sizable proportions of the registered electorate simply fail to show up at the polls. If 35 percent of the county is registered Democratic and 35 percent Republican, but only half of the registered Democrats vote while all the Republicans do, the difference in turnout will cause the county to be far more Republican than its registration figures would predict. The counties with the lowest turnout are most likely to show wide gaps between party balance and voting behavior. Since higher proportions of foreign-born residents and internal migrants are associated with low turnout, we would also expect these variables to be associated with party irregularity.

In fact, the results for Pennsylvania are mixed and vary from election to election (see table 7.3). The proportion of recent foreign-born residents is associated with party irregularity in most elections, but the effect is not always statistically significant. The proportion of out-of-state migrants seems to promote party *regularity* in most elections but in the 1990s has no statistically significant impact when other variables are included. This is contrary to the findings at the individual level, and for other states, where interstate migrants were *positively* associated with departures from partisanship. In Pennsylvania, however, the tendency for cross-state migration to generate party regularity must be understood in the context of the irregular partisanship of many rural Democrats, who often vote for Republicans. In western Pennsylvania, in particular, Republican candidates often do far better than registration figures would predict. In 1982, incumbent governor Richard Thornburgh, a Republican, won 48 percent of the Westmoreland County vote, though Republican registration was only at 29.1 percent. Thornburgh's opponent that year was a liberal congressman from eastern Pennsylvania, and eastern politicians are often eyed suspiciously by westerners. While the voting patterns of rural counties like Westmoreland are not easily predicted by their balance of party registrants, some counties did follow their registration patterns in the early 1980s. One of these is Chester County, in suburban Philadelphia, where high in-migration, Republican registration, and Republican voting coincide. Adjacent to Chester are Delaware and Montgomery Counties, also strongly Republican and quite regular in their behavior in spite of having a large population of nonnatives. Two things may account for the close alignment of party registration and voting in suburban Philadelphia. First, there is the

TABLE 7.3. Similarity of Party Registration to Party Voting in Pennsylvania Counties, 1980–94

Variable	1980	1982	1990	1992	1994	Pooled 1990s
% college educated	-.02	-.43	-.18	.40**	-.06	-.31*
	(.37)	(.38)	(.30)	(.18)	(.16)	(.17)
% born out of state	-.24*	-.33**	.02	-.02	-.06	.06
	(.13)	(.16)	(.18)	(.11)	(.09)	(.10)
% post-1970 immigrants	-.64	-1.96[a]	2.94[a]	.39[a]	.97[a]	5.13**
	(3.73)	(3.61)	(2.90)	(1.87)	(1.68)	(1.73)
% black	.07[a]	1.19**	-.67[a]	-.58[a]	.14[a]	-.28
	(.29)	(.30)	(.47)	(.31)	(.24)	(.27)
Population density	.0004	-.003**	.0005[a]	.0008[a]	-.001[a]	-.001
	(.001)	(.001)	(.002)	(.001)	(.001)	(.001)
% turnout	-.03	-.18	.23	.14	-.13	.19
	(.31)	(.23)	(.33)	(.29)	(.21)	(.15)
Spatial lag	.50**	.72**	.69**	.70**	1.20**	.14
	(.20)	(.18)	(.14)	(.19)	(.13)	(.10)
Presidential race	—	—	—	—	—	-6.81**
						(2.28)
Constant	11.03	20.91	-6.75	-12.13	6.89	3.62
N	67	67	67	67	67	201
R^2_a	.16	.42	.42	.41	.64	.21

Note: Spatial autoregressive model, weighted for population; dependent variable = Abs (% Republican vote − % Republican registration); high positive values indicate counties where voting differed from registration. See appendix A for a full description of variables.
[a]Variables with low tolerances and high standard errors due to multicollinearity.
*p < .10.   **p < .05.

"anticity" vote. The Philadelphia suburbs are more cohesively Republican than they might otherwise be because Philadelphia is so loyally Democratic. Second, the Philadelphia suburbs are known for being tightly organized and having strong party machines. This ensures a stronger measure of party discipline than one might find in a more rural Republican county where high costs prohibit the effective organization of a more dispersed population.

The inconsistent signs on the coefficients in table 7.3 for variables such as population density and percentage black may be due to multicollinearity—densely populated counties also contain large black populations. But the inconsistency of direction may have a more substantive meaning that points to the competitiveness of elections. In 1990 and 1982, both incumbents were considered easy candidates for reelection. The 1994 election, though, was the most competitive statewide governor's race in recent memory. Local patterns of turnout and party regularity are not as predictably stratified in Pennsylvania as they are in states where underlying demographic characteristics explain these outcomes independent of the particulars of a given election year. In other chapters, I have shown that the differences in turnout and party regularity usually hinge upon the proportion of nonnatives in an area and often upon the education and racial composition of the local population. In Pennsylvania, however, the role these factors play in distinguishing one place from another may depend upon the competitiveness of the election. In close elections, when mobilization and party loyalty count most, the state is more cleaved by region than in elections where strong incumbents have secured consensus behind their candidacy. Proof of this lies in the size and significance of the spatially lagged dependent variable for 1994 in tables 7.2 and 7.3. The 1994 election was the closest gubernatorial race in recent memory. For both turnout and party regularity, positive spatial dependency is stronger in 1994 than any other year, indicating that regional balkanization is more pronounced in competitive elections than in noncompetitive ones.

Changes in Party Registration in Pennsylvania

In previous chapters, I have repeatedly argued that growth in the population of U.S. internal migrants stimulates growth in the share of Republican registrants. Prima facie evidence for the connection between the two appears on map 7.5, where the shading bears a striking resemblance to the patterns of population growth depicted on map 7.1. Economically

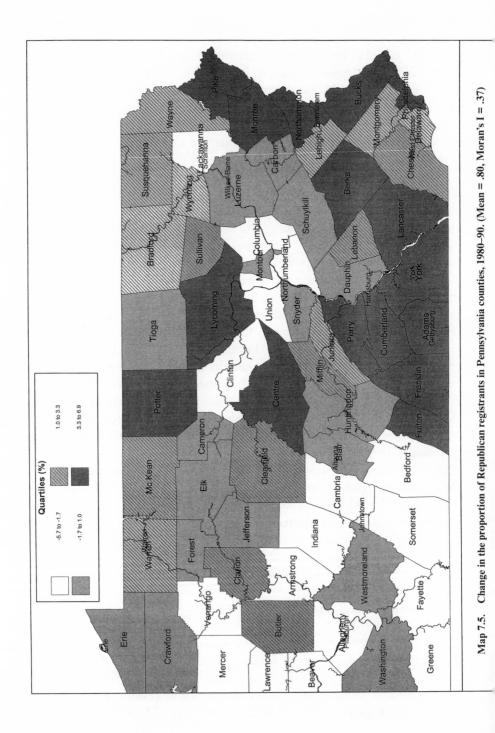

Quartiles (%)

-5.7 to -1.7   1.0 to 3.3

-1.7 to 1.0   3.3 to 6.9

Map 7.5.   Change in the proportion of Republican registrants in Pennsylvania counties, 1980–90. (Mean = .80, Moran's I = .37)

depressed areas have not been kind to the GOP, as we see in the lightly shaded regions in western Pennsylvania (map 7.5).

In the Pennsylvania case, Republican growth is associated with increases in the out-of-state population in both decades (table 7.4). For every percentage point of growth in the proportion of internal migrants, Republican registration growth moves up half a point during the 1970s and by .30 during the 1980s. Growth in the proportion of foreign-born residents is also associated with Republican growth in the 1970s and 1980s, reflecting the suburbanization of the immigrant population. It is noteworthy that increases in the proportion of foreign-born residents are associated with Republican growth in both decades. The places where Republicans seem to be gaining in the face of immigrant growth are in the southeastern Pennsylvania counties (York, Adams, and Lancaster) and several directly north of Philadelphia. This is no indication, of course, that

TABLE 7.4.   Impact of Population Mobility on Changes in Republican Party Registration in Pennsylvania Counties, 1970–80, 1980–90

Variable	1970–80	1980–90
% born out of state, 1970 (1980)	−.13*	.03
	(.08)	(.07)
Change in % born out of state	.46**	.30**
	(.22)	(.14)
% foreign born, 1970 (1980)	−.19	−.10
	(.35)	(.28)
Change in % foreign born	2.85**	3.02**
	(.77)	(.71)
% Republican registrants, 1970 (1980)	−.19**	−.05**
	(.03)	(.02)
Population density	−.001**	.0003**
	(.00004)	(.0002)
Spatial lag	−.48**	.56**
	(.18)	(.15)
Constant	4.66	3.72
N	67	67
R^2_a	.78	.68

Note: Spatial autoregressive model, weighted for population; dependent variable = change in Republican Party registration. See appendix A for a full description of variables.

[a]Variables with low tolerances and high standard errors due to multicollinearity.

*p < .10.   **p < .05.

the foreign born are necessarily registering and voting Republican. Many of the immigrants moving to such places are educated and skilled and have simply found their way to a better life in suburbia along with much of the native-born population. Suburbia's GOP orientation is coincidental to their arrival.

Much of the partisan change in Pennsylvania is directly related to deindustrialization. In chapter 1, I cited the evidence that Republicans are among the first to leave depressed areas. Republicans, therefore, lose registrants in economic hard times due to attrition. The results in table 7.4 are consistent with this explanation. In the 1970s, places of greater population density suffered heavy GOP losses. Areas that were strongly Republican in 1970 lost GOP strength from 1970 to 1980 and again from 1980 to 1990. Many of these losses occurred in areas where unemployment hit hardest, forcing the able bodied and well educated to move out. During the 1980s, Republicans lost five points to other parties in Armstrong County near Pittsburgh, and similar losses were incurred in western jurisdictions that were affected by the collapse of the steel industry.

Partisan change shows a pattern of negative spatial dependency during the 1970s, indicating that growth in GOP registration in a particular place was negatively related to growth in GOP registration in adjacent areas (see table 7.4; see also appendix B). Such a pattern of spatial clustering is consistent with the political development of suburban counties surrounding Pittsburgh and Philadelphia. At the same time that the state's largest cities are losing Republican registrants, the suburbs are gaining them. Hence, positive values for one observation are associated with negative values for geographically proximate observations. In the 1980s, though, the coefficient for the spatially lagged dependent variable in table 7.4 shows positive spatial dependency. This pattern indicates that Republican growth is occurring in "county clusters" or entire subsections of the state, independent of county boundaries or the redistribution of population between urban and suburban counties.

Pennsylvania's slow growth masks changes going on at the county level, which altered the balance of party registrants during the 1980s and early 1990s. Eastern Pennsylvania, in particular, has weathered difficult recessionary times to come out on top. Suburban Philadelphia has seen both population growth and Republican growth due to an influx of migrants from other states. Western Pennsylvania, on the other hand, has experienced population decline and Republican losses relative to those of other parties. Eastern Pennsylvania's restructured postindustrial economy, with its burgeoning share of white collar jobs in service industries and high technology manufacturing, is an especially suitable foundation for building a Republican-dominant politics. Western Pennsylvania still finds many of its interests best represented by Democrats.

The instrument for the economic balkanization of the state has been the uneven development of postindustrial enterprise. This uneven development has perpetuated, and to a great extent exacerbated, the separation of the state's population into two regions, east and west. The growth of Philadelphia's suburbs has been the result of in-migration from both other states and other countries. It is highly doubtful, of course, that many of the immigrants are naturalizing and registering as Republicans. The finding in table 7.4 suggesting that growth in the foreign-born population is closely linked to Republican growth could also be due to the native reaction to the growing number of immigrants in some Pennsylvania communities. Alternatively, immigration to an area is often a sign of an expanding economy. Immigrants are no less smart than native migrants. If they are going to the trouble to relocate, they want to settle in a place where there are economic opportunities. Coincidentally, expanding economies that are drawing population from all sources are often the places where the Republican share of the electorate is growing most rapidly. Democrats, on the other hand, gain most from immobility—from those who are left behind—which is one reason why Democrats have not lost their hold on the most deindustrialized and depopulated regions of the state.

Ethnicity and Political Behavior at the Individual Level

The aggregate data examined up to this point have revealed some interesting patterns in the Keystone State's recent development. We know that Asians and Mexicans are becoming more noticeable and concentrated in the areas where they have settled (table 7.1). There is also the important fact that recent statewide gubernatorial races have not always been competitive contests. Long-established generalizations in political science link turnout levels to the competitiveness of an election. Having added that important caveat, we have seen that out-of-state and foreign-born populations are associated with lower turnout in many major elections and that party regularity is higher in suburban Philadelphia than in other areas of the state. We have also seen that growth in the migrant and immigrant populations is linked to Republican growth. The inevitable ambiguities of ecological data do not allow us to conclude that the relationships examined in tables 7.2, 7.3, and 7.4 exist at the individual level. Drawing upon the statistical technique designed by Gary King (1997) to provide maximally descriptive individual level information from aggregate data, I estimated the proportion of blacks and whites who registered Republican for 1990, 1992, and 1994, based on county level observations of Republican registration and racial/ethnic composition. The proportion of white voters registering as Republicans hovered around 48 to 49 percent for all three years. Estimates of the proportion of the black population registered with the GOP were considerably lower, as we would expect them to be, but fluctuated more from presidential to gubernatorial election years: 24 percent for 1990, 6 percent for 1992, and 15 percent for 1994. Estimates for Hispanics and Asians showed greater Republican registration than among blacks, but less support for Republicans than among whites. The estimates for Asians and Hispanics, while clearly plausible, were not very precise due to severe aggregation bias in the data. State-level polling data may provide additional insight into the validity of inferences made at the aggregate level, especially on the question of whether ethnic groups in the state identify with the Republican or Democratic Party.

Whites are about evenly split between the parties, blacks are predictably Democratic, and Hispanics are, surprisingly, more Republican than in many other states, including California (see table 7.5; for the California comparison, see table 2.5). In 1994, a majority of Hispanic respondents reported that they were independents. Asians, on the other hand, were highly Republican in the 1994 contest. Only 10 percent of Pennsylvania's Asian population identified with the Democrats that year, compared to 58 percent in 1990. While the small numbers of Asians and Hispanics sampled are responsible for the volatility of these figures, it is also possible that Republicans do gain from the kind of established older immigrants one is likely to find in Pennsylvania. Philadelphia, for instance, shows stronger black versus white cleavages in voting behavior than any other area or city in the state. Philadelphia's nonblack minorities (Asians and Hispanics) are as likely to say they are independent as Democrat. Perhaps this is because the Democratic Party in Philadelphia is so dependent upon the majority black community for support that it has no incentive to reach out to the much smaller Hispanic and Asian communities. In Pittsburgh, where the black community is not nearly as influential, Hispanics are far more likely to report that they are Democrats. Asians, however, are more likely to be Republicans than Democrats in western Pennsylvania.

The patterns of party regularity described in the county-level analysis do have some basis in the traits of individual voters. Survey data reveal that Philadelphia's suburban voters were more consistent in their partisanship in the 1994 election than voters in the city proper, and more consistent than in Pittsburgh. That the suburbs should show such regularity is surprising given that whites are far more likely than ethnics to vote in a manner inconsistent with partisanship. But in highly polarized elections fierce competition enforces party regularity. Once again, the extent to which the state is geographically stratified into high and low turnout areas seems to depend crucially on the competition for given offices.

**Political Change and the Internal Composition of
Pennsylvania Counties**

Several of Pennsylvania's counties are worth close scrutiny because they present cases different from others in this book. None of the other states have experienced the kind of economic restructuring that has occurred in Pennsylvania. In a previous work, I argued that deindustrialization has

TABLE 7.5.   Party Identification by Race/Ethnicity in Pennsylvania Elections, 1990–94

Race/Ethnic Group	Year	Democrat	Independent	Republican
White	1990	42.4	20.6	37.0
	1992	40.5	19.8	39.6
	1994	35.2	21.0	43.7
Black	1990	78.1	14.6	7.3
	1992	75.5	20.2	4.3
	1994	80.6	15.2	4.2
Hispanic	1990	37.5	12.5	50.0
	1992	21.1	34.0	44.9
	1994	20.7	54.9	24.4
Asian	1990	58.3	25.0	16.7
	1992	38.2	12.3	49.5
	1994	10.3	27.6	67.1

Source: Voter Research and Surveys, General Election Exit Polls, 1990–94 (weighted data).

changed the electoral foundations of the state, contributing to a less predictably divided electorate than existed in the past and thereby generating a more candidate-centered politics (Gimpel 1996). Here I have posed a slightly different question: how the population changes accompanying the industrial restructuring of Pennsylvania have altered the social and political composition of counties, cities, and regions.

As in Florida and the other states I have studied, political change in Pennsylvania is related to demographic changes within the state. Of the various characteristics of an area that are relevant to politics, I have focused on patterns of ethnic and racial segregation. Spatially isolated minority groups practice a different kind of politics than spatially integrated ones. Isolated minorities are less likely to participate than more integrated groups, and they are more likely to practice a distinctively group-centered politics when they do get involved. Politicians from these communities have difficulty not practicing a racial or ethnic style of politics, for this is what is most likely to get them elected. While a group-centered politics may succeed in securing a few ethnically held seats in a city, state, or national legislature, these candidates usually have trouble moving any further because the race-based rhetoric that resonates so well in isolated communities turns off the broader majority. An additional perverse political effect of minority isolation is the election of electorally safe incumbents who rarely have to fear retribution at the polls for bad behavior. Finally, another noticeable effect of the isolation of minorities has been their inactivity in broad-based Democratic party-building efforts and the consequent strengthening of Republican prospects. But what of Pennsylvania? Is it any different?

Pennsylvania's patterns of ethnic and residential segregation are similar to those of the other states we have examined. The dissimilarity index in table 7.6 shows that blacks are the most spatially isolated minority population relative to whites (for a definition of the index, see chap. 2, n. 1). In 1990, nearly 80 percent of blacks would have had to move for them to be evenly distributed across the state's 3,166 census tracts. The degree of segregation has hardly changed since 1980. As in other states, Hispanics are the second most segregated population, more highly segregated than in Kentucky (chap. 5). Asians are the least segregated, although, interestingly, they are more highly segregated in Pennsylvania than in Florida (chap. 6).

The counties evaluated in table 7.6 run a wide gamut but do not necessarily represent the experience and composition of all areas in the state.

TABLE 7.6. Index of Dissimilarity for the Black, Asian, and Hispanic Populations Relative to Whites in Four Pennsylvania Counties, 1980 and 1990, by Census Tract

Variable	Pennsylvania		Allegheny		Adams		Chester		Erie	
	1980	1990	1980	1990	1980	1990	1980	1990	1980	1990
Asians	.46	.51	.44	.48	.31	.26	.32	.32	.37	.37
Blacks	.81	.79	.76	.74	.38	.43	.52	.50	.65	.65
Hispanics	.58	.61	.29	.29	.33	.32	.51	.47	.38	.49
N	3,166	3,166	499	499	19	19	113	113	69	69

Source: U.S. Census 1990, and author's calculations.
Note: Figures represent the percentage of each group that would have to move in order for the group to be evenly distributed across census tracts in the county.

In none of these jurisdictions is the population of recent immigrants much of a force. Pennsylvania's immigrant population is small, and the number of Asian immigrants is shrinking relative to the native population in Adams and Erie Counties. Hispanic immigrants increased as a proportion of the population in all four counties from 1980 to 1990. But in spite of their small numbers relative to the white population people of color are segregated to an extraordinary degree across all four places.

Adams County (Gettysburg) sits in the rural south-central region along the Maryland border. Never an area of heavy industry, between 1980 and 1992 this county experienced strong growth by Pennsylvania standards, moving from 68,000 to 81,000, a 19 percent increase. Republicans have also gained considerable ground, picking up about four points on Democrats and third parties during the 1980s. Adams shows comparatively low levels of racial segregation until one recognizes just how small the minority population is. With a black population of only 1 percent, less than 1 percent Asians, and about 2 percent Hispanics, it is difficult to imagine that there could be active racial exclusion. Nevertheless, according to the figures in table 7.6, 43 percent of the black population would have to move for this group to be evenly distributed across the nineteen tracts in the county.

Allegheny County is comprised of Pittsburgh and most of its suburbs, including McKeesport and Monroeville. Home to many Polish and Italian immigrants, as well as black migrants from the South and their descendants, Allegheny is a particularly good place to examine patterns of segregation in an urban area afflicted with significant population losses. Eight percent fewer people lived there in 1992 than in 1980. The figures in table 7.6 show that Allegheny County's Asian and black populations are nearly as isolated as in the state itself. Hispanics, on the other hand, are considerably less segregated from whites in the Pittsburgh area than they are statewide. In spite of the segregation, Democrats have done well here, probably because the first to leave the area were the most skilled, educated, and mobile of those laid off.

Chester County in the Philadelphia suburbs (see map 7.1) has experienced rapid economic growth. It has one of the largest non-Pennsylvanian populations in the state, as it has drawn many white collar workers from Delaware. Republicans gained some ground in Chester, though only a modest 1.3 percent, from 1980 to 1990. The population is only 6 percent black, but these blacks are more likely to be middle class than poor so there is less segregation between Caucasians and other races than is found in either Allegheny or poorer communities like Erie.

Finally, Erie County is in the northwest corner of the state, adjacent to New York and Ohio, bordering the shores of Lake Erie. Unlike Pittsburgh, Erie has experienced some growth since midcentury, but nearly all of that growth has occurred in the county rather than the city of Erie. From 1980 to 1990, the county lost less than 1 percent of its population, which stood at 280,000 by 1992. The county's black population is small (5 percent) but highly concentrated. Table 7.6 shows that two-thirds of the black population would be required to move for their numbers to be evenly distributed across the county's sixty-nine tracts. Hispanics are more segregated here than in Allegheny County, a surprising finding given that they only comprised 1 percent of the population in 1990. Republicans have done well in recent elections but have hardly improved their registration. From 1980 to 1990, there was a minuscule .1 percent increase in the share of GOP registrants. Erie County appears to violate the generalization that racially segregated populations benefit Republicans. Like other cities, though, the density of the population probably lessens the impact of spatial isolation on political activity.

Adams County

The Adams County economy is based on agriculture and tourism. Twenty thousand acres of apple and peach orchards cover the northern and western reaches of the county. Gettysburg is adjacent to the famous Civil War battlefield, now a national park. Growth has become an increasingly divisive issue, as commuters from the nearby cities of Baltimore, Washington, D.C., and Harrisburg have sought to escape urban life into more pastoral settings. "People like the rural life and will commute incredible distances to live here," said one local planner. Pennsylvania does not tax pension income, so elderly retirees from Maryland are also attracted to the area. Natives resent that Maryland commuters, with incomes much higher than those of the average Pennsylvania resident, have driven prices up and forced the natives into a kind of second-class status. The nonagricultural segment of the local economy is based on low-paying service sector jobs related to tourism, restaurant and hotel businesses mostly. In average annual wages, Adams County ranked among the lowest in the state in the early 1990s.

The new arrivals, often moving from more developed suburban areas, are accustomed to a wide range of public services. This puts pressure on

local governments to raise taxes to meet new demands. Natives, often living on fixed incomes or employed in low-paying service sector jobs, cannot
afford the taxes to support economic development. Still, the newcomers
have been slow to involve themselves in Pennsylvania politics, and natives
control most political offices. Local politicians proudly distinguish themselves from newcomers by proclaiming that they were born in the county.

The natives also look to the east and see the crowding of Lancaster
County. They are fearful that this pattern of change is in their future.
"People are not interested in a city moving here," said one local, himself a
California transplant (Eshleman 1991). Naturally these fears have translated into pressure for local growth control. The integrity of the Gettysburg battlefield itself has been at stake in some recent quarrels about
whether to build a shopping mall that abuts the park. Development has
won some of these battles. Route 30, the major east-west thoroughfare,
has been described as overburdened, a "homogenized, stripped-out
melange of 20th century motel and fast-food culture" (Goldstein 1991).

The areas of migrant settlement are shown on map 7.6. Even in this
sparsely populated area, one can see that immigrant and migrant settlements are in separate parts of the county. The area is home to a significant
population of Mexican migrant workers who pick apples on farms north
of Gettysburg. Haitians are a smaller but still significant portion of the
migrant work force. Given the location of the orchards, "upper Adams" is
where most of the Hispanic population is concentrated. South-central
Pennsylvania has long had the lowest unemployment rate in the state, so it
is not surprising that the migrant laborers have been a presence here since
the 1960s. Even family-owned farms hire them. Long-time Anglo natives
describe the migrant workers as "good citizens. They work, raise their
families, and do not go on welfare." They are also politically inactive and
"stick to themselves. The Catholic church is their only gathering point."
They are "not involved in criminal activity like minorities elsewhere," said
one local reporter.

The model of partisan change in table 7.4 suggested that growth in the
immigrant population is associated with growth in the Republican share
of registrants. In the case of Adams County, however, there is no direct
causal relationship at the individual level. Most Hispanics in Adams do
not vote, and many are not even citizens. Hispanics are drawn to Adams
County because of economic opportunities that are not available in the
declining areas of the state. This economic growth also happens to be
attracting an increasing number of Republican migrants from Maryland

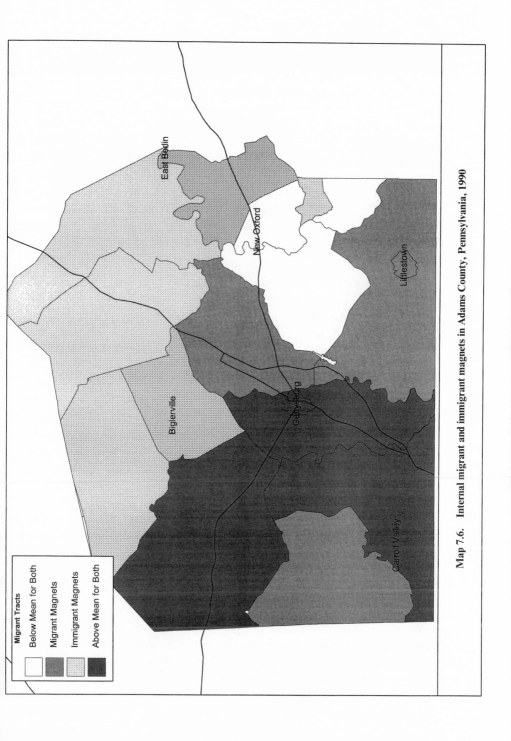

Migrant Tracts

Below Mean for Both

Migrant Magnets

Immigrant Magnets

Above Mean for Both

East Berlin

New Oxford

Littlestown

Biglerville

Gettysburg

Carroll Valley

Map 7.6.   Internal migrant and immigrant magnets in Adams County, Pennsylvania, 1990

and other states. Ethnic balkanization is on its way because Hispanics are settling down to raise families in rural Pennsylvania, only occasionally returning to their hometowns in Mexico.

The mechanism of the spatial segregation of the Hispanic population in Adams County is the location of jobs. It makes little sense for Hispanic migrants to commute to the apple farms when there is housing close by and commuting costs are high. Hispanic families (of all races) made only 65 percent of what non-Hispanic white families made in 1990. Ethnic tension is not much of an issue. Blacks constituted only 1 percent of the county population in 1990. There are few Asians, although Indians in the hospitality and convenience store businesses are a noticeable presence. Adams County is an excellent example of a case in which the isolation of the Hispanic population has hindered its assimilation and rendered it politically powerless. Like communities of immigrant agricultural laborers in California, Colorado, Florida, and other states, rural isolation has a far more adverse impact on participation in civic life than urban isolation has. While there are no signs of exploitation of Hispanics by farmers that compares to what is found in the meatpacking industry in Kansas and Colorado, the Latino population is vulnerable and excessively dependent upon the benevolence of their employers.

Pittsburgh and Allegheny County
Allegheny County's population loss can be attributed to younger middle and upper income out-migrants and semiskilled workers who finally realized that the old blue collar manufacturing jobs would not return. "You figured out the old jobs weren't going to come back when they started tearing down the mills in the early 1980s," said one local reporter. This left a large population of older residents, and a demoralized underclass, alongside established older wealth. By the early 1990s, Pittsburgh had made a comeback, bringing in high technology and service industries for the well educated (Stokes 1994). For the unskilled, the new industries offered lower paying nonunion employment, but this was better than nothing. Pittsburgh's effort to become the next Silicon Valley has been aided by the presence of excellent universities, but public school enrollment has declined, indicating that few people with families have been attracted to the area.

The Mon Valley, southeast of Pittsburgh, has not fared as well as the city itself. Along the Monongahela River lie the blighted, bombed-out remains of once thriving steel towns: Homestead, McKeesport, Duquesne, and Clairton (Serrin 1993; see map 7.7). In the early 1980s, 150,000 jobs

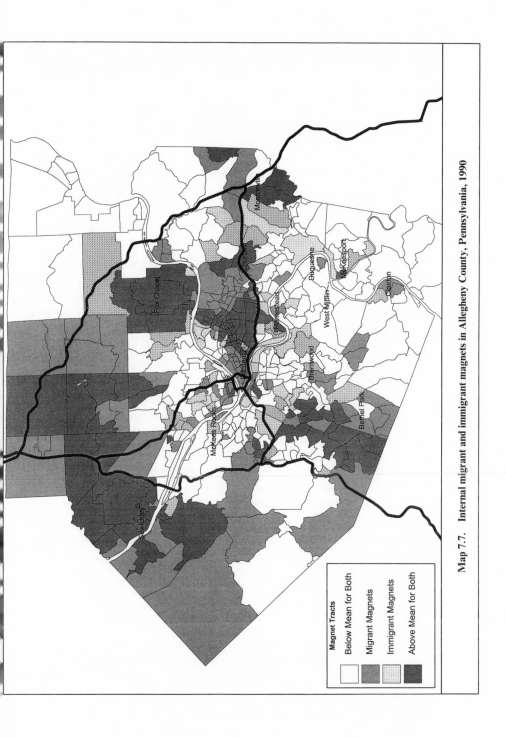

Magnet Tracts

☐ Below Mean for Both

▨ Migrant Magnets

▧ Immigrant Magnets

■ Above Mean for Both

Map 7.7. Internal migrant and immigrant magnets in Allegheny County, Pennsylvania, 1990

were permanently lost in this area. A few marginal businesses survive, mostly because the buildings they are in would be empty otherwise and are owned by elderly proprietors who have nothing else to do (Marsh 1987). With the sudden loss of the industrial tax base, these communities have been hard pressed to pay for basic public services. The remaining population consists mainly of two groups: the elderly, living on fixed incomes; and the poor, who are usually dependent on public assistance (Gittell 1992). The neighborhoods in these depressed areas are in a long-term state of decline typified by abandoned and dilapidated housing, drug activity, and crime. William Julius Wilson has found the same neighborhood dynamics at work in Chicago associated with depopulation and neighborhood disinvestment (1996). The Mon Valley has experienced no population growth, a situation that has aided Democrats, as the elderly and black populations are highly loyal. When asked why more young people do not leave, one local observer explained that "many residents do not think it would be better anywhere else. There is a lack of hope." Nor are there the resources in this population to pack up and go. Then there is the familiar gap in depressed areas everywhere between what a place provides and what it means (Marsh 1987). Some endure the social and economic hardship of remaining in a poor community because they have strong psychic ties to their neighborhood, church, family, and friends (Wilson 1996).

The wave of immigrants arriving since 1968 has largely bypassed Pittsburgh. Hispanic immigrants in search of work would not find it in a depressed economy. The Latino population is large enough, however (8,000 in 1990), to support a Spanish language newspaper. Map 7.7 shows that the areas of immigrant concentration tend to be in the poorer sections south of Pittsburgh rather than in the wealthier northern tracts. Areas where migrants and immigrants have mixed include the tracts on the east side of Pittsburgh (darkly shaded areas in map 7.7). Asians, particularly Chinese, Filipino, and Indian immigrants, have settled in the city's eastern tracts near Carnegie-Mellon University and the University of Pittsburgh in the neighborhoods of Garfield and Lawrenceville as well as in the eastern suburbs of Wilkinsburg and Monroeville. In the suburbs, Asians are more likely to be professionals than small business owners, and their level of education has facilitated their assimilation. Some of the brightest students in the Monroeville schools are from Vietnamese and Indian families. Since Asians comprised only 1 percent of the population in the 1990 census, their high degree of segregation is somewhat surprising, but it can be explained by the location of the universities and the tendency for Asians to chain migrate. Ethnic tensions between Asians and non-Asians are reportedly rare.

Many blacks came to the Pittsburgh area to take jobs in the steel mills as part of the "great migration" of the 1920s and 1930s (Gottlieb 1987). Their children and grandchildren have become the victims of deindustrialization. The black population is spatially segregated from the white population in both Pittsburgh and the Mon Valley towns. The black population in the valley is extremely poor, with 40 percent of the families living below the poverty line in 1990, compared to 14 to 15 percent for whites. In Pittsburgh, the only difference is that there are fewer white poor, so the income disparity is even greater in the city than in the suburbs. In the middle class eastern suburbs, such as Monroeville and Wilkinsburg, blacks have fared better. There have been isolated instances of racial intimidation but also concerted efforts to overcome this tension.

The mechanism of racial segregation is in part the county's unusual topography of hills, valleys, and rivers, which isolate neighborhoods in unique ways (Glasco 1989; Bodnar, Simon, and Weber 1982). But segregation has also been the product of industrial decline and differences between white and black birthrates. White, middle income neighborhoods were far better able to weather deindustrializing trends and have been the first to bounce back. In addition, more whites than blacks have decided to leave the county (and often the state) for better opportunities elsewhere. This has left the black population in some of the most impoverished and blighted areas in Pittsburgh and southwestern Pennsylvania. As the figures in table 7.6 show, the level of residential segregation of the black community has remained almost the same from 1980 to 1990. High birthrates among minorities and the out-migration of white families have created a highly segregated school system in which black children are a much larger proportion of the school population than blacks are in the general population. Population losses contribute to segregation because low-income minority groups are less mobile than wealthier whites.

Blacks are a minority in the city and the county, and nearly all of them vote Democratic. Pittsburgh is such an overwhelmingly Democratic town that the loyalty of the black wards to the Democratic Party has marginalized black influence. A recent move from at-large to district-level city council elections has helped elect several black council members who otherwise would not have been elected. But in countywide contests white Democratic politicians have been known to boast of not needing the black vote to win local elections. Local observers suggested that the black community has been afflicted with weak and inept leadership co-opted by Democratic machine politics. Ward leaders have a strong incentive to prevent aspiring and capable black leaders from gaining too much power.

By the 1990s, the Democratic Party machinery had ossified. Younger people were not drawn into the party leadership. As the suburbs have grown, and the city has declined, Republicans have sometimes taken advantage of Democratic factionalism. In the mid-1990s, the Allegheny County Commission was taken over by Republicans for the first time due to a feud within Democratic ranks. Party registration has remained heavily Democratic, and Republicans were still losing registrants as of the 1990s. Independent registration increased to 6 percent in 1994, up about one point since 1980, but there has been no massive abandonment of traditional party ties. Instead, party registration is stable because the population has not been replaced. The only changes are due to the attrition of voters, not to conversion or the addition of sizable new blocs.

The population trends in Allegheny County, its decline, the relative absence of immigrants, and the hopelessness of its unemployed population all speak to its isolation, from both the rest of the state and the nation. The reputable high-technology education centers in Pittsburgh have helped stabilize the area's economy, but the city is "just not on people's screens when they're looking for information about business markets. Not growing is a real clear signal from the market that you're not an attractive place to live," reported one *Post-Gazette* story in the mid-1990s (Heuck 1996). Rumors of Pittsburgh's recovery have been highly exaggerated. This area's long-term decline is favorable only to prolonged Democratic dominance.

Chester County
Chester County is a state away from Pittsburgh and worlds away in economic terms. Population growth started in the early 1970s, as Chester proved to be a second stop in the suburbanization of Philadelphia. Out-migrants from the city had first settled in Delaware County, but as Delaware became crowded the next move was to Chester. These are residential suburbs, then, where more people commute out to work to Delaware County, Philadelphia, and the state of Delaware than commute in. The population of newcomers consists mostly of affluent young families who, according to one long-time native, "want to convert Chester into the new Main Line. They want towns full of little shops that smell like lavender and serve cappuccino. They are obsessed with safety and crime. They lock their doors, don't allow their kids to go outside and expect someone to be

watching their children every minute." Wilmington, Delaware, started a busing program to integrate its schools in the late 1970s. Fearing the effects of integration, many white families fled across the border into Chester County. The new arrivals who have suburbanized Chester are distinct from the native population, which knew the county before the influx and grew up secure and comfortable in a rural way of life. Natives include affluent Italian and Quaker mushroom farmers at the southern end of the county and old wealth represented by the owners of Chester's sprawling horse farms, including descendants of William Penn himself.

The black and Asian populations are a minor presence. The Hispanic population, however, is growing (Garcia 1997). Mexican migrant laborers have settled at the south end of the county near the towns of Kennett Square and West Grove (see map 7.8). They are employed on the mushroom farms that have made Pennsylvania the nation's largest mushroom-producing state. Chester County became the nation's center of mushroom production in the 1920s as a secondary crop for florists (Hamm 1997). Mexicans are drawn to this area because unemployment is low and the black and Italian laborers who were once hired to work with the mushrooms are no longer willing to do so for the wages farmers are willing to pay. Low-wage labor is so scarce, in fact, that in the early 1990s businesses began paying workers' transportation costs from Philadelphia to suburban work sites. Working the mushroom farms is hot, smelly work, as mushrooms are grown in a manure and straw compost that must be mixed and "cooked out" before it is spread on the trays in dark, humid sheds where the fungus is grown. The original farm laborers were Italian immigrants. Now Italians own many of the farms. Mexican farm labor is prized for its low cost. In 1995, workers were paid one dollar above minimum wage (slightly over $5.30), and some growers also pay workers a bonus per pound harvested. A yearly salary for a Mexican migrant worker in the mid-1990s stood at $15,000 to $20,000.

The Mexican population has been greeted with hostility by the white newcomers and some natives who are unhappy with the prospect of low-income housing and integrated schools. In Kennett Square, internal migrants and immigrants have mixed uneasily. A local homeowners movement has tried to have the town declared a historic district with enforcement of strict architectural controls to force the Hispanic population to leave. Since a sizable percentage of the Mexican workers are either illegal or have forged papers, most are not politically active. The Mexicans all originate from one of several Mexican towns. Political activity by legal res-

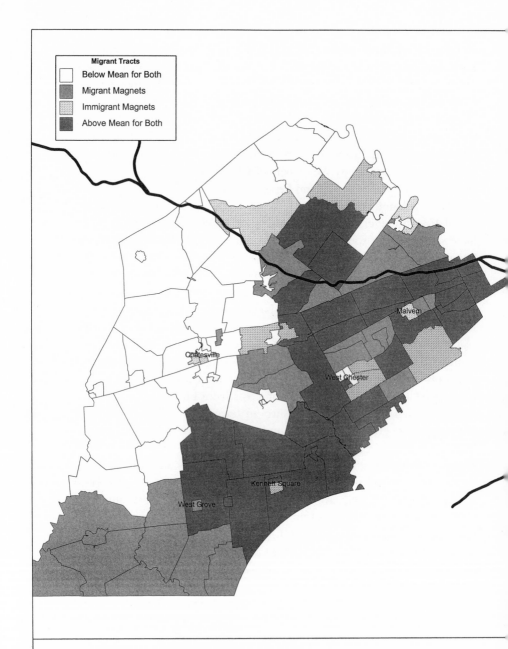

Migrant Tracts

☐ Below Mean for Both
▨ Migrant Magnets
▦ Immigrant Magnets
■ Above Mean for Both

Malvern
Coatesville
West Chester
Kennett Square
West Grove

Map 7.8.   Internal migrant and immigrant magnets in Chester County, Pennsylvania, 1990

idents and U.S. citizens is avoided for fear that retaliation could mean arrest and deportation of friends and relatives. Black residents, some of whom have lived here since before the Civil War, when Chester County was a stop on the underground railroad (Oblinger 1973), have been forced to move out by the rising cost of living (Garcia 1997). The ones who remain are people of some means. Only 14 percent of the black population lived in poverty in 1990, and this undoubtedly explains their relatively higher degree of integration compared to Erie or Allegheny Counties (see table 7.6). The small number of well-educated black residents are politically active. A few serve on local government boards in the southern boroughs and townships with mostly white constituencies.

Reflecting its rural roots, Chester County is one-party Republican turf and has been since before the New Deal. The Main Line WASP population combined with German and Dutch immigrants has made for a very conservative brew. Republicanism is also a reaction to the prevailing anti-Philadelphia sentiment that has differentiated the suburbs from the city for decades. Recent efforts to transfer money from the suburbs into the city to deal with Philadelphia's chronic fiscal problems have been met with hostility by all the suburban communities. "When Chester Countians see Philadelphia, they see business, money, traffic and crime. There is a hostility to diversity. People out here won't say they hate diversity, but their definition of diversity is very homogeneous," said one community reporter. In spite of cultural differences among natives and newcomers, population in-migration has not dented the county's Republican tradition as it has in other suburbs. Newcomers and natives may vote Republican for slightly different reasons. Natives, for instance, tend to be socially liberal, or even libertarian, on issues such as abortion. But the area is unified in its fiscal conservatism. No wonder Republican registration has remained stable through the 1980s while Democratic registration has declined slightly. Why haven't Republican gains been more positive? Many new voters from out of state have not registered and have been slow to develop an interest in state and local issues. New residents also know that juries are chosen from voter registration lists, an additional disincentive to regular participation. Finally, the population growth in this region has translated into strong gains for independent registration, which reached its historical peak of 12 percent of the electorate in 1994.

Erie County

At a convenient junction at the corners of Pennsylvania, Ohio, and New York, Erie was once a meeting place for rival Indian tribes seeking to resolve disputes on neutral ground. In the late twentieth century, Erie has found itself at the intersection of two major interstate highways (I–79 and I–90) and has emerged as a retail and wholesale trade center for the entire region. Small town residents from western New York, Pennsylvania, Ohio, and even Canada arrive in Erie for weekend sightseeing and shopping trips. While its population has been stable since 1980, Erie County is one of the few places that has grown in western Pennsylvania in the post–World War II period, suggesting some resilience in the face of the deindustrialization that wrecked Allegheny County and areas further south. The scale of industrial employment has always been smaller here. Economic hard times meant layoffs and plant closings, but the smaller size of plants meant that a closing rarely had the kind of ripple effect on the community that one found in the towns in the Mon Valley. Industrial employers in Erie include smaller shops that could more easily make the shift toward batch production than the hulking and inflexible steel mills to the south. When union laborers found themselves out of work in Erie, they either moved or were able to make the transition to jobs in nonunion employment, sometimes even changing careers. The outlying suburbs and towns have experienced a boom in low-wage retail and government employment. The university in Edinboro is a major employer, as is the state prison at the western end of the county. In the town of Albion, full of small retail employers typical of towns of this size, the school district is the single largest employer.

Originally settled by immigrants from Poland, Ireland, and Italy early in the twentieth century, the city of Erie, like cities elsewhere, has lost population to its suburbs and bedroom communities. This has left the city with the usual problems: increasing poverty, poorly equipped schools, dilapidated housing stock, an aging population, and crime. With good transportation links to the south, west, and east, the commute is short and tolerable for those wishing to shop and work in the city. The nonwhite population of Erie was only 15 percent by the mid-1990s, but the Hispanic population was growing rapidly. As in Adams and Chester Counties, Hispanics are employed in agriculture as seasonal labor on area grape farms. Judging from the figures in table 7.6, the segregation of the Hispanic population appears to be increasing along with its numbers. The Hispanic population of Erie is extremely poor, earning only half of what non-Hispanic white families earned in 1990, and isolated in neighborhoods on the east end of town. The city has also attracted recent waves of immigration from Russia, Asia, and Eastern Europe. Apparently, however, the arrival of these groups has not caused any controversy because the volume of in-migration has been small enough that they have not put much of a strain on local resources and services. Erie's strong and self-conscious ethnic heritage has made it more accepting of immigrants than it might otherwise be.

Reflecting its roots in the settlement of eastern and southern European Catholics, the city of Erie has been a Democratic stronghold for most of this century. The outlying areas are mostly Protestant and Republican. Like the rest of western Pennsylvania, the social values are conservative. Republicans represented the area in the U.S. House through the 1980s and 1990s. Local observers report that partisanship is not the strong cue that it once was. How else could Republicans get elected in a county where 57 percent of the registered voters are Democrats? Although the growth of the suburbs has come mostly from the Democratic city of Erie, Republicans have gradually improved their prospects in outlying areas, increasing their membership to about 40 percent of total registrants in 1994. The improvement in GOP registration is not clearly linked to any trends in migration from out of state but instead appears to be the result of generational change, suburbanization, and growth from sources internal to the state such as heavily Republican Crawford County to the south.

Large Numbers, Economic Opportunity, and Segregation

The Pennsylvania case is a good example of a place where numbers are a good indicator of an ethnic group's assimilation and economic well-being. In areas where a group is concentrated in large numbers, its economic prospects are poorer than where ethnics are few and far between (Frisbie and Neidert 1976; Tienda and Lii 1987). Hence, the small number of Asian families in Chester, Erie, and Allegheny Counties earn, on average, more than the average non-Hispanic white family. But in Philadelphia, with a far larger Asian population, Asian family income is only 65 percent of non-Hispanic white income.

The precise mechanism of cause and effect is unclear here. Do ethnic enclaves hold back economic progress and assimilation or is the causal direction the other way, with ethnics clustering in enclaves because they are poor, uneducated, and need the strength of numbers for survival? Variations in the well-being of the Hispanic population in Pennsylvania are also instructive and depend upon nativity and immigrant status. The small number of Hispanic families in Allegheny County earned nearly as much as non-Hispanic white families in 1990 because the vast majority were native born and English speaking. By contrast, in Adams, Chester, and Erie Counties, a far higher percentage were foreign born, in agricultural employment, and earning very low wages compared to the non-Hispanic white population.

Pennsylvania's varying patterns of population growth, stagnation, and decline add considerable texture to our understanding of the political consequences of demographic change. We have learned at least three things from this chapter. First, Pennsylvania's uneven development has lured more migrants and immigrants to the eastern than to the western region of the state. The instrument for the political and demographic balkanization of the state has been the uneven development of postindustrial enterprise. The geographic isolation of Pittsburgh and its reputation as a headquarters for costly union labor have been major barriers to new investment. By contrast, the proximity of Philadelphia and its suburbs to major East Coast markets has made for a much smoother transition to the service economy.

Second, and more important, population decline is far less likely to change the party balance of regions than population growth is. Those who remain behind when economic times turn sour are most likely to have entrenched patterns and ways of life and thought. Population loss leaves two kinds of people behind: the very old and the very poor—most of whom are unwilling or unable to move. With the most risk-averse citizens remaining behind, population loss has done little to alter the balance of party registration in Allegheny County. Population growth, on the other hand, has the capacity to upset the entire social and political balance of a community. This is why affluent white Pennsylvanians in Chester County have such a strong incentive to shut out the growing threat of the Hispanic population even as the local economy exploits their labor. In Adams County, the resentment is turned toward arrivals from other states, particularly Maryland, who with their superior incomes threaten to stratify an area that has been homogeneous with respect to income.

Finally, the spatial segregation of ethnic and racial minorities from the white majority, and from each other, can be exacerbated by either population growth or decline. In Chester County, and to a lesser extent in Adams, high-end development has taken the same track that it has in

Florida. It has made more neighborhoods off limits to low-income residents, many of whom are of color. While segregation in a rural county like Adams is a relatively benign function of Hispanic migrants who find living near the fruit orchards a practical measure, in the Philadelphia suburbs the mechanism of segregation is far from benign. White upper income residents are fiercely fighting to exclude low-income development from the southern end of Chester County in order to prevent the permanent settlement of Hispanic laborers. In the case of Allegheny County, we learn that spatial segregation is sustained through population losses because out-migrants are not a random mix of the area population. Those who leave are far more white, well educated, and motivated than those who stay behind. They are also those who can afford the costs of moving and are informed enough to know what opportunities lie elsewhere.

Segregation of minority from white population groups in Pennsylvania threatens to create homogeneous communities of interest, polarizing neighborhoods, cities, and counties in social and political terms. City-suburban polarization is nothing new. Philadelphia's inferiorities have always been accentuated by its suburbs (Muller, Meyer, and Cybriwsky 1976). Nor is the division between west and east in Pennsylvania especially new. The continuing polarization of such areas by race and class due to the mechanisms of either growth or decline are a matter of concern for those who value the practice of a pluralist politics of compromise where divisions in the community are temporary and subject to resolution. Overcoming the unpleasant political conflicts that occur along racial and ethnic lines has been a continuing battle in the history of the nation. Racial cleavages have been anything but temporary. The sustained segregation of racial and ethnic communities through contemporary migration and immigration processes places racial and ethnic harmony even further beyond our reach.

CHAPTER 8

New York: The Clustered Masses

New York, unlike California, has an immigrant-friendly reputation. In the 1840s and 1850s, when Irish immigrants were being persecuted for their Catholicism in the New England states, they often found a much less hostile reception in New York (Billington 1961; Glazer and Moynihan 1963). Although New York state lacks constitutional provisions for direct legislation, there was no serious consideration of Proposition 187-style bills in the state legislature as there was in other states. New York City's Republican mayor, Rudolph Giuliani, actively opposed GOP plans in Congress to place new restrictions on legal immigration in 1995 and 1996. When Congress gave states the option of ending or continuing certain welfare benefits for legal immigrants in 1996, Republican Governor George Pataki quickly acted to continue these programs at state expense while lobbying Congress to reconsider the decision to cut federal aid. Republican leaders in New York were hardly on the restrictionist bandwagon like the California GOP. Nor has there been much grassroots protest of immigrants.

New York receives fewer immigrants than California but its immigrant population is far from inconsequential. In 1990, the state was home to nearly 2.9 million immigrants—second only to the Golden State. These immigrants are clustered primarily in the state's largest cities, and, of these, the five New York City boroughs stand out. Only 3 percent of immigrants resided in New York's rural areas, compared with 18 percent of the native born in 1990.

The state's growth has been much slower than California, and this is an important difference that may explain the two states' differing reactions to immigrant influx. A large, but relatively slow-growing, foreign born population has been a steady feature of New York politics for the last 150 years. The ethnic composition of this population has changed with immigration law, but native New Yorkers rarely complain about their state being "overrun" as they frequently do in California.

Most of the state's growth has occurred in the counties containing the New York City suburbs (Suffolk, Nassau, Rockland, Westchester, and Orange Counties; see map 8.1). The lightly shaded counties upstate show that the population outside the New York City metropolitan area has been far more stable, with the exception, pehaps, of a few counties around Rochester (Monroe County) and Albany (Albany County) and scattered others (map 8.1). Between 1980 and 1992, the average county grew by about 5.3 percent with population decline occurring in Western New York, and particularly Erie (Buffalo) and Chautauqua (Jamestown) Counties.

As in Pennsylvania, the cultural and economic divide between New York City and the urban and rural areas upstate has repeatedly asserted itself in the state's politics. The cleavage between loyal Republican voters upstate and the Democratic boroughs of the city has been one of the most enduring divisions in American state politics (Gimpel 1996). While the lack of heavy industry on the Pittsburgh scale has made western New York less vulnerable to recession than it might otherwise be, economic decline has changed the occupational mix in Rust Belt cities such as Buffalo, Rochester, and Syracuse (Corrigan 1985; Wu and Korman 1987; Koritz 1991). Better educated workers and the wealthier among the elderly have moved out, leaving behind a less skilled and less mobile population forced into lower paying jobs and bearing up under a declining standard of living. Out-migration is also the product of the few new white collar jobs that have been created in areas upstate. Afflicted with one of the worst climates for new business creation during the 1970s and 1980s, college-educated, younger New Yorkers discovered that there were no opportunities for them once they entered the labor force (Alba and Trent 1986; Fitchen 1992). Population losses and economic decline in upstate New York have gradually eroded the registration edge the GOP has traditionally enjoyed, bolstering third-party and Democratic registration. The regional acculturation of the upstate voters to the Republicans is still strong, however, and the area is far less likely to vote Democratic in statewide races than New York City and its suburbs are.

The New York City boroughs have also lost population to the suburbs since the 1950s, with Queens and Manhattan (New York County) losing one-quarter of their population from 1950 to the mid-1990s. Only Staten Island (Richmond County) has grown, more than doubling in size over the same period. While the city has experienced a net loss in population, the housing stock remains inadequate in both supply and quality.

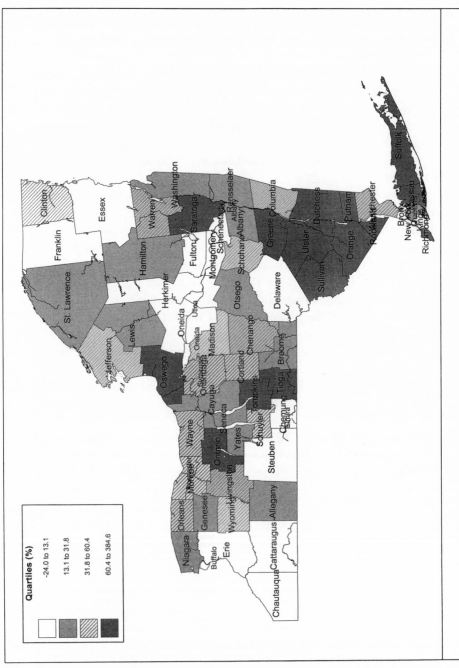

Map 8.1. Population growth in New York counties, 1950–92. (Mean = 48.5, Moran's I = .14)

Quartiles (%)

-24.0 to 13.1
13.1 to 31.8
31.8 to 60.4
60.4 to 384.6

"There are no true slum neighborhoods in New York," insisted one city planner in a 1996 interview. "Housing is in too short a supply for there to be slums." The population dynamics in the borough neighborhoods are extremely complex, with one demographic group moving out of an area only to be replaced by another (Denowitz 1980; Alba, Denton, Leung, and Logan 1993; Rosenbaum 1992). This phenomenon of population replacement, often termed "residential succession" by housing specialists, has been fueled by both out-migration to the suburbs and the arrival of immigrants (Denowitz 1980). In the early 1960s, it was possible to write about a city where most of the immigrants were still white and European (Glazar and Moynihan 1963; Moynihan 1979). By the 1990s, New York City was full of minorities of diverse origin, but this diversity was accompanied by racial segregation and economic polarization. Many neighborhoods that were racially mixed in the 1970s had become all-black by the 1990s (Alba, Denton, Leung, and Logan 1993). White and Asian immigrants have been among the first to move to the suburbs, leaving black and Hispanic residents to the older borough neighborhoods. New York City's increasing racial diversity has sustained and exacerbated the historical pattern of spatially isolating new groups in homogeneous pockets.

Contributing to this spatial segregation is the growing income inequality in New York City, characterized by opportunities for the well educated and skilled but not for the unskilled (Mollenkopf and Castells 1991; Waldinger 1996). Most of the city's manufacturing jobs had been lost by the early 1980s. The emergence of a postindustrial economy provided some well-paying white collar jobs but many more low-paying service sector positions (Bailey and Waldinger 1991). For low-income households that have missed out on the economic growth in the private sector, survival in New York has been aided only by public sector employment and services coupled with the high volume of out-migration (Waldinger 1996). Mollenkopf and Castells (1991) argue that it is an oversimplification to say that New York has been balkanized into two classes of people. The reason why the "dual city" metaphor does not seem to apply is that immigrants do better in the New York economy than many native minorities do. Foreign workers have substituted for natives in the manual labor market, taking many of the remaining manufacturing jobs (Marshall 1987). The labor market patterns of ethnic groups are often sector specific, reflecting the occupational paths that were established by their coethnic predecessors (Waldinger 1996; Foner 1987). Immigrants are also able to take advantage of the informal economy in enclave communities populated by coethnics, which helps to compensate for the discrimination they encounter (Waldinger 1996, 23; Kwong 1996; Portes and Rumbaut 1990; Zhou 1992). Reliance on ethnic enclaves and niches in the New York economy has paid off, as immigrants have proven better able to exit the city for the suburbs than native blacks and Hispanics.

While three of the five boroughs have minority white populations, the older suburbs in Nassau and Westchester Counties are also becoming more racially and economically diverse and gradually more Democratic in spite of the presence of strong Republican political machines. There are more all-black neighborhoods in Nassau than ever before—testimony to residential succession rather than spatial assimilation as the mechanism of neighborhood transition. Blacks may achieve a socioeconomic status close to that of whites, but the reluctance of whites to live near blacks has prevented the latter from translating socioeconomic achievement into improved living standards (Alba and Logan 1993; Rosenbaum 1992, 469; Wirt, Walter, Rabinovitz, and Hensler 1972). Further outside of New York City, the suburbs of Suffolk, Rockland, and Westchester Counties are home to the highly affluent residential development one can find in Chester County, Pennsylvania, and other commuter-shed areas. Like wealthy suburbs elsewhere, local control of public schools is a major issue. Several of the towns in this region have fought protracted battles against the development of low-income housing for minorities, including Yonkers and White Plains in Westchester County (Metzger 1995; Skinner 1995; Galster and Keeney 1993). Blacks, Hispanics, and Asians have found their way into older suburban neighborhoods, but the towns further out remain racially homogeneous, primarily residential, and white.

New York's uniqueness lies in the fact that the vast majority of suburban residents are not from out of state. Population growth in the New York suburbs has been the product of out-migration from the city rather than cross-state migration. Map 8.2 shows that the New York City area experienced overall decline in the proportion of internal migrants during the 1980s. By 1990, 87.3 percent of Suffolk County's population had been born in New York, far higher than the percentage for similar suburban counties in Kentucky, Florida, Kansas, Colorado, or California. Having a suburban population from elsewhere in New York, as opposed to elsewhere in the country, makes a difference for an area's politics. New Yorkers who move from one part of the state to another are more likely to have developed some knowledge of and interest in state and local politics than those who move from a different state. The likelihood that they will exercise this political capital by participating in state and local elections after they move is higher than for those who come from a greater distance.

Immigration has had an undeniably strong impact on the state's economy and politics (Torres 1995; Foner 1987; Glazer and Moynihan 1963). As in South Florida, immigrants socially and culturally demarcate New York City from the rest of the state (see map 8.3). The existence of immigrant enclaves has been well documented in New York City, and ethnic balkanization is nothing new (Ernst 1949; Glazer and Moynihan 1963). The racial diversity of immigrants who have arrived since 1970 is new. The bulk of the new immigration is from Asian, Latin American, and Caribbean countries. The racial composition of this new wave has served to harden divisions between upstate New York and the city by adding a component of racial balkanization to the more fundamental urban-rural differences that have existed for decades. The composition of the foreign-born population in 1990 reveals that European émigrés made up only 26 percent of the immigrant population in the state (see fig. 8.1). Forty-one percent come from Latin America and the Caribbean, and 20 percent are from Asian countries.

New York's racial heterogeneity is also the product of a large black population, numbering nearly three million in 1990. The black proportion of the population has increased in every borough since the 1960s and was well over one-third of the population in Brooklyn (Kings County) and the Bronx (Bronx County). Blacks comprise more than 10 percent of the population in only three counties outside the city: Erie (Buffalo), Monroe (Rochester), and Westchester (White Plains). This means that the black population is overwhelmingly concentrated in a small area of the state, although not quite so concentrated as in Pennsylvania. When a dissimilarity index is calculated for the state's sixty-two counties, it shows that nearly 50 percent of blacks would have to move for them to be evenly distributed, compared to two-thirds in Pennsylvania (see chap. 7). Unlike Pennsylvania, however, Asians and Hispanics are as concentrated in New York state (at the county level of aggregation) as blacks are. Nearly half of each group would be required to move for them to reside in balanced proportions across the state. Corresponding to this racial balkanization is political balkanization caused by the one-sidedness of party registration in many cities and counties. In terms of party registration, New York is less politically balanced than either Florida or Pennsylvania. A dissimilarity measure calculated for party registrants shows that about 40 percent of Republicans (or Democrats) would have to move for the parties to be equally proportioned across the state's counties.

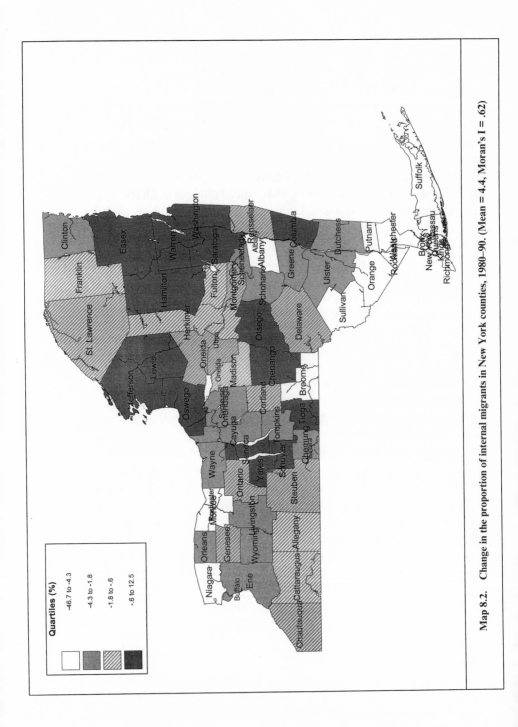

Map 8.2. Change in the proportion of internal migrants in New York counties, 1980–90. (Mean = 4.4, Moran's I = .62)

Quartiles (%)

-46.7 to -4.3
-4.3 to -1.8
-1.8 to -.6
-.6 to 12.5

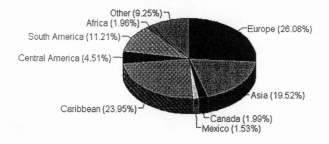

Fig. 8.1. Composition of the foreign-born population in New York, 1990

PUMS data for 1990 show that we have very little reason to expect that natives, migrants, and immigrants will be settling in next to each other anytime soon (see appendix A, table A8.1). Migrants from other states earned, on average, $17,118 annually, compared to $15,934 for native New Yorkers and just $12,946 for immigrants. The $4,200 gap in average earnings between immigrants and internal migrants is among the widest in the nation. The figures for *median* income indicate that immigrants earned only 66 percent of what internal migrants earned in 1990. The reasons why immigrants did not fare as well as other groups are straightforward. First, only 37 percent of foreign-born New Yorkers were non-Hispanic white, compared to 74 percent of internal migrants and 88 percent of natives (table A8.1). Immigrants also lag behind migrants and natives in terms of their educational attainment. On other measures of income and well-being, immigrants in New York lag well behind natives according to the PUMS data. They receive more in public assistance (but not Social Security) than either natives or internal migrants, and the average immigrant pays only about half of what the average native New Yorker pays in personal property taxes.

Settlement Patterns of Migrants and Immigrants in New York

Map 8.3 shows that growth in the concentration of immigrants has occurred in the New York City boroughs and the suburban counties along with Tompkins (Ithaca) County upstate. Internal migrants (map 8.2) were a decreasing presence in these locations and many others. The most notable growth in the concentration of interstate migrants has been in rural north-

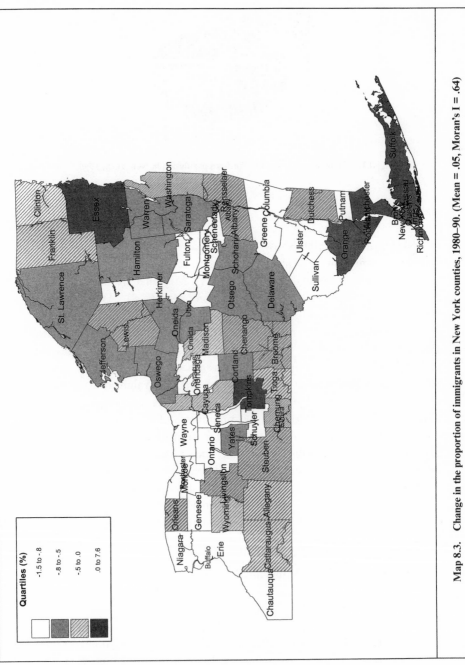

Quartiles (%)

☐ -1.5 to -.8

▨ -.8 to -.5

▥ -.5 to .0

■ .0 to 7.6

Map 8.3.   Change in the proportion of immigrants in New York counties, 1980–90. (Mean = .05, Moran's I = .64)

ern New York along I–87 above Albany and west along the Canadian border (map 8.2). Few counties have been strong magnets for both internal migrants and immigrants, and western New York, like western Pennsylvania to the south, is home mainly to native New Yorkers.

The analysis of settlement patterns in previous chapters has shown that Latin American and Asian immigrants are the most likely groups to be a growing presence in the areas where they have previously settled. This is also the case in New York, as table 8.1 shows. For Mexicans, a one-point increase in the Mexican-born population across counties in 1980 contributed to a nearly three-point increase in the Mexican proportion of the population by 1990. For South Americans, the results are similar, and for Asians the relationship is positive but not statistically significant. The more recent waves of immigrants are attracted to the destinations already settled by previous coethnic arrivals, particularly if they are of color. For Europeans, Africans, Canadians, and Central Americans, though, there is an inverse relationship between their growth throughout the 1990s and the size of their communities in 1980. This is no great surprise for the Caucasian groups, as these are the least likely to chain migrate or depend upon ethnic enclaves for employment at their destinations. The results for Central Americans and Africans are a bit more puzzling. They were a smaller proportion of the population in 1990 than in 1980 according to the coefficients in table 8.1. This result reflects the fact that, although their numbers have increased, their growth has been outstripped by the growth in other population groups settling in the same areas.

To what extent is the population mobility of these groups determined by employment prospects? Of all eight groups described in table 8.1, Europeans and Canadians appear to be best able to avoid increasing their relative presence in areas of New York that began the decade with high unemployment, while Asians, U.S. internal migrants, and Central and South Americans are an increasing proportion of the population precisely in those places that had the weakest job prospects in the early 1980s. As for increasing income, the proportion of the populations comprised of Asians, Central Americans, and internal migrants did increase with income growth, suggesting some sensitivity to economic conditions. Why don't internal migrants run from places with high unemployment rates, leaving only native New Yorkers behind? Perhaps it is because many of these migrants did not move to New York for economic reasons. New York's stagnant economy has not attracted people across state lines. The few recent migrants from elsewhere are retirees not in the labor force who have

TABLE 8.1. Influences on Population Concentration in New York Counties, 1980–90

Variable	U.S. Migrants	African Immigrants	Asian Immigrants	European Immigrants	Canadian Immigrants	Mexican Immigrants	Central American Immigrants	South American Immigrants
% 1980 group population	.42*	-.48*	.19	-.43**	-.38**	2.73**	-.44**	.90**
	(.23)	(.28)	(.14)	(.05)	(.04)	(.63)	(.12)	(.03)
% unemployment, 1980	1.86**	.003	.12**	-.08	-.01*	.007	.37**	.10**
	(.68)	(.009)	(.06)	(.10)	(.006)	(.01)	(.16)	(.02)
Change in real median income, 1980–90	.81**	-.002	.04**	-.02*	-.0002	-.004**	.05**	.008
	(.12)	(.002)	(.01)	(.02)	(.0009)	(.002)	(.02)	(.006)
% net population change	.18	.0005	-.01	-.03	.0004	.003	-.11**	-.007
	(.17)	(.002)	(.01)	(.02)	(.001)	(.003)	(.04)	(.005)
Population density	.00008	.000035**	-.00002**	.0000003	.000002**	-.000007**	.0001**	-.00003**
	(.0002)	(.000013)	(.00001)	(.00001)	(.0000006)	(.000002)	(.00002)	(.000002)
% college students	-.16	.007	.06**	.02	.006	-.008	-.06	-.005
	(.47)	(.006)	(.03)	(.06)	(.004)	(.007)	(.11)	(.01)
Spatial lag	1.62**	1.17**	.17	-3.28**	-.65**	1.04**	.59**	.47**
	(.22)	(.30)	(.18)	(.41)	(.18)	(.21)	(.28)	(.18)
Constant	-25.77	-.03	-1.35	-1.06	.007	-.009	-2.15	-.86
N	62	62	62	62	62	62	62	62
R^2_a	.80	.59	.70	.86	.82	.68	.51	.96

Note: Spatial autoregressive model, weighted for population; income coefficients expressed in thousands of 1992 dollars; dependent variable = change in population group as a percentage of total population. For a full description of variables, see appendix A.
*$p < .10$.   **$p < .05$.

moved to resort locations in northern New York near the Canadian border (Jefferson County on Lake Ontario and Essex County on Lake Champlain). U.S. internal migrants are gaining a larger share of the population in the areas where cross-state migration has been high in the past, mostly in upstate counties (see table 8.1 and map 8.2). Internal migrants are not dependent on ethnic enclaves, but the same amenities that attracted migrants to upstate locations in previous decades were also operating in the 1980s and 1990s.

Judging from the coefficients for population density, several groups increased their visibility in the state's most urban areas: Canadians, Africans, and Central Americans, for example, while Asians and South Americans were a growing presence in areas of lower density development. This is an important indication that the recent wave of immigrants is not entirely confined to big cities. Asians have been particularly successful in dispersing into the New York City suburbs in Nassau and Rockland Counties.

Ethnic Balkanization and Naturalization in New York

The spatial settlement patterns of migrants and immigrants illustrate some familiar patterns. Some populations are more dependent upon the presence of their coethnic predecessors than others. Nonwhite immigrants are less easily assimilated because they are more distinguishable from the white majority. Within cities, counties, and metropolitan areas, the size of the foreign-born population is highly related to its segregation from natives. But even at the state level, across geographic units as large as counties, differences among the settlement patterns of internal migrants, European and Canadian immigrants, and immigrants of color are of some consequence for predicting future patterns of economic, social, and political balkanization. Immigrant groups are not randomly mixed into the population. Instead they are "sorted by place according to their relative standing in society," and for this reason "group membership must be taken into account in analyzing locational processes" (Alba and Logan 1993, 1391). The stratification of groups by place of settlement would not be especially troubling if it did not also perpetuate economic, social, and political inequality. But some places have advantages that others do not (Logan 1978). That some immigrants are constrained to settle only in certain areas means that they will be confined to what those communities have to offer in terms of education, employment, community involvement, and attitudes toward government and political participation. In the final analysis, then, balkanization of ethnic and racial groups results in unhealthy political variations across communities that threaten the practice of pluralist democracy.

In previous chapters, we have seen that the spatial concentration of immigrant groups is often inversely associated with naturalization within the immigrant community. In New York, this is clearly the case, as table A8.2 (appendix A) shows. In 1980, a 10 point increase in the proportion of the population of foreign birth across the state's counties is associated with a 5.3 point drop in the percentage naturalized. In 1990, the effect is smaller but still highly significant. Moreover, the results also show that isolation of minorities from whites within counties is associated with diminished naturalization. Finally, the naturalization rates across the state display a pattern of positive spatial dependency in both 1980 and 1990, indicating that low naturalization counties are clustered together (in the areas of high immigrant concentration), while high naturalization counties are also found adjacent to one another upstate.

Migrants, Immigrants, and Voter Turnout in New York

In previous chapters, we have seen that it is quite common for turnout levels to be influenced by the composition of the electorate. The ecological data analysis suggests that places inundated with migrants from other states often have lower participation rates, particularly in nonpresidential election years. Average turnout rates for gubernatorial elections in 1990 and 1994 are shown on map 8.4 by quartile. Among the counties with the lowest turnout are the New York City boroughs, Suffolk County on Long Island, and scattered counties upstate, including Albany. High-turnout locations include the darkly shaded cluster of counties in central New York, including Onondaga (Syracuse), Tompkins (Ithaca), and Oneida (Oneida-Utica-Rome).

The results of a regression analysis of county-level demographic characteristics on turnout in recent presidential and gubernatorial races shows that the percentage of the population from out of state is often *positively* related to participation when other variables are taken into account (see table 8.2). Why is turnout slightly higher in places where large proportions of non–New Yorkers reside? One possible explanation is that many native New Yorkers are sufficiently disinterested in politics that by comparison the out-of-state population is relatively more active. New York's native

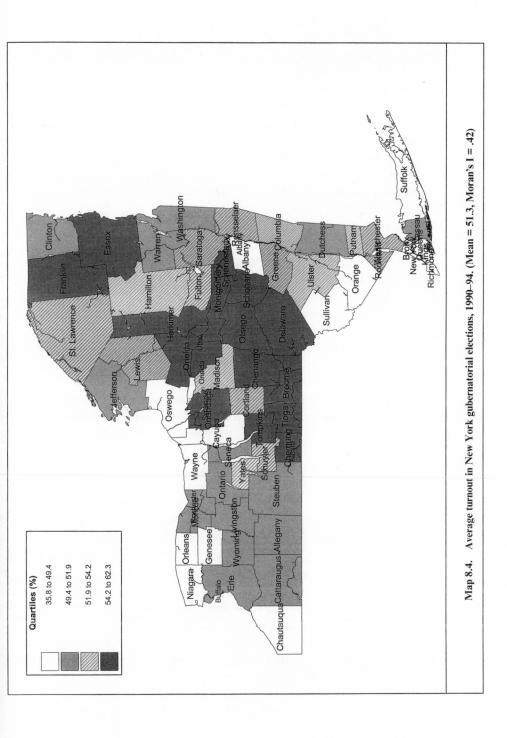

Map 8.4. Average turnout in New York gubernatorial elections, 1990–94. (Mean = 51.3, Moran's I = .42)

Legend:

Quartiles (%)

- 35.8 to 49.4
- 49.4 to 51.9
- 51.9 to 54.2
- 54.2 to 62.3

black population, for example, is known for its low participation. In table 8.2, the percentage of black residents in a county, for example, is associated with lower turnout for 1994 and in the pooled model. The low turnout of native populations, then, may account for the generally positive relationship between out-of-state residency and participation rates. Another explanation is that New York's out-of-state residents comprise an older, more established population, which, through longevity, has overcome the barriers to participation that newer migrants face. The 1990 PUMS data do reveal that the mean age of migrants over the age of eighteen was forty-seven, several years older than the average age for native New Yorkers (see table A8.1). Migrants in New York also earned more Social Security income than natives to the state.

The population of recent immigrants (those arriving after 1970) bolsters turnout in all of the elections except 1980. This is also contrary to the pattern in other states. The positive association between turnout and counties with a high percentage of recent immigrants reflects the influence of cases such as Tompkins (Ithaca) County, where recent waves of immigrants have included students and better educated residents associated with the universities and high-technology industries there. Note that the percentage of residents with college degrees is positively associated with turnout in all but one of the elections, as the individual-level relationship would predict (table 8.2). Population density is associated with lower turnout in all recent elections. It is not surprising that the densely populated urban counties have low participation. These are also the areas with the highest concentration of poor and uneducated residents (both natives and immigrants). Finally, the spatially lagged dependent variable shows that patterns of turnout in New York are highly regional in off-year elections such as 1982 and 1990. In these years, participation rates are similar across entire substate sections that cut across county boundaries.

Inequalities in turnout and participation across a state matter because they inevitably undermine the one person, one vote principle, effectively giving some people and places more control over government than their numbers merit. These results clearly show that many of New York state's elections are spatially balkanized by race, education, population growth or decline, and population density. The most urban areas, in particular, are underrepresented in all recent elections, giving city dwellers much less influence than they should have in statewide contests based on their numbers.

That demographic characteristics of areas explain turnout levels only reinforces the impression that the state is sectionally split. Like Pennsylva-

TABLE 8.2. Impact of Population Mobility on Voter Turnout in New York Counties, 1980–94

Variable	1980	1982	1990	1992	1994	Pooled 1990s
% college educated	.08	-.23	.37**	.62**	.16**	.37**
	(.20)	(.21)	(.08)	(.08)	(.08)	(.05)
Isolation of minorities from whites (within counties)	.08**	.02	.03**	-.03	.004	.02
	(.02)	(.03)	(.02)	(.02)	(.02)	(.01)
% post-1970 immigrants	-.65**	.10	.12[a]	.18[a]	.27[a]	.27
	(.17)	(.12)	(.25)	(.27)	(.27)	(.18)
% born out of state	-.07	.20**	.09[a]	.005	.09[a]	.08
	(.07)	(.07)	(.09)	(.10)	(.11)	(.07)
% black	-.03	.05	.03[a]	.05	-.37**	-.13**
	(.09)	(.10)	(.10)	(.10)	(.10)	(.07)
Population density	-.002**	-.0009	-.0003**	-.0003**	-.0003**	-.0003**
	(.001)	(.001)	(.0001)	(.0001)	(.0001)	(.0001)
Spatial lag	-.06	.59**	.98**	.02	.19	.84**
	(.15)	(.09)	(.23)	(.13)	(.19)	(.03)
Presidential race	—	—	—	—	—	4.08**
						(1.00)
Constant	73.33	8.60	-11.89	61.43	46.53	-2.76
N	62	62	62	62	62	186
R^2_a	.42	.74	.75	.69	.82	.93

Note: Spatial autoregressive model, weighted for population; dependent variable = percentage turnout by county. See appendix A for a full description of variables.

[a]Variables with low tolerances and high standard errors due to multicollinearity.

*$p < .10$.   **$p < .05$.

nia, the competitiveness of elections makes some difference. In the highly competitive 1982 gubernatorial contest and again in 1994, New York's turnout levels were highly stratified by the racial composition of counties. The 1990 contest, however, was far less competitive, and race played a very small role, as turnout levels sagged in many of the white (and Republican) areas upstate because the GOP candidate was dismissed early in the contest as a hopeless loser. That it takes a one-sided contest in which the outcome is known well in advance for the racial stratification in participation to subside reveals how competitive elections alone will not erase such inequalities. Indeed, the most highly competitive elections increase inequalities across these aggregate units, putting racially and economically heterogeneous places at a heightened disadvantage relative to their predominantly white and homogeneous counterparts.

Migration, Immigration, and Party Regularity in New York

Often turnout levels and patterns of party regularity are studied while their broader implications for democratic governance and representation are forgotten. Here I have tried to frequently remind the reader of the theoretical context that makes these analyses relevant. Party regularity refers to the extent to which party registration matches the balance of party voting. Differences between registration and voting in a neighborhood, city, or county can be the result of the level of turnout, the degree of independent and split-ticket voting, or some combination of the two. Following the theories offered at the individual level for the rise of independent political behavior in American politics, I have hypothesized that party regularity is a function of population stability (Brown 1988; Wattenberg 1991). Areas that have not undergone much population change are likely to have entrenched or institutionalized patterns of political behavior that the rapidly growing areas will lack.

For New York, table 8.3 provides a glimpse of the demographic characteristics of counties that are associated with differences between voting and registration. Positive coefficients indicate those variables that increase irregularity. The findings for various population characteristics are somewhat consistent with theoretical expectations. Party irregularity increases with the proportion of newly arrived immigrants in four of the five elections, particularly in the early 1980s. The population from out of state is associated with irregularity in 1994, where a 10 point increase in the pro-

TABLE 8.3. Similarity of Party Registration to Party Voting in New York Counties, 1980–94

Variable	1980	1982	1990	1992	1994	Pooled 1990s
% college educated	-.60**	-.73**	.19**	-.35**	-.55**	-.30**
	(.23)	(.20)	(.08)	(.11)	(.10)	(.06)
% born out of state	.03	.21	-.21**	-.03	.25*	-.01
	(.16)	(.15)	(.09)	(.09)	(.13)	(.07)
% post-1970 immigrants	1.62**	1.33**	-.75**	.12	.79**	.04
	(.37)	(.31)	(.25)	(.25)	(.35)	(.20)
% black	-.14	-.38**	.16*	-.09	-.09	-.02
	(.15)	(.14)	(.09)	(.09)	(.15)	(.07)
Population density	-.0001	-.00008	.00002	.00009	-.0002	.00002
	(.0001)	(.001)	(.003)	(.001)	(.001)	(.001)
% turnout	.06	-.20	.25**	.20	.65**	.49**
	(.21)	(.22)	(.13)	(.13)	(.20)	(.07)
Spatial lag	.57**	.48**	-.27	.64**	.11	.28**
	(.15)	(.18)	(.17)	(.21)	(.15)	(.08)
Presidential race	—	—	—	—	—	-14.85**
						(2.09)
Constant	12.11	19.50	-1.27	-5.17	-13.11	-7.98
N	62	62	62	62	62	186
R^2_a	.75	.51	.55	.37	.59	.65

Note: Spatial autoregressive model, weighted for population; dependent variable = Abs (% Republican vote – % Republican registration); high positive values indicate counties where voting differed from registration. See appendix A for a full description of variables.
[a]Variables with low tolerances and high standard errors due to multicollinearity.
*$p < .10$.   **$p < .05$.

portion of interstate migrants increases the difference between party registration and voting by about 2.5 points. But in other races, such as that of 1990, the impact is the reverse. The results are variable enough to suggest that much depends upon the idiosyncrasies of the election in question. New York is well known for having strong third parties, which frequently field candidates in gubernatorial races that draw strength away from the major party contenders (Gimpel 1996).

The 1990 contest is an anomaly in some noteworthy respects. In this lopsided election, Mario Cuomo coasted to an easy reelection victory. College education is positively associated with irregularity and the proportion of out-of-state migrants and foreign-born residents is associated with regularity. What is it about noncompetitive elections that makes them different from competitive contests? In the 1990 race, several of the most Republican areas upstate wound up splitting their votes between Herbert London (Conservative Party) and Pierre Rinfret (Republican Party), neither of whom stood much chance of unseating the popular Cuomo. These were areas such as Fulton, Saratoga, and Warren Counties (north of Albany; see map 8.1) that have few out-of-state residents and almost no immigrants. Second, Cuomo had considerable appeal in several areas with well-educated populations, including Tompkins (Ithaca) and Westchester (White Plains). Perhaps some of these voters could also sense that Cuomo's victory over two weak opponents was a sure bet and hence voted for the Democrat while others may have stayed home entirely. In more competitive contests, these areas are far less likely to depart from their basic party inclinations.

In highly competitive elections we can see that some patterns of spatial balkanization are consistent with patterns observed in other states, separating one area from another based on demographic composition. The more independent minded or irregular electorates in 1994, for instance, were less educated and comprised of both migrants from out of state and higher proportions of recent immigrants. In the less competitive contests, such as the 1990 gubernatorial election, these patterns almost totally reverse themselves.

New York's patterns of party irregularity are odd in one other respect. High turnout is associated with departures from party registration in the 1990 and 1994 gubernatorial races. Usually, when turnout matters at all, it reduces the difference between party registration and voting. In this state, however, there are some places where Republicans and Democrats are disloyal to their parties. These areas are often in high-turnout neighborhoods where swing voters are the focus of highly competitive party efforts and where third parties may garner strong support.

It is no trivial matter that some parts of New York state are less predictable in their behavior than others in competitive election contests. Political party organizations and candidates are charged with the complex and costly task of organizing and mobilizing support to win elections. The burden of carrying out this exercise is much heavier in the areas where voters have minds of their own (Gimpel 1996; Sorauf 1984). It is little wonder that political party organizations have endured far longer in densely populated urban areas where low-cost mobilization efforts translate directly and easily into votes for the dominant party. These spatial patterns of party regularity help to predict where political party organizations and candidates will be most effective in deploying a conventional mobilization strategy.

Changes in Party Registration in New York

The long-term dynamics of partisan change are perhaps best reflected in the changing balance of party registrants within a state. Changes in the vote, by contrast, are far more volatile, reflecting short-term forces, including the state of the economy, the popularity of incumbents, and the strategies of candidates and their campaigns. Party registration is more immutable to temporary forces, and this is the reason I have emphasized fluctuations in registration rather than votes throughout this book. From 1980 to 1990, Republicans did well in a number of unusual places in New York, including New York City, as the dark shading on map 8.5 plainly shows. Democrats countered by gaining party registrants in upstate New York in rural areas where they had not been much of a presence in times past. These gains upstate probably came more as the result of Republican out-migration than the conversion or realignment of long-time residents. Among the first to leave depressed cities such as Buffalo, Rochester, and Syracuse are the employable, the well educated, and upper income professionals who constitute the rank and file of the New York Republican Party. Others who may leave during economic hard times include New York's farmers, or their children, who by deserting the distressed farm economy reduce the balance of Republican Party registrants upstate.

Results from models that predict changes in the Republican share of party registrants from 1970 to 1980 and from 1980 to 1990 appear in table 8.4. The coefficients immediately indicate that New York is different from

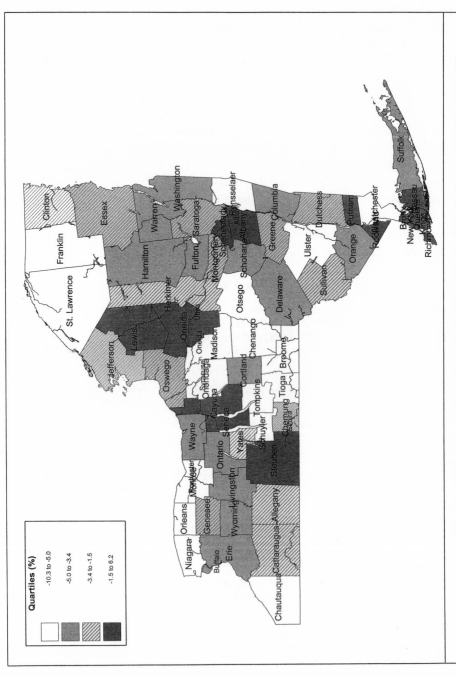

Quartiles (%)

- -10.3 to -5.0
- -5.0 to -3.4
- -3.4 to -1.5
- -1.5 to 6.2

Map 8.5. Change in the proportion of Republican registrants in New York counties, 1980–90. (Mean = –3.1, Moran's I = .20)

the states examined in earlier chapters. First, the proportion of the population from outside New York at the beginning of each decade does not necessarily strengthen Republican prospects like it does in some other states. A 1 point increase in the proportion of the population from outside New York in 1970 is associated with a .21 drop in GOP registration ten years later. These results are similar to those for Colorado, where the strong GOP inclinations of many of that state's counties in the early 1970s meant that almost any population influx from elsewhere would blunt the Republican edge (see table 3.4).

An examination of several cases explains why cross-state migration is not associated with Republican growth. Many out-of-state migrants have settled in New York City, including New York (Manhattan), Bronx, and Kings (Brooklyn) Counties. While the rate of out-of-state migration to New York City dropped drastically from the first to the second half of the twentieth century, a high proportion of the population in the Democratic

TABLE 8.4.   Impact of Population Mobility on Changes in Republican Party Registration in New York Counties, 1970–80, 1980–90

Variable	1970–80	1980–90
% born out of state, 1970 (1980)	−.21**	.31
	(.08)	(.29)
Change in % born out of state	−.31	−.11
	(.29)	(.18)
% foreign born, 1970 (1980)	−.89**	−.40
	(.19)	(.31)
Change in % foreign born	1.41**	.17
	(.33)	(.37)
% Republican registrants, 1970 (1980)	−.16**	−.10**
	(.04)	(.03)
Population density	.0001**	.0002**
	(.00004)	(.0001)
Spatial lag	−.66**	.31
	(.20)	(.29)
Constant	4.35	7.45
N	62	62
R^2_a	.57	.50

Note: Spatial autoregressive model, weighted for population; dependent variable = change in Republican Party registration. See appendix A for a full description of variables.

[a]Variables with low tolerances and high standard errors due to multicollinearity.

*$p < .10$.   **$p < .05$.

boroughs does come from elsewhere. A second area where growth from out of state has been associated with diminishing Republican prospects is northern New York, where the arrival of migrants from Connecticut and Massachusetts has politically diversified traditionally Republican communities. Albany and Schenectady are interesting cases in which the proportion of internal migrants dropped from 1980 to 1990 (map 8.2) while Republican registration growth was in the highest quartile (map 8.5). In these places, GOP growth has coincided with increases in the proportion of native New Yorkers due to natural increase (fertility) and migration from nearby locations.

Places with large immigrant settlements at the beginning of each decade became more Democratic through the 1970s and 1980s. But, on the other hand, counties where immigrants were a *growing* proportion of the population saw Republican prospects improve markedly in the 1970s. This is because established, upwardly mobile immigrants found their way to the Republican suburbs. The ecological results provide no evidence that immigrants are registering as Republicans, but growth in the immigrant population is an indicator of the pro-growth orientation of suburban areas, where Republican gains have been strongest. Many of the older immigrants, in particular, are more likely to be white and are better able to assimilate into the American economic mainstream. As their social and economic standing improves, they are just as likely to move to the suburbs as any native in the same situation. There is little individual evidence to suggest that immigrants are naturalizing and registering to vote in vast numbers, but their relocation to areas of Republican strength remind us that population growth in the United States is stimulated by strong and growing economies rather than impoverished and declining ones.

The coefficient for GOP registration at the beginning of each decade in table 8.4 also indicates that there may be an equilibration process occurring over time that is responsible for altering the balance of party registrants. Counties that began each decade with higher shares of Republican registrants, including those shaded in white in map 8.5, experienced slower Republican growth than those with low Republican registration. In a fiercely competitive two-party state like New York, these results come as no surprise. While regions of the state do have enduring traditions that align them with one party or the other, the Democratic and Republican Parties compete side by side in most areas. With time, even the strongest Republican counties will lose ground to Democrats and third parties. Similarly, the lopsided Democratic counties will become less Democratic as the two parties move back into competitive balance. More densely populated counties also saw high Republican growth rates during both decades, with several suburban counties (Nassau, Rockland, Putnam) picking up Republican registrants in spite of the increasingly high density of their development.

New York's patterns of partisan change provide some justification for doing state-by-state studies of the impact of migration and immigration on politics. States do differ, and New York's population trends are unique from those studied in the previous chapters. Out-of-state migration is a relatively inconsequential political phenomenon in New York compared to the significant impact of immigration and migration within the state from the boroughs to the suburbs.

Even so, some patterns of political stratification and change are similar to those observable in other states. Growth in the foreign-born population is occurring alongside Republican growth in suburbs and in the more prosperous counties upstate. The broader significance of the partisan changes occurring in New York is seen in how uneven the political and demographic development of the state continues to be. Migrants and immigrants have never dispersed randomly into New York's sixty-two counties. They select certain areas and avoid others. Hispanics and Asians, for example, go to areas in New York City where there are ethnic enclaves, and once established they move to Nassau, Westchester, and Rockland Counties. That these mobility patterns unevenly affect cities and towns invariably means that the political fallout from demographic change is not a random process either. Interestingly, several suburban areas that began the second half of the twentieth century with homogeneous white populations became more ethnically diverse during the 1970s and 1980s and have become *more* Republican. Whether this upward trend in GOP registration is a reaction against increasing ethnic diversity by native whites or a direct result of the foreign born registering as Republicans can only be determined through an examination of microlevel data. The aggregate variations detailed here raise enough questions to demand further exploration.

Migration, Ethnicity, and Political Behavior at the Individual Level

The aggregate data have shown that New York is a state where partisanship, ethnicity, race, and political participation are not evenly distributed.

As elsewhere, this unevenness is the result of the linkage of race, ethnicity, and education to partisanship and participation. Since racial and ethnic groups tend to cluster, especially if those populations are recently arrived, geographic patterns of clustered political participation and partisanship inevitably follow. Entire communities may go unrepresented due to massive nonparticipation. Other communities may become cohesively one-party Democratic (or Republican) because key members of that ethnic group find a reception in one party or the other.

Inferring individual level behavior from county level observations is difficult and potentially misleading. Using the standard model developed by King (1997, chap. 6), I evaluated party registration by ethnicity in New York based on the county level observations for 1990, 1992, and 1994. Using this method, I obtained reasonably precise estimates of the party registration of white voters—about 40 to 41 percent of this population is registered Republican. The proportion of blacks registered with the GOP was predictably low, ranging from 8 percent in 1990 to 6 percent in 1994. Estimates for the Hispanic population indicated far lower support for Republicans than in Pennsylvania, California, or many other states—only in the 5 to 6 percent range—but with a sizable margin of error. Estimates for the Asian population were not highly reliable due to the tiny fraction of Asians in most of the state's counties, and given the absence of additional information that would help to sharpen our image of this heterogeneous group's political leanings.

Limited individual-level data are available to determine the partisan orientation of New York voters by race and ethnicity (see table 8.5). While white voters are split between Republicans and Democrats, blacks are overwhelmingly Democratic. From 1990 to 1994, Hispanics were not as heavily Democratic as blacks but were solidly in the Democratic column nevertheless. Asians were more evenly divided between the parties than either Hispanics or blacks, and far more Asians were reported to be independents than in the other two minority groups. Still New York's Asians are far less likely to be Republican identifiers than those in California (see table 2.5 for comparison). That minority groups would identify so monolithically with a single party provides evidence of how ethnic and political identities go hand in hand, not only for black Americans but for other minorities as well. When controls for education and income are added, blacks and Hispanics are still highly likely to report Democratic affiliation, although Asians become far less Democratic (table not reported). Further analysis of polling data confirmed the tendency for voters upstate to be more irregular in their political behavior (e.g., they are more likely to disregard their partisanship when voting) than those in New York City or its suburbs in the three elections evaluated in table 8.5. African Americans are the most highly *regular* voters across all three regions.

Given that the majority of Asian, Hispanic, and black voters do identify with the Democratic Party in New York, it seems likely that the addition of immigrants from nations where these groups are the predominant population will only bolster Democratic registration. This means that the ecological regression analysis in table 8.4 does not point to a direct individual-level relationship when it shows growth in the Hispanic and Asian populations leading to Republican registration gains in New York's suburban counties.

While we have no way of verifying from the VRS exit polls which respondents are foreign born and which are not, these polls do suggest that some of the patterns in the ecological data are traceable to the individual level. Patterns of political party identification, for example, do hinge on ethnicity and whether respondents live in New York City, its suburbs, or the cities and towns upstate. Voters are spatially separated by party identification and propensity to participate in elections. The uneven distribution of ethnic groups and partisans in New York creates the kind of sin-

TABLE 8.5. Party Identification by Race/Ethnicity in New York Elections, 1990–94

Race/Ethnic Group	Year	Democrat	Independent	Republican
White	1990	39.0	24.2	36.9
	1992	38.4	25.2	36.4
	1994	32.9	31.2	35.9
Black	1990	83.5	10.3	6.2
	1992	80.1	14.2	5.7
	1994	84.6	11.5	3.8
Hispanic	1990	81.6	2.6	15.9
	1992	72.0	7.1	21.0
	1994	62.6	15.9	16.5
Asian	1990	62.5	30.6	7.0
	1992	45.7	12.8	41.5
	1994	61.8	25.5	12.7

Source: Voter Research and Surveys, General Election Exit Polls, 1990–94 (weighted data).

gle-party election districts that elect officeholders who are not as account-
able as they could or should be. Party responsibility and cohesion is eroded
in communities where the only meaningful competition occurs within the
primary of one party or the other. Finally, one-sided electioneering erodes
the value of political participation by marginalizing the value of voting in
general elections, thereby discouraging turnout and political activism.

Political Change and the Internal Composition of New York Counties

Describing political development and change across states utilizing
county-level data is convenient because comprehensive data exist that are
not available for smaller aggregate units or even individuals. It is highly
likely, though, that the mechanisms that create the interesting partisan and
political variations I have discussed are more clearly revealed by examining forces operating within counties at the neighborhood and tract levels.
Some counties are so large and heavily populated that figures aggregated
at the county level obscure crucial internal nuances and variations. I have
argued that GOP registration growth has often been assisted by the small
size and spatial isolation of ethnic groups within counties. Spatial isolation
may also inhibit overall turnout or the turnout of specific groups within an
area. In table 8.2 there was little relationship between minority isolation
from whites and overall participation because minority-white segregation
is so closely related to other variables I included in the model, including
the size of the black population and urbanization. A bivariate regression
model (not reported) revealed that a ten-point increase in the degree of
segregation within counties, as measured by the dissimilarity index, drops
overall turnout by 1.5 percent. In table A8.1, there is more convincing evidence that the spatial concentration of the foreign born inhibits assimilation by reducing the propensity of the immigrant population to naturalize.
Segregation within counties is also politically relevant because in places
where minorities are isolated, the politics that minorities practice is a
racially monolithic one. When those minorities are of a sufficiently small
number, a race-based politics contributes to their marginalization usually
within the politics of a minority party.

Examining the internal population dynamics of each of New York's
sixty-two counties is too big a task for a single chapter and would over-
whelm both the author and reader with data. Instead I have chosen to
investigate four counties that represent various electoral settings in the

state: Bronx (the Bronx), Chemung (Elmira), Nassau (Hempstead), and Onondaga (Syracuse). From 1980 to the mid-1990s, the populations of these four counties were stable, with Chemung and Nassau losing less than 3 percent of their population and Bronx and Onondaga increasing by about the same percentage. Bronx County has the highest proportion of immigrants of the four, followed by Nassau, Onondaga, and Chemung. Bronx also has the most internal (U.S.) migrants, although many of these are long-term residents. Chemung and Onondaga received a higher proportion of recent internal migrants (from 1980 to 1990) than the two counties downstate. GOP registration declined most precipitously in Onondaga County, where Republicans dropped from 59 percent of registered voters in 1970 to only 44 percent by the early 1990s. Chemung has also experienced decline in GOP registration, which was reported to be less than 50 percent for the first time in 1990. Nassau County's registration remained almost the same from the 1970s to the 1990s, hovering steadily at 48 to 49 percent. Bronx is the most Democratic county in the state, and Republicans have lost ground there. There is no hope for a restoration of two-party competition in this area, as GOP registration stood at a puny 10 percent in 1990.

The index of racial isolation is presented in table 8.6 for all census tracts in New York state as well as the four counties just mentioned. As in other places, blacks are the most spatially isolated minority group, followed by Hispanics and Asians. This has been an almost universal finding in this study and confirms the pattern found by Massey and Denton (1993) in their evaluation of metropolitan areas. Blacks are most isolated in Nassau and Onondaga Counties, and far less so in the Bronx, where they are a much larger share of the population, and Chemung, where they are much smaller. Hispanics are less segregated from whites in Nassau and Onondaga than in the more urban or rural counties but have grown more isolated from whites in all but the Bronx. Asians, too, seem to reside closer to whites in these four counties than in the state, but they grew more isolated from 1980 to 1990 in all four areas. Judging from the results in table A8.1, these patterns of minority concentration within counties appear to have some relation to both population loss and internal migration. For blacks in 1980, for example, a 10 percent loss in population in the previous ten years contributed to a nine-point increase in the isolation of blacks from whites. Population losses similarly impact the Hispanic and Asian populations. Gains from internal cross-state migration are related to the increasing segregation of Hispanics and Asians but have not affected

TABLE 8.6. Index of Dissimilarity for the Black, Asian, and Hispanic Populations Relative to Whites in Four New York Counties, 1980 and 1990, by Census Tract

Variable	New York		Bronx		Chemung		Nassau		Onondaga	
	1980	1990	1980	1990	1980	1990	1980	1990	1980	1990
Asians	.55	.55	.38	.41	.30	.36	.28	.30	.38	.43
Blacks	.79	.78	.57	.55	.59	.56	.82	.81	.73	.71
Hispanics	.68	.62	.50	.48	.44	.51	.34	.41	.38	.43
N	4858	4858	355	355	23	23	270	270	143	143

Source: U.S. Census 1990, and author's calculations.
Note: Figures represent the percentage of each group that would have to move in order for the group to be evenly distributed across census tracts in the county.

blacks who were already highly segregated. Internal migrants have contributed to the ethnic balkanization of the state based on their residential location choices.

The Bronx

The dynamics of partisan change suggested in table 8.4 indicated that Republican registration growth was associated with a high proportion of residents born in New York but few internal migrants. These figures predicted rapid GOP growth in the suburbs, on Staten Island, and in some upstate rural areas but Republican decline in the boroughs. Bronx County represents those cases that have a significant population of foreign-born residents but also many internal migrants. Some of these internal migrants are blacks who have migrated from Maryland, Virginia, and North Carolina but not from the Deep South. The majority of internal migrants, however, were born in Puerto Rico and have since settled in the Bronx, many in public housing projects. Immigrants, in general, are not as attracted to the Bronx as to other boroughs. The Asian population comprised a mere 2.6 percent of the total in 1990. This is understandable given the high crime rates and lack of job opportunities and housing. "High crime drives out anybody who can move," said one local planner. "The South Bronx has a higher crime rate than any other neighborhood. Immigrants don't come here to get robbed and killed." Aside from high crime, the Bronx is also the poorest of the New York boroughs. Immigrants who arrive to seek economic opportunity are least likely to find it here. Millions of dollars have been poured into the South Bronx in an effort to revitalize it but to little avail. During the early 1990s, the new trend was to encourage home ownership and private redevelopment. These efforts have displaced the established residents.

Residential mobility in the Bronx, as elsewhere in New York City, moves along the transit lines. This means that population groups that once settled in the south have since moved north to be replaced with others leaving Manhattan. The South Bronx was once the home of Polish, Italian, Irish, and Jewish immigrants. These residents have long since moved to the far north end of the county and into Westchester County to be replaced with blacks and Hispanics. The fastest growing foreign-born group in the Bronx is the Dominican population, which has spilled over from Washington Heights and nearby neighborhoods in Manhattan (Torres and Bonilla 1993). The black population constituted about one-third of the total in 1990, and it is highly clustered in two regions: poor blacks in the South Bronx housed mainly in public housing projects and a middle-class black population in the north-central Bronx in the Wakefield and Williams Bridge neighborhoods. The middle-income black population is primarily employed in government, and the northern Bronx neighborhoods are especially attractive to black workers employed in the New York City transit system because major transit yards are located nearby. The other major employer for middle-income blacks is the large number of public and private hospitals that offer a variety of steady semiskilled and skilled jobs.

The Bronx is not as segregated as other places in New York, perhaps because there are relatively few non-Hispanic whites there (21 percent in 1990). As in other large cities, the high population density mitigates the degree of spatial isolation among competing groups, and some studies have shown the black population to be politically well organized compared to other minorities (Torres 1995; Wilson 1960). The small and declining number of whites in the borough and the high proportion of minorities in an area where Democrats have firm control of all local offices have not made for a setting conducive to Republican Party growth. Throughout the 1990s, black and Hispanic animosity toward the Republican Giuliani administration has fueled a backlash in the activist nonwhite community. Giuliani's campaign against high crime was especially noticeable in lower-income black and Hispanic neighborhoods, where police brutality was commonly alleged. Giuliani's promises to reduce the size of municipal government also posed a significant threat to the Latino and black populations employed in the social services, transportation, and housing agencies. The majority of native blacks in New York, however, are convinced that the political system does not work for them, and this is particularly true for the citizens of the Bronx's poor neighborhoods. Blacks are sufficiently concentrated in the Bronx that they are assured of political representation by black city council members and state legislators, but the easily won election victories of black leaders have done little to improve turnout and participation rates.

Only 36 percent of adult Hispanics are registered to vote citywide. In the Bronx, Hispanic political participation rates are low because their inclination to naturalize is weak. Mexicans and Dominicans are the least likely of any group to change flags because they maintain closer ties to their home countries than other immigrants (Grasmuck 1984; Torres and Bonilla 1993). The Dominican population is also very young, and this youth translates into less interest in politics. Finally, the newer Hispanics who cluster in the Bronx are not inclined to get involved in politics because many cannot speak English. While these characteristics of the population make for easy Democratic victories, the long-term future for GOP candidates may not be entirely grim. Latinos are not wedded to the Democratic Party and seem to be more capable of playing off one party against the other than blacks. Citywide about 38 percent of Latinos supported Giuliani's first election and show themselves increasingly willing to vote against Latino candidates. Hispanics are more likely to vote for non-Hispanic candidates in neighborhoods where there is more integration with the white population, and this usually means that class is playing a role in preference formation.

Nassau County
Nassau County, lying just to the east of Queens and extending out onto Long Island, can be best described as a weakening Republican stronghold. Nassau's Republican tradition began with its establishment as a separate county in 1899. It had originally been a part of Queens. Democrats opposed the separation, but Republicans supported it, not wanting to be part of the Tammany Hall machine. The Republican inclination of the county was solidified early in the twentieth century when Irish immigrants who had settled the area from Queens took a strong dislike to President Wilson's warm relations with the British after World War I. As a result of the county's adversarial stance toward the city and the Democratic Party, many residents of Nassau County switched parties. By the 1990s, these historical events had faded from the collective memory, but the Republican tradition of the county was well entrenched. Republicans have maintained firm control over county government and public employment.

Just as the population migration in the Bronx flowed from north to south along the transit lines, population mobility in Nassau proceeded from Queens and Brooklyn eastward in two streams along the north and south shores. The north shore has typically been populated with wealthy residents from neighborhoods on the north end of Queens. Wealthy WASP communities such as Oyster Bay and Glen Cove (map 8.2) are home to the stately mansions of New York's old mainline Republicans. The southern part of the county drew migrants from the less affluent neighborhoods in the south end of Queens and Brooklyn. There are exceptions to these general patterns. The "five towns" along the south shore close to Queens are home to affluent, Democratic, Jewish residents. The north shore is drawing in a more diverse population, including wealthy Asian residents who have migrated out of the city.

Between the shores, Nassau is massively overdeveloped, with over-priced single-family housing in small crowded tracts, strip malls, shopping centers, and office buildings. Most Nassau County residents are com-muters. The white population in the county has declined with the loss of high-paying manufacturing jobs. The major local employer, Grumman Aircraft (with large plants in Bethpage and Calverton), employed nearly thirty thousand workers at its peak. By the early 1990s, employment at Grumman was less than two thousand. In the 1960s and 1970s, migrants went to Long Island because there was job growth. Now the only draw is the desire to get out of the city. Families from the boroughs move there to raise their children in a more peaceful setting with safer neighborhoods and better public school systems.

The population is increasingly heterogeneous, reflecting the outward flow of the changing population of Queens. While limited facility in Eng-lish and noncitizenship are barriers to assimilation for some groups, Asians and Hispanics are more dispersed and less segregated from whites than blacks are (see table 8.6 and map 8.6). Map 8.6 shows patterns of interstate and immigrant settlement in Nassau County. Wealthy internal migrants have been drawn to the far south shore and the far north. Lower-income black internal migrants have settled in Hempstead and Freeport alongside immigrants. Poorer, more recent immigrants are predominantly clustered on the western side of the county, with wealthier immigrants in the north. The patch of white tracts at the east end of the county (Levitt-town, Massapequa) is worth noting. These areas have been the least attractive to both immigrants and internal migrants and are occupied pre-dominantly by native New Yorkers.

In 1990, Hispanics did not constitute a majority of the population in any of the county's census tracts. A relatively higher degree of residential integration does not always indicate political involvement, of course. Among Asian groups, only around 20 percent of the thirty thousand eth-nic Koreans are citizens (Moritsugu and Guzman 1996). And many issues that are of interest to immigrants are handled at the national rather than the local level. With no possibility of electing members of their ethnic group to local office, Asians and Hispanics continue to work through the back channels of the party system. These groups, while smaller in number than blacks, are not nearly as tied to Democratic Party politics and are therefore in a stronger position of influence within Republican ranks.

The black population of Long Island increased by 10.6 percent between 1980 and 1990, with most of the growth occurring in Nassau.

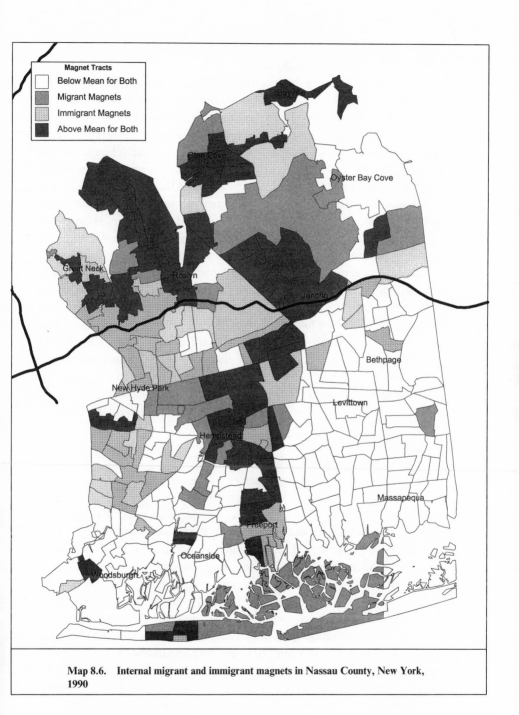

Map 8.6. Internal migrant and immigrant magnets in Nassau County, New York, 1990

Magnet Tracts
- Below Mean for Both
- Migrant Magnets
- Immigrant Magnets
- Above Mean for Both

Bayville

Glen Cove

Oyster Bay Cove

Great Neck

Roslyn

Jericho

Bethpage

New Hyde Park

Levittown

Hempstead

Massapequa

Freeport

Oceanside

Woodsburgh

Hempstead, Roosevelt, Wyandanch, and Freeport have large black populations. The black population is highly segregated from the white, reflecting the cost of housing. Segregation and Republican domination have undoubtedly reinforced habits of nonvoting among blacks whose political home is far more likely to be in the Democratic Party. In this respect, the black community in Nassau shares something in common with the black community in Dade County, Florida (see chap. 6). The village of Hempstead has more registered Democrats than Republicans, but Republicans have maintained a firm grip on local offices. The Republicans appear to be struggling to maintain this grip in the face of increasing diversity. Incidents of racial and ethnic violence and intimidation are more common, and this has brought pressure on the Republican leadership to open county government to the voices of the minority community. Lacking the numbers to directly elect minority legislators, minority groups have traditionally had to work behind the scenes in the political party organizations and make contributions to party coffers to gain access (Moritsugu and Guzman 1996). By the mid-1990s, blacks were sufficiently concentrated to have elected two black representatives to the county legislature with the help of specially drawn districts. If the white population continues to decline, as it did during the 1980s, and the black population remains politically cohesive, the emergence of a consistent black Democratic vote will help Democrats move into a competitive position vis-à-vis the Republicans.

Elmira and Chemung County

Chemung is typical of many counties in upstate New York with small cities that have struggled with the transition to the postindustrial economy. Population and economic losses have not been as catastrophic as in western Pennsylvania, but Republican Party registration has slowly eroded from 57 percent of all registered voters in 1970 to 47 percent in 1994, with independent and Democratic registration on the rise. Some of this erosion in GOP support has resulted from the deterioration of high-paying jobs accompanying industrial decline. Elmira was the site of the famous voting study conducted by Bernard Berelson, Paul Lazarsfeld, and William McPhee during the 1948 election campaign (1954). At that time, the authors described it as an "ordinary bustling industrial community," with nonmilitant unions and a predominantly white ethnic population, where the Democratic Party ran surprisingly well for upstate New York. In the 1990s, it could be described as an ordinary postindustrial northeastern city with a stable population and a lower standard of living than in the past. The city has declined relative to Chemung County, and all of the new housing development has occurred in outlying towns. Locals express the usual litany of complaints that are voiced about central cities everywhere: worsening schools, higher crime, and more illicit drug activity.

In the 1990s, Chemung County experienced a slight economic rebound, leading the state's counties in job growth. Some of the jobs were in manufacturing, such as in the Toshiba-Westinghouse color picture tube plant and Anchor Glass (as well as Corning Glass in nearby Corning, New York). But much of the job growth came in the low-paying retail trade sector and government employment. The county has two large state prisons. Local observers report that the area's bouts with unemployment have not resulted in population exodus because more households are relying on multiple wage earners and extra jobs than in the past, while others have turned to public assistance. Job growth in the health services sector has accompanied the aging of the population. As migration theory would predict, talented young people generally leave the area for greener pastures and few return. This leaves an older and poorer population behind.

There are few Asians or Hispanics in Chemung County. Map 8.7 shows patterns of immigrant and internal migrant settlement. Unlike areas with more noticeable immigrant populations, there is little spatial clustering of the tracts where immigrants reside. Like western Pennsylvania, its remoteness and its weak economy have not been attractive to many immigrants. "The Hispanic population works very hard at being invisible," said one local reporter. Constituting only 1.5 percent of the population in 1990, most of the Hispanics are immigrants from Central America or Puerto Ricans who have migrated from New York City. Reflecting the political turmoil in the countries from which they fled, the Central Americans are reluctant to involve themselves in civic affairs. According to the reporter, "They are hard working and willingly accept low-paying jobs on night shifts, so the natives don't notice them. The Puerto Ricans receive the brunt of the discrimination because they are accustomed to American life and more visible than the immigrant Hispanics." For Asians, who numbered just seven hundred in 1990, assimilation comes much easier, as the figures in table 8.6 suggest. Of those seven hundred Asians, less than two hundred lived in the city of Elmira in 1990. Some of the Asian families in suburbia are Japanese managers at the Toshiba plant, but they, too, remain politically indistinct.

The black community in Chemung County stood at 5,300 in 1990,

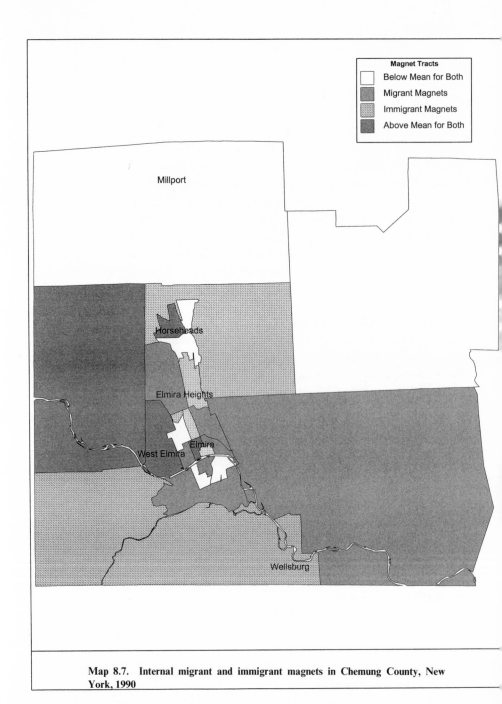

Map 8.7. Internal migrant and immigrant magnets in Chemung County, New York, 1990

Magnet Tracts

Below Mean for Both
Migrant Magnets
Immigrant Magnets
Above Mean for Both

Millport

Horseheads

Elmira Heights

Elmira
West Elmira

Wellsburg

about 5.5 percent of the population. Of those, 4,100 lived in the city of Elmira in black neighborhoods on the east side of town and mixed neighborhoods south of the Chemung River. According to locals, the occasional racial tension in the city may be the result of the proximity of the white and black populations rather than their separation. Certainly blacks and whites are more integrated in Chemung than in Nassau, Onondaga, or the state as a whole (see table 8.6). The black community is active enough to help make the city politically competitive in local races, usually coalescing with labor union votes to support Democratic candidates. Throughout the 1980s and 1990s, control of city government moved back and forth between the parties. "When you anger Elmira voters, you can be sure they will respond," said Steve Hughes, a Democratic city councilman. Democrats have a slight registration edge of about two thousand voters in Elmira, but that does not keep them from being tossed out of office for electorally unresponsive behavior. While the majority of blacks are Democrats, one black city councilman, a popular socially conservative minister of a mostly white suburban church, has won repeated reelection as a Republican. With such a small black population and elections that are so competitive, it is difficult and counterproductive to play a race-based politics in Elmira. Racial grievances, such as the lack of black employees in city government and incidents of police brutality, must be addressed gradually in coalition with other forces at the local level. The county government, on the other hand, is firmly in Republican hands, and so are the local governments of the smaller towns. Democrats have difficulty recruiting candidates outside of Elmira. Republican registration strength has eroded, but not necessarily to the benefit of Democrats. Independent registrants (those outside the two major parties) rose from 13.7 percent of the electorate in 1980 to 19.3 percent by 1994.

Syracuse and Onondaga County

"The last ten years has been a story about the destruction of the local economy," said one county planner about the economic decline of Syracuse. Although its population has been stable since the 1970s, Onondaga County has struggled with the transition to the postindustrial economy. Surprisingly, unemployment has not gone up—people who don't leave can find work—but, as in Elmira, the standard of living for blue collar families has diminished. Economic losses in chemical and automotive parts manufacturing and corporate consolidation at the area's major defense contractor, General Electric, have contributed to the disappearance of high-paying jobs in blue collar occupations. The response of the less mobile blue collar labor force was often to take lower-paying service sector jobs while putting a spouse to work to maintain the same standard of living. In many cases, household income still declined, but where it did not it was often because more people in the family were working, sometimes in multiple jobs. Politically many of these workers have found themselves part of the burgeoning class of independent voters. Convinced that the Democratic Party and their old labor unions have let them down, but still associating Republicans with wealth and privilege, the struggling service sector household has dealigned. Registration outside the major parties rose from 23 to 29 percent between 1980 and 1994.

Even the city's largest employer, Syracuse University, has downsized, cutting six hundred nonacademic positions in the early 1990s and restructuring its major programs. Of the local corporations that have survived, many have been bought by national corporations. With the disappearance of local corporate wealth goes the benevolent association of companies with the local community. The decline of local ownership and management of remaining manufacturing facilities has resulted in the export of many high-paying management jobs. Carrier Corporation, the local air conditioning manufacturer, is a good example. When its plant was bought in the late 1980s, the local management jobs were eliminated or transferred to a new headquarters in Connecticut. In the 1970s, Syracuse was home to several locally owned and managed banks. By the mid 1990s, only one was locally owned, and the others were branches whose headquarters were located elsewhere. Since skilled professionals are among the most highly mobile workers in the labor force, they are the first to leave an economically depressed area. Republican Party registration has suffered from this kind of attrition as professional positions have dried up.

The city of Syracuse has steadily lost population since the 1950s, and this has left the population poorer, older, and more racially diverse. Ethnic minority populations are far less likely to migrate during hard times, so the Asian, Hispanic, and black populations have increased. About one-fourth of Syracuse's population was nonwhite by 1990, and this population was highly segregated. Contributing to this segregation are the patterns of immigrant and internal migrant settlement pictured on map 8.8. Internal migrants are concentrated on the east and southeast sides of the city and in the suburb of Manlius. Natives, including many native blacks, are clustered in the eastern and southern tracts shown in white. More recent immigrants have been drawn to neighborhoods at the north and

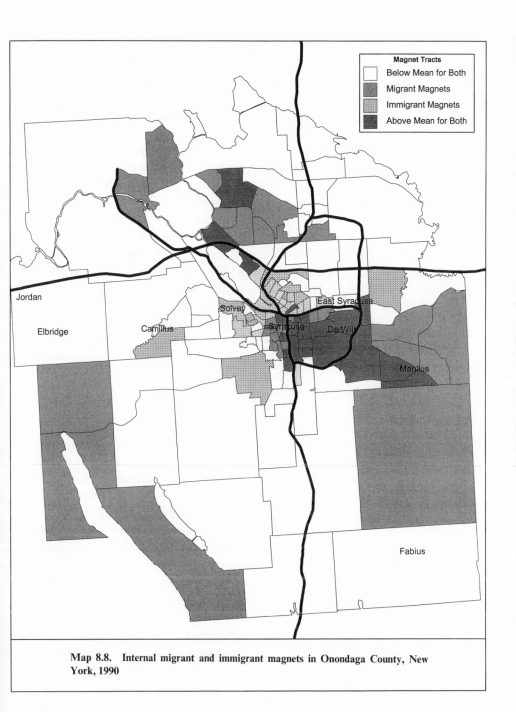

Map 8.8. Internal migrant and immigrant magnets in Onondaga County, New York, 1990

west ends of Syracuse. Older and more established immigrants reside alongside internal migrants and natives on the south and east sides of city.

According to the dissimilarity index reported in table 8.6, 71 percent of the black population would have to move for it to be equally distributed across the county's 143 census tracts, indicating a high level of residential segregation. The population losses in Syracuse created a major housing glut in the 1980s and 1990s. The lower-cost housing has slowly helped the black and Hispanic communities spread out of their traditional enclaves on the south, east, and southwest sides of the city into the older suburbs. Like other urban counties in upstate New York, Onondaga is highly balkanized internally in racial, economic, and political terms. The segregation that has accompanied white flight and black immobility has helped consolidate the Democrats' control of the city while making the suburbs nearly as homogeneously Republican. The county is governed by Republicans and the city by Democrats. Syracuse elected a Republican mayor in 1995 for the first time since 1970 as the result of fierce Democratic infighting, but the city council was still in Democratic hands. The city is perpetually broke. For a string of twelve years in the 1980s and 1990s, the Syracuse municipal government outspent its revenues. This had some politicians considering city-county consolidation by the mid 1990s.

The minority black population of Syracuse has forced black politicians to use nonracial appeals to get elected to city and county office, but primaries are the only locus of political competition. In the predominantly black areas of town, Republicans are hard pressed to slate a candidate. Racial tension between blacks and whites has sometimes flared in the administration of law enforcement and a major federal investigation in the early 1990s found the county jail to be a racially hostile environment for both black employees of the sheriff's department and prisoners. The suburban communities have the typical attitudes toward the central city that one finds in suburbia nationwide. People view Syracuse as crime ridden and a place to be escaped. The retail sector in the city has collapsed, so it is not even viewed as a place to shop. There are some commuters, but many new industrial parks and white collar jobs are located in the suburbs. "You could shoot a cannon ball down main street at 5:30 P.M. and not hit anybody," said one local reporter.

Hispanics and Asians are not a political force in either the county or Syracuse. The Hispanic population is predominantly of Puerto Rican and Mexican ancestry. In the 1980s and 1990s, this population was joined by Dominican immigrants, many of whom were suspected to be involved in the illicit drug trade. Whites made no distinctions between Dominicans and Puerto Ricans, and the negative stereotypes created a rift between the Puerto Rican community and the newer Hispanic arrivals. Asians are a small and growing population, including three hundred families of Vietnamese, Cambodian, and Laotian boat people relocated with the help of local churches. Language barriers have prevented them from developing an interest in politics. In the mid 1990s, they were still struggling to integrate into the local economy, trying to overcome language and skill deficits. Immigration is not an issue in Syracuse because it has been small in its overall volume. The absence of foreign and domestic in-migration has kept the supply of labor remarkably consistent, with stable demand even in the face of economic restructuring. Since the foreign born do not pose a threat to native workers, the immigrant influx has not resulted in a backlash, which in so many other places has benefited Republican Party registration.

Two States, Even More Separate Than Before

New York is a diverse and complicated state, differing significantly from all the other states studied in this book. In the last twenty years, it has experienced the waves of immigration that are typical of New York City but very little internal migration anywhere. Among the nonimmigrant population, the proportion of locally born persons is extraordinarily high: 89 percent in Nassau and 82 percent in Onondaga in the 1990s. With its terrible business climate, few persons have entered New York from outside the state to take advantage of economic gains. Consequently, few areas have experienced the kind of political change, evidenced in northern Kentucky, Florida, and California, that has been so kind to Republicans. As the results in table 8.4 showed, growth in the population from out of state seems to *depress* Republican prospects.

Ethnic balkanization is occurring across as well as within counties. Immigration to New York City and its suburbs will further isolate this part of the state from the upstate cities and towns. Once a massive collection of white ethnic enclaves, the new wave of immigration since 1968 has transformed New York into a city of mixed race enclaves. While the city's boroughs are internally varied, their heterogeneity separates their politics even more from that of the rest of New York than in 1960. Given the prevailing patterns of party support among racial and ethnic groups, it is unsurprising that boroughs like the Bronx and Brooklyn are becoming even more Democratic than in the past. Reflecting established migration patterns along transit lines from city to suburbs, blacks, Hispanics, and Asians are finding their way out of the boroughs and into the New York City suburbs. The monolithic identification of blacks with the Democratic Party has put increasingly competitive pressures on the GOP machines in Nassau and Westchester Counties. Republicans must find a way to either incorporate the black population in these areas and win black party converts or eventually cede power. In Nassau, the black population is more highly segregated than in any other part of the state (table 8.6). Republicans finally responded to the pressure of black leaders in the early 1990s by carving out two county council districts with majority black populations. Asians and Hispanics who migrate to the suburbs are not nearly as likely as African Americans to vote Democratic. They have shown only limited interest in political involvement, preferring to focus on activities that will further their economic integration.

Republicans are losing ground upstate and in New York's suburban counties as the result of attrition due to deindustrialization. As companies left New York during the 1970s, 1980s, and 1990s, those who could afford to move did so. These were often the skilled and well-educated white collar employees whose management jobs had disappeared. The blue collar workers were not nearly so mobile. They were left behind to scrounge for new jobs in low-paying service sector employment, often putting their spouses to work to maintain their standards of living. The demise of Republican registration and the rise of third-party and Democratic registration can be linked to deindustrialization through the mechanisms of out-migration and declining living standards that have led to a large class of economic and political malcontents.

Throughout this book, I have underlined the importance of consistent two-party competition as an instrument for obtaining full representation and good government. Forces restoring and promoting two-party competition to states and localities are good. Forces that promote and extend one-party politics are bad. Current economic forces appear to be restoring a two-party balance of power in New York's upstate counties. While a large number of entrenched Republican machines still exist and may hang on for some time, the long-term trends are favoring Democrats and third parties. Some of the suburbs are standing on a similar threshold. Ethnic and racial diversity may finally bring needed representation to residents who heretofore have had no voice in the politics of Long Island and Westchester Counties. New York City is a more troubling case. Mayor

Giuliani's election and reelection in the 1990s is a function of his strong and forceful personality rather than a resurgence of Republican Party strength. Giuliani's claim to represent the Republican alternative to the governance of New York City can legitimately be called into question given his endorsement of statewide and national Democratic candidates. There is no true Republican Party in New York City in the sense in which the party label finds its expression in national terms.

While a glance across counties reveals that population diversity has stimulated a movement toward two-party politics in many one-party areas, within counties the mechanism of spatial balkanization by race and ethnicity continues to create many single-party-dominated cities, townships, and neighborhoods. Chemung and Onondaga Counties are good examples of this common pattern: one-party municipalities, with occasionally competitive general elections, surrounded by overwhelmingly Republican suburbs. This gives the politics internal to counties an areal foundation that erodes accountability and cheapens the value of votes in local elections. City council members from Syracuse have safe seats. One party usually controls the mayoralty. Suburban council members in the county legislature have equally safe seats. With a politics that is so closely tied to the segregated residential settlement patterns of contemporary metropolitan areas, it is little wonder that turnout and participation in local elections is so low, that urban leadership has been at such a loss when confronting long-standing urban problems, and that suburban leadership turns its back on urban problems entirely.

CHAPTER 9

Population Mobility and Ethnic Divisions in
the American Electorate

In this book I have detailed a number of ways in which population movement has reconfigured American electoral politics in the waning decades
of the twentieth century. The fundamental fact is that native migration
flows do not closely parallel those of the most recent immigrants. Asians,
Mexicans, and Central Americans, while not always drawn to ethnic
enclaves, are far more likely to settle in areas of established coethnic settlement than other groups. Even for states such as Pennsylvania, where the
rate of immigrant influx has been rather slow over the last thirty years,
Asians and Mexicans are an increasing presence in the places of already
established Asian and Mexican settlement but not always where economic
prospects are brightest (see table 7.1). With few exceptions, internal
migrants are far more capable of avoiding areas of high unemployment
than the newer immigrant groups are. Only in states where the internal
migrant population is comprised mainly of elderly retirees do we find a sizable proportion of domestic migrants increasing their presence in destinations independent of prevailing employment and economic conditions.
This serves to remind us that not all internal migration is occurring for
economic reasons. Even if the elderly are not moving to find work, however, they are looking to improve their quality of life, and their choice of
destinations is nothing like that of most new immigrants.

Table 9.1 presents a pooled model of the change in the proportion of
internal migrants and several immigrant groups across counties for all
seven states evaluated in this study. These are cross-sectional results predicting the change in population *concentration* between 1980 and 1990
because more preferable time-series data on these populations are not
available. With that methodological caveat in mind, the results serve as a
convenient summary of the separate tables presented in chapters 2 through

324

TABLE 9.1. Influences on Population Concentration in Counties across Seven States, 1980–90

Variable	U.S. Migrants	Asian Immigrants	Mexican Immigrants	Canadian Immigrants	Central American Immigrants
% 1980 group population	-.18**	.35**	.20**	-.29**	.33**
	(.03)	(.03)	(.02)	(.01)	(.02)
% unemployment, 1980	.51**	-.06**	-.05**	-.002	-.01
	(.22)	(.02)	(.02)	(.002)	(.03)
Change in real median income, 1980–90	.06**	-.002**	-.0005	-.0001	.001
	(.01)	(.001)	(.005)	(.0009)	(.01)
% net population change	.15**	-.003	.004**	.0009**	-.008**
	(.02)	(.002)	(.002)	(.0001)	(.003)
Population density	.0001**	.00002**	.000005	.000007**	.00001**
	(.001)	(.00001)	(.000037)	(.000003)	(.000005)
% college students	-.52**	.08**	.003	.03**	-.11**
	(.14)	(.02)	(.005)	(.001)	(.02)
Spatial lag	1.37**	.95**	.55**	.008	.14
	(.07)	(.08)	(.04)	(.04)	(.10)
Constant	-2.18	.27	.34	.01	-2.15
N	541	541	541	541	541
R^2_a	.61	.72	.81	.67	.55

Note: Spatial autoregressive model, weighted for population; pooled data for California, Colorado, Kansas, Kentucky, Florida, Pennsylvania, and New York. Income coefficients are expressed in thousands of 1992 dollars; dependent variable = change in population group as a percentage of total population. For a full description of variables, see appendix A.

*p < .10.   **p < .05.

8 for several population groups: Canadian, Mexican, Central American, and Asian immigrants and U.S. internal migrants. Two of the groups, Canadians and U.S. internal migrants, were a generally smaller proportion of the population in 1990 than they were in 1980. The other groups, Mexicans, Asians, and Central Americans, gained a larger share of the population in the areas where they had settled in 1980. U.S. migrants grew more noticeable in areas that began the decade with high unemployment, but their increasing concentrations were also associated with income growth. Growth in the Asian presence across counties is associated with real income losses from 1980 to 1990. The foreign-born groups in table 9.1 became a larger proportion of the population in more densely populated areas, a finding consistent with earlier work showing that immigrants are slow to disperse into suburban and rural areas (Lieberson 1963).

What does it mean that so many of the new immigrants and internal migrants are not drawn to the same destinations? Because immigrants are drawn to areas where economic opportunities are limited and upward mobility is highly constrained, class cleavages across states and substate regions may increasingly parallel racial ones (Morales and Ong 1993, 77). The selection process in migration sorts people by both race and economic standing, generating a more class-based and race-based politics. Blacks and other minorities, because they lack marketable skills, education, and (in the case of immigrants) English, occupy especially weak positions in local labor markets (Kossoudji 1988; McManus 1985). This restricts their mobility and contributes to their geographic concentration and the increasing size of ethnic enclaves. White migrants, for their part, prefer to live in neighborhoods where whites predominate (Farley et al. 1994; Massey and Denton 1993). Their high mobility patterns contribute to the homogeneity of suburbs and suburban counties. Even in places where there are relatively few immigrants and internal migrants, a sorting process is observable that sends immigrants and internal migrants to different destinations.

Since the apportionment of political representation in most legislative bodies in the United States is spatially based (as opposed to at-large) and not proportional, the concentration of racially and economically monolithic populations inevitably exacerbates racial and economic cleavages in national politics. At the local level, of course, the close linkage of race, economic position, and political views ensures that legislative districts will be internally homogeneous. There can be no racial divisiveness in a city, county, or congressional district constituted by only one group. But the political representatives from districts lacking internal diversity are less likely than those elected from heterogeneous districts to practice a nonracial politics upon reaching a state or national legislature. Representing homogeneous areas that are most readily identifiable by their racial and ethnic composition, as opposed to some more mutable trait, ensures that the most obvious constituency characteristic determining the nature of representation will be the race or ethnicity of the people who are represented.

Mobility and Balkanization across Neighborhoods

In the foregoing pages, I have examined the settlement patterns of racial and ethnic groups within counties by examining the concentration of those groups relative to whites in census tracts. It is important to note at the outset that there are clear differences across states in the degree of residential segregation of whites from minorities. Pennsylvania and New York show the highest level of residential isolation for blacks and Hispanics. In these states, urban enclaves and ethnic neighborhoods are older, larger, and more entrenched. Industrial decline and economic restructuring have also left black and Hispanic neighborhoods more destitute and hopeless than in southern and western states. Black neighborhoods in Florida, Kentucky, and California are the next most isolated areas.

Hispanic populations in California and Kentucky are also highly isolated, but in Florida the segregation of Hispanic and Anglo populations is minimized due to the fact that there are fewer nonwhite Hispanics there than in the other states. The two most rural states, Colorado and Kansas, show the lowest degrees of racial balkanization across census tracts because they have the fewest minorities. Outside of Denver and Kansas City, comparatively few neighborhoods have reached their tipping point as the result of growing black and Hispanic populations.

As for Asians, the most urban states, Pennsylvania, New York, and California, show the highest degree of spatial isolation of Asians from whites. These states contain significant Asian concentrations within their largest cities. In spite of its small immigrant population, Kansas shows a stunningly high degree of segregation between whites and Asians. The concentration of this population in certain low-skill sectors of the Kansas economy, such as meatpacking, is responsible for their degree of residential isolation in spite of their small numbers. Asians are least concentrated in Florida and Colorado, where their numbers are far smaller and their levels of skill and education are higher.

The segregation of these groups from white natives is therefore highly variable across states and depends mostly upon the size of the minority population in the state. One clear conclusion is that small and dispersed minority populations may sometimes face discrimination and consequent economic hardship but large and concentrated minority populations are even more likely to struggle with prejudice in labor and housing markets. The reasons for this difference in the experience of dispersed and concentrated minority communities are straightforward. There are two kinds of deconcentrated minority populations. First, there are those with education and means who have easily integrated into the Anglo-dominant society and, because of their small numbers, are not threatening to non-Hispanic whites. The few, but relatively wealthy, immigrants in Kentucky seem to mix well with the native and internal migrant populations in Louisville, Lexington, and suburban Cincinnati. A second group of dispersed minorities are those clustered in isolated rural areas in places like the Central Valley of California or the isolated border towns of South Texas, far from contact with Anglo neighborhoods, business districts, and institutions. These communities do not make regular demands on the majority and are left to their own devices (Lamare 1977; Garcia 1973). Sizable minority communities in urban areas, on the other hand, not only make demands on the institutions of Anglo-white society but enter into direct competition with the majority for jobs, housing, schools, public services, and control of government. Not surprisingly, then, the more blacks reside in a state the more residentially segregated they will be. The same is true of Asians and Hispanics. The association of size with residential segregation is related to the established social scientific finding that income inequality and the concentration of minority populations are directly related (Tienda and Lii 1987; Frisbie and Neidert 1976; Jiobu 1988; Brown and Fugitt 1972; Lieberson 1963). The one exception to this rule seems to be Kentucky, where a relatively small black population is accompanied by an extraordinary degree of residential segregation. This anomaly is perhaps best explained by the legacy of race relations in the southern and border states, where segregated settlement patterns were more likely to be a function of official law and policy than in the northern and western states. Even small numbers of blacks were a threatening prospect to authorities in the Old South.

The geographic isolation of black, Asian, and Hispanic populations from whites across census tracts is clearly a function of recent immigration trends. The more immigrants in an area, the more racial and ethnic segregation one can expect to find, even after controlling for variables such as the high-density neighborhoods where most immigrants find their first homes. The proportion of immigrants arriving since 1970 is particularly related to the segregation of blacks from whites. That blacks would wind up more isolated from whites as the result of recent waves of immigration is a provocative discovery verifying the contention by some that blacks actually lose out to Hispanics and Asians in urban labor markets (Waldinger 1996; Mollenkopf and Castells 1991; Bailey and Waldinger 1991; Waldinger 1986–87; Skerry 1993).

A third influence on the spatial balkanization of ethnic and racial groups has been patterns of internal migration by wealthier white populations. To be sure, the effect of internal migration on residential segregation is more pronounced in some states than in others. For states with high rates of population influx from other states, the locational choices made by the new residents increase segregation. Internal migration has contributed to segregation not only across tracts within counties but across counties themselves, as internal migrants have decided to avoid entire municipalities and metropolitan areas on the basis of their racial makeup and the location of job opportunities (Burns 1994).

Mobility and Participation

To argue that the kind of ethnic balkanization flowing from these population changes has an impact on politics, politically distinguishing states and substate regions, requires evidence that inequalities across neighborhoods and counties in political participation, party registration, and party regularity are causally related to the settlement patterns of migrants and immigrants. Does such an association exist? Certainly the connection between education and participation is well established. Affluent people are better informed and more interested in civic affairs than the poor and uneducated. At the aggregate level, then, we should not be surprised to find lower naturalization and turnout rates in areas with large populations of poorly educated recent immigrants. The county level may be too gross of an aggregation for these familiar patterns to appear in every state, but clearly in California there is a relationship even at this level, with the more homogeneous white counties reporting the highest participation rates. It is well known that areas with high concentrations of minority voters have been underrepresented for decades due to their low turnout. But it is clear that this pattern of low participation in areas of minority concentration is increasing inequalities in representation across substate regions, cities, and neighborhoods.

Table 9.2 presents summary information on the relationship between patterns of ethnic settlement and turnout rates across counties for all seven states in the early 1990s. Residential isolation of whites from minorities within counties depresses turnout in 1990 and 1994 but not in 1992. Apparently the interest and mobilization generated by presidential contests is sufficient to overcome disparities in turnout generated by segregated neighborhoods within counties. Equally interesting is the result that inequalities in participation can be explained by the proportion of recent immigrants across counties. In 1992, a ten-point increase in the proportion

TABLE 9.2.   Impact of Population Mobility and Settlement Patterns on Voter Turnout in Seven States, 1990–94

Variable	1990[a]	1992	1994[a]
% college educated	−.15**	.39**	.15**
	(.03)	(.03)	(.03)
Isolation of minorities from	−.04**	.01	−.02**
whites (within counties)	(.008)	(.008)	(.008)
% post-1970 immigrants	−.04**	−.09**	−.06**
	(.01)	(.01)	(.01)
% born out of state	.04**	−.09**	.01
	(.01)	(.01)	(.01)
% black	−.03	.14**	−.05*
	(.03)	(.03)	(.03)
Population density	−.0002**	−.0002**	−.0002**
	(.0001)	(.0001)	(.0001)
Spatial lag	.71**	.16**	.73**
	(.03)	(.04)	(.03)
Constant	18.18	53.14	18.54
N	534	534	534
R^2_a	.76	.42	.58

Note: Spatial autoregressive model, weighted for population; pooled data for California, Colorado, Kansas, Kentucky, Florida, Pennsylvania, and New York; dependent variable = percentage turnout by county. See appendix A for a full description of variables.

[a]Kentucky data are for election years 1991 and 1995.

*$p < .10$.   **$p < .05$.

of recent immigrants dropped countrywide turnout by almost one percentage point.

Densely populated urban areas have lower turnout rates than rural ones, but this commonplace finding obscures a particularly noteworthy pattern of mobilization inequality in some states. Rural minority populations may be at a greater disadvantage in politics than urban minority populations because rural minorities have less contact with whites. The issue is distance. Immigrant minorities and native blacks who have settled outside of metropolitan areas face a degree of political isolation far more extreme than the segregation presented by the more widely studied urban setting (Lamare 1977). While minority-dominant urban neighborhoods may be just a few blocks from the schools, housing, and jobs present in affluent white neighborhoods, or at most just a few miles away, rural ethnic enclaves can be tens of miles away from affluent locations. Having even less contact than residents of urban ghettos with the Anglo population, rural minorities may experience less interethnic tension. But the absence of interracial contact in the highly class-homogeneous rural enclave has a demobilizing effect on the minority community. Under such isolated conditions, demands are voiced only within the community. Lacking the large and concentrated numbers of an inner city ward, rural enclaves in places like California's Central Valley, eastern Colorado, and southwestern Kansas are usually not the focus of much attention by political campaigns and party organizations either. The rural enclave is less attractive to the political organizer than the city ward not simply because of its smaller size but because its population is highly transient. With no outside pressure on the rural minority population to engage in civic affairs, these enclaves are typified by an inactivity that makes urban minority neighborhoods participatory hotbeds by comparison (Lamare 1977).

The news is not all good for white suburbia's participation, either. While residents are generally well educated in these places, there are some countervailing forces at work in the fast-growing suburbs that may contribute to low turnout in young neighborhoods. The influx of white internal migrants to a locale dampens turnout in some states, particularly in local elections. With the exception of Florida, there was evidence that places inundated with populations from elsewhere have lower participation rates than those with predominantly stable or declining populations. Within states, there were differences between places with migrants and those without across election years, with presidential elections erasing such differences across jurisdictions but off years heightening them.

Florida is an exception because the peculiar character of the internal migration, consisting of a large number of elderly retirees of long tenure, has been conducive to high participation rates across the peninsular counties. I have argued with the support of a long line of work on the impact of residential mobility on turnout that barriers to reregistration are partly responsible for the low participation rates of suburbs (Teixeira 1992; Squire, Wolfinger, and Glass 1987; Wolfinger and Rosenstone 1980; Campbell, Converse, Miller, and Stokes 1960). But mobility also disrupts (at least temporarily) a voter's social connectedness—that network of family, work, and friendship groups that lowers information costs and rewards good citizenship (Rosenstone and Hansen 1993, 23–24).

Although mobility may place a temporary damper on participation by affluent, upwardly mobile, suburban whites, the combined forces of poor education, low efficacy, and few resources put minority voters trapped in low-income neighborhoods at a more constant disadvantage. The wealthy and well educated are not only better able to learn about politics and participation but they have more resources and so do not persistently face the same difficult tradeoffs that limit the participation of the have-nots. For the poor, participation is often an alien luxury to be pursued after more basic needs have been met (Rosenstone and Hansen 1993; Rosenstone 1982). For immigrants who lack even the most basic knowledge of the American political system, the barriers to political participation are even greater than for native-born minorities (Tam 1996). These barriers to political involvement can be overcome, and usually they are in the second generation, but this often requires English proficiency, a goal that many first-generation Asian and Latin American immigrants never attain.

Still, the sheer volume of immigration in the last twenty years promises to enhance the influence of minorities in the politics of the nation and has already ensured their influence in New York, Florida, and California. Whether their political power in the coming decades will be directly proportional to their numbers depends upon the group's capacity to assimilate. The new immigrants are hampered not only by their lack of English proficiency but by their inferior position in the economy, which is determined by both their lack of skills and discrimination by natives. Political participation is so often contingent upon progress up the economic ladder that whatever holds such progress back is likely to restrain political participation as well. Given that geographic isolation and the expanding size of ethnic enclaves are associated with economic disadvantage, the new immigrant communities retard rather than promote political participation.

Mobility and Party Regularity

Party regularity measured at the aggregate level refers to the extent to which an area's political behavior in major elections can be predicted by its balance of party registrants. Regular areas are those where the balance of party registrants and the outcome of elections neatly match. Irregularity, on the other hand, is observable when either sizable proportions of the electorate consistently fail to turn out or when those who do vote are not loyal to their registration. In democratic systems, party regularity matters because partisanship is a reflection of what divides, animates, and mobilizes the electorate. Party labels provide an accurate guide to the stands incumbent and aspiring officeholders take as well as a standard by which their performances can be judged. When the lines of partisanship are blurred as the result of the relocation of partisans with widely differing attitudes and political orientations, judgments based on party cues are more error prone and electoral accountability can be undermined. In addition, the regularity of an electorate is an important consideration when planning an election campaign. Reliable electorates need not be the focus of the candidate or party organization's attention (Gimpel 1996). Volatile ones, on the other hand, must be carefully studied, targeted, and mobilized. The more areas of a state are unpredictable the more campaign and organization resources must be diffused.

I have theorized that places where recent migrants and immigrants settle are more likely to be irregular—primarily on the basis of their erratic participation rates. The evidence supporting this hypothesis is mixed, depending upon the state. Florida and Kentucky, it should be noted, are more irregular than the other states due to the ubiquity of dual partisans— Democratic identifiers who regularly vote Republican—in the parts of those states that most closely resemble the Old South. Overall, however, it appears that the areas where the recent waves of immigrants have settled are more *regular* than the areas they have avoided—the precise opposite of my conjecture. This makes sense if the majority of naturalized foreign-born minorities are loyal to one party, probably the Democrats. Certainly the individual-level data from exit polls suggests that Asians and Hispanics were strongly Democratic in the early 1990s and less likely to split their ballots than whites were. Regularity in immigrant receiving areas is also understandable given that the places where the recent foreign born are most concentrated are highly urbanized areas dominated by Democratic officeholders and where strong Democratic identifiers greatly outnumber weaker partisans. That so many immigrants reside in predictably Democratic cities is itself an explanation for their low participation. Individual votes matter least in the one-sided electoral settings Peter Skerry has referred to as rotten boroughs (1993). Abstention in such areas is a highly rational act.

In table 9.3, I have pooled the data from all seven states to generalize about demographic correlates of party irregularity in 1990, 1992, and 1994. The presence of large numbers of blacks in an area will usually ensure that party irregularity is kept to a minimum. In 1990, a 10 percent increase in the percentage of blacks across counties was associated with a two-point drop

TABLE 9.3.   Similarity of Party Registration to Party Voting in Seven States, 1990–94

Variable	1990[a]	1992	1994[a]
% college educated	−.12**	.02	−.22**
	(.04)	(.04)	(.03)
% born out of state	−.02	−.02	−.10**
	(.02)	(.02)	(.01)
% post-1970 immigrants	.03	−.009	.06**
	(.02)	(.02)	(.01)
% black	−.21**	−.08**	−.08**
	(.04)	(.03)	(.03)
Population density	−.00004	−.00003	−.0002**
	(.0003)	(.0001)	(.0001)
% turnout	−.02	−.21**	.05
	(.04)	(.05)	(.04)
Spatial lag	.61**	.52**	.67**
	(.05)	(.04)	(.03)
Constant	7.84	18.58	6.34
N	541	541	541
R^2_a	.38	.23	.59

Note: Spatial autoregressive model, weighted for population; pooled data for California, Colorado, Kansas, Kentucky, Florida, Pennsylvania, and New York; dependent variable = Abs (% Republican vote − % Republican registration). High positive values indicate counties where voting differed from registration. See appendix A for a full description of variables.

[a]Kentucky data are for election years 1991 and 1995.

*$p < .10$.   **$p < .05$.

in the difference between party registration and voting outcomes. Providing that blacks turn out, their loyally Democratic ballots will ensure minimal differences between party registration and actual vote choice.

As for internal U.S. migrants, the evidence that they are responsible for party irregularity is not uniformly strong across states. In table 9.3, the evidence indicates that the presence of interstate migrants is consistent with regularity rather than deviation from partisanship. In Pennsylvania, for instance, the areas with the highest proportion of internal migrants, including the wealthy Philadelphia suburbs, are quite regular in highly competitive elections. Similarly, in Florida and Kentucky it is the local, indigenous populations with their dual partisanship that by comparison make areas with out-of-state migrants easy to forecast in the early 1980s. By the 1990s, though, the continued high volume of cross-state migration was showing a marked tendency to increase the difference between registration and voting in Florida. Much of this discrepancy is related to the lower turnout levels of the newest residents. California's out-of-state populations are also associated with party irregularity, particularly in presidential contests and less so in state-level elections. While individual-level data are required to determine precisely whether the out-of-state migrants are the ones that are creating this electoral chaos by their unpredictable behavior, it is a good bet based on survey data that they are (Brown 1988).

Mobility and the Changing Balance of Partisanship

Finally, I investigated the impact of mobility on changes in party registration, hypothesizing that population growth from domestic sources is a sign of expanding economic opportunity likely to attract the best educated, most upwardly mobile populations and therefore likely to benefit the GOP at the expense of Democrats and third parties. Across states, of course, this would predict Republican growth in the Sunbelt and decline in the Rust Belt. GOP registration growth was especially brisk in Florida and California during the 1980s and 1990s. New York and Pennsylvania saw their Republican share of registrants diminish on average. In some states (Kentucky, Kansas) the benefits of migration for the GOP are not decisive, perhaps because the total volume of migration to these states has been low. Any Republican gains have been offset by similar losses. In these slower growth states, Republicans have gained more from generational replacement, specifically the death of old Democrats, than from population mobility.

Keeping in mind that we are dealing with cross-sectional data, a summary analysis of the change in Republican registration from 1980 to 1990 is presented in table 9.4. As expected, the proportion of internal migrants in a place in 1980 is positively associated with increasing GOP registration between 1980 and 1990. Population density is associated with Republican gains, but the more urban places where the foreign born concentrated in 1980 wound up with low Republican growth rates or even decline relative to other parties. Notably, however, *change* in the proportion of foreign-born residents enhances GOP growth. This is not necessarily the reflection of the voting tendencies and political preferences of these populations. But it is striking that in spite of the advance of immigrant populations in the

TABLE 9.4.   Impact of Population Mobility on Changes in Republican Party Registration in Seven States, 1980–90

Variable	1980–90
% born out of state, 1980	.03**
	(.01)
Change in % born out of state	.07
	(.05)
% foreign born, 1980	–.12*
	(.07)
Change in % foreign born	.42**
	(.10)
% Republican registrants, 1980	–.03**
	(.01)
% over age 65 in 1980	–.14**
	(.04)
Population density	.00007**
	(.00002)
Spatial lag	.82**
	(.03)
Constant	3.07
N	541
R^2_a	.70

Note: Spatial autoregressive model, weighted for population; pooled data for California, Colorado, Kansas, Kentucky, Florida, New York, and Pennsylvania; dependent variable = change in percentage of Republican Party registrants.
   $*p < .10.$ $**p < .05.$

suburbs, Republicans have still gained some work. After all, the majority of Hispanic and a large proportion of Asian immigrants migrating to the suburbs identify with the Democratic Party. Immigrants are finding their way into the suburbs, and their relocation is apparently not putting a complete damper on Republican registration.

Glimpses of what is occurring within states reveal that Republicans have benefited from the movement of new populations into Southern California, northern Kentucky, and the Florida Gulf Coast, particularly in the 1980s and 1990s. The notion that the Democratic Party remains the political hope of those living in declining, impoverished areas is not a mythical one. The results suggest that the socioeconomic distinction between the parties in American politics may only grow wider in years to come and that one instrument of this division is the selective process behind population mobility.

Party support is dynamic and cyclical. Natural equilibrating tendencies in two-party politics militate against the permanent dominance of a single party in a particular area (Sellers 1965; Stokes and Iverson 1962). The two-party, winner-take-all structure of American elections encourages the intense effort by out-parties to build support, recruit more attractive candidates, and work their way into competitive positions. This is a potentially important countervailing force to the trends that shape political stratification that I have discussed throughout this book. While it is easy to see how the balance of party strength has been maintained at the national level and in most states, it is less clear whether localities are ruled by the balancing forces that ensure regular shifts in the political control of government. Indeed, there is some evidence that at the local level these equilibrium cycles are at work to prevent the sustained domination of a single party. Places that began the 1970s and 1980s with a high proportion of GOP registrants often experienced Republican losses. Examples include the waning Republican strength of several counties in upstate New York (including Tompkins and Onondaga) that have seen Democrats make considerable gains since the early 1970s.

Whatever incentives are at work in some areas to keep out-parties struggling to win elections, there are as many areas where the dominance of one party is more secure than ever. Whether a locality is potentially two-party competitive or electorally one sided remains contingent upon the racial and ethnic composition of the local electorate (Huckfeldt and Kohfeld 1989). Blacks and nonwhite Hispanics are sufficiently dedicated to one party that the spatial sorting that has led to the segregation of neighborhoods, counties, and regions inevitably translates into single-party domination in geographically tied election districts. A state may be two-party competitive, but if that bipartisanship is constructed on the basis of homogeneous, ethnically pure electoral districts that are spatially segregated from one another, it will mean that state (and ultimately national) politics will become even more of an ethnic and racial battleground than it has been in the past.

The Future of Racial Divisions in the American Polity

I have argued that existing patterns of racial and ethnic segregation have not only been very slow to break down but are now being reinforced by both white mobility patterns and the influx of immigrants of color whose upward mobility and capacity to assimilate is limited in a variety of ways: by low skill levels, a lack of English proficiency, and the discrimination of native whites and in some cases native minorities. I have also indicated that sustained residential segregation by race will have an impact on politics as the minority communities grow larger, exacerbating racial and ethnic cleavages in the American political system. One could well argue that it is the nature of politics to cleave the community in one way or another. If race were not the dividing line, something else surely would be, say, class or religion or ideology. Why should we be so concerned that our politics divides us by race and ethnicity?

The answer is that race is the most unpleasant of dividing lines because it is not something people can change about themselves (Rothbart and John 1993). It is a permanent trait, with clear physical markers, even more difficult to disguise than gender and impossible to alter. A person can change his or her ideology through learning and compromise, convert to a new religion, or adopt no religion at all. Economic inequality can be addressed by combinations of individual action and government policy. For many issues that divide communities, resolutions have been achieved, even if they are often temporary. But no amount of government action can make those who are white black or vice versa. Of course, the immutable quality of race is what makes the issue so difficult to resolve.

While people cannot change their race, they can change their racial attitudes, and this leaves room for hope. Integration—or, to use a less politically charged term, "contact"—is the usual mechanism for constructing cross-racial friendships (Sigelman, Bledsoe, Welch, and Combs

1996; Sigelman and Welch 1993; Allport 1954). As Donald Kinder and Lynn Sanders have recently pointed out, segregation reduces incentives for coalition building and only widens the racial divide in opinion (1996, 286–87). The data presented in this book show that some progress has been made toward residential integration in the last thirty years. Asians, blacks, and Hispanics are moving out of central city neighborhoods. But for blacks and nonwhite Hispanics the suburbs they move to are only slightly less segregated than the urban neighborhoods they left behind (Massey and Denton 1993). Further progress will require vigorous enforcement of antidiscrimination laws by state and national governments. But the separation between ethnic groups is only partly kept in place by the prejudices of the majority. Many groups desire to maintain their own identity, language, and subculture, and this collective decision is averse to the type of contact that will reduce prejudice. As sociologist Milton M. Gordon observed in the mid-1960s:

> The fulfillment of occupational roles, the assignment of living space, the selection of political leaders and the effective functioning of the educational process, among others, demand that universalistic criteria of competence and training, rather than considerations based on racial, religious, or nationality background, be utilized. The subversion of this principle by ethnic considerations would appear bound to produce, in the long run, confusion, conflict and mediocrity. (1964, 236)

Aside from residential integration, there are only a few alternatives that might help to diminish racial divisiveness in American politics. One possibility is that minorities will leave the Democratic Party and move into the GOP. But usually minority conversions to the Republican Party are associated with upward mobility—rising incomes, educational attainment, and middle-class status. If the economic position of native blacks and new immigrants slips further behind that of native whites, it is difficult to imagine that many of these voters will abandon the Democratic Party, which, for all its faults, capably maintains the image of the party of the downtrodden. For immigrants who have skills, English proficiency, and access to capital, the path to economic and geographic mobility is less blocked—and so, too, is the route to Republican Party identification. Upward mobility comes more easily to most Asians than to nonwhite Hispanics or blacks. Consequently, the prospects for increasing Asian influence within Republican ranks are quite promising (Horton 1995). Asian communities like

Monterey Park, California, are already showing some measure of two-party competition, therefore reducing the level of political balkanization that stems directly from insular settlement patterns.

The other possibility that may contribute to the dissipation rather than the increase in the level of racial tension in American politics is that national immigration policy will be changed, perhaps altering legal immigration preferences to favor more highly skilled and better educated immigrants. More highly skilled immigrants would have more geographic and socioeconomic mobility than the unskilled. In turn, a renewed focus on skilled immigration would lessen the reliance of the immigrant on the coethnic enclave and greatly facilitate the assimilation of the admitted immigrants into the mainstream economy. Moreover, native minorities and older immigrants are concerned about job competition from newly arriving groups. Even economists who favor unrestricted immigration have indicated that the influx of immigrants has the effect of depressing wages in low-skill occupations. Restricting entrance to skilled immigrants would lessen the competition for the unskilled positions and stabilize the wages and employment prospects for low-skill natives. Restricting the flow of legal immigrants would also directly address the anxieties of native minorities, particularly those in low-skill, low-wage occupations. In turn, the prosperity of native minorities and already settled immigrant groups would diminish the extent to which economic grievances based on racial inequities become the foundation for political demands.

Finally, racial cleavages have persisted because of the way in which political jurisdictional boundaries have been drawn. Residential settlement patterns, as I have repeatedly indicated, remain highly segregated by race and ethnicity in most urban and many rural areas. Even when minority populations are small, they are often isolated in a particular area or neighborhood within a county. Spatial isolation confines whatever political influence they have to just one or a few legislative districts (Lublin 1997). While the move from at-large to district-tied elections has succeeded in electing minority representatives to local, state, and national office, it has also wasted minority votes by blocking them into politically homogeneous, ethnically pure election districts characterized by little electoral competition. Inevitably the votes of many minorities in these districts are wasted because the politicians that represent them face only minimal opposition. Lani Guinier, a critic of geographically based, winner-take-all election districts, complains that the votes in support of losing candidates in gerrymandered districts are wasted (Guinier 1994,121). Guinier neglects to add that when winning candidates are coasting to easy 75 percent victories even the votes in the majority's favor are wasted. The answer to bad representation is not to give voters who supported the loser proportional representation but to draw district lines that promote two-party political competition—and that means, in present times, the abolition of race-based districting. Wasted votes are not just those cast for the losing candidate, as Guinier insists, but all votes that are cast in any noncompetitive election setting. Whereas Guinier objects to territorial districts that encompass heterogeneous groups that are not of like mind, maximizing the value of individual votes requires just these kinds of districts—since these are the districts most likely to generate competitive party politics. Gerrymandering should be designed not to group people on the basis of their similarity but on the basis of their *dissimilarity*! The guiding criteria for drawing boundaries should be to maximize racial, economic, and political diversity within a district. Inevitably, given the concentration of certain economic and racial groups, there are limits to the extent to which any set of boundary adjustments will promote this diversity. Given their small minority populations, Kansas and Kentucky districts are likely to be racially homogeneous regardless of how much the lines are redrawn, although they may still be politically diverse.

The proposal to draw districts that maximize rather than minimize racial and economic heterogeneity is likely to strike some as simply a return to white-dominated, at-large schemes of representation that many municipalities have recently rejected on grounds of inequity. But it is a mistake to assume that a group is well or poorly represented because of the race or economic class of the politicians who are elected. The political presence of a group in a legislature is not determined by the presence of a member of that group in that legislature. Minorities in big cities and white voters in wealthy suburbs are often poorly represented not because the politicians elected to represent them are the wrong race but because the election contests in these areas are not politically competitive. In the absence of competitive contests, voters become cynical and apathetic and refuse to participate—further contributing to the erosion of the threat of electoral sanction. Until the success of candidates is entirely independent of the ethnic and racial composition of district populations, race-based districting should be eliminated at all levels of elective office.

Conflict between groups with differences on some salient dimension is the hallmark of politics in a democratic system. But it is important to distinguish between healthy and unhealthy divisions. The unhealthy divisions are ones rooted in unalterable traits like race, which divide people based on permanent group memberships. The healthy divisions are those that can be resolved more easily by the movement of individuals into and out of penetrable coalition groupings. It is not inevitable that political conflict in the United States must be based on race and ethnic differences; it only seems that way given the nation's long struggle with this issue. Redefining notions of minority political empowerment to recognize the importance of competitive electoral districts while maintaining efforts to promote minority opportunity and advancement in the economy is essential to creating a democracy in which the issues dividing the polity are more temporary and soluble.

Variables and Variable Definitions

All demographic county-level variables have been drawn directly from the 1970, 1980, and 1990 U.S. *Censuses of Population,* published by the U.S. Department of Commerce, Bureau of the Census. Variables for political party registration and party voting originate from the state agency in each state in charge of administering elections.

% 1980 Group Population	Immigrant group's percentage of total population residing in the county in 1980
% Unemployment 1980	Unemployment rate in 1980
Change in Real Median Income 1980–90	Dollar change in real median family income from 1980–90 expressed in thousands of 1992 dollars
Net Population Change	Percentage of population growth 1970–80, 1980–90
Population Density	Population/square mile of land area (in 1980, 1990)
% College Students	Percentage of county population enrolled in colleges within the county in 1980
Median Income	Median family income (in 1980 and 1990)
% College Educated	Percentage of population within county with four-year college degree (in 1980 and 1990)
% Born Out of State (or % Internal Migrants)	Percentage of population born outside the state where currently residing, 1980 and 1990, exclud-

ing the foreign-born population and those born in U.S. territories such as Guam or Puerto Rico

% Pre-1965 Immigrants — Percentage of population that is foreign born arriving in the United States prior to 1965 (in 1980 and 1990)

Isolation of Minorities from Whites — Dissimilarity index calculated across tracts within counties for white-Asian, white-Hispanic, and white-black concentration and then summed (in 1980 and 1990) (*See Chapter 2, footnote 1*)

Asian Segregation — Dissimilarity index calculated across tracts within counties for white-Asian concentration (in 1980 and 1990) (*See Chapter 2, footnote 1*)

Hispanic Segregation — Dissimilarity index calculated across tracts within counties for white-Hispanic concentration (in 1980 and 1990)

% Post-1970 Immigrants — Percentage of population that is foreign born arriving in the United States after 1965 (in 1980 and 1990)

% of Foreign Born Naturalized — Percentage of the foreign-born population that is naturalized (in 1980 and 1990)

% Black — Percentage of the population that is African American (in 1980 and 1990)

% Turnout — Percentage of registered voters voting in either a gubernatorial or presidential election in year

Party Irregularity — Percentage of voters registered Republican in a year minus percentage of vote for the Republican

	candidate leading the ticket (either president or governor) in year, expressed in absolute terms
Change in % Born Out of State	Percentage born out of state (but in the United States) in 1990 minus percentage born out of state (but in the United States) in 1980 and the same for 1970 to 1980
% Foreign Born	Percentage foreign born (in 1980 and 1990)
% Hispanic	Percentage of Hispanic ancestry of any race, (in 1980 and 1990)
% Asian	Percentage of Asian ancestry (in 1980 and 1990)
Change in % Hispanic	Percentage Hispanic in 1990 minus percentage Hispanic in 1980 and the same for 1970 to 1980
Change in % Asian	Percentage Asian in 1990 minus percentage Asian in 1980 and the same for 1970 to 1980
% Republican Registrants	Republicans registered as a percentage of total registrants, 1980 and 1990
Change in % Republican Registrants	Republicans registered as a percentage of total registrants in 1990 minus the same figure for 1980 and the same for 1980 to 1970
Change in % Unemployment	Percentage unemployment in 1990 minus percentage unemployment in 1980 and the same for 1970 to 1980
% Over Age 65	Percentage of residents over age sixty-five (in 1980 and 1990)
Spatial Lag	Dependent variable spatially weighted to account for the influence of nearby observations. (*see appendix B*)

TABLE A2.1.   Characteristics of California Natives, Immigrants, and
Internal Migrants

Demographic	Native	Migrant	Immigrant
Mean age	37.8	49.4	40.0
Mean education	10.9	11.0	8.8
Mean wage and salary income	$22,687	$26,342	$18,624
Median wage and salary income	$10,000	$8,230	$6,213
Mean Social Security income	$2,061	$3,118	$1,840
% non-Hispanic white	70.7	80.0	20.0

Source: 1990 U.S. Census Public Use Microdata Sample for California, 1 percent sample, respondents over age eighteen. Figures are percentages unless otherwise indicated.

Note: These data reflect individual responses, not households.

TABLE A2.2.   Influence of Spatial Segregation
Internal to California Counties on Naturalization
Rates, 1980 and 1990

Variable	1980	1990
Population density, 1980–90	.0008**	.0006**
	(.0003)	(.0003)
% foreign born	−.86**	−.41**
	(.17)	(.10)
Asian segregation	.33**	.10
	(.09)	(.09)
Hispanic segregation	−.41**	−.26**
	(.11)	(.12)
% college education	.47**	.53**
	(.18)	(.11)
Spatial lag	.44**	.14
	(.14)	(.20)
Constant	31.51	29.66
N	58	58
R^2_a	.85	.65

Note: Spatial autoregressive model, weighted for population;
dependent variable = percentage of the immigrant population
naturalized. See appendix A for a full description of variables.

   $*p < .10.$ $**p < .05.$

TABLE A2.3   Logistic Regression of the Influence of Nativity on Presidential Vote Choice, Controlling for Party Identification, Education, Income, Length of Residence, and Urban/Rural Location, by Ethnic Background

Variable	European and Canadian	Hispanic	Asian
Birthplace (native = 0, foreign born = 1)	.14	.31	.49
	(.21)	(.51)	(1.09)
Rural	.04	.55	−.13
	(.10)	(.58)	(1.24)
Urban	−.18	.48	1.01
	(.11)	(.41)	(1.13)
Income	.12**	.33**	−.32
	(.04)	(.19)	(.47)
Education	−.05*	.01	.63
	(.03)	(.13)	(.57)
Age	.0003	.004	.02
	(.003)	(.02)	(.05)
Length of residence	.003	−.016	−.05
	(.003)	(.015)	(.05)
Black	−.52	−.04	—
	(1.09)	(1.15)	
Party identification	1.69**	1.97***	2.35***
(1 = D, 2 = I, 3 = R)	(.05)	(.28)	(.63)
Constant	−3.09	−4.86	−7.52
N	4037	218	51
% correctly classified	81.1%	83.5%	84.3%
Null model	59.9%	61.0%	56.0%
Model χ^2	1,814.1	104.1	31.4
Significance	$p < .0001$	$p < .0001$	$p < .0001$

Source: ICPSR, *American National Election Studies Cumulative Datafile 1980–1994.*
Note: Dependent variable = presidential vote choice coded: 0 = Democrat, 1 = Republican.
*$p < .10$.   **$p < .05$.   ***$p < .01$.

TABLE A3.1.   Characteristics of Colorado Natives, Immigrants, and Internal Migrants

Demographic	Native	Migrant	Immigrant
Mean age	41.0	44.4	42.3
Mean education	10.4	11.3	9.9
Mean wage and salary income	$12,365	$16,101	$11,651
Median wage and salary income	$5,600	$7,530	$6,000
Mean Social Security income	$2,218	$2,570	$2,101
% non-Hispanic white	77.1	88.6	51.5

Source: 1990 U.S. Census Public Use Microdata Sample for Colorado, 1 percent sample, respondents over age eighteen. Figures are percentages unless otherwise indicated.
Note: These data reflect individual responses, not households.

TABLE A3.2. Influence of Spatial Segregation Internal to Colorado Counties on Naturalization Rates, 1980 and 1990

Variable	1980	1990
Population density, 1980–90	.001	−.001
	(.001)	(.002)
% foreign born	.49	−1.99*
	(1.19)	(1.07)
Asian segregation	.26	−.17
	(.20)	(.20)
Hispanic segregation	−.43**	.08
	(.20)	(.25)
% college education	−.49**	.01
	(.23)	(.12)
Spatial lag	.34**	.40**
	(.13)	(.13)
Constant	43.07	40.82
N	63	63
R^2_a	.30	.23

Note: Spatial autoregressive model, weighted for population; dependent variable = percentage of the immigrant population naturalized.
*$p < .10$.   **$p < .05$.

TABLE A4.1. Characteristics of Kansas Natives, Immigrants, and Internal Migrants

Demographic	Native	Migrant	Immigrant
Mean age	47.1	45.7	46.6
Mean education	10.3	10.7	9.7
Mean wage and salary income	$10,986	$13,993	$11,216
Median wage and salary income	$5,600	$7,530	$6,000
Mean Social Security income	$1,400	$1,166	$636
% non-Hispanic white	92.9	87.9	41.6

Source: 1990 U.S. Census Public Use Microdata Sample for Kansas, 1 percent sample, respondents over age eighteen. Figures are percentages unless otherwise indicated.
Note: These data reflect individual responses, not households.

TABLE A4.2. Influence of Spatial Segregation
Internal to Kansas Counties on Naturalization Rates,
1980 and 1990

Variable	1980	1990
Population density, 1980–90	−.0007	.007
	(.006)	(.005)
% foreign born	−5.88**	−3.45**
	(1.34)	(.83)
Asian segregation	−.04	−.14
	(.08)	(.13)
Hispanic segregation	−.10	−.09
	(.18)	(.15)
% college education	−.10	−.35**
	(.39)	(.17)
Spatial lag	−.17	.17
	(.16)	(.13)
Constant	80.25	62.15
N	105	105
R^2_a	.17	.32

Note: Spatial autoregressive model, weighted for population;
dependent variable = percentage of the immigrant population
naturalized. See appendix A for a full description of variables.
    *$p < .10$.   **$p < .05$.

TABLE A5.1. Characteristics of Kentucky Natives, Immigrants, and
Internal Migrants

Demographic	Native	Migrant	Immigrant
Mean age	45.4	42.2	41.6
Mean education	9.2	10.5	11.1
Mean wage and salary income	$10,250	$13,823	$14,045
Median wage and salary income	$3,671	$6,400	$3,725
Mean Social Security income	$1,113	$925	$641
% non-Hispanic white	92.4	90.0	57.1

Source: 1990 U.S. Census Public Use Microdata Sample for Kentucky, 1 percent sample,
respondents over age eighteen. Figures are percentages unless otherwise indicated.
    Note: These data reflect individual responses, not households.

TABLE A5.2. Influence of Spatial Segregation
Internal to Kentucky Counties on Naturalization Rates,
1980 and 1990

Variable	1980	1990
Population density, 1980–90	.004	.008**
	(.004)	(.004)
% foreign born	–4.77*	.36
	(2.91)	(4.59)
Asian segregation	–.29*	–.32*
	(.17)	(.18)
Hispanic segregation	.08	–.01
	(.23)	(.08)
% college education	–2.99**	–1.35**
	(.81)	(.53)
Spatial lag	–.11	.02
	(.15)	(.14)
Constant	100.42	74.78
N	120	120
R^2_a	.19	.08

Note: Spatial autoregressive model, weighted for population;
dependent variable = percentage of the immigrant population
naturalized. See appendix A for a full description of variables.
    *$p < .10$.   **$p < .05$.

TABLE A6.1. Characteristics of Florida Natives, Immigrants, and
Internal Migrants

Demographic	Native	Migrant	Immigrant
Mean age	38.8	50.5	47.7
Mean education	10.0	10.5	9.4
Mean wage and salary income	$12,163	$12,475	$10,662
Median wage and salary income	$7,800	$4,500	$5,000
Mean Social Security income	$2,061	$3,335	$2,672
% non-Hispanic white	67.7	89.0	28.4

Source: 1990 U.S. Census Public Use Microdata Sample for Florida, 1 percent sample,
respondents over age eighteen. Figures are percentages unless otherwise indicated.
    Note: These data reflect individual responses, not households.

TABLE A6.2. Influence of Spatial Segregation
Internal to Florida Counties on Naturalization Rates,
1980 and 1990

Variable	1980	1990
Population density, 1980–90	.006**	−.0004
	(.002)	(.002)
% foreign born	−.69**	−.41**
	(.10)	(.14)
Asian segregation	−.54**	.23
	(.20)	(.28)
Hispanic segregation	.19	−.10
	(.12)	(.17)
% college education	−1.29**	−.63**
	(.47)	(.29)
Spatial lag	.04	.33
	(.18)	(.21)
Constant	85.62	43.88
N	67	67
R^2_a	.55	.31

Note: Spatial autoregressive model, weighted for population;
dependent variable = percentage of the immigrant population
naturalized. See appendix A for a full description of variables.
  $*p < .10.$ $**p < .05.$

TABLE A7.1. Characteristics of Pennsylvania Natives, Immigrants, and
Internal Migrants

Demographic	Native	Migrant	Immigrant
Mean age	45.6	44.3	48.7
Mean education	9.9	10.8	9.5
Mean wage and salary income	$12,106	$15,208	$11,953
Median wage and salary income	$6,000	$6,899	$1,594
Mean Social Security income	$1,004	$943	$1,229
% non-Hispanic white	95.5	88.5	66.7

Source: 1990 U.S. Census Public Use Microdata Sample for Pennsylvania, 1 percent sample, respondents over age eighteen. Figures are percentages unless otherwise indicated.
  Note: These data reflect individual responses, not households.

TABLE A7.2. Influence of Spatial Segregation
Internal to Pennsylvania Counties on Naturalization
Rates, 1980 and 1990

Variable	1980	1990
Population density, 1980–90	−.001	−.0004
	(.001)	(.002)
% foreign born	4.68**	−.41**
	(1.28)	(.14)
Asian segregation	−.37**	.23
	(.17)	(.28)
Hispanic segregation	−.19**	−.10
	(.07)	(.17)
% college education	−2.41**	−.63**
	(.45)	(.29)
Spatial lag	.47**	.33
	(.16)	(.21)
Constant	64.47	43.88
N	67	67
R^2_a	.55	.31

Note: Spatial autoregressive model, weighted for population;
dependent variable = percentage of the immigrant population
naturalized. See appendix A for a full description of variables.
  *$p < .10$.   **$p < .05$.

TABLE A8.1. Characteristics of New York Natives, Immigrants, and
Internal Migrants

Demographic	Native	Migrant	Immigrant
Mean age	43.9	47.2	46.7
Mean education	10.6	10.9	9.2
Mean wage and salary income	$15,934	$17,118	$12,946
Median wage and salary income	$8,600	$7,596	$5,000
Mean Social Security income	$1,162	$1,352	$1,017
% non-Hispanic white	87.9	73.7	37.2

Source: 1990 U.S. Census Public Use Microdata Sample for New York, 1 percent sample,
respondents over age eighteen. Figures are percentages unless otherwise indicated.
  Note: These data reflect individual responses, not households.

TABLE A8.2.   Influence of Spatial Segregation
Internal to New York Counties on Naturalization
Rates, 1980 and 1990

Variable	1980	1990
Population density, 1980–90	−.00002	−.0001*
	(.00005)	(.00006)
% foreign born	−.53**	−.38**
	(.12)	(.11)
Asian segregation	−.29**	−.17*
	(.10)	(.10)
Hispanic segregation	−.05	−.08
	(.05)	(.06)
% college education	−.28**	.04
	(.11)	(.07)
Spatial lag	.33**	.42**
	(.15)	(.16)
Constant	63.89	47.16
N	62	62
R^2_a	.85	.82

Note: Spatial autoregressive model, weighted for population;
dependent variable = percentage of the immigrant population
naturalized. See appendix A for a full description of variables.
   $*p < .10.$ $**p < .05.$

Basics of Spatial Regression Analysis

Boundaries around geographical units (counties, cities, census tracts, districts) are usually arbitrarily drawn. This gives rise to the problem of spatial dependence among observations that are spatially related. When the values of a variable across units of analysis are spatially related, the standard regression assumption of independence among the observations is violated. Fortunately, recent developments in statistics and econometrics have provided potential corrections or controls for the effects that the spatial arrangement may have on the values of given observations for a variable. When the values of an observation are closely related to the values of nearby observations, the condition is analogous to time-series autocorrelation when the values at a particular time for a given observation are related to the values of previous times for that observation:

Time series autocorrelation

Time:	$t-4$	$t-3$	$t-2$	$t-1$	t
Observation:	15	25	35	45	55

The analogy is imperfect, however, because spatial autocorrelation may occur in multiple "directions." In the time-series case, the dependency is only backward in time. Typically, the values at time t are modeled as a function of the values at $t-1$ and other explanatory variables. The values at time t can also be modeled as a function of the values at $t-2, t-3, \ldots$ $t-n$. But the directionality is always unidimensional, making temporally lagged variables very easy to compute.

In the case of *spatial autocorrelation,* the dependency can be in multiple directions, in two dimensions:

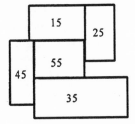

As in time-series autocorrelation, the dependency can extend to more than just the immediately adjacent observations to observations that are more distant.

Just as the goal in time-series analysis is to account for the influence of serial correlation on the dependent variable, the goal in spatial data analysis is to eliminate the influence of spatial dependence. According to Anselin, spatial dependence is the existence of a functional relationship between what happens at one point in space and what happens elsewhere (1988, 11). Since county, tract, and other jurisdictional boundaries are arbitrarily drawn, it is likely that observations from one point on a map are similar to those of nearby points, violating classical regression assumptions. Certainly for geographically arranged data, where the observations are determined by boundaries that do not truly separate observations from one another, it is safer to assume that observations are related to one another than to assume that all observations are independent.

One of the most difficult areas of spatial data analysis is to determine the precise nature of the relationship among observations arranged in space (Haining 1990, 341–42). In time-series analysis, it is straightforward to lag a variable by one time period or more, and econometric theory often provides clear direction for specification. But in spatial analysis some units in the geographic vicinity of a given observation may have more influence than others (Anselin 1988, 16–17). It is a safe assumption that closer neighbors make more of a difference than those that are far away, but a given county may be more closely related to its close neighbors to the north and west than to equally contiguous neighbors to the south and east. This could be the case, for instance, if highways ran to the north and west but not in the other two directions.

After considering the complications involved in attempting to specify the precise nature of spatial dependency for every observation across seven states, I decided on a simpler distance criteria for the analysis in this book.

Ideally one should run models using a variety of different specifications of spatial dependency. Space constraints, and the desire to write a book about the political consequences of population mobility, rather than one about methodology, prevented me from reporting models using other weighting schemes. The reader should note, however, that different weighting schemes will produce different regression results than the ones reported here.

Taking each state separately, I calculated the arc (great circle) distance between county centroids for all observations using the statistical software SPACESTAT. This produced an $N \times N$ matrix specifying the distance between each observation (county) in each state. I then converted the distance matrix to a binary contiguity matrix (1,0) based on the minimum distance necessary to link each observation to at least one other observation. For example, if the minimum distance necessary to establish that every California county has at least one neighboring county is 77.2 miles, then this was the distance criteria used to calculate the number of neighbors for each county in the state. An especially small California county could have many neighboring counties whose centroids were within 77.2 miles, and each of these counties are scored a "1," as neighbors. In adopting this method of defining the values of the spatial weights matrix, then, I assumed that no county in any of the states was totally isolated from, or independent of, all other counties in the state. Counties that are small in land area obviously have more neighbors than those that are large in land area. The conversion of the distance matrix to a binary contiguity matrix results in a $N \times N$ matrix, W, of ones and zeros, with ones indicating linkages to the most proximate observation(s), and zeros indicating no such linkage (see table B1.1).

The spatial weight matrix, once constructed, is then standardized such that the row elements sum to one. This facilitates later interpretation of the coefficients in spatial regression analysis (Anselin 1988, 23).

The goal of creating the spatial weight matrix in my analysis is to calculate spatially lagged dependent variables. Once the spatial weights matrix of ones and zeros is generated, it can be used with a program such as GAUSS or SPACESTAT to construct a spatial lag for any variable. Briefly, the spatial lag is a weighted sum of the observations adjacent to a given observation (those nearby observations given a value of 1) for a given variable. The terms of the sum are obtained by multiplying the dependent variable by the associated weight in the spatial weights matrix (Anselin 1988).

The resulting regression model, in matrix form, appears as follows:

$$y = \rho W_1 y + X + X\beta + \varepsilon$$
$$\varepsilon = \lambda W_2 \varepsilon + \upsilon$$

where y is an $N \times 1$ vector of observations on the dependent variable, $W_1 y$ is the spatially lagged dependent variable, and X symbolizes an $N \times K$ matrix of other explanatory variables. β is a vector of K regression coefficients, ρ is the spatial autoregressive coefficient, and ε is the random disturbance term. ε, in turn, is a function of the errors of adjacent observations ($W_2\varepsilon$) plus random error, υ.

Spatial autocorrelation of the type I focus on here is the condition where the dependent variable at each location is correlated with observations on the dependent variable at other locations:

$$E(y_i, y_j) \neq 0.$$

If there is no spatial autocorrelation, $\rho = 0$ and OLS estimation will be unbiased. If spatial autocorrelation is present, however, $\rho <$ or > 0 and OLS estimation will be biased in the same manner as if one had omitted an important explanatory variable.

By including the spatially lagged dependent variable as an explanatory variable, I can directly test the degree of spatial dependence while controlling for the effects of other explanatory variables. This appendix was designed to provide only an intuitive and general grasp of the method I used to specify the weights matrix from which I calculated the spatially lagged dependent variables in my regression models. Replications using alternative weighting schemes would be most welcome. For additional detail on spatial regression analysis, the reader may want to consult Anselin 1988, Haining 1990, or Cressie 1993.

Characteristics of the Weights Matrices for States

In addition to providing useful mathematical and data analytic functions for spatial analysis, SPACESTAT commands allow researchers to examine characteristics of the weights matrices used in computing spatial lags. The characteristics of the weights matrices used in the regression models for each state appear in table B1.1. One of the more helpful figures is the average number of links for counties in each state appearing in the last column. Based on the distances used to compute the weights used in my analysis, it is no surprise that California has the largest average number of links. California has some of the smallest and largest counties in terms of land area, so the average distance between county centroids will be sufficiently large that some counties will have many "influential neighbors" while others will have only one. Yolo County, for example, in northern California, had 19 observations to which it was linked, while much larger counties, including Inyo and Modoc, had only 1. New York is similar in that the state contains very small and large counties. The average New York county has 6.9 linked observations or "influential neighbors." Tompkins County, in upstate New York, was linked in my analysis to eleven nearby neighbors. Suffolk County, on the eastern end of Long Island, had only one link, Nassau.

Computation of Moran's I Statistic for Spatial Autocorrelation

For the state maps I present in the text for various variables, I have included a measure of spatial autocorrelation present in the observations. This measure of spatial autocorrelation is known as the "I statistic" or as "Moran's I" (Moran 1948; Cliff and Ord 1981; Anselin 1988). Moran's I can be applied to test both variables and regression residuals for the presence of spatial autocorrelation. Moran's I is defined as:

TABLE B1.1.   Characteristics of Spatial Weights Matrices for Each State

State	Dimension of Matrix	Nonzero Links	% Nonzero Weights	Average Weight	Average Number of Links
California	58	464	14.0	.13	8.0
Colorado	63	204	5.2	.31	3.2
Kansas	105	388	3.6	.27	3.7
Kentucky	120	462	3.2	.26	3.9
Florida	67	212	4.8	.32	3.2
Pennsylvania	67	228	5.2	.29	3.4
New York	62	428	11.3	.14	6.9

Source: Figures based on weights matrices computed in SPACESTAT for spatial data analysis in chapters 2 through 8.

$$I = [N/S] \times \{[e'We]/e'e\}$$

where e is a variable or a vector of OLS residuals, W is a spatial weight matrix whose (i, j)th element is either 1 or 0, N is the number of observations and S is a standardization factor, equal to the sum of all elements in the weight matrix (Anselin 1988, 101). For a row standardized weight matrix, Moran's I can be expressed as:

$$I = e'We/e'e.$$

Because the mathematics of calculating Moran's I is similar to that of calculating the correlation coefficient (r), the values it takes on ranges from –1 to +1. Values of Moran's I that approach +1 indicate positive spatial autocorrelation—where similar values are clustering in spatially adjacent areas on a map. The generally rarer condition of negative autocorrelation is present when values approach –1. Here dissimilar values are clustering together. When $I = 0$, the values of the variable (or residuals) are randomly scattered, indicating no spatial autocorrelation.

References

Abbott, Carl, Stephen J. Leonard, and David McComb. 1982. *Colorado: History of the Centennial State.* Boulder: Colorado Associated University Press.

Agnew, John. 1996. "Mapping politics: How context counts in electoral geography." *Political Geography* 15.2: 129–46.

Aguirre, B. E. 1976. "Differential migration of Cuban social races: a review and interpretation of the problem." *Latin American Research Review* 11.1: 103–24.

Aguirre, B. E., Kent P. Schwirian, and Anthony J. LaGreca. 1980. "The residential patterning of Latin American and other ethnic populations in metropolitan Miami." *Latin American Research Review* 15.2: 35–64.

Alba, Richard D. 1981. "The twilight of ethnicity among American Catholics of European ancestry." *Annals of the American Academy of Political and Social Science* 454:86–97.

Alba, Richard D., Nancy A. Denton, Shu-yin Leung, and John R. Logan. 1993. "Neighborhood change under conditions of mass immigration: the New York City region, 1970–90." *International Migration Review* 29.3: 625–56.

Alba, Richard D., and John R. Logan. 1993. "Minority proximity to whites in suburbs: an individual-level analysis of segregation." *American Journal of Sociology* 98.6: 1388–1427.

Alba, Richard D., John R. Logan, and Katherine Crowder. 1997. "White ethnic neighborhoods and assimilation: The greater New York region." *Social Forces* 75:883–912.

Alba, Richard D., and Katherine Trent. 1986. "Population loss and change in the north: an examination of New York's migration to the Sunbelt." *Social Science Quarterly* 67.3: 690–706.

Alford, Robert E., and Eugene C. Lee. 1968. "Voting turnout in American cities." *American Political Science Review* 62: 796–813.

Allport, Gordon W. 1954. *The Nature of Prejudice.* Cambridge, MA: Addison-Wesley.

Ambrecht, Biliana C. S., and Harry P. Pachon. 1974. "Ethnic political mobilization in a Mexican American community: An exploratory study of East Los Angeles." *Western Political Quarterly* 27:500–519.

American Demographics. 1985. "Migration's toll: lessons from New York state." *American Demographics* (June): 38– 42.

Andreas, Carol. 1994. *Meatpackers and beef Barons: Company Town in a Global Economy.* Niwot: University Press of Colorado.

Anselin, Luc. 1988. *Spatial Econometrics: Methods and Models.* Boston: Kluwer.

Anselin, Luc. 1995. *SpaceStat Version 1.80 User's Guide.* Morgantown, WV: Regional Research Institute. Copyright by the Author.

Antunes, George, and Charles M. Gaitz. 1975. "Ethnicity and participation: a study of Mexican Americans, blacks, and whites." *American Journal of Sociology* 80:1192–1211.

Arizona Business. 1988. "Migration still from north and east to south and west." *Arizona Business* (June): 4–5.

Arizona Business. 1994. "Out-migration from California increased in 1992–93." *Arizona Business* (May): 8.

Associated Press. 1995. "Hazard's path to peace in race relations." *Lexington Herald-Leader,* October 30, B1.

Azicri, Max. 1981–82. "The politics of exile: trends and dynamics of political change among Cuban Americans." *Cuban Studies* 11.2: 55–73.

Bailey, Kenneth R. 1985. "A judicious mixture: Negroes and immigrants in the West Virginia mines, 1880–1917." In *Blacks in Appalachia,* edited by William H. Turner and Edward J. Cabbell. Lexington: University Press of Kentucky.

Bailey, Thomas, and Roger Waldinger. 1991. "The changing ethnic/racial division of labor." In *Dual City: Restructuring New York,* edited by John Millenkopf and Manuel Castells. New York: Russell Sage Foundation.

Barff, Richard, and Robert Walker. 1992. "Linked migration systems: immigration and internal labor in the United States." *Economic Geography* 68:234–48.

Barrera, Mario. 1979. *Race and Class in the Southwest: A theory of Racial Inequality.* Notre Dame, IN: University of Notre Dame Press.

Barsby, Steven L., and Dennis R. Cox. 1975. *Interstate Migration of the Elderly.* Lexington, MA: D. C. Heath.

Bartel, Ann P. 1989. "Where do the new U.S. immigrants live?" *Journal of Labor Economics* 7.4: 371–91.

Barth, Gunther. 1975. *Instant Cities: Urbanization and the Rise of San Francisco and Denver.* New York: Oxford University Press.

Bass, Jack, and Walter DeVries. 1976. *The Transformation of Southern Politics.* New York: Basic Books.

Beatty, Kathleen Murphy. 1981. "Colorado: increasingly unpredictable." *Social Science Journal* 18.3: 31–40.

Beck, Paul Allen. 1982. "Realignment begins: the Republican surge in Florida." *American Politics Quarterly* 10.4: 421–38.

Becker, Gary S. 1964. *Human Capital.* New York: Columbia University Press.

Beggs, John J., Wayne J. Villemez, and Ruth Arnold. 1997. "Black population concentration and black-white inequality: expanding the consideration of place and space effects." *Social Forces* 76.1: 65–91.

Belanger, Alain, and Andrei Rogers. 1992. "The internal migration and spatial redistribution of the foreign-born population in the United States: 1965–70 and 1975–80." *International Migration Review* 27.4: 1342–69.

Benson, Janet E. 1990. "Good neighbors: ethnic relations in Garden City trailer courts." *Urban Anthropology* 19.4: 361–85.

Benson, Janet E. 1994. "The effects of packinghouse work on Southeast Asian refugee families." In *Newcomers in the Workplace: Immigrants and the Restructuring of the U.S. Economy,* edited by Louise Lamphere, Alex Stepick, and Guillermo Grenier. Philadelphia: Temple University Press.

Berelson, Bernard R., Paul F. Lazarsfeld, and William N. McPhee. 1954. *Voting: The Study of Opinion Formation in a Presidential Campaign* Chicago: University of Chicago Press.

Berry, Mike. 1992. "A tale of two regions: water buoys southwest while northwest dries up," *Wichita Eagle,* February 23, 3K.

Billings, Dwight. 1974. "Culture and poverty in Appalachia: a theoretical discussion and empirical analysis." *Social Forces* 53:315–23.

Billington, Ray A. 1963. *The Protestant Crusade, 1800–1860: A Study of the Origins of American Nativism.* Gloucester, MA: Peter Smith.

Bizjak, Tony. 1993. "Foreigners flock to recession-hit Golden State." *Sacramento Bee,* September 3, A1.

Black, Merle, and Earl Black. 1988. *Politics and Society in the South.* Cambridge: Harvard University Press.

Black, Merle, and Earl Black. 1992. *The Vital South.* Cambridge: Harvard University Press.

Blalock, Hubert. 1956. "Economic discrimination and Negro increase." *American Sociological Review* 21:584–88.

Blanco, C. 1963. "The determinants of interstate population movements." *Journal of Regional Science* 5:77–84.

Blau, Peter M. 1977. *Inequality and Heterogeneity.* New York: Free Press.

Bodnar, John, Roger Simon, and Michael P. Weber. 1982. *Lives of Their Own: Blacks, Italians, Poles, in Pittsburgh, 1900–1960.* Urbana: University of Illinois Press.

Bonacich, Edna. 1972. "A theory of ethnic antagonism: the split labor market." *American Sociological Review* 37:547–59.

Bonacich, Edna. 1976. "Advanced capitalism and black/white race relations in the United States: a split labor market interpretation." *American Sociological Review* 41:34–51.

Borjas, George J. 1990. *Friends or Strangers: The Impact of Immigrants on the U.S. Economy.* New York: Basic Books.

Borjas, George J., Stephen G. Bronars, and Stephen J. Trejo. 1992. "Self-selection and internal migration in the United States." *Journal of Urban Economics* 32:159–85.

Borjas, George J., and Richard Freeman. 1992. *Immigration and the Work Force.* Chicago: University of Chicago Press.

Bouvier, Leon F., William Leonard, and John L. Martin. 1994. *Shaping Florida: The Effects of Immigration, 1970–2020.* Washington, DC: Center for Immigration Studies.

Bowman, Mary Jean, and W. Warren Haynes. 1963. *Resources and People in East*

Kentucky: Problems and Potentials of a Lagging Economy. Baltimore: Johns Hopkins University Press.

Brackman, Harold, and Steven P. Erie. 1998. "At rainbow's end: empowerment prospects for Latinos and Asian Pacific Americans in Los Angeles." In *Racial and Ethnic Politics in California,* edited by Michael B. Preston, Bruce E. Cain, and Sandra Bass. Vol. 2. Berkeley: Institute of Governmental Studies.

Broadway, Michael J. 1987. "The origins and determinants of Indochinese Secondary In-migration to Southwestern Kansas." *Heritage of the Great Plains* 20.2: 17–29.

Broadway, Michael J. 1994. "Beef stew: cattle, immigrants, and established residents in a Kansas beefpacking town." In *Newcomers in the Workplace: Immigrants and the Restructuring of the U.S. Economy,* edited by Louise Lamphere, Alex Stepick, and Guillermo Grenier. Philadelphia: Temple University Press.

Broadway, Michael J., and Susan D. Snyder. 1989. "The persistence of urban deprivation: the example of Wichita, Kansas, in the 1970s." *Growth and Change* 20.2 :50–61.

Brown, David L,. and Glenn V. Fuguitt. 1972. "Percent nonwhite and racial disparity in nonmetropolitan cities in the South." *Social Science Quarterly* 53:573–82.

Brown, Thad. 1988. *Migration and Politics.* Chapel Hill: University of North Carolina Press.

Burbank, Matthew J. 1995. "The psychological basis of contextual effects," *Political geography* 14:6/7: 621–635.

Burns, Nancy. 1994. *The Formation of American Local Governments.* New York: Oxford University Press.

Button, James W. 1989. *Blacks and Social Change: Impact of the Civil Rights Movement in Southern Communities.* Princeton: Princeton University Press.

Cabbell, Edward J. 1985. "Black invisibility and racism in Appalachia: an informal survey." In *Blacks in Appalachia,* edited by William H. Turner and Edward J. Cabbell. Lexington: University Press of Kentucky.

Cadwallader, Martin. 1992. *Migration and Residential Mobility: Macro and Microlevel Approaches.* Madison: University of Wisconsin Press.

Cain, Bruce E., and D. Roderick Kiewiet. 1987. "Latinos and the 1984 election: A comparative perspective." In *Ignored Voices: Public Opinion Polls and the Latino Community,* edited by Rodolfo de la Garza. Austin TX: The Center for Mexican American Studies.

Cain, Bruce E., D. Roderick Kiewiet, and Carole J. Uhlaner. 1991. "The acquisition of partisanship by Latinos and Asian Americans." *American Journal of Political Science* 35.2: 390–422.

Camp, Scott D. 1995. *Worker Response to Plant Closings: Steelworkers in Johnstown and Youngstown.* New York: Garland.

Campa, Arthur. 1990. "Immigrant Latinos and Resident Mexican Americans in Garden City, KS: Ethnicity and Ethnic Relations." *Urban Anthropology* 19:345–60.

Campbell, Angus, Philip E. Converse, Warren E. Miller, and Donald E. Stokes. 1960. *The American Voter.* New York: John Wiley and Sons.

Carnahan, Ann. 1992. "Suburbia shedding its lily-white image." *Rocky Mountain News,* June 1, 8.

Castro, Max J. 1992. "The politics of language in Miami." In *Miami Now! Immigration, Ethnicity, and Social Change,* edited by Guillermo Grenier and Alex Stepick. Gainesville: University Press of Florida.

Cebula, R. J. 1980. "Voting with one's feet: a critique of the evidence." *Journal of Regional Science and Urban Economics* 10:91–107.

Charland, William. 1995. "Today's service employees must leap cultural barriers." *Rocky Mountain News,* May 21; 3C.

Citrin, Jack, Donald P. Green, Christopher Muste, and Cara Wong. 1997. "Public opinion toward immigration reform: the role of economic motivations." *Journal of Politics* 59.3: 858–81.

Clark, G. L. 1989. *Unions and Communities under Siege: American Communities and the Crisis of Organized Labor.* New York: Cambridge University Press.

Clark, G. L., and K. P. Ballard. 1980. "Modeling outmigration from depressed regions: the significance of origin and destination characteristics." *Environment and Planning A* 12:799–812.

Clark, G. L., and J. Whiteman. 1983. "Why poor people do not move: job search behavior and disequilibrium amongst local labor markets." *Environment and Planning A* 15:85–104.

Clark, W. A. V. 1991. "Residential preferences and neighborhood racial segregation: a test of the Schelling segregation model." *Demography* 28.1: 1–19.

Clark, W. A. V. 1995. "Scale effects in international migration to the United States." Typescript to be published in *Regional Studies.*

Clark, W. A. V., and Peter A. Morrison. 1992. "Gauging Hispanic voting strength: paradoxes and pitfalls." *Population Research and Policy Review* 11.2: 143–53.

Clark, W. A. V., and Peter A. Morrison. 1995. "Demographic foundations of political empowerment in multiminority cities." *Demography* 32.2: 183–201.

Cliff, A. D., and J. K. Ord. 1973. *Spatial Autocorrelation.* London: Pion.

Cliff, A. D., and J. K. Ord. 1981. *Spatial Processes: Models and Applications.* London: Pion.

Cobb, James C. 1982. *The Selling of the South.* Baton Rouge: Louisiana State University Press.

Cohen, Cathy, and Michael Dawson. 1993. "Neighborhood poverty and African-American politics." *American Political Science Review* 87.2: 286–302.

Corrigan, Richard. 1985. "No smoke, no growth?" *National Journal,* July 27, 1732–36.

Craig, Stephen C. 1991. "Politics and elections." In *Government and Politics in Florida,* edited by Robert J. Huckshorn. Gainesville: University of Florida Press.

Crain, Jan. 1993. "A whole new world." *Colorado Business* 20.5: 20–26.

Cressie, Noel A. C. 1993. *Statistics for Spatial Data.* New York: John Wiley and Sons.

Cummings, Scott. 1977. "Racial prejudice and political orientations among blue-collar workers." *Social Science Quarterly* 57:907–20.

Cummings, Scott. 1980. "White ethnics, racial prejudice, and labor market segmentation." *American Journal of Sociology* 90:938–50.

Dauer, Manning J. 1972. "Florida: the different state." In *The Changing Politics of the South,* edited by William C. Havard. Baton Rouge: Louisiana State University Press.

de la Garza, Rodolfo. 1987. *Ignored Voices: Public Opinion Polls and the Latino Community.* Austin, TX: Center for Mexican American Studies.

de la Garza, Rodolfo, and Louis DeSipio, eds. 1992. *From Rhetoric to Reality: Latino Politics in the 1988 Elections.* Boulder: Westview.

de la Garza, Rodolfo, and Louis DeSipio. 1994. "Overview: the link between individuals and electoral institutions in five Latino neighborhoods." In *Barrio Ballots,* edited by Rodolfo De La Garza, Martha Menchaca, and Louis DeSipio. Boulder: Westview.

de la Garza, Rodolfo, Martha Menchaca, and Louis DeSipio, eds. 1994. *Barrio Ballots.* Boulder: Westview.

Deaton, Brady J., and Kurt R. Anschel. 1974. "Migration and return migration: a new look at the eastern Kentucky migration stream." *Southern Journal of Agricultural Economics* 6.1: 185–90.

Deitrick, Sabina, and Robert A. Beauregard. 1995. "From front-runner to also-ran—the transformation of a once-dominant industrial region: Pennsylvania, USA." In *The Rise of the Rustbelt,* edited by Philip Cooke. New York: St. Martin's.

DeJong, Gordon F. 1977. "Residential preferences and migration." *Demography* 14.2: 169–78.

Denowitz, Ronald M. 1980. "Racial succession in New York City, 1960–1970." *Social Forces* 59:440–55.

DeSipio, Louis, and Gregory Rocha. 1992. "Latino influence on national elections: the case of 1988." In *From Rhetoric to Reality: Latino Politics in the 1988 Elections,* edited by Rodolfo de la Garza and Louis DeSipio. Boulder: Westview.

DeVrooman, Sacha. 1995. "Apartment freeze proposed." *Kentucky Post,* June 14, 1K.

Dubin, Jeffrey A., and Gretchen Kalsow. 1997. "An aggregate nested logit model of political participation." Social Science Working Paper 998, California Institute of Technology.

Duncan, Cynthia. 1992. "Persistent poverty in Appalachia: scarce work and rigid stratification." In *Rural Poverty in America,* edited by Cynthia M. Duncan. New York: Auburn House.

Duncan, Otis Dudley, and Beverly Duncan. 1955. "Residential distribution and occupational stratification." *American Journal of Sociology* 60: 493–503.

Dunn, Marvin. 1997. *Black Miami in the Twentieth Century.* Gainesville: University Press of Florida.

Dunn, Marvin, and Alex Stepick. 1992. "Blacks in Miami." In *Miami Now! Immi-*

gration, Ethnicity, and Social Change, edited by Guillermo Grenier and Alex Stepick. Gainesville: University Press of Florida.

Edmundson, Brad. 1987. "Is Florida our future?" *American Demographics* 9:38–44.

Elazar, Daniel J. 1970. *Cities of the Prairie: The Metropolitan Frontier and American Politics.* New York: Basic Books.

Ellison, Christopher G., and Daniel A. Powers. 1994. "The contact hypothesis and racial attitudes among black Americans." *Social Science Quarterly* 75.2: 385–400.

Epple, Dennis, and Thomas Romer. 1991. "Mobility and Redistribution." *Journal of Political Economy* 99.4: 828–58.

Erie, Steven. 1988. *Rainbow's End: Irish Americans and the Dilemmas of Urban Machine Politics, 1840–1985.* Berkeley: University of California Press.

Ernst, Robert. 1949. *Immigrant Life in New York City, 1825–1863.* New York: King's Crown.

Eshleman, Russell. 1991. "Barrage of criticism for retreat plan." *Philadelphia Inquirer,* August 27, B6.

Espenshade, Thomas, and Haishan Fu. 1997. "An analysis of English language proficiency among recent immigrants." *American Sociological Review* 62:288–305.

Eulau, Heinz, and Kenneth Prewitt. 1973. *Labyrinths of Democracy: Adaptations, Linkages, Representation, and Policies in Urban Politics.* Indianapolis: Bobbs-Merrill.

Farley, Reynolds, Charlotte Steeh, Maria Krysan, Tara Jackson, and Keith Reeves. 1994. "Stereotypes and segregation: neighborhoods in the Detroit area." *American Journal of Sociology* 100.3: 750–80.

Ferraro, Cathleen. 1994. "Newcomers pour into Colorado, even new residents say growth is too fast." *Rocky Mountain News,* December 25, 24A.

Fiedler, Tom, and Margaret Kempel. 1993. *The Almanac of Florida Politics.* Miami: Miami Herald.

Filer, Randall K. 1992. "The effect of immigrant arrivals on migratory patterns of native workers." In *Immigration and the Workforce,* edited by George J. Borjas and Richard B. Freeman. Chicago: University of Chicago Press.

Fitchen, Janet M. 1992. "Rural poverty in the Northeast: the case of upstate New York." In *Rural Poverty in America,* edited by Cynthia M. Duncan. New York: Auburn House.

Flynn, Nickie. 1991. "McCray hitches ambition to conservative machine." *Wichita Eagle,* May 28, 1D.

Foner, Nancy, ed. 1987. *New Immigrants in New York.* New York: Columbia University Press.

Foster, Dick. 1995. "INS targets illegals in ski towns." *Rocky Mountain News,* July 28; 10A.

Frazier, Deborah. 1994. "Growth rattles rural Colorado; the reason: gambling, resorts, prisons." *Rocky Mountain News,* December 26; 30A.

Frendreis, John P. 1989. "Migration as a source of changing party strength." *Social Science Quarterly* 70.1: 211–20.

Frey, William H. 1993. "Interstate migration and immigration for whites and minorities, 1985–1990: the emergence of multi-ethnic states." University of Michigan, Population Studies Center, research report.

Frey, William H. 1994. "Immigration and internal migration for U.S. states: 1990 census findings by poverty status and race." University of Michigan, Population Studies Center, research report.

Frey, William H. 1995a. "Immigration and internal migration 'flight' from U.S. metropolitan areas: toward a new demographic balkanization." *Urban Studies* 32:733–57.

Frey, William H. 1995b. "Immigration and internal migration 'flight': a California case study." *Population and Environment* 16:353–75.

Frey, William H. 1996. "Immigration, internal out-movement, and demographic balkanization in America: new evidence for the 1990s." University of Michigan, Population Studies Center, research report.

Frey, William H. Forthcoming. *New Spatial Divisions in America: Immigration, Race, and Region.*

Frisbie, W. Parker, and Lisa Neidert. 1976. "Inequality and the relative size of minority populations: a comparative analysis." *American Journal of Sociology* 82.5: 1007–30.

Gabriel, Paul, and Susanne Schmitz. 1995. "Favorable self-selection and the internal migration of young white males in the United States." *Journal of Human Resources* 30.3: 460–69.

Galderisi, Peter F., Michael S. Lyons, Randy T. Simmons, and John G. Francis. 1987. *The Politics of Realignment: Party Change in the Mountain West.* Boulder: Westview.

Galster, George, and Heather Keeney. 1993. "Subsidized housing and racial change in Yonkers, NY." *Journal of the American Planning Association* 59.2: 172–81.

Gannon, Michael. 1991. "A history of Florida to 1990." In *Government and Politics in Florida,* edited by Robert J. Huckshorn. Gainesville: University Press of Florida.

Garcia, F. Chris. 1973. *Political Socialization of Chicano Children: A Comparative Study with Anglos in California Schools.* New York: Praeger.

Garcia, F. Chris, John A. Garcia, Rodolfo O. de la Garza, Angelo Falcon, and Cara J. Abeyta. 1991. *Latinos and Politics: A Select Research Bibliography.* Austin, TX: Center for Mexican American Studies.

Garcia, John A. 1981. "The political integration of Mexican immigrants: explorations into the naturalization process." *International Migration Review* 15: 608–25.

Garcia, John A. 1987. "The political integration of Mexican immigrants: examining some political orientations." *International Migration Review* 21:372–87.

Garcia, Maria Cristina. 1996. *Havana USA.* Berkeley: University of California Press.

Garcia, Victor Q. 1997. "Mexican enclaves in the U.S. Northeast: immigrant and migrant mushroom workers in southern Chester County, Pennsylvania."

JSRI Research Reports, no. 27. Julian Samora Research Institute, Michigan State University. Mimeo.

Garling, Tommy, and Reginald G. Golledge, eds. 1993. *Behavior and Environment: Psychological and Geographical Approaches.* Amsterdam: Elsevier Science Publishers.

Gerber, Alan, and Donald P. Green. 1998. "Rational learning and partisan attitudes." *American Journal of Political Science* 42: 794–818.

Giarratani, Frank, and David B. Houston. 1989. "Structural change and economic policy in a declining metropolitan region: implications of the Pittsburgh experience." *Urban Studies* 26:549–58.

Giles, Michael W. 1977. "Percent black and racial hostility: an old assumption reexamined." *Social Science Quarterly* 58:412–17.

Giles, Michael W., and Arthur Evans. 1985. "External threat, perceived threat, and group identity." *Social Science Quarterly* 66:50–66.

Giles, Michael W., and Kaenan Hertz. 1994. "Racial threat and partisan identification." *American Political Science Review* 88.2: 317–26.

Gimpel, James G. 1996. *National Elections and the Autonomy of American State Party Systems.* Pittsburgh: University of Pittsburgh Press.

Gimpel, James G., and James R. Edwards Jr. 1999. *The Congressional Politics of Immigration Reform.* Boston: Allyn and Bacon.

Gittel, Ross J. 1992. *Renewing Cities.* Princeton: Princeton University Press.

Glasco, Laurence. 1989. "Double burden: the black experience in Pittsburgh." In *City at the Point,* edited by Samuel Hays. Pittsburgh: University of Pittsburgh Press.

Glaser, James M. 1994. "Back to the black belt: racial environment and white racial attitudes in the South." *Journal of Politics* 56:21–41.

Glaser, James M., and Martin Gilens. 1997. "Interregional migration and political resocialization: a study of racial attitudes under pressure." *Public Opinion Quarterly* 61:72–81.

Glazar, Nathan, and Daniel Patrick Moynihan. 1963. *Beyond the Melting Pot.* Cambridge: MIT Press.

Gober, Patricia. 1994. "Americans on the move." *Population Bulletin* 48:3.

Goldstein, Steve. 1991. "Battle lines drawn in Gettysburg." *Philadelphia Inquirer,* June 30, B1.

Goode, Judith. 1990. "A wary welcome to the neighborhood: community responses to immigrants." *Urban Anthropology* 19.1–2: 125–53.

Goodenough, Richard. 1992. "The nature and implications of recent population growth in California." *Geography* 77:123–33.

Gordon, Milton M. 1964. *Assimilation in American Life: The Role of Race, Religion and National Origins.* New York: Oxford University Press.

Gottlieb, Peter. 1987. *Making Their Own Way: Southern Blacks' Migration to Pittsburgh, 1916–1930.* Urbana: University of Illinois Press.

Gouveia, Lourdes, and Donald D. Stull. 1995. "Dances with cows: beefpacking's impact on Garden City, Kansas, and Lexington, Nebraska." In *Any Way You Cut It: Meat Processing and Small Town America,* edited by Donald D. Stull,

Michael J. Broadway, and David Griffith. Lawrence: University Press of Kansas.

Grasmuck, S. 1984. "Immigration, ethnic stratification, and native working class discipline: comparisons of documented and undocumented Dominicans." *International Migration Review* 18:3–20.

Green, Donald P., and Eric Schickler. 1996. "The grim reaper, the stork, and partisan change in the North and South, 1952–1994." Paper presented at the annual meeting of the Midwest Political Science Association, Chicago, IL, April 18–20.

Greenwood, Michael J. 1975. "Research on internal migration in the United States: a survey." *Journal of Economic Literature* 13:397–433.

Gregory, James N. 1989. *American Exodus.* New York: Oxford University Press.

Grenier, Guillermo J., et al. 1992. "On machines and bureaucracy: controlling ethnic interaction in Miami's apparel and construction industries." In *Structuring Diversity: Ethnographic Perspectives on the New Immigration,* edited by Louise Lamphere. Chicago: University of Chicago Press.

Grenier, Guillermo J., and Alex Stepick. 1992. *Miami Now! Immigration, Ethnicity and Social Change.* Gainesville: University Press of Florida.

Grey, Mark A. 1996. "Meatpacking and the migration of refugee and immigrant labor to Storm Lake, Iowa." Paper presented at the Iowa Meeting of Immigration and the Changing Face of Rural America Conference Series. July 11–13.

Griffith, David. 1995. "Hay trabajo: poultry processing, rural industrialization, and the Latinization of low-wage labor." In *Any Way You Cut It: Meat Processing and Small Town America,* edited by Donald D. Stull, Michael J. Broadway, and David Griffith. Lawrence: University Press of Kansas.

Gross, Andrew B., and Douglas S. Massey. 1991. "Spatial assimilation models: a micro-macro comparison." *Social Science Quarterly* 22.2: 347–60.

Guinier, Lani. 1994. *The Tyranny of the Majority: Fundamental Fairness in Representative Democracy.* New York: Free Press.

Hahn, Harlan, and Timothy Almy. 1971. "Ethnic politics and racial issues: voting in Los Angeles." *Western Political Quarterly* 24:719–30.

Hahn, Harlan, David Klingman, and Harry Pachon. 1976. "Cleavages, coalitions and the black candidate: the Los Angeles mayoralty elections of 1969 and 1973." *Western Political Quarterly* 29:521–30.

Haining, Robert. 1990. Spatial Data Analysis in the Social and Environmental Sciences. Cambridge: Cambridge University Press.

Halley, Robert M., Alan C. Acock, and Thomas Greene. 1976. "Ethnicity and social class: voting in the Los Angeles municipal elections." *Western Political Quarterly* 29:507–20.

Hamel, Ruth, and Tim Schreiner. 1989. "Thinking small in Denver." *American Demographics* (November): 52–53.

Hamel, Ruth, and Tim Schreiner. 1990. "At the summit." *American Demographics* (April): 48–50.

Hamm, Shannon Reid. 1997. "The future of mushroom production in the United States: fewer producers and expanding output." Paper presented at the conference The Changing Face of Delmarva, September 11–13, 1997, University of Delaware.

Handlin, Oscar. 1952. *The Uprooted.* Boston: Little, Brown.

Harkman, Anders. 1989. "Migration behavior among the unemployed and the role of unemployment benefits." *Papers of the Regional Science Association* 66:143–50.

Harwood, Richard C. 1993. "Managing the politics of change." *Colorado Municipalities* 69.2: 24–25.

Hein, J. 1994. "From migrant to minority: Hmong refugees and the social construction of identity in the United States." *Sociological Inquiry* 64:281–306.

Hero, Rodney E. 1987. "The election of Hispanics in city government: an examination of the election of Frederico Pena as mayor of Denver." *Western Political Quarterly* 40:93–105.

Hero, Rodney E. 1989. "Multiracial coalitions in city elections involving minority candidates: some evidence from Denver." *Urban Affairs Quarterly* 25:342–51.

Herron, Mat. 1998. "Hispanics living in fear in wake of raid by INS." *Lexington (KY) Herald-Leader.* June 5.

Hershberg, I. 1981. *Philadelphia.* New York: Oxford University Press.

Heuck, Douglas. 1996. "How're we doing?" *Post-Gazette* (Pittsburgh), June 30, A1.

Hewstone, Miles, and Rupert Brown, eds. 1986. *Contact and Conflict in Intergroup Encounters.* New York: Basil Blackwell.

Hing, Bill Ong. 1993. *Making and Remaking Asian America through Immigration Policy, 1850–1990.* Stanford: Stanford University Press.

Hirschman, Charles. 1996. "Studying immigrant adaptation from the 1990 population census: from generational comparisons to the process of 'becoming American.'" In *The New Second Generation,* edited by Alejandro Portes. New York: Russell Sage Foundation.

Hobbs, A. H. 1942. "Specificity and selective migration." *American Sociological Review* 7:772–81.

Honeycutt, Valarie. 1998. "Mayor plans task force on migrants, other efforts in works to help laborers." *Lexington (KY) Herald-Leader,* June 2.

Hood, M. V., and Irwin L. Morris. 1997. "¿Amigo o enemigo? Context, attitudes, and anglo public opinion toward immigration." *Social Science Quarterly* 79.2: 309–23.

Hood, M. V., and Irwin L. Morris. 1998. "Give us your tired, your poor . . . but make sure they have a green card: the effects of documented and undocumented migrant context on anglo opinion toward immigration." *Political Behavior* 20.1: 1–15.

Horton, John. 1995. *The Politics of Diversity.* Philadelphia: Temple University Press.

Huckfeldt, Robert,. 1986. *Politics in Context: Assimilation and Conflict in Urban Neighborhoods.* New York: Agathon Press.

Huckfeldt, Robert, and Carol Kohfeld. 1989. *Race and the Decline of Class in American Politics.* Urbana: University of Illinois Press.

Huckfeldt, Robert, and John Sprague. 1995. *Citizens, Politics, and Social Communication.* New York: Cambridge University Press.

Hull, Susan Ferriss Tupper. 1994. "Latin assemblywoman bucks anti-demo trend." *San Francisco Examiner,* December 12, A7.

Humphrey, Craig R., Ralph R. Sell, John A. Krout, and R. Thomas Gillaspy. 1977. "Net migration turnaround in Pennsylvania nonmetropolitan minor civil divisions, 1960–70." *Rural Sociology* 42.3: 332–51.

Ignatiev, Noel. 1995. *How the Irish Became White.* New York: Routledge.

Jackson, Byran O. 1987. "The effects of racial group consciousness on political mobilization in American cities." *Western Political Quarterly* 40:631–46.

Jackson, Byran, and Michael B. Preston, eds. 1991. *Racial and Ethnic Politics in California.* Berkeley: Institute of Governmental Studies.

James, Franklin J. 1995. "Research plan for studying minority neighborhoods in Denver." Paper prepared for the Rockefeller Institute of Government, State University of New York.

James, Franklin J. with Jeff Romine and Peter Zwanzig. 1997. "The effects of immigration on urban communities." Graduate School of Public Affairs, University of Colorado at Denver.

Jewell, Malcolm E., and Everett W. Cunningham. 1968. *Kentucky Politics.* Lexington: University of Kentucky Press.

Jiobu, Robert M. 1988. *Ethnicity and Assimilation.* Albany: State University of New York Press.

Kain, John F., and John M. Quigley. 1975. *Housing Markets and Racial Discrimination: A Microeconomic Analysis.* New York: National Bureau of Economic Research.

Kelly, Guy. 1994. "Resorts face urban woes." *Rocky Mountain News,* September 4, 12A.

Kelly, Guy. 1996. "Race relations on edge." *Rocky Mountain News,* March 17, 4A.

Kerven, Anne. 1992. "Douglas County: balancing the boom." *Colorado Business* 19.1: 23–29.

Key, V. O., Jr. 1949. *Southern Politics in State and Nation.* New York: Knopf.

Key, V. O., Jr. 1956. *American State Politics: An Introduction.* New York: Knopf.

Kinder, Donald R., and Lynn M. Sanders. 1996. *Divided by Color: Racial Politics and Democratic Ideals.* Chicago: University of Chicago Press.

King, Gary. 1996. "Why context should not count." *Political Geography* 16.2: 159–64.

King, Gary. 1997. *A solution to the Ecological Inference Problem.* Princeton: Princeton University Press.

Knapp, Tim. 1995. "Rust in the wheatbelt: the social impacts of industrial decline in a rural Kansas community." *Sociological Inquiry* 65.1: 47–66.

Kolbe, Richard L. 1975. "Culture, political parties, and voting behavior: Schuylkill County." *Polity* 8.2: 241–68.

Koritz, Douglas. 1991. "Restructuring or destructuring? deindustrialization in two industrial heartland cities." *Urban Affairs Quarterly* 26.4: 497–511.

Kossoudji, Sherrie A. 1988. "English language ability and the labor market opportunities of Hispanic and East Asian immigrant men." *Journal of Labor Economics* 6.2: 205–28.

Kritz, Mary M., and June Marie Nogle. 1994. "Nativity concentration and internal migration among the foreign born." *Demography* 31.3: 509–24.

Kwong, Peter. 1996. *The New Chinatown.* New York: Hill and Wang.

Ladinsky, Jack. 1967. "Sources of geographical mobility among professional workers: a multivariate analysis." *Demography* 4:293–309.

Lamare, James W. 1977. "The political world of the rural chicano child." *American Politics Quarterly* 5.1: 83–108.

Lamis, Alexander P. 1988. *The Two-party South.* New York: Oxford University Press.

Lamphere, Louise, ed. 1992. *Structuring Diversity: Ethnographic Perspectives on the New Immigration.* Chicago: University of Chicago Press.

Lamphere, Louise, Alex Stepick, and Guillermo Grenier. 1994. *Newcomers in the Workplace: Immigrants and the Restructuring of the U.S. Economy.* Philadelphia: Temple University Press.

Lansing, John B., and James N. Morgan. 1967. "The effect of geographical mobility on income." *Journal of Human Resources* 2:449–60.

Leslie, Gerald R., and Arthur H. Richardson. 1961. "Lifecycle career patterns and the decision to move." *American Sociological Review* 26:894–902.

Lessner, Lori. 1997. "Jobs lure illegal aliens to Kansas." *Wichita Eagle,* December 18, A3.

Lewis, Paul G. 1996. *Shaping Suburbia: How Political Institutions Organize Urban Development.* Pittsburgh: University of Pittsburgh Press.

Liang, Zai. 1994. "Social contact, social capital, and the naturalization process: evidence from six immigrant groups," *Social Science Research* 23:407–37.

Lieberson, Stanley. 1961. "The impact of residential segregation on ethnic assimilation." *Social Forces* 40:52–57.

Lieberson, Stanley. 1963. *Ethnic Patterns in American Cities.* Glencoe, IL: Free Press.

Lieberson, Stanley, and Donna K. Carter. 1982. "Temporal changes and urban differences in residential segregation: a reconsideration." *American Journal of Sociology* 88.2:296–311.

Logan, John R. 1978. "Growth, politics, and the stratification of places." *American Journal of Sociology* 84.2: 404–16.

Long, Larry. 1988. *Migration and Residential Mobility in the United States.* New York: Russell Sage Foundation.

Lovrich, Nicholas P., and Otwin Marenin. 1976. "A comparison of black and Mexican American voters in Denver: assertive versus acquiescent political orientations and voting behavior in an urban electorate." *Western Political Quarterly* 29:284–94.

Lublin, David. 1997. *The Paradox of Representation.* Princeton: Princeton University Press.

Lyons, William, and Robert F. Durant. 1980. "Assessing the impact of in-migration on a state political system." *Social Science Quarterly* 61.3: 473–84.

MacDonald, Karin, and Bruce E. Cain. 1998. "Nativism, partisanship and immigration: an analysis of proposition 187." In *Racial and Ethnic Politics in California,* edited by Michael B. Preston, Bruce E. Cain and Sandra Bass. Vol. 2. Berkeley: Institute for Governmental Studies.

Marsh, Ben. 1987. "Continuity and decline in the anthracite towns of Pennsylvania." *Annals of the Association of American Geographers* 77.3: 337–52.

Marshall, Adriana. 1987. "New immigrants in New York's economy." In *New Immigrants in New York,* edited by Nancy Foner. New York: Columbia University Press.

Marshall, Harvey, and Robert Jiobu. 1975. "Residential segregation in United States cities: a causal analysis." *Social Forces* 53.3: 449–59.

Massey, Douglas S. 1988. "The dimensions of residential segregation." *Social Forces* 76:281–315.

Massey, Douglas S. 1989. "Hypersegregation in U.S. metropolitan areas." *Demography* 26:373–92.

Massey, Douglas S. 1995. "The new immigration and ethnicity in the United States." *Population and Development Review* 21.3: 631–44.

Massey, Douglas S., and Nancy A. Denton. 1987. "Trends in the residential segregation of blacks, Hispanics, and Asians: 1970–1980." *American Sociological Review* 52:802–25.

Massey, Douglas S., and Nancy A. Denton. 1993. *American Apartheid: Segregation and the Making of the Underclass.* Cambridge: Harvard University Press.

Matthews, Donald R., and James W. Prothro. 1963a. "Social and economic factors and Negro voter registration in the South." *American Political Science Review* 57:24–44.

Matthews, Donald R., and James W. Prothro. 1963b. "Political factors and negro voter registration in the South." *American Political Science Review* 57:355–67.

McBurnett, Michael. 1991. "The instability of partisanship due to context." *Political Geography Quarterly* 10:132–43.

McManus, Walter S. 1985. "Labor market costs of language disparity: an interpretation of Hispanic earnings differences." *American Economic Review* 75.4: 818–27.

McVeigh, Rory. 1995. "Social structure, political institutions and mobilization potential." *Social Forces* 74.2: 461–85.

Menchaca, Martha. 1995. *The Mexican Outsiders: A Community History of Marginalization and Discrimination in California.* Austin: University of Texas Press.

Metzger, John T. 1995. "The politics of housing in the New York metropolitan region." In *Contested Terrain: Power, Politics, and Participation in Suburbia,* edited by Marc L. Silver and Martin Melkonian. Westport, CT: Greenwood.

Miller, Michael V. 1975. "Chicano community control in South Texas: problems and prospects." *Journal of Ethnic Studies* 3.3: 70–89.

Miller, Penny M., and Malcolm E. Jewell. 1990. *Political Parties and Primaries in Kentucky.* Lexington: University Press of Kentucky.

Milne, Dann. 1980. "Migration and income opportunities for blacks in the South." *Southern Economic Journal* 46:913–17.

Mohl, Raymond. 1988. "Ethnic politics in Miami 1960–1986." In *Shades of the Sunbelt: Essays on Ethnicity, Race, and the Urban South,* edited by Randall M. Miller and George E. Pozzetta. New York: Greenwood.

Mollenkopf, John, and Manuel Castells, eds. 1991. *Dual City: Restructuring New York.* New York: Russell Sage Foundation.

Morales, Rebecca, and Frank Bonilla, eds., 1993. *Latinos in a Changing U.S. Economy.* Newbury Park, CA: Sage.

Morales, Rebecca, and Paul M. Ong. 1993. "The illusion of progress: Latinos in Los Angeles." In *Latinos in a Changing U.S. Economy,* edited by Rebecca Morales and Frank Bonilla. Newbury Park, CA: Sage.

Moran, P. A. P. 1948. "The interpretation of statistical maps." *Journal of the Royal Statistical Society B* 10:243–51.

Moreno, Dario, and Nicol Rae. 1992. "Ethnicity and partnership: the eighteenth congressional district in Miami." In *Miami Now! Immigration, Ethnicity, and Social Change,* edited by Guillermo Grenier and Alex Stepick. Gainesville: University Press of Florida.

Morgan, Dan. 1992. *Rising in the West.* New York: Random House.

Moritsugu, Ken, and Isaac Guzman. 1996. "Rallying the minority vote." *Newsday.* (New York), March 20, A29.

Morrill, Richard. 1995. "Racial segregation and class in a liberal metropolis." *Geographical Analysis* 27.1: 22–41.

Morrill, Richard, and Ernest H. Wohlenberg. 1971. *The Geography Of Poverty in the United States.* New York: McGraw-Hill.

Moynihan, Daniel Patrick. 1979. "Patterns of ethnic succession: blacks and Hispanics in New York City." *Political Science Quarterly* 94.1: 1–14.

Muller, Peter O., Kenneth C. Meyer, and Roman A. Cybriwsky. 1976. *Metropolitan Philadelphia: A Study of Conflicts and Social Cleavages.* Cambridge, MA: Ballenger.

Muller, Thomas. 1993. *Immigrants and the American City.* New York: New York University Press.

Muller, T., and T. Espenshade. 1985. *The Fourth Wave: California's Newest Immigrants.* Washington, DC: Urban Institute.

Nakanishi, Don. T. 1991. "The next swing vote? Asian Pacific Americans and California politics." In *Racial and Ethnic Politics in California,* edited by Byran Jackson and Michael B. Preston. Berkeley, CA: Institute of Governmental Studies.

Newbold, K. Bruce. 1998. "Outmigration from California: the role of migrant selectivity." *Geographical Analysis* 30.2: 138–52.

Nie, Norman H., Jane Junn, and Kenneth Stehlik-Barry. 1996. *Education and Democratic Citizenship in America.* Chicago: University of Chicago Press.

Nogle, June Marie. 1996. "Immigrants on the move: how internal migration increases the concentration of the foreign born." *Center for Immigration Studies Backgrounder* 1:96.

Oblinger, Carl. 1973. "Alms for oblivion: the making of a black underclass in southeastern Pennsylvania, 1780–1860." In *The Ethnic Experience in Pennsyl-*

vania, edited by John E. Bodnar. Cranbury, NJ: Associated University Presses.

Olsen, Marvin E. 1970. "Social and political participation of blacks." *American Sociological Review* 35:682–96.

Olzak, Susan. 1990. "The political context of competition: lynching and urban racial violence, 1882–1914." *Social Forces* 69.2: 395–421.

Olzak, Susan. 1992. *The Dynamics of Ethnic Competition and Conflict.* Stanford: Stanford University Press.

Oppenheimer, Robert. 1985. "Acculturation or assimilation: Mexican immigrants in Kansas, 1900 to World War II." *Western Historical Quarterly* 16:429–48.

Ord, J. K., and Arthur Getis. 1995. "Local spatial autocorrelation statistics: distributional issues and an application." *Geographical Analysis* 27.4: 286–306.

Pachon, Harry. 1987. "Naturalization and determinants and process in the Hispanic community." *International Migration Review* 21:299–311.

Pachon, Harry. 1991. "U.S. citizenship and Latino participation in California politics." In *Racial and Ethnic Politics in California,* edited by Byran Jackson and Michael B. Preston. Berkeley, CA: Institute of Governmental Studies.

Pachon, Harry, and Lourdes Arguelles with Rafael Gonzalez. 1994. "Grassroots politics in an East Los Angeles barrio: a political ethnography of the 1990 general election." In *Barrio Ballots,* edited by Rodolfo de la Garza, Martha Menchaca, and Louis DeSipio. Boulder: Westview.

Parker, Suzanne L. 1988. "Shifting party tides in Florida: where have all the Democrats gone?" In *The South's New Politics: Realignment and Dealignment,* edited by Robert H. Swansbrough and David M. Brodsky. Columbia: University of South Carolina Press.

Patty, Mike. 1996. "Hispanics on the rise in suburbs." *Rocky Mountain News,* May 5, 36A.

Perez, Lisandro. 1992. "Cuban Miami." In *Miami Now! Immigration, Ethnicity, and Social Change,* edited by Guillermo Grenier and Alex Stepick. Gainesville: University Press of Florida.

Perkins, Jerry. 1974. "Bases of partisan cleavage in a southern urban county." *Journal of Politics* 36.1: 208–13.

Peterson, Paul. 1981. *City Limits.* Chicago: University of Chicago Press.

Petrocik, John R. 1987. "Realignment: new party coalitions and the nationalization of the South." *Journal of Politics* 49.2: 347–75.

Porter, Bruce, and Marvin Dunn. 1984. *The Miami Riot of 1980: Crossing the Bounds.* Lexington, MA: D.C. Heath.

Portes, Alejandro. 1984. "The rise of ethnicity: determinants of ethnic perceptions among Cuban exiles in Miami." *American Sociological Review* 49:383–97.

Portes, Alejandro, ed. 1995. *The Economic Sociology of Immigration: Essays on Networks, Ethnicity, and Entrepreneurship.* New York: Russell Sage.

Portes, Alejandro, and Robert L. Bach. 1985. *Latin Journey: Cuban and Mexican Immigrants in the U.S.* Berkeley: University of California Press.

Portes, Alejandro, and John W. Curtis. 1987. "Changing flags: naturalization and its determinants among Mexican immigrants." *International Migration Review* 21.2: 352–71.

Portes, Alejandro, and Rafael Mozo. 1985. "The political adaptation process of Cubans and other ethnic minorities in the United States: a preliminary analysis." *International Migration Review* 19.1: 35–63.

Portes, Alejandro, and Ruben G. Rumbaut. 1990. *Immigrant America: A Portrait.* Berkeley: University of California Press.

Portes, Alejandro, and Richard Schauffler. 1996. "Language and the second generation: bilingualism yesterday and today." In *The New Second Generation,* edited by Alejandro Portes. New York: Russell Sage Foundation.

Portes, Alejandro, and Min Zhou. 1992. "Gaining the upper hand: economic mobility among immigrant and domestic minorities." *Ethnic and Racial Studies* 15:491–522.

Powers, Daniel A., and Christopher G. Ellison 1995. "Interracial contact and black racial attitudes: the contact hypothesis and selectivity bias." *Social Forces* 74:205–26.

Preston, Michael B., Bruce E. Cain, and Sandra Bass, eds., 1998. *Racial and Ethnic Politics in California.* Vol. 2. Berkeley: Institute of Governmental Studies.

Reis, Jim. 1994. *Pieces of the Past.* 3 vols. Covington: Kentucky Post.

Rice, Tom W., and Meredith L. Pepper. 1997. "Region, migration, and attitudes in the United States." *Social Science Quarterly* 78.1: 83–95.

Ritchey, P. Neal. 1976. "Explanations of migration." *Annual Review of Sociology* 2:363–404.

Rolph, Elizabeth S. 1992. *Immigration Policies: Legacy from the 1980s and Issues for the 1990s.* Santa Monica: CA: Rand Corporation.

Rose, Harold M. 1964. "Metropolitan Miami's changing Negro population." *Economic Geography* 40:221–38.

Rosenbaum, Emily. 1992. "Race and ethnicity in housing: turnover in New York City, 1978–1987." *Demography* 29.3: 467–86.

Rosenbaum, Walter A., and James W. Button. 1989. "Is there a gray peril? Retirement politics in Florida." *The Gerontologist* 29.3: 300–306.

Rosenbaum, Walter A., and James W. Button. 1993. "The unquiet future of intergenerational politics." *The Gerontologist* 33.4: 481–90.

Rosenstone, Steven J. 1982. "Economic adversity and voter turnout." *American Journal of Political Science* 26:25–46.

Rosenstone, Steven J., and John Mark Hansen. 1993. *Mobilization, participation, and democracy in America.* Needham Heights, MA: Allyn and Bacon.

Rosenstone, Steven J., and Raymond Wolfinger. 1978. "The effect of registration laws on voter turnout." *American Political Science Review* 72:22–45.

Rothbart, Myron, and Oliver John. 1993. "Intergroup relations and stereotype change: a social cognitive analysis and some longitudinal findings." In *Prejudice, Politics, and the American Dilemma,* edited by P. Sniderman, P. Tetlock, and E. Carmines. Stanford: Stanford University Press.

Saenz, Rogelio, and Robert N. Anderson. 1994. "The ecology of Chicano interstate net migration, 1975–1980." *Social Science Quarterly* 75.1: 37–52.

Salter, Paul S., and Robert C. Mings. 1972. "The projected impact of Cuban settlement on voting patterns in metropolitan Miami, Florida." *Professional Geographer* 24:123–31.

Sandefur, Gary, Nancy Tuma, and George Kephart. 1991. "Race, Local Labour Markets, and Migration in the United States, 1975–1983." In *Migration Models,* edited by John Stillwell and Peter Congdon. London: Belhaven.

Scavo, Carmine. 1995. "Patterns of citizen participation in edge and central cities." In *Contested Terrain: Power, Politics, and Participation in Suburbia,* edited by Marc L. Silver and Martin Melkonian. Westport, CT: Greenwood.

Schelling, Thomas. 1969. "Models of segregation." *American Economic Review* 59.2: 169–85.

Schelling, Thomas. 1972. "A process of residential segregation: neighborhood tipping." In *Racial Discrimination in Economic Life,* edited by Anthony H. Pascal. Lexington, MA: Lexington Books.

Schelling, Thomas. 1978. *Micromotives and Macrobehavior.* New York: Norton.

Schlichting, Kurt, Peter Tuckel, and Richard Maisel. 1998. "Racial segregation and voter turnout in urban America." *American Politics Quarterly* 26.2: 218–35.

Schneider, Mark. 1976. "Migration, ethnicity, and politics: a comparative state analysis." *Journal of Politics* 38.1: 938–62.

Schultz, T. W. 1963. *The Economic Value of Education.* New York: Columbia University Press.

Schwarzweller, Harry K., James S. Brown, and J. J. Mangalam. 1971. *Mountain Families in Transition.* University Park: Pennsylvania State University Press.

Sellers, Charles G. "The equilibrium cycle in American two-party politics." *Public Opinion Quarterly* 29 (1965): 16–37.

Serow, William J. 1981. "An economic approach to population change in the South." In *The Population of the South,* edited by Dudley L. Poston Jr. and Robert H. Weller. Austin: University of Texas Press.

Serrin, William. 1993. *Homestead: The Glory and Tragedy of an American Steel Town.* New York: Vintage.

Shelley, Fred M., and Curtis C. Roseman. 1978. "Migration patterns leading to population change in the nonmetropolitan South." *Growth and Change* 9:14–23.

Shryock, Henry S. 1964. *Population Mobility within the United States.* Chicago: Community and Family Study Center, University of Chicago.

Sigelman, Lee, Timothy Bledsoe, Susan Welch, and Michael W. Combs. 1996. "Making contact? Black-white social interaction in an urban setting." *American Journal of Sociology* 101.5: 1306–32.

Sigelman, Lee, and Susan Welch. 1993. "The contact hypothesis revisited: interracial contact and positive racial attitudes." *Social Forces* 71:781–95.

Sjaastad, Larry. 1962. "The costs and returns of human migration." *Journal of Political Economy* 70:80–93.

Skerry, Peter N. 1993. *Mexican Americans: The Ambivalent Minority.* New York: Free Press.

Skinner, Ellen J. 1995. "The war against the housing of the minority poor: White Plains, NY." In *Contested Terrain: Power, Politics, and Participation in Suburbia,* edited by Marc L. Silver and Martin Melkonian.Westport, CT: Greenwood.

Sly, David F., and Jeff Tayman. 1977. "The ecological approach to migration reexamined." *American Sociological Review* 42:783–95.

Smith, Michael M. 1981. "Beyond the borderlands: Mexican labor in the central plains, 1900–1930." *Great Plains Quarterly* 1:239–51.

Sniderman, Paul M., and Thomas Piazza. 1993. *The Scar of Race.* Cambridge, MA: Belknap Press.

Sonenshein, Raphael J. 1990. "Can black candidates win statewide elections?" *Political Science Quarterly* 105:219–41.

Sonenshein, Raphael J. 1993. *Politics in Black and White: Race and Power in Los Angeles.* Princeton: Princeton University Press.

Sorauf, Frank J. 1984. *Party Politics in America.* 5th ed. Boston: Little, Brown.

Squire, Peverill, Raymond E. Wolfinger, and David P. Glass. 1987. "Residential mobility and voter turnout." *American Political Science Review* 81.1: 45–65.

Stack, John F., and Christopher L. Warren. 1992. "The reform tradition and ethnic politics: metropolitan Miami confronts the 1990s." In *Miami Now! Immigration, Ethnicity, and Social Change,* edited by Guillermo Grenier and Alex Stepick. Gainesville: University Press of Florida.

Stanley, Harold W. 1988. "Southern partisan changes: dealignment, realignment or both." *Journal of Politics* 50.1: 64–87.

Stark, Oded, and J. Edward Taylor. 1991. "Migration incentives, migration types: the role of relative deprivation." *Economic Journal* 101:1163–78.

Stein, Robert M., Stephanie Shirley Post, and Allison L. Rinden. 1997. "The effect of contact and context on white attitudes toward immigrants and immigration policy." Paper presented at the annual meeting of the American Political Science Association, Washington, DC., August 28–31.

Stepick, Alex, Guillermo Grenier, Steven Morris, and Debbie Draznin. 1994. "Brothers in wood." In *Newcomers In the Workplace: Immigrants and the Restructuring of the U.S. Economy,* edited by Louise Lamphere, Alex Stepick, and Guillermo Grenier. Philadelphia: Temple University Press.

Stevens, A. Jay. 1975. "The acquisition of participatory norms: the case of Japanese and Mexican American children in a suburban environment." *Western Political Quarterly* 28:281–95.

Stokes, Bruce. 1994. "Out of the rubble." *National Journal* 26.44: 2398–2403.

Stokes, Donald E., and Gudmund R. Iverson. 1962. "On the existence of forces restoring two-party competition." *Public Opinion Quarterly* 26:159–71.

Stonecash, Jeffrey. 1989. "Political cleavage in gubernatorial and legislative elections: party competition in New York, 1970–1982." *Western Political Quarterly* 42:69–81.

Straetz, Ralph, and Frank J. Munger. 1960. *New York Politics.* New York: University Press.

Stull, Donald D. 1990. "I come to the garden: changing ethnic relations in Garden City, KS." *Urban Anthropology* 19:303–20.

Stull, Donald D. 1994. "Knock 'em dead: work on the killfloor of a modern beef-packing plant." In *Newcomers in the Workplace: Immigrants and the Restructuring of the U.S. Economy,* edited by Louise Lamphere, Alex Stepick, and Guillermo Grenier. Philadelphia: Temple University Press.

Stull, Donald D., and Michael J. Broadway. 1990. *Changing Relations: Newcomers and Established Residents in Garden City, KS.* Reports, no. 172. Lawrence: University of Kansas, Institute for Public Policy and Business Research.

Stull, Donald D., and Michael J. Broadway. 1995. "Killing them softly: work in meatpacking plants and what it does to workers." In *Any Way You Cut It: Meat Processing and Small-Town America,* edited by Donald D. Stull, Michael J. Broadway, and David Griffith. Lawrence: University Press of Kansas.

Stull, Donald D., Michael J. Broadway, and Ken C. Erickson. 1992. "The price of a good steak: beef packing and its consequences for Garden City, KS." In *Structuring Diversity: Ethnographic Perspectives on the New Immigration,* edited by Louise Lamphere. Chicago: University of Chicago Press.

Stull, Donald D., Michael J. Broadway, and David Griffith, eds. 1995. *Any Way You Cut It: Meat Processing and Small-Town America.* Lawrence: University Press of Kansas.

Taeuber, Karl, and Alma F. Taeuber. 1969. *Negroes in Cities: Residential Segregation and Neighborhood Change.* New York: Atheneum.

Tam, Wendy K. 1995. "Asians: a monolithic voting bloc?" *Political Behavior* 17.2: 223–49.

Tam, Wendy K. 1996. "Minorities and the calculus of voting." Manuscript.

Taylor, J. Edward, Philip L. Martin, and Michael Fix. 1997. *Poverty amid Prosperity: Immigration and the Changing Face of Rural California.* Washington, DC: Urban Institute Press.

Teaford, Jon C. 1997. *Post-Suburbia: Government and Politics in the Edge Cities.* Baltimore: Johns Hopkins University Press.

Teixeira, Ruy A. 1992. *The Disappearing American Voter.* Washington, DC: Brookings Institution.

Tiebout, Charles. 1956. "A pure theory of local expenditures." *Journal of Political Economy* 64:416–24.

Tienda, Marta, and Ding-Tzann Lii. 1987. "Minority concentration and earnings inequality: blacks, Hispanics, and Asians compared." *American Journal of Sociology* 93.1: 141–65.

Torres, Andres. 1995. *Between Melting Pot and Mosaic: African Americans and Puerto Ricans in the New York Political Economy.* Philadelphia: Temple University Press.

Torres, Andres, and Frank Bonilla. 1993. "Decline within decline: the New York perspective." In *Latinos in a Changing U.S. Economy,* edited by Rebecca Morales and Frank Bonilla. Newbury Park, CA: Sage.

Tuch, Steven A., and Michael Hughes. 1996. "Whites' racial policy attitudes." *Social Science Quarterly* 77.4: 723–45.

Tuckel, Peter, and Richard Maisel. 1994. "Voter turnout among European immigrants to the United States." *Journal of Interdisciplinary History* 24.3: 407–30.

Turner, William H. 1985. "The demography of black Appalachia: past and present." In *Blacks in Appalachia,* edited by William H. Turner and Edward J. Cabbel. Lexington: University Press of Kentucky.

Turner, William H., and Edward J. Cabbell, eds. 1985. *Blacks in Appalachia.* Lexington: University Press of Kentucky.

Uhlaner, Carole J. 1991. "Perceived discrimination and prejudice and the coalition prospects of blacks, Latinos, and Asian Americans." In *Racial and Ethnic Politics in California,* edited by Byran Jackson and Michael B. Preston. Berkeley: Institute of Governmental Studies.

Uhlaner, Carole J., Bruce E. Cain, and D. Roderick Kiewiet. 1989. "Political participation of ethnic minorities in the 1980s." *Political Behavior* 11.3: 195–229.

United States Department of Commerce, Bureau of the Census. 1970. *1970 Census of Population: General Social and Economic Characteristics,* in various parts. Washington, DC: U.S. Government Printing Office.

United States Department of Commerce, Bureau of the Census. 1972. County and City Databook. Washington, DC: U.S. Government Printing Office.

United States Department of Commerce, Bureau of the Census. 1980. *1980 Census of Population: General Social and Economic Characteristics,* in various parts. Washington, DC: U.S. Government Printing Office.

United States Department of Commerce, Bureau of the Census. 1983. *County and City Databook.* Washington, DC: U.S. Government Printing Office.

United States Department of Commerce, Bureau of the Census. 1990. *1990 Census of Population: General Social and Economic Characteristics,* in various parts. Washington, DC: U.S. Government Printing Office.

United States Department of Commerce, Bureau of the Census. 1994. *County and City Databook.* Washington, DC: U.S. Government Printing Office.

Vest, Donald R. 1994. *City of Pueblo 1994 Data Book.* Pueblo: Department of Planning and Development.

Viviano, Frank. 1991. "A rich ethnic mix in the suburbs: census reveals a new kind of metropolis in the Bay Area." *San Francisco Chronicle,* May 11, A1.

Voter News Service. 1994. "General election exit polls." Made available through ICPSR.

Voter Research and Surveys. 1992. "Presidential primary exit polls." Made available through ICPSR.

Waldinger, Roger. 1986–87. "Changing ladders and musical chairs: ethnicity and opportunity in post-industrial New York." *Politics and Society* 15.4: 369–402.

Waldinger, Roger. 1996. *Still the Promised City?* Cambridge: Harvard University Press.

Walker, Robert, Mark Ellis, and Richard Barff. 1992. "Linked migration systems: immigration and internal labor flows in the United States." *Economic Geography* 68:234–48.

Wallace, David. 1962. "Shifts in one suburb's voting patterns." *Public Opinion Quarterly* 26:486–87.

Wattenberg, Martin. 1991. *The Rise of Candidate-Centered Politics.* Cambridge: Harvard University Press.

Weaver, J. L. 1976. "The elderly as a political community." *Western Political Quarterly* 29.3: 610–19.

Weber, Brian. 1995a. "Good from the bad: positive aspects emerge from contentious campaign." *Rocky Mountain News,* June 11, 93A.

Weber, Brian. 1995b. "Denver mayor's race exposes racial sensitivities issue." *Rocky Mountain News,* May 28, 12A.

Welch, Susan, and Timothy Bledsoe. 1988. *Urban Reform and Its Consequences.* Chicago: University of Chicago Press.

Weller, Robert. 1994. "Western slope groans under the pressure of a surging population." *Rocky Mountain News,* April 26, 14A.

White, M. J., and Y. Imai. 1994. "The impact of immigration on internal migration." *Population and Environment* 15:189–209.

White, M. J., and G. Kaufman. 1997. "Language usage, social capital, and school completion among immigrants and native-born ethnic groups." *Social Science Quarterly* 78.2: 385–98.

Williams, J. Allen, and Suzanne T. Ortega. 1990. "Dimensions of ethnic assimilation: an empirical appraisal of Gordon's typology." *Social Science Quarterly* 71.4: 697–710.

Wilson, James Q. 1960. *Negro Politics: A Search for Leadership.* Glencoe, IL: Free Press.

Wilson, William Julius. 1987. *The Truly Disadvantaged: The Inner City, the Underclass, and Public Policy.* Chicago: University of Chicago Press.

Wilson, William Julius. 1996. *When Work Disappears: The World of the New Urban Poor.* New York: Knopf.

Winsberg, Morton D. 1979. "Housing segregation of a predominantly middle class population: residential patterns developed by the Cuban immigration into Miami, 1950–74." *American Journal of Economics and Sociology* 38.4: 403–17.

Winsberg, Morton D. 1983. "Ethnic competition for residential space in Miami, Florida, 1970–80." *American Journal of Economics and Sociology* 42.3: 305–14.

Winsberg, Morton D. 1985. "Flight from the ghetto: the migration of middle class and highly educated blacks into white urban neighborhoods." *American Journal of Economics and Sociology* 44:411–21.

Winsberg, Morton D. 1993. "The changing South: regional migration streams to different parts of Florida." *Southeastern Geographer* 33.1: 110–21.

Wirt, Frederick M., Benjamin Walter, Francine F. Rabinovitz, and Deborah R. Hensler. 1972. *On the City's Rim: Politics and Policy In Suburbia.* Lexington, MA: D. C. Heath.

Wolfinger, Raymond. 1965. "The development and persistence of ethnic voting." *American Political Science Review* 59:896–908.

Wolfinger, Raymond. 1974. *The Politics of Progress.* Englewood Cliffs, NJ: Prentice-Hall.

Wolfinger, Raymond, and Robert B. Arseneau. 1978. "Partisan change in the South, 1952–1976." In *Political Parties and Political Decay,* edited by Louis Maisel and Joseph Cooper. New York: Sage.

Wolfinger, Raymond, and Michael G. Hagen. 1985. "Republican prospects: southern comfort." *Public Opinion* 8.5: 8–13.

Wolfinger, Raymond E., and Steven J. Rosenstone. 1980. *Who Votes?* New Haven: Yale University Press.

Wright, Gavin. 1986. *Old South, New South: Revolutions in the Southern Economy since the Civil War.* New York: Basic Books.

Wright, Sharon. 1995. "Electoral and biracial coalition: possible election strategy for African-American candidates in Louisville, KY." *Journal of Black Studies* 25.6: 749–58.

Wu, Sen-Yuan, and Hyman Korman. 1987. " Socioeconomic impacts of disinvestment on communities in New York State." in *American Journal of Economics and Sociology* 46.3: 261–71.

Yezer, Anthony M. J., and Lawrence Thurston. 1976. "Migration patterns and income change: implications for the human capital approach to migration." *Southern Economic Journal* 42:693–702.

Zaller, John. 1992. *The Nature and Origins of Mass Opinion.* New York: Cambridge University Press.

Zelinsky, Wilbur 1978. "Is nonmetropolitan American being repopulated? The evidence from Pennsylvania's minor civil divisions." *Demography* 15.1: 13–39.

Zhou, Min. 1992. *Chinatown: The Socioeconomic Potential of an Urban Enclave.* Philadelphia: Temple University Press.

Author Index

Grey, Mark A., 21
Griffith, David, 147
Guinier, Lani, 340
Guzman, Isaac, 312, 314

Hagen, Michael G., 6, 24
Haining, Robert, 38, 355, 357
Hamel, Ruth, 81
Hamm, Shannon Reid, 273
Handlin, Oscar, 6
Hansen, John Mark, 211, 332
Harkman, Anders, 10
Haynes, W. Warren, 161, 194
Hein, Jeremy, 11
Hensler, Deborah, 284
Hero, Rodney E., 89, 108
Herron, Matt, 159
Hertz, Kaenan, 22, 37, 66
Heuck, Douglas, 272
Hewstone, Miles, 22
Hirschman, Charles, 123
Hobbs, A. H., 12
Honeycutt, Valarie, 159
Hood, M. V., 22, 37
Horton, John, 61, 339
Houston, David, 238
Huckfeldt, Robert, 8, 20, 337
Hull, Susan F. T., 75

Ignatiev, Noel, 6
Iverson, Gudmund, 98, 337

Jewell, Malcolm E., 161, 170, 177, 178,
    183, 192, 195
Jiobu, Robert M., 18, 45, 46, 67, 197,
    328
John, Oliver, 22, 338

Kain, John F., 8, 12
Kalsow, Gretchen, 6
Kaufman, G., 48
Keeney, Heather, 284
Kelly, Guy, 80, 81, 82
Kephart, George, 12
Kerven, Anne, 114
Key, V. O., 9, 22, 37, 66, 181, 199, 200

Kieweit, D. Roderick, 6, 7, 48, 61, 62
Kinder, Donald R., 339
King, Gary, 8, 64, 95, 103, 141, 223,
    260, 304
Kohfeld, Carol, 337
Kolbe, Richard L., 238
Koritz, Douglas, 281
Korman, Hyman, 281
Kossoudji, Sherrie, 326
Kritz, Mary M., 16
Kwong, Peter, 17, 129, 144, 284

Ladinsky, Jack, 12
LaGreca, Anthony J., 202, 228
Lamare, James W., 17, 77, 144, 328,
    331
Lamis, Alexander P., 6
Lamphere, Louise, 147
Lansing, John B., 12
Lazarsfeld, Paul, 20, 314
Lee, Eugene, 66
Leonard, Stephen J., 28, 81
Leonard, William, 202
Leslie, Gerald R., 12
Lessner, Lori, 147
Leung, Shu-yin, 15, 16, 283
Lewis, Paul G., 10, 81, 115
Liang, Zai, 45, 47, 129, 210
Lieberson, Stanley, 9, 39, 45, 169, 210,
    326, 328
Lii, Ding-Tzann, 129, 277, 328
Logan, John R., 6, 15, 16, 283, 284,
    291
Long, Larry, 9, 12, 162
Lovrich, Nicholas, 103
Lublin, David, 340
Lyons, Michael, 6

McBurnett, Michael, 5, 20
McComb, David, 28, 81
McManus, Walter S., 326
McPhee, William N., 20, 314
McVeigh, Rory, 108
Mangalam, J. J., 161, 194
Marenin, Otwin, 103
Marsh, Ben, 238, 270

Subject Index

Jim Crow system in Florida, 234

Latino population. *See* Hispanic population; Mexican population

Mexican population
Colorado, 86, 88–89
political participation of, 103
Florida
Brevard County, 230
central region, 206
Kansas, in southwestern region, 149
Kentucky
as immigrants, 162
and U.S. guest worker program,
159–61
Pennsylvania
Chester County, 273–75
settlement patterns, 324
Migrants, internal
adaptation and political assimilation
of, 18–21
California
characteristics of, 32–33, 36, 346
migration to, 33
as proportion of population
(1980–90), 42–44
settlement patterns, 37–45
Colorado
Denver County, 108–9
as majority of population, 92
settlement patterns of migrants
and immigrants, 84–90
spatial concentration, 87, 90
Florida
blacks moving from north, 234
Brevard County, 229–31, 236
differences in income from immigrants, 206–7
from out of state, 203, 209
party regularity among voters
from out of state, 217
Republican affiliation of voters,
223
to rural north Florida from out of
state, 234–36

settlement patterns, 204–5, 207–10
as source of population growth,
200–206
influence on political landscape,
23
Kansas
Johnson County, 155–56
Kansas City and Wyandotte
County, 151, 153–54
settlement patterns, 125–28, 130,
144
in southwestern Kansas, 147–49
in Wichita and Sedgwick County,
150–52
Kentucky, 162–64
Louisville and Jefferson County,
190–92
in northern region, 187–88
relation to Republican registration growth, 181, 183
settlement patterns, 166–69
voter participation, 170–71
New York, 184–85, 321
the Bronx, 309
characteristics of, 287, 352
Elmira and Chemung County,
315–16
settlement patterns, 287–91
Syracuse and Onondaga County,
318–21
Pennsylvania
effect on residential segregation,
247
incomes of, 241
settlement in Adams County,
266–67
settlement patterns, 242–43,
245–47
voter participation and party regularity, 248–59
possible political effects of, 11–15
Republican social profile of, 135–
36
United States
avoidance of high unemployment
areas, 324